VALUE-FOCUSED THINKING

VALUE-FOCUSED THINKING

A Path to Creative Decisionmaking

Ralph L. Keeney

Harvard University Press
Cambridge, Massachusetts
London, England

Copyright © 1992 by the President and Fellows of Harvard College
All rights reserved
Printed in the United States of America

This book has been digitally reprinted. The content remains
identical to that of previous printings.

Library of Congress Cataloging-in-Publication Data

Keeney, Ralph L., 1944–
    Value-focused thinking / Ralph L. Keeney.
        p. cm.
    Includes bibliographical references and index.
    ISBN 0-674-93197-1 (cloth)
    ISBN 0-674-93198-X (pbk.)
    1. Decision-making. 2. Values. I. Title.
HD30.23.K354   1992   91-31496
658.4'03—dc20   CIP

To Howard Raiffa

whose ideas, encouragement, and actions
have guided and inspired me
and so many others

Preface

Many books have been written about decisionmaking. They tell us how to solve decision problems. They do not tell us how to identify potential decision opportunities. They tell us how to analyze alternatives to choose the best one. They do not tell us how to create alternatives. They tell us how to evaluate alternatives given some quantitative objective function. They do not tell us how to articulate the qualitative objectives on which any appraisal of alternatives must rest. This book is different. It does what the others do not.

Almost all of the literature on decisionmaking concerns what to do *after* the crucial activities of identifying the decision problem, creating alternatives, and specifying objectives. But where do these decision problems, alternatives, and objectives come from? This book describes and illustrates the creative processes that you should follow to identify your decision problems, create alternatives, and articulate your objectives. These prescriptions are quite different from the way people typically pursue these activities.

Most people do not like problems, and since decisions are problems to most people, they typically do not create their own decision problems. Instead, decision problems are usually thrust upon them by others or by happenstance. If your firm no longer needs your services, you have a decision problem. If consumers are not purchasing your product as expected, you have a decision problem. If you are diagnosed as having a serious illness, you have a decision problem. If hurricanes hit a populated area, many decision problems arise.

Once the decision problem is imposed from outside, the so-called solving begins. Typically, the decisionmaker first focuses on alternatives, until either an appropriate set of alternatives or one acceptable one is found, and only then begins to concentrate on objectives or criteria to evaluate the alternatives. I refer to this general problem-solving approach as *alternative-focused thinking.*

Focusing on alternatives is a limited way to think through decision situations. It is reactive, not proactive. If you wish to be the master of your decisionmaking, it makes sense to have more control over the decision situations you face. You do not control decision situations that you approach through alternative-focused thinking. This standard mode of thinking is backward, because it puts the cart of identifying alternatives before the horse of articulating values.

It is values that are fundamentally important in any decision situation. Alternatives are relevant only because they are means to achieve your values. Thus your thinking should focus first on values and later on alternatives that might achieve them. Naturally there should often be iteration between articulating values and creating alternatives, but the principle is "values first." Such thinking, which I refer to as *value-focused thinking,* can significantly improve decisionmaking because the values guide not only the creation of better alternatives but the identification of better decision situations. These better decision situations, which you create for yourself, should be thought of as *decision opportunities* rather than as decision problems.

This book shows how you should think about decision situations. It addresses how to create better alternatives for any decision problem that you face, how to identify decision opportunities more appealing than the decision problems that confront you, and how to articulate and use your fundamental values to guide and integrate all of your decisionmaking activities. The ideas are relevant to your personal decisions and to the decision situations of firms, organizations, and governments.

Value-focused thinking addresses the large void between unstructured creative thinking without bounds and very structured approaches to decision problems. It is the structuring of thinking to address decision opportunities and problems in creative ways. In short, it is directed creativity applied to decisions. The basis for the creativity is the values appropriate to the decision situation.

The purpose and thought processes of value-focused thinking are different from those of alternative-focused thinking. Alternative-focused thinking is to solve decision problems. Value-focused thinking is a way to identify desirable decision situations and then reap the benefits of these situations by solving them. Therefore, value-focused thinking suggests a different paradigm for addressing decisions from the standard alternative-focused-thinking paradigm. It is different in three important ways. First, significant effort is allocated to articulating values. Second, this articulation of values in decision situations comes before other activities. Third, the articulated values are explicitly used to identify decision opportunities and to create alternatives. A value-focused orientation will help you to create better decision situations with better alternatives, which should lead to better consequences.

Part One of the book presents the conceptual ideas of value-focused thinking. Numerous examples in Chapter 1 demonstrate the usefulness of the approach. Chapter 2 introduces a framework that relates objectives, values, and alternatives. This chapter also discusses how decisions should be related to one another and outlines the shortcomings of alternative-focused thinking as a way to think about decisions.

The core of value-focused thinking is thinking about values. Part Two presents procedures and theoretical background for value-focused thinking. Chapter 3, about identifying and structuring objectives, is entirely qualitative and provides the foundation on which further thinking about values rests. To gain a better understanding of the meaning of qualitatively stated objectives, it is useful to consider how to measure the achievement of objectives. This measurement is the topic of Chapter 4. Chapter 5 is quantitative. It indicates how to build a value model (that is, an objective function) to integrate the achievement of a set of objectives. The value model can be used for clarification of qualitative values and for quantitative analyses.

Uses of value-focused thinking are detailed in Part Three. Chapter 6 describes how to uncover hidden objectives relevant to a decision situation. Chapters 7 and 8 present ways to facilitate the creative development of alternatives. Chapter 9 has several suggestions for identifying decision opportunities. Chapter 10 discusses the usefulness of value-focused thinking in guiding information collection, evaluating alternatives, interconnecting decisions, improving communication, facilitating involvement in multiple-stakeholder decisions, and guiding strategic thinking.

Part Four presents several applications of value-focused thinking. Chapter 11 stresses different aspects of value-focused thinking in six decision contexts: options for future NASA missions, the transporting of nuclear waste, research on climate change, air pollution in Los Angeles, the designing of an integrated circuit tester, and a small negotiation on a book project. Chapter 12 describes the in-depth use of value-focused thinking to guide strategic thinking at a major international corporation, the British Columbia Hydro and Power Authority. Chapter 13 is my attempt to convince you that value-focused thinking can be useful for your personal decisionmaking. Using my own life as an example, I discuss in detail how I have used value-focused thinking to facilitate my decisionmaking in many contexts, including professional decisions, decisions about health and safety, and personal decisions such as whether to have a child.

The audience for this book is thoughtful decisionmakers and people who help others in their decisionmaking. These others may be individuals, firms, organizations, or governments. Thus, there are four main groups who should find this book most interesting. One group is analysts and consultants who make a living providing insights and advice to others with responsibilities for important decisions. The second group is students concerned with any aspect of decisionmaking. Such students may study management, policy, psychology, economics, law, design, engineering, or operations research. The third group is individuals in government agencies or organizations concerned with big issues that transcend well-established individual or organizational decision processes. Such issues include hazardous waste, global warming, disarmament, fair international trade, and immigration policy. The fourth group is people who find decisionmaking interesting, intriguing, and challenging, who enjoy the process of thinking through tough problems.

Depending on your interests, you may not wish to read all of the book. In particular, essentially all of the material requiring any mathematical knowledge has been included in Chapters 5 and 6 and designated sections of Chapters 4, 11, and 12. The reader who is not mathematically inclined can skip these passages with no loss of qualitative ideas.

If you want to begin by answering the question "What can this book do for me?" start with Chapter 1, with its many examples, then go to Part Four and choose any of the applications that are appealing. If your main interest is very broad strategic thinking, start with the early sections of Chapter 12. If your interest is major organizational decisions, select sections in Chapters 11 and 12. If your main concern is how to think better about personal decisions, read Chapter 13 first. Then go back and read the earlier chapters for a thorough grounding in the principles, procedures, and uses of value-focused thinking.

Acknowledgments

It is my good fortune to have David Bell and Howard Raiffa of the Harvard Business School and Detlof von Winterfeldt of the University of Southern California as friends and colleagues. I have benefited from their ideas about essentially all the contents of this book. My first paper on value-focused thinking was presented at a conference organized by David and Howard and Amos Tversky at the Harvard Business School in 1983. Three of the six applications in Chapter 11 involved Detlof, and there are many other situations in which we have collaborated on applying ideas of value-focused thinking.

Several other people have also contributed to my thoughts on this topic. Fruitful suggestions and ideas have arisen from discussions with Janet Beach of U.S. Marketing Services, Ward Edwards of the University of Southern California, Robin Gregory of Decision Research, Tim McDaniels of the University of British Columbia, Ken Peterson of the British Columbia Hydro and Power Authority, Franz-Josef Radermacher of the University of Ulm, Richard Richels of the Electric Power Research Institute, and Robert Winkler of Duke University. Others, too, at various stages in my life, have contributed significantly to my thinking. It is a pleasure to acknowledge Rita Boulet and Herman Peterson of the Lewistown Junior High School (Montana), Howard Dissly, John Dracup of U.C.L.A., Al Drake of M.I.T., Richard Meyer of the Harvard Business School, Joyce and Bill Lee, my aunt Louise Nance, and especially my mother, Anne Keeney. It is also a pleasure to recognize the superb editing by Camille Smith of Harvard University Press.

In the course of crystallizing my ideas about value-focused thinking,

I have been supported by numerous organizations. Partial support for this work has been provided by the National Science Foundation with grants SES-8942884 and SES-8520167, the Office of Naval Research contract N00014-84-K-0332, and the Electric Power Research Institute. In addition to my home Department of Systems Management at the University of Southern California, I have had the privilege of extended visits at the University of Passau in Germany in the fall of 1985 and at the Harvard Business School in the spring and summer of 1990 to complete this book.

My wife, Janet, and our son, Gregory, have been extremely patient and supportive during my writing of the book. My hope is that some of the ideas presented here will help me identify additional ways to enrich their lives as they do mine.

Contents

PART ONE

CONCEPTS

CHAPTER 1

Thinking about Values

Values are what we care about. As such, values should be the driving force for our decisionmaking. They should be the basis for the time and effort we spend thinking about decisions. But this is not the way it is. It is not even close to the way it is.

Instead, decisionmaking usually focuses on the choice among alternatives. Indeed, it is common to characterize a decision problem by the alternatives available. It seems as if the alternatives present themselves and the decision problem begins when at least two alternatives have appeared. Descriptively, I think this represents almost all decision situations. Prescriptively, it should be possible to do much better.

Values are more fundamental to a decision problem than are alternatives. Just ask yourself why you should ever make the effort to *choose* an alternative rather than simply let whatever happens happen. The answer must be that the consequences of the alternatives may be different enough in terms of your values to warrant attention. Your reason for interest in any decision problem is the desire to avoid undesirable consequences and to achieve desirable ones. The relative desirability of consequences is a concept based on values. Hence, the fundamental notion in decisionmaking should be values, not alternatives. Alternatives are the means to achieve the more fundamental values.

In this book I consider the role of values in decisionmaking. The approach is prescriptive: it concerns how values *should be* used to improve decisionmaking. The premise is that focusing early and deeply on values when facing difficult problems will lead to more desirable consequences, and even to more appealing problems than the ones we currently face. In short, we should spend more of our decisionmaking time concentrating on what is important: articulating and understanding our values and using these values to select meaningful decisions to ponder, to create better alternatives than those already identified, and to evaluate more carefully the desirability of the alternatives.

1.1 Value-Focused Thinking

Value-focused thinking essentially consists of two activities: first deciding what you want and then figuring out how to get it. In the more usual approach, which I refer to as alternative-focused thinking, you first figure out what alternatives are available and then choose the best of the lot. With value-focused thinking, you should end up much closer to getting all of what you want. Consider an illustration.

■ *Job Choice*
John is a senior at the University of Wisconsin. He plans to work for a few years before attending graduate school in business. How should he find "the right" job? The standard approaches would be to interview with firms that recruit graduates on campus and to pursue possibilities back home. Suppose that after reading short descriptions of job placement possibilities John selects six firms to interview, and from these interviews he gets three offers. He also mentions to some people back home that he is graduating and in the job market. From this, two good prospects for offers come up, but these are not yet actual offers.

At this stage, John considers that he has five alternatives, and that seems like plenty. Now he must choose one. Most likely, this selection process will take place entirely in his head. Somehow he will balance the pros and cons. First, he may eliminate alternatives that seem to be noncontenders, reducing the possibilities to three. Here the choice gets difficult. He may rank the remaining alternatives in terms of his personal feelings about them and in terms of their probable effects on his career. He may talk to his friends, teachers, and parents about the options before he decides.

Let us examine John's decision making process more closely. First, he looks around in the standard places for alternatives. As a result, he ends up with five possible jobs that are entirely defined by others. Next, he cuts off the search for further options, and begins to evaluate the alternatives. His evaluation addresses both professional and personal concerns, but in a rather ad hoc manner. He selects a job. John makes no attempt to reopen the search for alternatives based on his evaluation criteria, which are not clearly articulated, or on his thinking during the evaluative process.

Finding the right job is one of those decisions that are important enough to address in a much more organized and careful manner. Suppose we allow John to start again.

John's situation is ideal for value-focused thinking. He can begin by clarifying what he wants to achieve by working for the next few years. After hard thinking and perhaps some serious study, he may break his objectives into four categories broadly concerned with (1) learning valuable skills for his career, (2) finding out for sure whether he wants to go to graduate school in business, (3) enhancing his chances of acceptance at the best business schools, and (4) experiencing a different geographical region and lifestyle. Under each of these categories he should get specific. For example, valuable skills to learn may include technical skills like marketing and finance as well as interpersonal skills like how to work on teams, how to cope with office politics, and how to manage subordinates and superiors (yes, managing one's boss is a skill). Thinking specifically about his wish to experience a different region and lifestyle, John may decide this means to live near the ocean in a major metropolitan area that has a diversity of nationalities and a rich cultural life.

Using his interests to guide his thinking, John should be able to identify jobs that may well satisfy his desires. These jobs should be in places interesting to him, perhaps with firms that did not recruit on campus. The jobs may be of a type that will enable him to meet people who are knowledgeable about business schools and who may be of assistance when he applies. And these jobs may be in fields that are recognized as good career starters but that are not plentifully available back home. Once John has identified particularly desirable jobs in each category, he should rank them using all of his objectives, or at least he should determine which ones rank near the top of the list.

Now begins the process of making one—at least one—of those best jobs into a bona fide offer. This process should be recognized as a decision opportunity: one involving entirely different alternatives from those presented by job offers. There are many ways to turn a specific job or a type of job (such as account executive at a marketing firm in Northern California) into a real offer. It may take work to identify the alternatives and more work to implement them. Part of John's task is to identify the resources he has available to assist him, including his experiences and skills, his contacts, professional organizations, sources for ideas (such as books), and of course campus recruiting. Follow-through using such resources should produce job offers. Any of these offers should be at least as good and is likely to be much better than the best of the jobs available from alternative-focused thinking. ■

Value-focused thinking involves starting at the best and working to make it a reality. Alternative-focused thinking is starting with what is readily available and taking the best of the lot.

The Pervasiveness of Alternative-Focused Thinking

The easy way out of a decision problem is to focus narrowly on obvious alternatives and select one. This "solves" the problem, but a price is to be paid later when the consequences accrue. This is alternative-focused thinking. Value-focused thinking is more difficult and meant to be penetrating. There are mental costs and time associated with the exercise, but the benefits should well reward the effort as the consequences unfold.

Is John's initial approach to decisions unusual? Absolutely not! The same narrowly focused thinking occurs in the offices of physicians and lawyers, in the boardrooms of multinational organizations, in the chambers of regulatory agencies and legislative bodies, and routinely in our homes and schools. Alternative-focused thinking is the "natural" way we all have learned to deal with decisions. It is not that we were taught to make decisions this way, because most of us weren't taught to make decisions. Rather we picked up this habit by observing others making decisions and by having decisions throughout life posed to us as choices between given alternatives. Would you like to wear your red pajamas or your green ones? You can do your homework either before dinner or after dinner. On the menu today, we have swordfish, cannelloni, and filet mignon. You have three choices: chemotherapy, radiation treatment, or surgery, or there are possible combinations. Basically, there are two options, burial and cremation. So the habit of alternative-focused thinking is deeply engrained—but it can be kicked. The place to begin is with values.

What Are Values?

Values are principles used for evaluation. We use them to evaluate the actual or potential consequences of action and inaction, of proposed alternatives, and of decisions. They range from ethical principles that must be upheld to guidelines for preferences among choices.

We can identify our values by hard thinking. We make them explicit through statements expressing value judgments. To render value judgments useful for decisionmaking, we must be precise about their meaning. We can articulate this meaning qualitatively by stating objectives, and, if desirable, we can embellish it with quantitative value judgments.

Ethics, desired traits, characteristics of consequences that matter, guidelines for action, priorities, value tradeoffs, and attitudes toward risk all indicate values. Consider the following examples:

Ethics: Do not exploit the misfortune of others.

Traits: It is important to be trustworthy, loyal, and dependable.

Characteristics: Any proposed national energy policy should be appraised in terms of national security, economic cost, environmental impacts, and health and safety.

Guidelines: It is better to try and fail than not to try at all.

Priorities: Safety is more important than economy when purchasing an automobile.

Value tradeoffs: If cutbacks are necessary, laying off one person is as bad as limiting ten persons to four days of work per week.

Attitude toward risk: The risks of introducing the new product immediately are outweighed by the possible increase in market share from the introduction.

Statements like these can clearly represent a person's values. They may also represent the values of an organization or even a society. In these situations, the group's values should reflect the values of the individuals in it.

Constraint-Free Thinking

Thinking about values is constraint-free thinking. It is thinking about what you wish to achieve or what you wish to have. All of this thinking need not be self-centered; what you want may be for others or for society. Thinking of desirable alternatives is also constraint-free thinking. Selecting among alternatives, however, is constrained thinking. Even though some of the choices may be difficult, constrained thinking is easier than constraint-free thinking, because the former significantly limits the range of concerns. But the payoffs of constraint-free thinking are potentially much greater.

Many methodologies and techniques to aid decisionmaking have been developed over the past forty years. So why bother with yet another approach? Invariably, existing methodologies are applied to decision problems once they are structured, meaning after the alternatives and objectives are specified. Such methodologies are not very helpful for the ill-defined decision problems where one is in a major quandary about what to do or even what can possibly be done. Certainly if the alternatives are not known, one cannot characterize the decision problem by the alternatives.

In addition, most decision methodologies try to find the best alternatives from a prespecified list. But where does this list come from? In contrast, value-focused thinking does not simply accept prespecified problems or prespecified lists of alternatives. It either creates them or changes them. Value-focused thinking should lead both to more appealing decision problems and to choices among better alternatives than those generated by happenstance or conventional approaches.

Decision Problems Aren't Problems

There is something odd about referring to a situation in which a decision has to be made as a "decision problem." Is it really a problem? If you were looking for a job, would the prospect of having only one alternative thrill you? You might have to accept the job whether or not it was particularly desirable, but there would definitely be no decision problem. There would be no required choices. But this "no decision problem" might be a big problem. On the other hand, suppose you were faced with several job alternatives, some of which were quite appealing. This presumably would not be a bad situation to be in, but it is what is referred to as a decision problem.

It is useful to recognize that before any decision there is an opportunity—an opportunity to create alternatives. By beginning with values, we can think of situations not as decision problems but rather as decision opportunities. Periodically, we may examine our achievement in terms of our values and ask if we can do better. The thinking process may suggest further creative alternatives. This is a better allocation of time than spending most of it choosing among readily apparent alternatives. What is missing in most decisionmaking methodologies is a philosophical approach and methodological help to understand and articulate values and to use them to identify decision opportunities and to create alternatives. The way to remedy that situation is to focus on what matters: on values.

1.2 Creating Alternatives

The range of alternatives people identify for a given decision situation is often unnecessarily narrow. There are several reasons for this. There is a tendency in all problem solving to move quickly away from the ill-defined to the well-defined, from constraint-free thinking to contrained thinking. There is a need to feel, and perhaps even measure, progress toward reaching a "solution" to a decision problem. To get that feeling of progress, one often quickly identifies some viable alternatives and proceeds to evaluate them, without making the effort to broaden the search for alternatives.

The first alternatives that come to mind in a given situation are the obvious ones, those that have been used before in similar situations and those that are readily available. Once a few alternatives—or perhaps only one, such as the status quo—are on the table, they serve to anchor thinking about others. Assumptions implicit in the identified alternatives are accepted, and the generation of new alternatives, if it occurs at all, tends to be limited to a tweaking of the alternatives already identified. Truly creative or different alternatives remain hidden in another part of the mind, unreachable by mere tweaking. Deep and persistent thought is required to jar them into the consciousness.

Focusing on the values that should be guiding the decision situation makes the search for new alternatives a creative and productive exercise. It removes the anchor on narrowly defined alternatives and allows clear progress toward "solving" the problem. Let us discuss some examples.

■ *A Hawaiian Vacation*
A professional couple, the Lees, are considering a two-week vacation in Hawaii. After investigating several options through their travel agent, they have tentatively selected a vacation package that includes a week each on Oahu and Maui. But now, just before they sign up, the agent mentions another possibility. The Lees could extend their stay by one week and visit a third island, Kauai, at a good price. Even though their vacations from work are for two weeks, the Lees believe they could get the additional week off without pay. They decide to do it.

With the range of vacation ideas somewhat expanded, the Lees are now dreaming about enjoying the tranquillity of the islands. An image comes to mind of the South Seas, which they feel might be more exotic than Hawaii. They have often talked about a big South Seas trip sometime in the future. Maybe the future is now. They call their travel agent and ask about changing their plans to include two weeks in Hawaii and two weeks in Micronesia. And they decide that as long as they are taking their once-in-a-lifetime trip they should do it first class and "not worry about the cost." The travel agent custom-designs such a vacation package, and now the Lees are again ready to sign up.

This alternative is significantly different from the various two-week Hawaiian trips they initially appraised. Four weeks of time, a substantial sum of money, and "goodwill chips" needed to obtain four weeks away from their jobs are the resources the Lees will utilize for their vacation. Their investment may well be worth its value. However, it would be reasonable at this point to consider whether the contemplated four-week trip is the best use of those resources. The Lees may ask themselves what they would like to achieve with four weeks of free time and the funds they intend to spend. They may conclude that they wish to learn about other cultures, understand a bit more of their world, and meet people very dissimilar to themselves in background and experience. Thinking about four-week trips that would satisfy these desires, the Lees may come up with alternatives such as an African picture safari, a tour of the Soviet Union, an Amazon cruise, or an intensive German course in Heidelberg. These alternatives are ones they clearly would not have considered in the context of two-week vacations in Hawaii. ∎

The general principle here is that the implementation of any alternative requires the use of valuable resources. Before expending these resources, you should consider explicitly what valued consequences you would like to achieve, and create alternatives that will allow you to achieve them.

∎ *Leave of Absence*

The four-week vacation creates another decision "problem" for both Mr. and Ms. Lee. They have to request and receive the additional two weeks off from work to extend their vacations. Let us consider Ms. Lee's problem. Suppose she is an environmental scientist in a medium-sized consulting firm. She is currently working full time five days a week on the potential environmental consequences of a proposed seabed mining project several miles offshore from Cape Cod, Massachusetts. This large project will continue for several months. In addition, the company wants her to undertake an environmental assessment of a proposed waste-burning power plant near Providence, Rhode Island. So far, she has not agreed to do this, citing her heavy commitment to the seabed mining project.

In order to take the additional two weeks of vacation time, Ms. Lee needs to get an okay from the project leader of the seabed project, Mr. Turbo, and from Mr. Turbo's boss, Ms. Hawkes, who has managerial and fiscal responsibility for the division. The obvious alternative for Ms. Lee in this situation is simply to ask for leave from Mr. Turbo and Ms. Hawkes. If she does so, it will either be approved or not, but the consequences of either outcome will not be particularly desirable to Ms. Lee. The firm is rumored to have an unstated policy of not granting leave for vacation, especially in the first few years of work for the company as in Ms. Lee's case. If leave is not granted, Ms. Lee will miss a very special vacation. If leave is granted, she may find she owes large goodwill debts. Knowing she is valuable to the company, Ms. Lee could respond to a rejection by threatening to quit. Consequences of either possibility here would not be desirable either, as she enjoys both her work and her colleagues. So what should Ms. Lee do?

This situation is akin to many negotiation contexts. Ms. Lee could "negotiate" the two-week leave without pay. A better strategy might be to use her understanding of the values of Mr. Turbo and Ms. Hawkes to create proactive alternatives that give her what she wants—two weeks off without goodwill debt, and maybe even with goodwill credits and with pay—and also improve circumstances for both Mr. Turbo and Ms. Hawkes.

Turbo's values in this situation are clear. He wants good work done on time on the seabed project and the ability to rely on Ms. Lee any time an environmental crisis occurs in the project. Ms. Hawkes's values are probably contributing to profit, getting the environmental work done on the power plant project, and not setting a precedent for an implied policy of "leave on request." With these values identified, it should be possible to create an alternative that all three, Ms. Lee, Mr. Turbo, and Ms. Hawkes, will consider preferable to the status quo. Some care may be required in the actual discussions, but here is the essence of an alternative Lee might propose: Upon returning from her vacation, Ms. Lee will shift two days a week to the power plant project until it is completed. The other three weekdays will be spent on the seabed project. The actual timing can be directed by Mr. Turbo, which means that Ms. Lee will be present whenever he needs her. In case the environmental part of the seabed project begins to lag behind the overall project, Ms. Lee will work evenings or weekends. In exchange, she will go on leave with pay for the two additional weeks. In the negotiations she can "give up" the pay if necessary, but it probably will not be necessary.

Everybody appears better off with this proposed agreement. Mr. Turbo gets good work generated on time from Ms. Lee and her word that his project has priority. He doesn't have to worry that her future responsibility to the power plant project will lessen her commitment to his project. Ms. Hawkes can foresee a stream of profit from Ms. Lee's work, as her time will be billed to projects at forty hours per week at least. In addition, Ms. Hawkes has Ms. Lee's commitment to do the environmental work on the power plant project. And because the arrangement is proactive, and good for the company, it does not set a precedent for granting leave on request. Ms. Lee, of course, also wins. She gets her vacation, with pay, and goodwill credit for turning a potentially difficult situation into a benefit for all. ■

The general principle used here is relevant to wide classes of problems where you want something from someone else. The idea is to create an alternative that gets you what you want and at the same time makes others better off. This requires thinking of their values at the same time as you think of yours. The idea is to create a win-win situation with the novel twist that you are negotiating both for yourself and for the others.

■ *Fire Department Operations*

Chief Cullinan heads the fire department in a major city that has suffered a recent series of unfortunate fires. Three fires in the last month have taken civilian lives, and in two of these firemen also died. Local politicians and citizen groups are pushing for better fire protection. The wisdom on the street is that the fire department just doesn't have the equipment or the personnel to provide necessary service. One of the local newspapers prints an editorial recommending purchasing four to six new fire trucks and hiring approximately eighty more firefighters. Mayor Seavey is in a very difficult situation: demands for a significant increase in fire department resources on the one hand and a fiscal crisis that has led to a budget freeze in all city departments on the other hand. This situation is widely perceived as a problem with no good alternatives. What can possibly be done?

Mayor Seavey arranges personal meetings with Chief Cullinan and a few staff members. These are working sessions, intended to get down to basics. Just what are the fundamental objectives of the fire department? What are the mechanisms that can achieve those fundamental objectives? How well is the department doing in terms of those mechanisms, and where might changes improve matters? The exercise results in the following understandings:

The major objectives of the department are to protect residents, minimize property loss, and reduce fears in the community. There are numerous mechanisms available for achieving those objectives. There are fire-prevention activities, ranging from building inspections to educational campaigns. The department has not been doing much of these in the past year because of the budget freeze. Then there are communication activities that might take place from the onset of a fire to the time when the fire crews arrive on scene. The population might be better informed about when and how to report fires. Fire department personnel could be better trained in eliciting needed information and in communicating it to the crews. Response time to reach the scene of a fire is important for saving lives and property. One reason for slow response time is the high number of false alarms, which have been running at 60 percent for the past few years. Even the other 40 percent of the time, most of the equipment responding to the fire is not needed. Five trucks, three engines and two ladders, respond to every alarm. In only one out of ten cases of genuine alarms are these needed; the other nine cases involve limited fires (such as chimney fires, oven fires, garbage fires) that are handled by the first crew on the scene.

With this basic understanding of the fundamental objectives of the fire department and several possible ways to achieve them, numerous potential alternatives and classes of alternatives can be created. One class of alternatives is to reinstitute and stress fire prevention programs. A second class of alternatives involves communication. An educational program to educate and train people about how to report fires could be developed. Local fire alarm boxes might be wired to ring simultaneously in the nearest fire station and in a central dispatching center. Perhaps an additional dispatcher could be assigned to the busy evening shift. A system might be developed to assign a communication channel to each fire, and communication equipment might be installed on each fire truck.

Response time might be drastically reduced if the number of fire trucks initially dispatched to an alarm were decreased—yes, decreased.

More than one truck is needed on only four percent of all alarms. With the current strategy of sending five trucks, all the nearby trucks are often unavailable, responding elsewhere when a local fire alarm occurs. Hence, the response to that alarm must come from much farther away, lengthening response time. For the four percent of the alarms that need more equipment, a quick initial appraisal by the crew of one truck that traveled only a short distance might actually get other vehicles to the scene sooner than with the standard five-truck response, as these vehicles too would be traveling a shorter distance.

Policies to reduce false alarms might be appropriate. Such policies could range from educational coaxing to severe penalties. Other alternatives, such as photographing individuals who ring an alarm box, might result in a greater likelihood of apprehending people who turn in false alarms. Perhaps requiring them to do community service or to view bodies burned in fires might deter them from turning in more false alarms.

Mayor Seavey and Chief Cullinan now have a solid list from which they can expand and more carefully define alternatives. Any combination of their generated suggestions might lead to major improvements in the department. They might provide better fire department service, reduce departmental workload by reducing false alarms, and thus improve department morale. Chief Cullinan should be pleased. In addition, almost all of the suggestions should be less costly than increases in fire trucks and personnel. So Mayor Seavey should also be pleased. She not only has a feasible alternative, she has several feasible alternatives and quite probably several *good* feasible alternatives. ■

The general principle used to suggest alternatives here is relevant to almost all decisions. You begin with the fundamental objectives that indicate what you really care about in the problem. Then you follow simple logical reasoning processes to identify the mechanisms by which the fundamental objectives can be achieved. Finally, for each mechanism, you create alternatives or classes of alternatives by asking what control you have over that mechanism.

■ Reducing Automobile Fatalities
Automobile fatalities are one of the major causes of death in the United States. Before the mid-1970s, speed limits varied from state to state, with a few states having no speed limits at all. Then, because of the oil crisis, the Congress passed a law making 55 miles per hour the national

speed limit in order to reduce consumption of gasoline. Apparently as a result, the number of annual fatalities due to vehicle accidents dropped about 10,000, to approximately 45,000. By 1980, the oil crisis had passed. But many then argued that the speed limit should be kept at 55 because raising it would also raise the number of deaths in auto accidents. A national debate raged that basically focused on two alternatives, speed limits of 55 mph and 65 mph. This is an incredibly limited range of alternatives. Highly charged debates unfortunately too often turn out this way. If you were responsible for traffic safety in the United States, what might you do to reduce fatalities?

First it would be useful to understand some realities of the problem. It is very easy to reduce traffic deaths. Setting a speed limit of 45 mph would save 10,000 fatalities per year relative to the number of deaths at 55 mph. Lowering the speed limit to 35 mph would save another 10,000 more. And forbidding vehicles to move at all would eliminate automobile fatalities entirely. But nobody is advocating a speed limit of 25 or 35 mph. Why not? Because such decisions involve naturally conflicting values, only one of which is reducing the number of deaths. Others have to do with convenience, opportunities to do many worthwhile things, saving time, and cost. Such values should always be kept in mind when appraising life-saving programs.

Having recognized that, you could then focus on the detailed meaning of the objective "minimize vehicle fatalities" and the means that affect the degree to which the objective is achieved. This thinking should help you generate alternatives.

You might divide the objective of minimizing fatalities into subsets of adults and children and drivers and passengers. Other subsets might be pedestrians, motorcyclists, and road workers. It might also be useful to categorize fatal accidents into those involving few fatalities and those involving several. Each of these sets might be broken down further. For example, drivers might be categorized as novice (less than three years experience), adult, and senior. Children might be classified as teens, preteens, and under four.

Focusing on how to reduce fatalities to any group of individuals might suggest alternatives. For example, novice drivers might be required to have external identification on their vehicles similar to that on cars involved in driver education. They might be issued provisional licenses that would be more easily revoked. Similar rules might apply to seniors. Seniors might also be required to repeat certain parts of the test for a driving license, such as those involving reflexes and eyesight, at more frequent intervals. Focusing on fatalities to children under age four, you might first collect data on what contributes to their deaths. If a major factor is failure to use mandated child safety seats, then perhaps drivers of vehicles transporting children without a child's seat should be fined or even lose their licenses. If many fatalities are due to head injuries, perhaps children should be required to wear helmets in the car. Even child-seat airbags would be a possibility. In appraising any alternative, you should consider the implications for other objectives in addition to safety. But for now you should simply create alternatives; appraisal comes later.

Next it would be useful to examine why fatalities occur. Obviously they occur because of accidents, so why do accidents occur? For our purposes, let us identify just two contributing factors: drunk drivers and speeding drivers. You can now think of alternatives that might reduce the impact of each of these factors on accidents. For drunk drivers, you might have a light go on outside the car when there was an indication of impaired reflexes or judgment. The "smart car" might even refuse to start if the driver registered as drunk. An exterior light might also go on at a given speed to deter speeding. Maybe analysis of accident data would suggest that drunk speeders are much worse than either drunk drivers or speeding drivers. Perhaps a particularly harsh penalty should be placed on such individuals, in an attempt to keep drunk drivers from speeding. ■

This example illustrates two general principles that are helpful in creating alternatives. Specifying the meaning of the fundamental objective, in this case by dividing the reduction of vehicle fatalities into categories, can suggest alternatives. Similarly, identifying the means contributing to the achievement of any aspect of the fundamental objective can also indicate potential alternatives.

1.3 Identifying Decision Opportunities

Who should be making your decisions? The answer is obvious: You should. Well then, who should be deciding what decision situations you face and when you face them? The answer here is the same: You should. At least you should control far more of the decision situations you face than many of us do. Controlling what decision situations you face may have a greater influence on the achievement of your objectives than controlling the alternatives selected for those decisions.

Most decision situations are created by the normal course of events, actions of others, and happenstance, and force the decisionmaker(s) to be reactive. Personal decisions required by the normal course of events include what employment to seek and accept, where to live, whether to marry, how many children to have, and when to retire. Additional decision situations are caused by others: Your teenager didn't come home last night and showed up at seven o'clock this morning with a lame explanation. You were just offered a promotion at work, but it requires moving to suburban New Jersey and you like the high desert of New Mexico. Then there is happenstance, which includes good luck, bad luck, and acts of God: laboratory tests recently confirmed that you have the initial stages of lung cancer. You just won the Big Lottery. Like it or not, each of these circumstances also puts you in a decision situation.

Decision situations are also sprung upon businesses and organizations and nations. A competitor introduces a new product or offers significant price incentives for existing products. A legislative body passes a law or a budget and numerous agencies must adapt to it. Scientists discover that global warming is occurring, and decisive national action is needed. The Berlin Wall falls. Each circumstance sets up a potentially critical decision situation, a situation that was not created by the respective decisionmaking entity.

But not all decision situations have to be created by outside forces. It is worthwhile to seek out decision situations, situations I refer to as decision opportunities rather than decision problems. Such decision situations do not occur outside your control; they occur because of your control.

There are two ways to create decision opportunities. One is to convert an existing decision problem into a decision opportunity. Often this involves broadening the context of the problem, as Mayor Seavey did in deciding what to do about the fire department. Rather than limiting concern to how many additional fire trucks and personnel were needed, she broadened the problem to address the goal of improved fire protection. The other way to create decision opportunities is from scratch. You use your creative genius, which can be stimulated by value-focused thinking, to examine whether and how you can better achieve your objectives.

▪ *Jackets from Scraps*
In the 1980s, The North Face was a successful manufacturer of outdoor clothing and supplies based in Berkeley, California. Many of the company's clothing and tent products used colorful nylon cloth. Even

though the cutting procedures minimized the amount of scrap cloth, there still were many scraps. Hap Klopp, the company president, created a decision opportunity. He posed the question of what could productively be done with the scraps. This decision situation was not externally forced. There was no requirement that any decision be made concerning the scrap cloth. But Mr. Klopp recognized this as a potential opportunity. So what happened? The company formulated and appraised alternatives, including the status quo alternative of discarding the scraps. The chosen alternative was a multicolored duck-down parka made from sewn scraps. The parkas readily sold at a premium over the single-colored parka in certain markets. ■

How many billions of dollars could companies produce or save annually by posing similar questions? Asking questions such as "Could we use this waste as a resource?" or "Is there a better way to . . .?" creates potentially valuable decision opportunities.

■ *Life after Retirement*
The day you retire, you face a very broad range of possibilities. Planning what to do in retirement requires using constraint-free thinking, understanding your objectives for the rest of your life, creating opportunities, and making the most of them. It is a wonderful decision opportunity, but one that can frighten the timid and be a major hassle to some of the adult children of the retirees. It helps if these children can view the situation as an opportunity for their parents, not as a problem for themselves.

Mrs. Lyons retired at age sixty-five after having been a bookkeeper all her working life. Twenty years earlier she had left Montana and moved to Los Angeles. She did not wish to remain there, nor did she wish to return to Montana. She did try a readily available alternative, moving to the Seattle area to live with her sister. This didn't turn out to be such a great life either. Mrs. Lyons and her only son agreed there was a major problem. Quite simply, she was not happy with her life. On the positive side, her physical and mental health were very good, and although she was not wealthy, financial considerations would not limit most activities she might like to pursue. The tough issues were to recognize that almost any activity that interested her could become a part of her life and to identify the activities she valued.

It took some time for Mrs. Lyons to recognize that she could control her future. Then came the issue of what was important to her. Mrs. Lyons realized that it would be nice to have some good friends nearby.

Previous moves had resulted in more acquaintances and fewer friends. Now other thoughts seemed to flow more readily. She hadn't golfed in forty years, but thought she might like to try it again. Her son jumped at this suggestion. One afternoon during the next week, he took her to a golf driving range to foster further interest. His objective was to get his mother doing anything that she might enjoy.

Mrs. Lyons also stated other desires. She preferred to have a lot of warm sunny weather and very little of the Seattle winter drizzle. She was skilled in several art forms and liked the idea of pursuing those interests. Last, but she insisted not least, she wanted to be able to see her son and daughter-in-law often.

The decision opportunity was now framed, at least in a preliminary way, by her values. The next task was to identify some alternative places to live, preferably in California, Arizona, or New Mexico because of the climate and proximity to her son and daughter-in-law. She gathered information by reading up on retirement living and by writing to several Chambers of Commerce for information. After this research, Mrs. Lyons and her son visited five communities and selected one. They both recognized that moving there was an experiment, not necessarily a commitment for life. As it happened, Mrs. Lyons made some good friends, began to play golf regularly, took up jewelry making and Japanese painting, and saw her son and daughter-in-law often as they lived only an hour away. Life was never the same again; it was much better. ■

The principle of this example is that you should monitor your life just as you monitor your health. A physical examination may identify health problems and suggest how to improve your health. It is proactive to avoid health problems in the future. By analogy, a life examination to identify discontentment or unrecognized potential achievement of your values may suggest decision opportunities to improve your quality of life and avoid possible future problems.

■ *Communicating about Risks*
Many business organizations and regulatory agencies are enlightened about the importance of informing the public about life-threatening risks. Unfortunately, they are not so enlightened about how to do this well. Communication about risks is a big problem to many organizations.

This problem is not well formulated in most organizations. The objective of risk communication is rarely explicitly stated. It is more or less assumed that the objective is to inform the public about risks facing them, and perhaps to insure that the public understands the implications of these risks. Often, the risk communication problem is not recognized as a decision situation: only one alternative is recognized, so no choice can be made among alternatives. The alternative normally followed is to deliver the "risk numbers" to the public either orally by handing them a report with the advice "Read the report, the risks are included in it." As a result, the public is confused and frustrated, which in turn renders the communicating organization confused and frustrated.

Communication about risk offers an organization a major decision opportunity. It is important to recognize that decisions can be made about risk communication and that these decisions are distinct from decisions that may influence the risks themselves. Several possible objectives articulating values that help to frame this decision opportunity can be identified (Keeney and von Winterfeldt, 1986). They include the following:

1. To inform the public about specific risks.
2. To inform the public about actions to alleviate specific risks.
3. To educate the public about risks, risk analysis, and risk management.
4. To encourage personal measures to reduce risk.
5. To improve the understanding of public values and concerns regarding risks.
6. To increase mutual trust and credibility between an organization and the public.
7. To resolve conflicts and controversy.

Using these objectives to focus thinking, it should be possible to create a large number of alternatives for communicating about risk. These alternatives would include various possible measures of risk to use in communicating with the public, various uses of media and graphical representations to aid the communication, processes that involve feedback and two-way communication over time as well as one-shot communication, and ways to obtain information that would facilitate learning and adaptation of the communication process to better achieve objectives. ∎

∎ *Providing Services for People with AIDS*
Dr. Fos had just been appointed to a newly created post to manage and integrate all municipal activities concerning AIDS in a major metropolitan area. Although managing and integrating would be difficult, he

knew he could do them well. He also recognized there would be opportunities to view the recognized problems in a different light and do things about them differently and better.

The area had many programs involving research, public health, social service, and education, but these had been set up separately and were operated by the professionals in the research facilities, health departments, social agencies, and schools. None had been established in response to direct input from people with AIDS. Nobody had asked them what they wanted or needed most; nobody had explicitly determined their values. In fact, almost all of the work Fos knew of in the field referred to people with AIDS as AIDS patients; it approached them from the perspective of the medical community.

Fos recognized a major decision opportunity to articulate the strategic values that should guide all the efforts under his control. Since he wished to have a broad perspective, he formed three distinct panels to specify values: a health panel, an education panel, and a panel of persons with AIDS. Each panel of from five to seven members was guided through a process of listing and defining strategic values concerning AIDS. Although there was overlap in the panels' values, the health panel stressed medical treatment and medical research, the education panel stressed prevention and the elimination of misperceptions about AIDS, and the persons with AIDS stressed their quality of life. Each of the identified values opened up decision opportunities that Fos could pursue. Let us outline just two of these.

The medical panel naturally wanted to practice medicine consistent with the law. The panel of persons with AIDS quite reasonably wanted unencumbered access to current drugs, such as AZT, or future drugs that might slow the progression of the disease or even cure it. These obvious values conflict on at least two important facets. First, there are very stringent licensing laws that essentially prohibit the fast entry of new drugs into the market, in case these drugs may be ineffective or have serious side-effects. While these laws are reasonable in many situations, many people with AIDS would rather take the chance of ineffectiveness or side-effects rather than go without an experimental treatment. Second, once a drug such as AZT is licensed for testing, it is often available only to people who agree to participate in a controlled experiment. Half of the participants are given the new drug and half are given a placebo. All must agree in a contract not to simultaneously try any other drugs, legal or illegal. This framework seems cruel and absurd in a situation where the disease has no known cure. It is hard to justify giving some patients a placebo just because certain types of testing are mandated by existing law.

The conflict between the medical community's wish to observe the laws and the wish of persons with AIDS to be able to pursue any avenue that might improve their chances of survival set up a decision opportunity for Fos. He developed a project to design new laws specifically for AIDS drugs that could reasonably balance the legitimate concerns of the medical and legal communities and persons with AIDS. The project included representatives from each of these groups.

Another decision opportunity was suggested by one of the objectives identified by the panel of persons with AIDS. This objective was to reconcile persons with AIDS with any estranged family members before it was too late. A study was begun that involved people with AIDS, families of people with AIDS, family counselors, and a psychiatrist. The intent was to develop a series of self-help and assisted procedures to facilitate the reconciliation process. ∎

1.4 Thinking about Values

The decision situations I have outlined have three characteristics in common. First, each is based on a real decision. Second, each was a very important decision to the person or organization facing it. And third, each was a complex decision with no clear "solution." Decisions with these characteristics are ideal for value-focused thinking. Values should and can guide all the effort that should be expended on these decisions. But how should one begin to identify the values relevant to a decision situation?

When you are faced with a difficult decision situation, start by thinking about your values. Do not start by thinking about alternatives, as that will limit you. Ask what you hope to achieve in the decision context you face. Write down a list of your responses. Then push yourself to think of anything else that should be on the list.

Once you have a preliminary list of your objectives written down, scrutinize each of these carefully. First ask why each objective is important. The responses will probably add objectives to your list. Suppose you are considering buying a new automobile and good gasoline mileage is one of your objectives. Thinking about why this is important, you may decide that better mileage is a means to lower operating costs, fewer stops to fill the tank, and less pollution of the atmosphere. Each of these objectives should also be subjected to the "why is it important" test. For example, having to stop for gas less often will save you time and inconvenience. At this stage, you can recognize that mileage should be thought of in terms of its implications for operating costs, convenience, time savings, and pollution. These objectives are more fundamental than mileage, and they are influenced by aspects of automobiles other than mileage.

Once you feel the list of objectives is reasonably complete, it is important to specify clearly what each objective includes. For example, the convenience you care about should be specified in detail. Aspects may include the car's durability, meaning that it is always ready to go when you need it, storage space, easy control of instruments, and features of handling such as the turning radius, which affects parking as well as safety. This list may stimulate you to consider another fundamental objective, namely safety. Continuing the thinking process, you may find that several aspects of an automobile and its operation are means that affect the attainment of fundamental objectives or parts of fundamental objectives. For example, license fees and insurance are part of operating costs; scheduled and unscheduled maintenance affect time savings; oil leaks and ability of the engine to stay in tune affect pollution; and the brake system, steering, and weight distribution affect safety.

The general principle of thinking about values is to discover the reasoning for each objective and how it relates to other objectives. Values are identified by the responses to a large number of questions about the meaning of and reasoning for objectives. Each response can be considered to be a "value bit" of information useful in guiding value-focused thinking. Any of these value bits may suggest the insight that leads to the breakthrough thought that eventually enables the decisionmaker to make a much better choice than would otherwise have been possible. Taken together, the value bits should indicate everything you really care about in a decision context. Using these to stimulate thought about how to get what you care about makes good sense. It makes much better sense than trying to get what you care about without thoroughly understanding what it is that you care about.

1.5 The Uses of Value-Focused Thinking

The central role of thinking about values is illustrated in Figure 1.1. Here, I will briefly describe the advantages to be gained from this kind of thought; details are found in Part Three.

Uncovering Hidden Objectives

It is often difficult to pinpoint the values that should be driving a decision situation. Sometimes you may have a gut feeling for what values seem relevant to a decision, but you may find them hard to articulate. At other times, you may not even know what you want in a complicated decision situation. To enhance the likelihood of getting what you want, it is important—perhaps essential—to know what you want.

Thinking about values naturally provides an initial list of your conscious values. This thinking may also provide many keys to identify previously subconscious values. Bringing these values to consciousness allows you to uncover hidden objectives, objectives you didn't realize you had.

Guiding Information Collection

The values relevant to a given decision situation indicate what information is important. Once you have specified your values, you should then

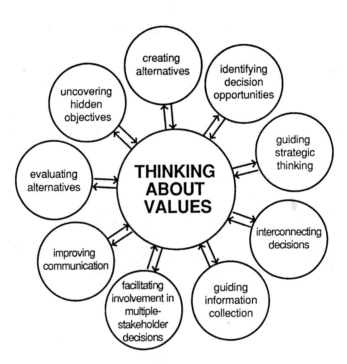

Figure 1.1. Overview of value-focused thinking

collect information on alternatives only if the information will help you judge the alternatives in terms of achieving those values. With carefully quantified objectives, it is conceptually straightforward to do calculations to determine the potential usefulness of gathering information. There are too many tales about expensive and time-consuming efforts to collect data that turned out to be worthless. Data have value only if they will help lead you to better consequences, either through the creation of better alternatives or through the wiser choice of alternatives.

Improving Communication

The language of value-focused thinking is the common language about the achievement of objectives in any particular decision context. It is not the technical language of many specialties. This basis in common language should facilitate communication and understanding.

Value judgments specify what is important in the decision problem. They are what should be discussed when people talk about the pros and cons of alternatives. For most public problems, values, rather than facts, are the aspect of the problem about which many members of society will have knowledgeable viewpoints. Discussion of the details of the consequences of various alternatives often depends on technical and complex concepts from various professional fields. Hence, without discussion of values, many people are excluded from participation and others are limited to minor contributions.

Facilitating Involvement in Multiple-Stakeholder Decisions

Many decisions, including those categorized as bargaining or negotiation, involve multiple stakeholders who must interact to produce decisions. Value-focused thinking can contribute to the productivity of such interactions.

If you as one participant explicitly include values in your analysis of alternatives, the appeal of the values will lend support to your choice of a particular alternative. To support other alternatives, adversaries may be forced either to select values at odds with the "reasonable" values in the analysis or to question the adequacy of the "reasonable" factual data used in the analysis. This may weaken an adversary's position and strengthen yours.

If values are not explicitly considered, disagreements must be addressed in a general discussion about alternatives. If values are made explicit, the discussion can separate disagreements about possible consequences from disagreements about the relative desirability of those consequences. This should help identify the basis for conflicts. Only when the basis for conflicts is clearly known can a group constructively begin to reduce them.

Interconnecting Decisions

A decisionmaker naturally faces numerous decisions. It is desirable that these decisions be made in a consistent manner. This means that alternatives chosen in different situations should not work at cross-purposes. It does not mean that all alternatives chosen must further the same specific objectives, but that all alternatives should be chosen to further the same set of ultimate objectives. It is desirable to explicitly state these objectives, which are the decisionmaker's strategic objectives.

Evaluating Alternatives

Value judgments can be quantified and used to build what I refer to as a value model (that is, an objective function). By linking this to a model that describes the consequences of various alternatives, it is possible to derive implications for the relative desirability of the alternatives. Furthermore, sensitivity analyses of the relative desirability of these alternatives to specific value judgments, as well as to specific factual data, can be made.

Conventional decisionmaking methodologies have always attempted to evaluate alternatives; the difference is in the basis for that evaluation. If the objectives are incomplete or not clearly defined, the data for evaluating alternatives are probably not as useful as could be the case. If values are not explicitly specified, the implicit value judgments may not be appropriate for the decision being faced. Most importantly, if the value model is not based on sound judgment and logic, the insights based on evaluation with that value model cannot be sound.

Creating Alternatives

It may be much more important to create alternatives than to evaluate readily available ones. The creativity necessary to design new alternatives is often neglected by decision methodologies. Many decision methodologies not only do not promote creativity, they inhibit it. Value-focused thinking is intended to do just the opposite, to enhance the creation of desirable alternatives.

In decision problems, there is usually an alternative such as the status quo or "an obvious choice." If no better alternatives are found, this alternative will probably do. Often the entire analysis uses this alternative as an anchor and tries to find alternatives that are incrementally better. Even dimensions of thought are anchored by those objectives felt to be sufficient for evaluating existing alternatives. The anchor plays a role similar to that in the assessment of probabilities (see Tversky and Kahneman, 1974) but the implications are potentially far worse. One's thought processes about what alternatives are possible are anchored, and so one is not creative in devising alternatives, and one may settle for an alternative considerably less desirable than others that could have been developed. In value-focused thinking, in contrast, the value model guides the search for creative alternatives in the direction in which one should go.

Identifying Decision Opportunities

What about the cases where decision problems do not appear? Should we just sit and wait? Maybe so. But only if sitting and waiting is an explicit choice made because we have decided that it is the best thing to do. Often, instead of sitting and waiting, it may be preferable to identify decision opportunities, that is, opportunities to better achieve our overall values by formulating a decision situation. Typically, the initial stimulus for this decision opportunity will be a disenchantment with something or a perceived possibility to do something better. But it is also worthwhile to think routinely about how things are going and whether we can do better. Systematically appraising how well we are doing in terms of our values may suggest fruitful decision opportunities to formulate and pursue.

Guiding Strategic Thinking

A decisionmaker's strategic values should be identified to guide all decisions. These strategic values can suggest when and where potentially productive decision opportunities may be lurking. They also suggest the objectives for those decision opportunities, which are more specific than strategic objectives.

Strategic objectives do not vary from day to day. Indeed, if well-stated, they should be stable over years. If the objectives change easily, they simply are not strategic objectives. An individual may want to ski and party one month and work hard to get ahead the next month. To ski, to party, and to work hard may all be important, but they are not strategic objectives for most people. Having a high quality of life is a strategic objective. Whether you get your high quality of life from skiing, partying, or working hard can change, as these activities are only means to your ends. Stating your strategic objectives very clearly and unambig-uously can give you a stable point of reference to guide all of your decisionmaking for a long time. It is a very sound place to begin your thinking when faced with a situation in which you don't even know where to begin.

CHAPTER 2

The Framework of
Value-Focused Thinking

We have seen through a wide range of cases that value-focused thinking has significant advantages over alternative-focused thinking for both identifying decision opportunities and creating alternatives. But, if value-focused thinking is such a good approach for addressing decision situations, why isn't it used all over the place? Why does alternative-focused thinking prevail as *the* mode for addressing decision problems? Although some decisionmakers intuitively follow some of the ideas of value-focused thinking, they do not explicitly use its concepts. The main explanation for this lack of use is obvious: the concepts and procedures have not been developed or integrated into an explicit approach. That is the role of this book.

Let me review the typical decisionmaking process. First, a decision problem is identified. Often this occurs because of dissatisfaction with the current state of affairs and a wish to do something about it. Then the decisionmaker thinks about what can be done and quickly generates some "obvious" alternatives. In other situations, an unanticipated alternative appears (such as a chance to switch jobs), forcing a choice between the status quo alternative and the new one. In both cases, the decisionmaker next selects some criteria to indicate the consequences of the alternatives. The focus is on easy-to-measure "hard" data rather than "soft" objectives like goodwill, quality of the product, amount to be learned, or fun. Therefore, the criteria often only indirectly indicate the fundamental consequences of alternatives. For example, sulfur dioxide emissions are measured as a proxy to indicate the environmental consequences of acid rain. Most of the time spent analyzing the problem is used to estimate the impacts of the alternatives in terms of the proxy measures. The decisionmaker then reviews the information to help make the decision.

This process has many shortcomings. The values should provide the guidance for all the effort on a problem, and yet they are usually treated cursorily and considered only after the set of alternatives is known. The process of identifying alternatives often consists of just choosing those readily apparent. The interaction between values and the creation of alternatives receives essentially no attention. Almost all the effort is reserved for a partial evaluation of the given alternatives. It is partial because the set of objectives is not complete, the criteria (or measures) do not reflect the fundamental objectives but rather proxies, and the achievement of different objectives (or proxies) is not integrated.

Clearly, many good decisionmakers, whether they use analysis or not, and many analysts are much more sophisticated than this. But for too many decision problems this is not an inadequate description of the decisionmaking process (see Russo and Schoemaker, 1989). It is alternative-focused thinking. And it is possible to follow a much better process, value-focused thinking.

2.1 Framing a Decision Situation

A decision is framed by the alternatives and the values considered in making that decision. Since the concepts related to the decision frame are central to understanding value-focused thinking, it is important to clarify the concepts with several definitions.

The *decision context* and the *fundamental objectives* together provide the *decision frame*. The decision context defines the set of alternatives appropriate to consider for a specific decision situation. The fundamental objectives both make explicit the values that one cares about in that context and define the class of consequences of concern. In other words, the fundamental objectives are the ends objectives, as opposed to the means objectives, of a given decision context. It is critical that the decision context and the fundamental objectives be compatible, as they are interdependent concepts.

■ *Investing Personal Funds*
Consider the decision context where an individual wishes to invest personal funds. And suppose that his or her overall fundamental objective

in that context is to maximize the financial return on the investment. This decision context and fundamental objective frame the decision situation, which is represented by the three-dimensional box in Figure 2.1. The left wall of the decision frame is the decision context. The right wall is the fundamental objective.

Within the decision context of investing personal funds, Figure 2.2a suggests several more limited decision contexts that may be appropriate for a particular investor at a particular time:

1. Invest personal funds through a brokerage firm.
2. Invest personal funds with banks.
3. Invest personal funds in stocks.
4. Invest personal funds in certificates of deposit.
5. Invest personal funds in real estate.

As is easily seen, each of these decision contexts limits the set of alternatives to be considered. Each decision context could be related to the same fundamental objective of maximizing the financial return on the investment. In Figure 2.2a we see that these five decision contexts are collectively less broad than the context "invest personal funds." Other

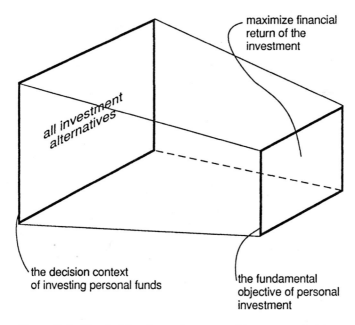

Figure 2.1. The decision frame for personal investment decisions

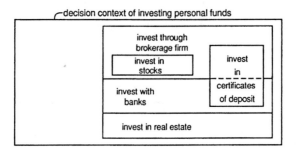

a. the relationships between several decision contexts concerning personal investment

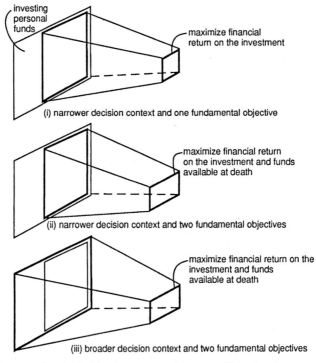

b. expanding the decision frame concerning personal investment

Figure 2.2. Relating decision frames

options would include investing with insurance companies, buying a small business, or simply keeping the funds in the proverbial mattress. Also, we see that some decision contexts are mutually exclusive, such as investing in real estate and investing through a brokerage firm. Other decision contexts are included within broader contexts, as investing in stocks is within investing through brokerage firms, which itself is within the context of investing funds. And some decision contexts overlap; for example, certificates of deposit can be purchased through brokerage firms or at banks.

The framing of the decision situation changes if the investor has a second fundamental objective, such as maximizing funds available for heirs after the investor's death. Having two fundamental objectives broadens the scope of consequences relevant to the decision context. The framing of the decision to invest personal funds in real estate, banks, or brokerage firms combined with the single fundamental objective and with the two fundamental objectives is illustrated in Figure 2.2b. It is not necessary to expand the set of alternatives to account for the broadened fundamental objectives. However, once funds available at death are recognized as an important objective, it may be useful to expand the list of alternatives to include investment in insurance. ■

Both Figures 2.1 and 2.2 show the decision context to be much larger than the fundamental objectives, because there may be billions of alternatives and yet at most only ten to twenty fundamental objectives. This partially indicates the usefulness of focusing on values to frame a decision situation. Even with the difference in numbers of alternatives and objectives, these two categories can be referred to as a match. They match because the objectives are sufficient to evaluate all the alternatives considered and the alternatives are sufficient to describe all the ways that those objectives can be achieved.

2.2 Fundamental Objectives

Values of decisionmakers are made explicit with objectives. Hence, the set of objectives developed for a decision frame is absolutely critical. The fundamental objectives are the basis for any interest in the decision being considered. These objectives qualitatively state all that is of concern in the decision context. They also provide guidance for action and the foundation for any quantitative modeling or analyses that may follow this qualitative articulation of values.

As a simple example of why objectives are so important, consider a study of alumni ten years out of Harvard, conducted by Forrest H. Patton and summarized by McGarvey (1989). Only 3 percent of those responding had written down their objectives, and an additional 14 percent had objectives but had not written them down. The other 83 percent indicated that they did not have explicit objectives. McGarvey reports that alumni with written objectives were earning ten times as much as those with no objectives, while those with objectives, even though unwritten, earned three times as much as those with no objectives.

If the set of objectives selected for a decision context is inadequate, meaning for example incomplete or vague, the power and insights potentially available from value-focused thinking based on the objectives are diminished. The quality of insights from thinking about values can be no better than the quality of the objectives through which the values are expressed. If objectives are missing or vague, alternatives may not be recognized, time and energy may be wasted collecting unnecessary information while useful information may be ignored, and communication about the pros and cons of the alternatives will suffer.

What Are Objectives?

An objective is a statement of something that one desires to achieve. It is characterized by three features: a decision context, an object, and a direction of preference. For example, with respect to traveling in automobiles, one objective is to maximize safety. For this objective, the decision context is automobile travel, the object is safety, and more safety is preferred to less safety. Specification of this objective does not require the identification of a measure to indicate the degree to which safety is achieved, nor does it quantify the relative desirability of different levels of safety. However, both of these concerns are important for a full representation of values (see Chapters 4 and 5).

There are two types of objectives that are important to distinguish. I refer to these as *fundamental objectives* and *means objectives*. Both are context-dependent. A fundamental objective characterizes an essential reason for interest in the decision situation. A means objective is of interest in the decision context because of its implications for the degree to which another (more fundamental) objective can be achieved. Simply stated, the means objectives are important because they are means to the achievement of the fundamental objectives.

Consider a decision context of managing an outpatient health care facility. One objective might be to minimize the time that patients are required to be in the facility. Here minimization is the preference orientation and patient time at the facility is the object. This is a means objective, however, because it is of interest only because of its implications for objectives such as maximizing the quality of health care, minimizing the cost of health care, and minimizing inconvenience to patients. These last three objectives are fundamental objectives because they are essential reasons for operating outpatient facilities.

Means objectives can be very useful for developing models to analyze decision problems and for creating alternatives. However, it is the fundamental objectives that are essential to guide all the effort in decision situations and in the evaluation of alternatives.

2.3 The Decision Context

The decision context is most readily specified by the activity being contemplated. As an example, one decision context facing an electric utility company may be to choose a site for a coal-fired power plant. It directly follows that the set of alternatives of interest are the potential sites for the power plant. Fundamental objectives in this context may include health and safety, environmental, social, and economic concerns.

It is worth noting that a decision context could be an alternative itself in a broader decision context. In the decision context of "supply the electricity our customers need," the utility company may consider alternatives such as building a coal-fired power plant, building a nuclear plant, purchasing electricity from other sources, or encouraging conservation measures by customers.

The decision context and the fundamental objectives that frame a decision situation must be compatible. This issue is addressed when the fundamental objectives for a given decision context are specified. A few examples illustrate this critical concept.

■ *Air Pollution Standards*
The Environmental Protection Agency has a major responsibility for managing air pollution in the United States. For simplicity, let me con-

sider only carbon monoxide (CO) air pollution (see Keeney, Sarin, and Winkler, 1984). The decision context for this case might be defined as to manage CO pollution. To be a little more precise, the decision context is to manage CO pollution while conducting activities deemed to be desirable (such as operating factories and vehicles). Even with this elaboration, the decision context does not clearly characterize the set of possible alternatives that should be considered, because of different possible interpretations of the word *manage*. These interpretations are defined by the fundamental objectives for the decision context. In other words, the fundamental objectives define the set of alternatives that are appropriate to consider in the decision context.

Four different possible fundamental objectives for the decision context of managing CO pollution are as follows:

1. Minimize CO emissions.
2. Minimize CO concentrations.
3. Minimize population exposure to CO.
4. Minimize health effects due to CO.

The meaning of the decision context of managing CO pollution directly follows from these respective fundamental objectives. For objective 1, managing CO pollution means managing CO pollution emissions. For objective 2, it means controlling CO concentrations, and for objectives 3 and 4, the decision contexts are respectively controlling population exposure to CO and controlling the health effects due to CO.

With each of these clearer descriptions of the decision context, it appears as if the decision context and the fundamental objective are almost one and the same. For example, the decision context of managing CO emissions and the fundamental objective of minimizing CO emissions sound the same. But the former refers to the alternatives, such as putting air pollution devices on smokestacks, and the latter refers to implications of those alternatives, such as tons of CO emitted into the atmosphere.

The relative breadth of the four decision contexts characterized by "manage CO pollution" is illustrated in Figure 2.3a. It is important that the breadth of the decision context match the breadth of the fundamental objectives. If this match is not made properly, the range of alternatives considered may be too narrow. To illustrate, suppose the decision situation is framed by the context of controlling CO emissions and by the fundamental objective of minimizing health effects attributable to CO, as indicated in Figure 2.3b. Then the class of alternatives to be

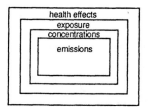

a. four decision contexts for managing CO pollution

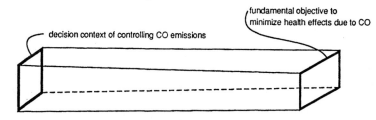

b. an inappropriate match of decision context and fundamental objective

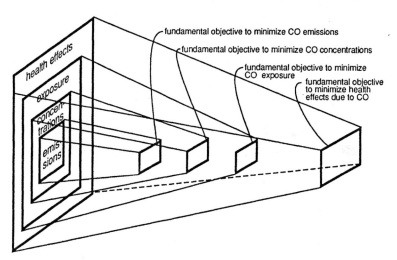

c. several appropriate matches of decision context and fundamental objective

Figure 2.3. Relationships of four decision frames concerning carbon monoxide pollution

considered is only those that bear on CO emissions, which are only a subset of those that bear on the health effects of CO. Alternatives that reduce CO concentrations but do not affect CO emissions are not considered, nor are alternatives that directly effect exposure or health effects but not emissions. Such alternatives are clearly relevant to the fundamental objective of reducing health effects. Figure 2.3b illustrates an inappropriate match between decision context and fundamental objective. Figure 2.3c illustrates several appropriate matches, where the decision context and the fundamental objectives are compatible. Once the fundamental objective is articulated, the decision context should be set or reset to match that fundamental objective. ∎

∎ *Ambulance Service*

It is easy to state the decision context concerning ambulance service. The decision context is to provide high-quality ambulance service. In this case, the precise meaning of high-quality service is crucial to defining the decision context. This meaning is clarified by the fundamental objectives. Let me indicate how four different fundamental objectives help define the decision context and relate to one another in this context. The fundamental objectives are as follows:

1. Minimize response time to reach the patient.
2. Maximize quality of ambulance personnel.
3. Minimize time until patient is at a hospital.
4. Maximize the number of people saved.

Different alternatives should be considered for each of these objectives, as illustrated in Figure 2.4.

With objective 1, appropriate alternatives to consider involve purchasing more ambulances, improving dispatching service, changing locations of ambulances, and training drivers to select quicker routes. The last alternative is also relevant to objective 2, as are alternatives that place better-trained medical personnel on ambulances or give better training to ambulance personnel.

All of the alternatives for minimizing response time and for maximizing the quality of ambulance personnel can contribute to the broader objective 3 of minimizing travel time. Thus the decision context to match objective 3 includes the contexts for objectives 1 and 2. But some other alternatives may also contribute to objective 3 that do not influence objectives 1 and 2. Examples include furnishing ambulances with special equipment to allow quicker at-the-scene evaluation of pa-

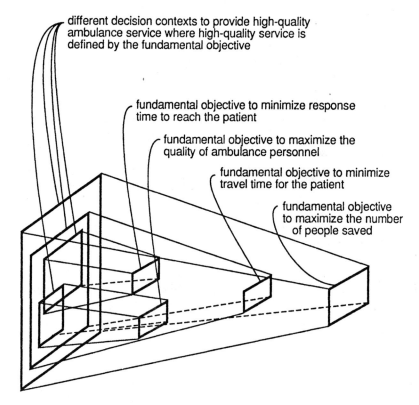

different decision contexts to provide high-quality ambulance service where high-quality service is defined by the fundamental objective

fundamental objective to minimize response time to reach the patient

fundamental objective to maximize the quality of ambulance personnel

fundamental objective to minimize travel time for the patient

fundamental objective to maximize the number of people saved

Figure 2.4. Four decision frames concerning high-quality ambulance service

tients or to assist in placing patients in an ambulance and preparing them for any travel.

Objective 4, maximizing the number of people saved, is the broadest of the listed objectives. The associated decision context includes all those for objectives 1 through 3. Hence all of the alternatives in those contexts are legitimate to consider in this broader decision context. Additional alternatives that might be appropriate include placing better equipment on ambulances that might save lives and improving facilities for receiving ambulance patients at the hospital. ∎

▣ *Business Management*
Management decisions are clearly critical to a firm. The decision context is critical to examining any of these decisions. To indicate this in a simple manner, consider three possible decision contexts:

1. Provide the best product.
2. Manage sales of the product.
3. Enhance shareholders' wealth.

These contexts could be relevant to a firm that produces physical products, such as breakfast cereals or integrated circuit testers (see Section 11.5), or a service firm.

With decision context 1, a crucial question concerns the fundamental objectives that characterize best product. Two distinct possibilities are minimizing the cost of the product and maximizing the quality of the product. The two decision contexts defined by these objectives are likely to overlap: some alternatives will influence product quality as defined by either of the two objectives. A third decision context is indicated by specifying both of the two objectives. Clearly the precise decision context is different for these three situations.

Decision context 2 is naturally broader. All of the alternatives that might contribute to providing the best product are relevant, and additional alternatives that concern sales volume, marketing strategy, distribution policy, and so forth are also possibilities to be considered. The precise decision context will be controlled by the specific fundamental objective, which may be to maximize sales or to maximize profits from the product. The latter is clearly broader, as sales is only one of the means to profits.

The broadest of the decision contexts is enhance shareholders' wealth. The exact definition of the decision context will depend on the meaning of *enhance* and the fundamental objectives. It is safe to conclude, however, that decision context 2 is contained within decision context 3, meaning that all the alternatives relevant to decision context 2 are also relevant to decision context 3. ∎

2.4 Guiding Strategic Thinking and Action

The broadest decision context facing any decisionmaker (I define *decisionmaker* to mean an individual or organization or any other decisionmaking entity) is the *strategic decision context*. It is defined by the set of all possible alternatives, including dynamic decision strategies, available to that decisionmaker. The fundamental objectives corresponding to the strategic decision context are the decisionmaker's ultimate end objectives. By definition, I will refer to these ultimate end objectives as *strategic objectives*. All objectives of any decision context, other than the strategic decision context, facing that decisionmaker must be means to achieve the strategic objectives. The strategic decision frame is illustrated in Figure 2.5.

Strategic Objectives

Every individual and every organization has strategic objectives. Although they are often not explicitly written down, these objectives are intended to guide all decisionmaking. The separate decisions made over time are the means by which strategic objectives are pursued. These same decisions collectively determine how well the individual or organization performs. The strategic objectives should provide common guidance to all decisions and to all decision opportunities. In an organization, they also serve as the mechanism by which management can guide decisions made by different individuals and groups within the organization. If these strategic objectives are not carefully defined and communicated, the guidance is minimal and some separate decisions simply won't make sense in the larger context of the organization's affairs.

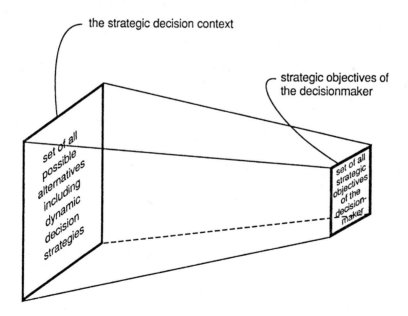

Figure 2.5. The strategic decision frame facing a decisionmaker

So why is it that strategic objectives are often not completely and unambiguously stated? I believe the reason is alternative-focused thinking, the precise curse that value-focused thinking about strategic objectives would break. Strategic objectives, if they are written down at all, are usually vague statements that everyone would easily agree with. They are too vague to be useful for guidance. In my terminology, these "strategic objectives" are not objectives at all; they are value statements that need to be interpreted to be useful. Furthermore, specifying strategic objectives is often not recognized as a decision opportunity. A person or an organization can choose to have clearly defined strategic objectives or not. The decision opportunity to structure strategic objectives has a tremendous potential to aid decisionmaking. It establishes a sound basis for decisionmaking that can be repeatedly used, and it provides a stable reference point for even the most turbulent of decision situations.

The Strategic Decision Context

For an individual, the strategic decision context is managing one's life. I will refer to the fundamental objective in this decision context as "to maximize the quality of life," a notion closely related to self-actualization as described in Maslow (1968). A great deal of effort is necessary to define quality of life, but nevertheless that is the strategic objective. The set of alternatives defined by the decision context is all possible alternatives for the individual.

By analogy, the strategic decision context for a firm is management of the firm. The strategic objective may be something like to be the best, meaning most profitable, most prestigious, and most growth-oriented. The class of alternatives implied by the decision context is the entire set of options available to the firm. In the strategic decision context of managing the United States, the class of alternatives might be all alternatives available to the federal government. The strategic objective in this context might be stated as "to maximize the quality of life for all citizens."

Rarely are decisions addressed on the strategic level. The focus is almost always on more limited decision situations, which are also important and worthy of being addressed with significant time and effort. It is necessary to reduce the decision frame to foster useful thinking and analyses. This is done in two ways: the decision context is reduced so fewer alternatives are appropriate, and, the fundamental objective for the decision context is reduced to limit the set of consequences of concern.

Recall the decision context of an individual investing personal funds, framed in Figure 2.1. This context can be placed inside the strategic context of managing one's life shown in Figure 2.5. This nesting is done in Figure 2.6, which indicates that the decision context of investing personal funds is naturally a subset of the decision context of managing one's life. Figure 2.6 also indicates that the fundamental objective of financial return is more limited than the strategic objective of quality of life. Financial return is one of the means to quality of life, as is represented by the shortened frame of the investment context relative to the life context in Figure 2.6.

There is another way in which the strategic decision frame may be reduced. Only a subset of the alternatives in the strategic decision con-

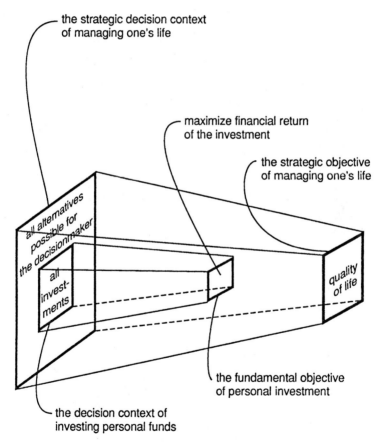

Figure 2.6. The decision frame for personal investment decisions nested in the strategic decision frame facing a decisionmaker

text may influence some of the strategic objectives, so when considering these objectives the decisionmaker need address only a part of the strategic decision frame.

2.5 The Framework

There is a vast discrepancy between the way decision situations are usually examined and the way they should be in order to be consistent with the decisionmaker's values and information. Value-focused thinking will help overcome this discrepancy.

The major shortcomings of alternative-focused thinking are that (1) viable alternatives, possibly much better than the alternatives considered, are not identified; (2) the objectives identified are often only means to the consequences that are of fundamental concern; and (3) there is not a logical match between alternatives and objectives. In short, alternative-focused thinking is too narrow.

Figure 2.7a illustrates alternative-focused thinking in the framework of the strategic decision frame. The framework is drawn with broken lines to make the point about what is missing: namely, the fundamental objectives and the decision context are not usually made explicit with alternative-focused thinking. The alternatives are represented by points A, B, and C in the set of all decisions. These alternatives are evaluated using a means objective or a set of means objectives. There is not necessarily a match between these objectives and the available alternatives. Pictorially, there are several points representing alternatives near alternatives A, B, and C in Figure 2.7a, that are not identified and yet could contribute to the same means objectives.

Value-focused thinking can significantly alleviate the shortcomings of alternative-focused thinking. The process of framing the decision situation is likely to begin with an intuitive rough-cut that may not be very distinct from the frame provided by alternative-focused thinking. The first step of value-focused thinking is to broaden the decision situation and define it more carefully.

The critical task at this stage is to define the fundamental objectives for the decision context. To do this, we work from two directions. The means objectives in Figure 2.7a are pushed out using a means-ends logic (see Chapter 3) until fundamental objectives for the evolving decision situation are found. From the other direction, we work back from our strategic objectives, or from other stated sets of broad objectives, to

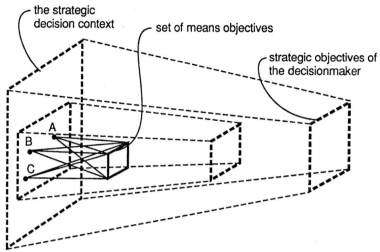

a. alternative-focused thinking with alternatives A, B, and C

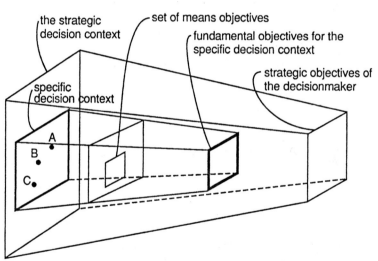

b. the decision frame based on value-focused thinking

Figure 2.7. Contrasting alternative-focused thinking and value-focused thinking for the same decision frame

generate fundamental objectives for the given decision. There may be some give and take owing to this push-pull thought process, but a reasonable set of fundamental objectives will emerge. These fundamental objectives will be much broader than the means objectives that we began with but naturally narrower than the strategic objectives.

At this point we return to the decision context to broaden it, that is, to increase the range of potential alternatives, and to match the decision context to the fundamental objectives. Essentially the decision context is the answer to the question "What is the set of all alternatives that can affect achievement of the fundamental objectives?"

Now we have a well-defined decision frame with what I refer to as a preliminary decision context and a preliminary set of fundamental objectives. Then it is appropriate to check back and forth until the decision context and fundamental objectives consistently match and, in our judgment, define all that is important for the decision situation. Figure 2.7b illustrates this decision situation within the framework of all decisions.

Figure 2.8 indicates the value-focused thinking framework for a

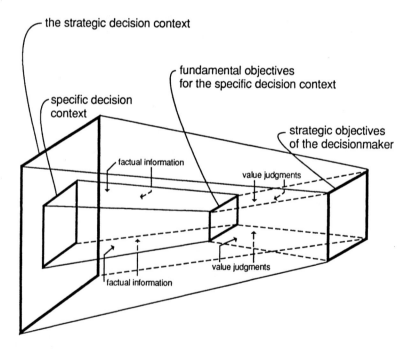

Figure 2.8. The value-focused-thinking framework with flow of information indicated

specific decision within the framework of a decisionmaker's strategic decision context. The small box inside the larger one represents the specific decision situation. It is framed by the decision context on the left and the fundamental objectives on the right. The decision context defines the set of possible alternatives for the decision situation, and the fundamental objectives define the set of consequences of interest. The decision context is drawn much larger than the fundamental objectives, because there are usually far more alternatives than fundamental objectives.

The decision frame distinguishes those concerns relevant to the specific decision situation from concerns relevant to all decision situations that may face the decisionmaker. Facts and values are necessary links between the specific decision context and all other decisions. Facts are needed to relate alternatives to fundamental objectives. In a sense, these facts come externally from other decision situations through the upper, lower, and side walls of the specific decision frame. Values are needed to relate the fundamental objectives to the strategic objectives. These values, expressed as value judgments, are also introduced externally to the specific decision situation, as indicated in Figure 2.8.

2.6 Comparing Alternative-Focused and Value-Focused Thinking

Value-focused thinking and alternative-focused thinking are not merely two different approaches to "solving" decision problems. Solving decision problems is the sole aim of alternative-focused thinking. Value-focused thinking is much broader. One of its aims is to solve decision problems, but value-focused thinking is also concerned with the identification of decision opportunities—a process that is sometimes called problem finding.

It is typically a need that leads to problem solving. A decision situation is dropped in our laps by someone else or by circumstances beyond our control, and we need to take some action. The standard ways to address such decision problems use alternative-focused thinking. Alternative-focused thinking is reactive.

Rather than a need, it is a desire to do better, to strive toward the best possible consequence in terms of our values, that leads to the identification of decision opportunities. Value-focused thinking is proactive. It is our job, our opportunity, to create a decision opportunity.

Since value-focused thinking and alternative-focused thinking are both ways to address decision situations, it is only natural that they have some activities in common, as indicated in Table 2.1. They differ in how these activities are conducted, the order in which they are carried out, and ultimately how good the implications are. Value-focused thinking also includes activities that have no obvious analogue in alternative-focused thinking. Let me describe in oversimplified terms both alternative-focused and value-focused thinking in order to detail their similarities and differences.

Alternative-Focused Thinking

As shown in Table 2.1, there are five major activities associated with alternative-focused thinking. The first activity is recognizing that a decision problem has arisen. The decision problem usually occurs as a result of actions that are not controlled by the decisionmaker. Sometimes an alternative to the status quo is proposed, as when someone is offered a new job. At other times, the decision problem is recognized in response to a need. A company may have an unprofitable division or be losing market share to a competitor, or a government program may be evaluated as ineffective. In each such case, the cry goes out that something must be done.

The next activity is to identify alternatives. The status quo alternative exists and perhaps other proposed alternatives. Sometimes the decision context for the problem is cast narrowly so that identifying all alternatives is easy. For example, if a decision problem is defined as to close or not to close a facility, then all alternatives are stated by definition. Since many decision problems are characterized by the words "Choose the best among the alternatives," the set of alternatives is de facto determined.

Decisionmakers employing alternative-focused thinking do sometimes search for additional alternatives. However, the already-stated alternatives anchor the thought process, stifling creativity and innovation. As a result, newly created alternatives often share many features with the original alternatives. As an example, if two existing alternatives to supply a part necessary to manufacture your product are to make it yourself or buy it from Nanosystems, Inc., you may come up with the new alternative of purchasing the part from Picosystems, Inc. Alternatives like using a different part or redesigning the product so the part is not necessary may less readily come to mind.

The third activity is specifying the values for evaluation of the alternatives. With alternative-focused thinking, this activity can be carried out with various degrees of formality. At one level, without deep thought, a decisionmaker may select an objective such as maximizing sales. If analysis is used, first criteria to distinguish the alternatives are chosen. These criteria are typically selected based on thinking about the alternatives, not about the fundamental objectives to be achieved. The criteria should then be appraised to be sure they adequately describe the range of possible consequences.

The evaluation of alternatives and the selection of an alternative are the final activities. The evaluation addresses the degree to which the alternatives measure up in terms of the criteria. Then the selection of an alternative is based on an interpretation of the implications of an analysis and/or on an intuitive appraisal of the alternatives.

Table 2.1. Comparing sequences of activities with alternative-focused and value-focused thinking

Alternative-focused thinking for decision problems

1. Recognize a decision problem
2. Identify alternatives
3. Specify values
4. Evaluate alternatives
5. Select an alternative

Value-focused thinking

For decision problems	For decision opportunities	
	Before specifying strategic objectives	After specifying strategic objectives
1. Recognize a decision problem	1. Identify a decision opportunity	1. Specify values
2. Specify values	2. Specify values	2. Create a decision opportunity
3. Create alternatives	3. Create alternatives	3. Create alternatives
4. Evaluate alternatives	4. Evaluate alternatives	4. Evaluate alternatives
5. Select an alternative	5. Select an alternative	5. Select an alternative

Value-Focused Thinking

As shown in Table 2.1, the activities involved in value-focused thinking are somewhat different for the two types of decision situations: decision problems and decision opportunities. Furthermore, decision opportunities may be recognized either before or after the decisionmaker specifies strategic objectives.

For decision problems, the five activities of value-focused thinking are the same as those of alternative-focused thinking. However, the procedures used in conducting the activities and their order are different.

Values come before alternatives in value-focused thinking. Hence, after a decision problem is recognized, the full specification of values is the next activity. For many decisions, these values should first be qualitatively explored at length and then possibly quantified. The qualitatively articulated values, and any quantitative embellishments, are then directly used in the third activity, the creation of alternatives. The intent is to broaden the range of alternatives considered by eliminating any anchoring on already-identified alternatives.

The evaluation process and the selection of an alternative can then be explicitly based on an analysis relying on any established evaluation methodology. These activities are very similar to what should be done with alternative-focused thinking when an analysis of the alternatives is conducted.

Unlike decision problems, decision opportunities are identified and defined by the decisionmaker rather than precipitated by external parties or events. Decision opportunities that occur before the specification of the decisionmaker's strategic objectives come up in two distinct ways. First, in addressing a decision problem, the decisionmaker may realize that it is desirable to broaden the decision context. The values made explicit in consideration of the decision problem stimulate the thought necessary to identify a decision opportunity. Second, a decisionmaker may discover a decision opportunity out of a desire to do something better. The decisionmaker may notice that a resource is being underused or unused. For example, the realization that a waste product may be useful identifies a decision opportunity. Often the decision opportunity grows out of an intuitive appraisal of how well objectives, stated or unstated, are being met. Recognizing the desire to make certain improvements sets up a decision opportunity.

Once the decision opportunity has been identified, the next activity is the specification of relevant values. The concepts and procedures used are identical to those used to address values in decision problems. Then the concern shifts to creating alternatives to achieve the specified values. There may be significant interplay between the identification and structuring of values and the creation of alternatives.

At some stage in the process, the decisionmaker ends the search for alternatives, at least temporarily. At this time, the decision opportunity has been structured exactly like a decision problem. With the objectives and alternatives fixed for the time being, the evaluation and selection processes begin. The evaluation may lead to insights that cause one to create additional alternatives, but typically a decision will eventually be made in this decision context. There may, however, be additional iteration if the decision context is again changed to recognize a different, and presumably better, decision opportunity.

Before specifying strategic objectives, a decisionmaker may use alternative-focused thinking in one decision situation and use value-focused thinking in another decision situation. It is perhaps a bit schizophrenic, but one can jump back and forth from one approach to another on different "problems." But after the decisionmaker does the deep thinking necessary to identify and structure strategic objectives and spends the time to understand the guiding significance of these objectives for decisionmaking, the decisionmaker should naturally use value-focused thinking in all decision situations. The decisionmaker will now view the world "through value-focused glasses."

The additional activity of value-focused thinking in this case is identifying and structuring the strategic objectives. These objectives provide a guide for all of the other activities associated with decisionmaking. The specification of values leads to many insights that enable the decisionmaker to perform these activities better. Perhaps the most significant benefit is that the decisionmaker can productively create, rather than simply identify, decision opportunities.

2.7 Ethics and Value Neutrality

Values and ethics are related concepts in most people's minds. Ethics are meant to guide all one's actions, so it is natural that they should guide decisions resulting from value-focused thinking.

Ethics represent the absolute values that are unalterable. Evaluating alternatives according to ethical principles divides the possible alternatives into two groups, those consistent with the principles and those inconsistent with them. For example, an executive may have an ethical principle that the firm is not to cheat its customers. An individual may have an ethical principle not to discriminate against others for any reason. In any specific case, it may be difficult to ascertain if the ethical principle is being followed, but the assumption is that the principle either is or is not being followed. You cannot be 65 percent consistent with an ethical principle.

A decisionmaker's ethics have two major influences on value-focused thinking. Ethical principles eliminate alternatives and guide the specification of objectives. Thus ethics have a natural influence on the decision frame by their effect on both the decision context and the fundamental objectives.

Alternatives in the decision frame are eliminated in an implicit manner. Alternatives that violate ethical principles simply are not selected, evaluated, or often even thought of as possible contenders. An executive who follows the principle of not cheating customers will not consider price-fixing in collaboration with competitors as a legitimate alternative to improve profit. The alternative simply will not come to mind or will be dismissed without serious consideration.

The other role of ethics is in guiding the identification of objectives. This influence is particularly clear with fundamental objectives, as they are the broadest set of objectives for a specific decision context. In the case of the ethical principle of not cheating customers, a fundamental objective in a specific decision context might be to provide the best product for the least cost.

Value-focused thinking is value neutral. Any application of the approach, naturally enough, is not value neutral but value laden. Saying that value-focused thinking is value neutral means that the approach can be utilized in a manner that is consistent with any set of ethical principles (Keeney, 1984). If a decisionmaker wishes to follow the utilitarian ethical principle of the "greatest good for the greatest number," it is straightforward to do this in an application of value-focused thinking. It is also easy to develop strategic objectives that are consistent with and promote acting in accord with these principles. On the other hand, a decisionmaker may be concerned with treating different individuals or groups equitably. Many nonutilitarian ethical theories espouse this principle. It is also straightforward to implement value-focused thinking in a manner consistent with such principles. Likewise, strategic objectives can conform to such principles.

PART TWO

FOUNDATIONS

CHAPTER 3

Identifying and Structuring Objectives

The achievement of objectives is the sole reason for being interested in any decision. And yet, unfortunately, objectives are not adequately articulated for many important decisions. There are several explanations for this state of affairs. First, decisionmakers may think they understand their objectives well, although often this is not the case. Second, decisionmakers are routinely under pressure to "produce tangible results" so they don't have the time to carefully articulate their objectives. And third, there is a serious lack of structured approaches to promote systematic and deep thinking about objectives. All decision gurus state "list objectives" somewhere in their schemes. But they do not clearly address what objectives to list, how to go about listing them, or how to use them. Simply listing objectives is shallow. Identifying, structuring, analyzing, and understanding objectives should be much deeper. If you really care about a decision, objectives are worth deep and serious thought. This chapter discusses how to direct that thought.

3.1 Identifying Objectives

Values provide the foundation for interest in any decision situation. Since the values that are of concern in a given decision situation are made explicit by the identification of objectives, this process is crucial. Before discussing the devices that may help individuals identify objectives, let us briefly consider who such individuals should be.

Who Should Specify Objectives

The main purpose of identifying and structuring objectives is to provide insight for better decisions. However, decisionmakers themselves do not necessarily need to be the ones who specify objectives. Indeed, for many complex decision problems, there are neither obvious decisionmakers nor clear decision processes. For decisions involving reproductive freedom, illegal immigration, gun control, or the quality of education, the decision processes evolve over time and the decisionmakers are identified during this evolution. Yet it is particularly true in such situations that a logical identification and structuring of objectives can provide significant help for all those who end up involved in the decision process.

The objectives for a decision situation should come from individuals interested in and knowledgeable about that situation. This section will focus on circumstances where objectives are specified by a single entity, such as an individual or group with responsibility for a decision or for recommending a decision. The entity may specify its own objectives or its perception of the objectives of the decisionmakers or stakeholders affected by the decision. In some cases, these objectives may represent large groups, such as the public, with diverse interests. In other cases, they may represent an individual facing his or her own decision problem. A second type of decision situation, where the objectives are elicited from more than one entity, is discussed in Section 3.8.

The Process

The process of identifying objectives requires significant creativity and hard thinking about a decision situation. Therefore, it is often helpful to enlist a facilitator to guide the process. I will address the rest of this section to the facilitator. But all the questions and devices suggested to elicit objectives from others are also appropriate when an individual is analyzing a decision situation alone. If you are that individual, you address the questions to yourself rather than to some other respondent.

The most obvious way to identify objectives is to engage in a discussion of the decision situation. Early in the discussion, either the decision context or some objectives should be roughly outlined. With this rough description of the decision situation, you begin an iterative process by asking "What would you like to achieve in this situation?" The responses provide a list of potential objectives and a basis for further probing.

When eliciting objectives from more than one individual, first ask each one to provide a written list of objectives, and then move on to group discussion of the lists. This sequence will promote thinking from every individual. If general discussion began immediately, it would be too easy for group members to anchor on the ideas presented by the first speakers.

There are several devices that can help to stimulate the identification of possible objectives. As will be obvious, these devices provide redundant guidance for identifying objectives. The major purpose in identifying objectives is to be as complete as possible. Redundancy is not an issue at this stage, as it is much easier to recognize redundant objectives when they are explicitly listed than it is to identify missing objectives. The devices for identifying objectives are listed in Table 3.1.

Use of a Wish List. When asking any individual to express objectives, make it clear that what is needed is a qualitative list of objectives without ranking or priorities. To expand the list, you may ask "If you had no limitations at all, what would your objectives be?" Similarly, you may ask what elements constitute the bottom line for the decision situation and for the decisionmaker.

There are many words that should trigger questions that will make implicit objectives explicit. Such words include *tradeoffs, consequences, impacts, concerns, fair, balance,* and so forth. For example, if a respondent says "Tradeoffs are necessary," ask tradeoffs between what and what.

Table 3.1.   Devices to use in identifying objectives

1. A wish list

2. Alternatives

3. Problems and shortcomings

4. Consequences

5. Goals, constraints, and guidelines

6. Different perspectives

7. Strategic objectives

8. Generic objectives

9. Structuring objectives

10. Quantifying objectives

If a respondent says "The consequences should be fair," ask fair to whom, and what is fair. If the respondent seems to stop and think, ask what the thoughts are. Responses to any of these questions may lead into the use of other devices as appropriate.

Use of Alternatives. Often one begins to think hard about a decision situation only after at least two alternatives become apparent. The question then is which of the alternatives is best. This raises the issue of what makes one alternative better than another. An articulation of the features that distinguish existing alternatives provides a basis for identifying some objectives for the decision problem (see Buede, 1986). For example, in a consideration of alternative sites for an airport, the alternatives might be differentiated by the amount of disruption of nearby residents' lives due to high noise levels. This would suggest the obvious objective of minimizing disruption from noise. You might also ask respondents to list particularly desirable and undesirable features of alternatives and use these to stimulate thought about objectives.

Existing alternatives are a useful source of objectives. You might simply ask what the objectives of each alternative are. Pushing slightly further, you might ask what alternatives or programs are considered to be very successful or failing. These extreme cases can serve to highlight objectives that should be considered in future decisions.

Hypothetical alternatives can also be useful. You might ask respondents to describe a "perfect" alternative or a "terrible" alternative, then ask what makes it perfect or terrible. Similarly, you might ask respondents to describe their pet project or an alternative that they would personally not like to have chosen, and again pursue their reasons. Or you might discuss whether a slight modification of either an existing or a hypothetical alternative would make the alternative better or worse, and why. In any of these cases, the reasoning should suggest possible objectives.

A useful way to generate hypothetical alternatives is as follows. For an already stated objective, ask for an alternative that would probably be excellent in terms of that objective. Then ask what other implications that alternative would have. In this manner, the creation of real or hypothetical alternatives can also help in identifying objectives.

Use of Problems and Shortcomings. At any given time, a decisionmaker is working on problems and recognizing shortcomings with respect to achievement. The basic idea for generating objectives from either circumstance is to articulate the reasons for the concern.

You may ask what major problems the respondent is working on now, or what major problems are confronting the decisionmaker. If an individual says she is trying to "bring some order into her life," pursue the precise objectives that define such order for her. If "inventory problems" are the major problem facing a company, pursue specific objectives to alleviate these problems.

A slightly different twist to stimulate thinking is to ask what needs to be changed from the status quo. In other words, ask how matters could be or should be improved. If this suggestion does not bear fruit, consider what areas are less than perfect even if matters generally seem fine. It is sometimes useful in situations with stakeholders to ask if any of them are less pleased than others or if some groups of stakeholders are not as well treated as others. Following up the reasons why different stakeholders may be more or less satisfied should suggest objectives.

Use of Consequences. Consequences are descriptions of the impacts of alternatives described in terms of the degree to which objectives are met. Therefore, if one can articulate consequences that matter, it is quite easy to identify associated objectives.

To begin, you might ask if there are any consequences that would be unacceptable. Responses to this often indicate consequences that are undesirable rather than truly unacceptable. For example, in numerous contexts involving consumption (for example, of food, energy, medicine, transportation), I have heard people state that health and safety risks are unacceptable. The fact is, such risks are unavoidable. They may be reduced or minimized, but not to zero, so these unacceptable consequences suggest objectives. Related to this device, you might ask a respondent to describe an undesirable "future history" and say why it would be undesirable.

There are various ways to expand the list of objectives. A simple way is to sum up the discussion in terms of objectives on the list and ask if there are any more. For example, you might say that all of the consequences of concern seem to be economic ones, and ask if there are any other types of consequences that matter. Another way is to ask if there are any consequences the respondent cares about but feels unable to influence. The response helps to identify objectives that have not been on the table, but perhaps should be. Once they are articulated, that choice can be easily made. During discussions of operating policies for hydroelectric dams, one respondent mentioned that some "environmental disturbance" was inevitable. We then identified several environmental objectives that could be influenced by decisions being contemplated.

Value tradeoffs may help identify objectives. In one case, suppose that minimizing cost (or maximizing profit) has already been identified as an objective. You might ask respondents what they would have to receive to be willing to bear more cost, or what they could forgo to make costs lower. In a similar vein, you might ask if there are tradeoffs that the respondent thinks should not be entertained. A response like "We cannot give up one iota of quality" suggests that important objectives relate to quality.

Use of Goals, Constraints, and Guidelines. In normal conversation, the term *goal* is often used to describe the same concept that I have defined as an objective. I use *goal* to refer to a different, but related, concept. To avoid confusion, let me give an example. In a decision context of transporting hazardous waste material to a disposal site, say that two objectives are to minimize the annual cost of transportation and to maximize the safety of the operations. Goals related to these objectives are to keep the annual transportation cost less than $10 million and to insure that no accidents occur.

A goal substitutes a level or standard with respect to a specific measure of an objective for the orientation of preferences provided for that objective. The goal is either achieved or it is not. Therefore, goals are sometimes useful for motivating greater achievement of objectives. However, objectives are much better for creating and evaluating alternatives and for focusing attention on the important aspects of decision situations.

Constraints are similar to goals in that they have a standard. This standard is meant to screen unacceptable alternatives from consideration. Constraints in the context of transporting hazardous waste may be avoiding transportation at night, presumably to reduce the chances of accidents, and traveling by the shortest route on paved highways, presumably to reduce costs while avoiding less safe roads. Both of these constraints eliminate possible alternatives from further consideration. Even though the intent of constraints is to limit alternatives, they are sometimes stated in terms of the achievement of objectives. For instance, a constraint might be that the cost of transporting hazardous waste should not exceed $10 million annually. Clearly, in this case, the constraint is the reciprocal of a goal, in that it states what not to do whereas a goal states what to do. Constraints applied directly to the decision context are useful if they eliminate clearly inferior alternatives, thus allowing more time and resources to be directed to creating and evaluating contending alternatives.

Both goals and constraints can suggest objectives. For instance, if a goal of a mail-order house is to ship 90 percent of its orders within two days and the reciprocal constraint is that no more than 10 percent of the orders should take more than two days, an obvious associated objective is to minimize the time between order and shipment. Less obvious, but perhaps more important, are the objectives that led to the establishment of the goal or constraint in the first place. Thinking about who set the goal or constraint and why may help identify appropriate objectives for the problem at hand.

In many contexts, regulations set constraints that limit the alternatives that can be legitimately considered in a decision situation. For instance, if a military regulation states that 20 percent of a particular type of aircraft should be in the air at any given time in a given area, then alternatives that would result in less than 20 percent being in the air should not be considered. This regulation suggests that an objective might be to maximize the percentage of aircraft in the air. It should be clear that in such a problem there would be other objectives, such as minimizing aircraft operating costs and minimizing aircraft accidents (which would require time on the ground for maintenance), that would naturally conflict with maximizing the percentage of aircraft in the air. All decision problems have such conflicting objectives that must be weighed in any consideration of alternatives.

Guidelines are less definitive than either goals or constraints. They only indicate, perhaps strongly, either objectives or alternatives that should or should not be considered. Guidelines come from many sources, including mission statements, policy guidelines, strategic plans, or incentive systems. Typically, they cover broad issues. Hence, in any decision context, you should consider how a specific guideline might help define a relevant objective. If a bank has a policy of "providing superior service to customers," you should ask in any decision context for that bank how the alternatives may influence the quality of customer service. The responses you receive will suggest objectives.

Use of Different Perspectives. When people are asked to state objectives, they naturally begin to think of the objectives from their own perspectives at the time. This is useful. It is also useful to vary the perspective.

If you ask physicians to specify objectives for a hospital, they are likely to begin with objectives relevant to themselves at the time. After they have identified a set of objectives, you might ask them to take the perspective of other stakeholders, such as nurses, administrative staff, or patients, and list objectives from that perspective. To push the thought further, ask what objectives the physicians have for each of these stakeholder groups. Many of the devices already mentioned can be used to stimulate thinking. For example, you might ask what alternatives would be either unacceptable or highly desirable to each stakeholder and why.

Viewing today from the future can also provide a distinct perspective that suggests objectives. An individual may contemplate where he would like to be in ten years and work back to see what objectives this implies for today. A U.S. company's wish to have a market for products in Eastern Europe in five years should suggest specific objectives for today. A thought experiment may help visualize objectives: ask respondents to imagine they are shipwrecked for ten years and then come back to find that circumstances are intolerable. Asking why they are intolerable will help pinpoint objectives.

Still another way to change perspectives is to eliminate some of the realism of any situation. Ask respondents to suppose they are the "ultimate decisionmaker," able to act with no limitations from anyone or anything. Considering what they would do and why should suggest possible objectives.

Use of Strategic Objectives. Strategic objectives, which I introduced in Chapter 2, are the ultimate objectives of a decisionmaker. All other objectives of that decisionmaker must be means objectives to the strategic objectives. Thus, the purpose of any decision is to contribute to the achievement of the strategic objectives. You should carefully consider how alternatives in the current decision context may contribute to the strategic objectives. The responses indicate potential fundamental objectives for the problem at hand.

There are chains of means objectives linking a particular decision frame to the decisionmaker's strategic objectives. Correspondingly, a specific decision context is only part of a larger one, which is itself only a part of a still larger one, until the strategic decision context is reached. Achieving the objectives in a narrower decision context is one of the means to achieving the objectives in the broader decision context. If the fundamental objectives of the broader context have been articulated, you can generate objectives for the narrower context by asking, for each fundamental objective in turn, what can be done in the present decision context to contribute to its achievement.

Use of Generic Objectives. Whereas strategic objectives are intended to define the concerns of a single decisionmaker for all decision situations, generic objectives attempt to define the concerns for all decisionmakers in a single decision situation. For some classes of decisions, von Winterfeldt (1980) suggests the development of generic objectives hierarchies to outline the key concerns of interest. The generic hierarchy provides a basis for identifying specific objectives in a given decision situation. One decision context in which I have used generic objectives hierarchies involves the siting of energy facilities, where major categories of objectives concern economic impacts, health and safety, environmental impacts, socioeconomic impacts, and political implications (see Keeney, 1980). This is not necessarily a complete set of categories, but it does stimulate thinking. With the category health and safety, for example, you can ask whether one objective in the given decision context is to maximize health and safety. If the response is yes, you should follow up by asking what effects on health and safety are of concern, who they affect, and how they can occur. Discussion of these questions should lead to the development of specific objectives.

It is possible to develop generic objectives for a specific decision context by generating sets of all possible objectives, usually with the help of a computer. As an example, suppose a firm makes a product by assembling several parts purchased from different sources. One major objective may be to reduce the cost of producing the product. A logical analysis might define the set of objectives to be (1) reduce the cost of acquiring each part; (2) reduce the cost of transporting each part; and (3) reduce the cost of assembling each combination of parts. Once such a complete specification is available, the list of generic objectives should be reviewed to eliminate any that are nonsensical. If part A would never be individually combined with part B, the objective to reduce this cost should be dropped. This type of systematic analysis is probably reasonable only for large decisions. It was used, for example, to develop an initial set of scientific objectives for the space exploration of NASA (see Dole et al., 1968).

Use of Structuring Objectives. Once the list of objectives seems somewhat complete, it is time to begin to separate the means objectives from the fundamental objectives, and to structure both sets. The processes of identifying and structuring objectives cannot be completely separated, because additional objectives are typically identified during structuring (for details, see Sections 3.2–3.5).

Briefly, in structuring objectives you try to define listed objectives more clearly, to relate them to one another, and to relate them to objectives not yet identified. To define an objective, you might ask the respondent to describe in detail a particular objective, such as "raise morale in the organization." For listed objectives X and Y, you might ask how X could lead to Y. If one path is that X interacts with Z which leads to W which influences Y, then Z and W may suggest objectives. For example, in a job choice decision, let us say that X and Y are commuting distance and commuting convenience. Together, X, commuting distance, and Z, time of day (rush hour or not) of the commute, influence W, total commuting time, which influences Y, commuting convenience. Naturally, objectives such as "optimize the time of day of the commute" and "minimize total commuting time" are reasonable in this decision context. With regard to other objectives, simply asking a question like "Other than commuting concerns, does anything else matter?" often stimulates thought. The question opens up the discussion by removing the anchor, namely commuting concerns, that had kept the focus of discussion narrow.

Use of Quantifying Objectives. After an original list of objectives has been identified and structured, it is often useful to quantify the fundamental objectives. As outlined in Chapters 4 and 5, this process involves the identification of attributes and the construction of a value model. In proceeding through each of the steps involved, it is possible to identify additional objectives for a decision situation. The understanding that the quantification of objectives is a powerful tool to aid in qualitatively identifying and clarifying objectives in a specific decision context is an important part of value-focused thinking. Chapter 6 is devoted to this topic, so discussion here will be brief.

The identification of objectives and the specification of attributes are intertwined processes. Attributes measure the degree to which an objective is met by various alternatives. The objectives give a preference orientation with respect to these attributes. In some cases the attributes are identified before the objectives, and in other cases the objectives are identified first. You can identify attributes by examining similar decision problems and their consequences that have already occurred or by simply asking what important consequences might occur.

Identifying an attribute often makes it possible to better understand the meaning of a stated objective. For instance, in a decision context involving the control of forest pests, one objective might be to minimize impacts on unemployment in the lumber industry (see Bell, 1977a). One attribute for this objective might be the number of workers laid off in the lumber industry, and another might be the number of unemployed in the lumber industry. The former attribute concerns changes in unemployment and relates to the trauma of losing a job, whereas the latter concerns the hardship of not being employed. The selection of either attribute would put a particular focus on the stated objective. In fact, the two attributes might be representative of two separate but related fundamental objectives in a given decision context.

Quantifying objectives involves the assessment of a value model, such as a utility function or a value function as discussed in Chapter 5. In either case, specific judgments are required about the value tradeoffs between different attributes and about the relative desirability of different levels of given attributes. Each specific judgment provides insights about the objectives that are important for the problem. For instance, in one assessment I was concerned with, the loss of a small number of salmon in a river was accorded an importance equal to that of a large economic loss. As we pursued the reasoning, it became clear that the loss considered so important was of native salmon indigenous to the stream and not of hatchery-bred salmon. Further probing indicated that the relative values of a loss of an equal number of fish of these two types was greater than 1,000 to one. The true fundamental objective in the problem was not to minimize the loss of salmon, but to minimize the loss of indigenous salmon. Numerous other examples of insights for fundamental objectives from assessing value models are given in Chapter 6.

3.2 Identifying Fundamental Objectives

Any initial list of proposed objectives for a complex problem will include both means objectives and fundamental objectives. It is important to separate the fundamental objectives on this list from the means objectives. You can do this by examining the reasons for each item on the list. Two important concepts are repeatedly used. One involves linking objectives through means-ends relationships; the other involves specifying fundamental objectives.

Linking Means and Ends Objectives

Repeatedly tracing ends objectives for specific means objectives should lead to at least one fundamental objective in a given decision situation. For each objective, ask, "Why is this objective important in the decision context?" Two types of answers seem possible. One answer is that the objective is one of the essential reasons for interest in the situation. Such an objective is a candidate for a fundamental objective. The other response is that the objective is important because of its implications for some other objective. In this case, it is a means objective, and the response to the question identifies another objective. The "Why is it important?" test must be given to this objective in turn to ascertain whether it is a means objective or a candidate for a fundamental objective.

Consider the decision situation involving the transportation of hazardous material. One objective may be to minimize the distance the material is transported by trucks. The question should be asked, "Why is this objective important?" The answer may be that shorter distances would reduce both the chances of accidents and the costs of transportation. However, it may turn out that shorter transportation routes go through major cities, exposing more people to the hazardous material, and this may be recognized as undesirable. Again, for each objective, concerning traffic accidents, costs, and exposure, the question should be asked, "Why is that important?" For accidents, the response may be that with fewer accidents there would be fewer highway fatalities and less exposure of the public to the hazardous material. And the answer to why it is important to minimize exposure may be to minimize the health impacts of the hazardous material. To the question "Why is it important to minimize health impacts?" the response may be that it is simply important. This indicates that the objective concerning impacts on public health is a candidate to be a fundamental objective in the decision context.

Why have I hedged by saying that minimizing health impacts is only a candidate for a fundamental objective? One might intuitively ask, if that objective is not fundamental in the context of transporting hazardous material, what objective could be? Such intuition is usually correct, and in those cases we can simply conclude that the "Why is it important?" test has identified a fundamental objective. The reason to call such designated objectives only candidates for a fundamental objective is that the means-ends logic may be carried too far. It may be followed all the way from the alternatives to the decisionmaker's strategic objectives. By definition, the strategic objectives have to indicate the essential reasons for being interested in a specific decision situation, as they indicate the reasons for being interested in *any* decision situation.

Control of Consequences. Clearly, the strategic objectives are too all-encompassing for most decision situations. Therefore, fundamental objectives must have some property that narrows the focus from the strategic objectives to match the decision context. This property has to do with the control of consequences.

For an objective to be a fundamental objective, all alternatives that can significantly influence the achievement of that fundamental objective need to be included in the corresponding decision context. If a candidate fundamental objective is too broad, alternatives in addition to those in the decision context can influence its achievement, so it is not controlled by alternatives in the decision context and therefore not a legitimate fundamental objective. In such a case, some means objective to that candidate fundamental objective must be an actual fundamental objective in the specified context.

As a simple illustration of the control of consequences, consider the decision context of investing funds. The fundamental objective here might be to maximize the net worth of those funds in five years. The decisionmaker could reasonably state that the only interest she has in the funds is to use them to enhance her quality of life, which is her strategic objective. However, enhancing her quality of life is an inappropriate fundamental objective in this investment context. The consequences affecting her quality of life would depend on many decisions outside the investment decision context.

As another example, consider a telephone company addressing the decision context of expanding its line capacity on certain links in its network. Appropriate fundamental objectives might be to maximize the capacity of the network or to maximize the quality of service provided. An inappropriate fundamental objective would be to minimize the number of complaints filed about blocked circuits. Clearly, complaints are related to the quality of service, but alternatives that would influence (that is, partially control) the number of complaints might include education programs about why blockage occurs and free calls to compensate customers for blocked calls, and such alternatives would not be included in the decision context of expanding capacity.

Timing. It is useful to recognize that timing is sometimes relevant in determining whether an objective is a fundamental objective or a means objective. If an organization is trying to improve its ability to plan, fundamental objectives now may be to "understand planning concepts" and "develop planning skills." Obviously, these concepts and skills will be useful for planning in the future. The fundamental objective now is to learn, whereas the fundamental objective later will be to use that knowledge. For a more personal example, at a job interview your fundamental objective should be to obtain a job offer. This is a means to a future decision about whether or not to accept the offer. You can always turn down a job offer, but you cannot accept a job rejection.

Specifying Fundamental Objectives

Another important concept in identifying fundamental objectives is that of specification. For instance, one fundamental objective for shipping hazardous materials may be to minimize impacts on the natural environment. However, it may be useful to make this more specific. Thus, you ask "What environmental impacts should be minimized?" The response, which may be one specific environmental impact or many, should lead to a clarification of the objective and a better focus for thinking and action.

There are many ways to phrase questions aimed at specification, and it is often worthwhile to pursue several questions. Suppose the CEO of a service firm identifies one objective as "to minimize nonproductive time spent by employees." To better understand this objective, you might ask the executive to be more specific, or to list characteristics of nonproductive time, or to define nonproductive time. You might ask how nonproductive time occurs and whose nonproductive time is of concern. After getting a response, you can ask for other aspects of nonproductive time. All responses should help specify the objective.

Specification generally aims to break an objective into logical parts. The same concept can be used, however, to indicate a broader objective of which a given objective is a part. A common example involves the objective of minimizing risks to health from a specific cause. When a utility company is contemplating building a nuclear power plant, one common objective is to minimize health and safety risks from the proposed plant. But if the decision is either to build the plant or not, the objective should be generalized to include the health and safety risks of *not* building the plant. Any alternative other than the nuclear plant that is pursued, including conservation, has risks also. These risks may be less or greater than those of the nuclear plant, but they are not zero. If the nuclear plant is chosen, policies and procedures to reduce risks to health and safety have risks themselves. These risks should also be a part of the fundamental objective of minimizing risks to health and safety.

3.3 Structures of Objectives

The process of structuring objectives results in a deeper and more accurate understanding of what one should care about in the decision context. Structuring helps to clarify the decision context and to define the set of fundamental objectives. This leads to a clearer distinction between the fundamental objectives and the means objectives.

Structured objectives provide the basis for any use of quantitative modeling. The fundamental objectives hierarchy indicates the set of objectives over which attributes should be defined. The value model is then developed to evaluate consequences in terms of that set of objectives. The means-ends objectives network indicates the objectives that should be considered in developing a model to relate the alternatives to their consequences. The process of structuring helps identify missing objectives in both the objectives hierarchy and the objectives network. Essentially the structures indicate where the holes are and what types of objectives are needed to fill them. The basic ideas used in structuring objectives are introduced here through illustrations concerning automobile travel, air pollution, and the transportation of nuclear waste. The processes used to structure objectives are discussed in the following section.

■ *Automobile Safety*
Every Department of Motor Vehicles is concerned about the safety of automobile travel. Consider a decision situation framed by the fundamental objective "maximize safety" and the decision context of automobile travel. Figure 3.1 presents a simplified fundamental objectives hierarchy and a partial means-end objectives network for this decision situation. In both cases, the overall objective, illustrated at the left, is the fundamental objective of broadest concern in the decision context.

In the fundamental objectives hierarchy, the three objectives immediately under the overall objective specify the meaning of "maximize safety" in more detail. These objectives are to minimize loss of life, to minimize serious injuries, and to minimize minor injuries. The objec-

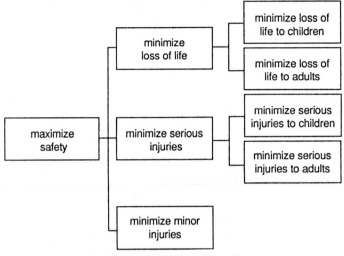

a. a fundamental objectives hierarchy

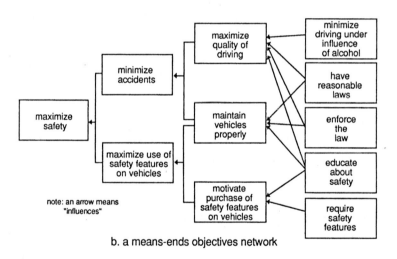

b. a means-ends objectives network

Figure 3.1. Objectives structures for the safety of automobile travel

tives under the first two of these further specify their meaning. This specification categorizes loss of life and serious injuries into those to children and those to adults. The objective "minimize minor injuries" is not further specified.

With the means-ends objectives network, the objectives of minimizing accidents and maximizing use of safety features are both means to the overall objective of maximizing safety. These in turn are broken down into more means. For example, accidents might be reduced by maximizing the quality of driving and by maintaining vehicles properly. Maximizing the quality of driving can be furthered by minimizing driving under the influence of alcohol, having reasonable laws, enforcing these laws, and educating the public about automobile safety. The last three are also means to the objective of maintaining vehicles properly.

In a fundamental objectives hierarchy, the lower-level objectives under any higher-level objective are the answer to the question "What aspects of the higher-level objective are important?" In Figure 3.1a, the safety impacts that are important are loss of life, minor injuries, and serious injuries. In a means-ends objectives network, the lower-level objectives under any higher-level objective are the answer to the question "How can the higher-level objective be better achieved?" Hence, in Figure 3.1b, safety is better achieved by reducing accidents, which is better achieved by maximizing the quality of driving, which is better achieved by reducing driving under the influence of alcohol.

It is important to recognize that the objectives structures in Figure 3.1 do not intermingle means-ends relationships and specification relationships. For example, the specification of the objective "minimize loss of life" in the fundamental objectives hierarchy does not include means objectives such as maintaining vehicles properly and minimizing driving under the influence of alcohol. Note, however, that to some degree all of the means objectives in Figure 3.1b are means to all of the fundamental objectives in Figure 3.1a. ∎

∎ *Carbon Monoxide Standard*

One specific air pollution problem, introduced in Section 2.3, concerns setting an air quality standard for carbon monoxide (CO). Because blood hemoglobin has a stronger affinity for CO than for oxygen, breathing CO lowers the amount of oxygen that can be carried in the blood. This has adverse affects on the cardiovascular, central nervous,

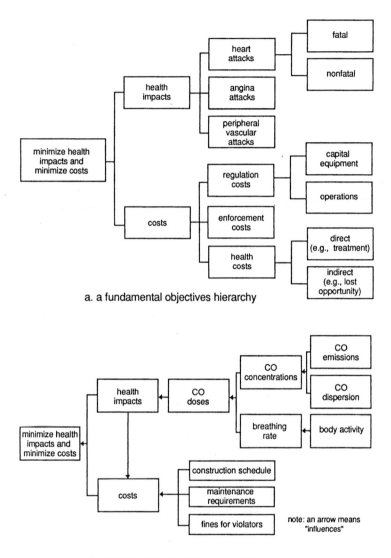

a. a fundamental objectives hierarchy

b. a means-ends objectives network

Figure 3.2. Objectives structures for setting a carbon monoxide air quality standard

pulmonary, and other systems that rely on the ability of the blood to deliver oxygen (see U.S. Environmental Protection Agency, 1980).

Figure 3.2 illustrates both a fundamental objectives hierarchy and a means-ends objectives network for health impacts and costs in the carbon monoxide problem. Because there is no single word for health impacts and costs, both of these hierarchies begin with the fundamental objective "minimize the health impacts of and the costs of controlling carbon monoxide in the air." To save space I have omitted the words *minimize* and *maximize* from the objectives hierarchies in the figure, but the orientation should be clear.

For the fundamental objectives hierarchy in Figure 3.2a, the health impacts of concern are specified as heart attacks, angina attacks, and peripheral vascular attacks. Heart attacks are further specified as fatal or nonfatal. A specification of the fundamental objective "minimize costs" lists regulation costs for capital equipment and operations, enforcement costs of ensuring that individuals and institutions complying with any rules to limit CO pollution, and health costs. The health costs are broken into the direct costs of treatment for the health impacts of CO and the indirect costs due to lost opportunities resulting from fatalities or impairment.

With the means-ends objectives network in Figure 3.2b, the first division of the overall objective is one of specification, as in the fundamental objectives hierarchy. This helps to classify the means-ends structure by illustrating which parts of the overall objective are influenced by what. The means to the health effects go from emissions to concentrations to doses of CO. One of the significant means to the dose is the body activity rate when CO concentrations are present in the air. Increased activity rates increase breathing rate and hence expose the blood to more carbon monoxide.

Alternatives can be identified that affect each of the means objectives. For instance, using smog control devices reduces CO emissions from autos, and this in turn reduces concentrations of CO in the air. However, the weather is also a means that can significantly affect concentrations. This is not categorized as a means objective (such as "maximize the inversion level") because there are no alternatives to influence the weather in the context of this decision. Similarly, the level of fitness of the population affects the breathing rate. However, in the context of setting a national ambient air quality standard, increasing the fitness of the public via some alternative is unrealistic.

Four different means objectives for minimizing costs are identified in Figure 3.2b. These include a shorter construction schedule for capital improvements, a reduction of maintenance requirements for such equipment, and an increase in fines for violators of standards. The most interesting means objective for reducing costs is to minimize the health impacts, since this is also the fundamental objective for health impacts. ∎

∎ *Transportation of Nuclear Waste*
The Nuclear Waste Policy Act of 1982 (now amended) established guidelines for governmental handling of spent nuclear fuel generated by nuclear power plants in the United States. Specifically, the Act stated that in 1998 the government will begin accepting spent nuclear fuel for permanent storage in a geologic repository. There may or may not be intermediate storage at what is referred to as a monitored retrievable storage facility. In any case, there will be the need to transport spent nuclear fuel from power plants across the nation to the geologic repository. The fuel will probably be packed in either metal or ceramic casks and shipped by either truck or train.

Many decisions must be made to provide for efficient operation of the overall system. These include what type of casks to use, where to locate the repository, by what routes to ship the material, whether a monitored retrievable storage is necessary or desirable, and more specific decisions involving such items as the size and weight of the casks and whether specifically trained escorts should accompany all transfers of spent fuel. For all of these decisions, the fundamental objectives are similar. One study, utilizing inputs from a variety of viewpoints concerning nuclear waste, structured fundamental objectives that pertained to health and safety, environmental impacts, costs, socioeconomic impacts, political implications, equity, and flexibility (see Section 11.2).

Figure 3.3a illustrates the portion of the fundamental objectives hierarchy pertaining to health and safety. The first level of specifying the impacts on health and safety of transporting spent nuclear fuel is impacts on the current generation and impacts on future generations. The impacts on future generations are further specified as genetic effects and cases of cancer, some that will be fatal and some that will not be fatal. Impacts on the current generation are divided into cancer cases and other (noncancer) effects, and are categorized by whether they affect the public or workers in the nuclear industry. The cancer implications are further specified as fatal or not, and the noncancer implications are specified as resulting in deaths or in serious injuries.

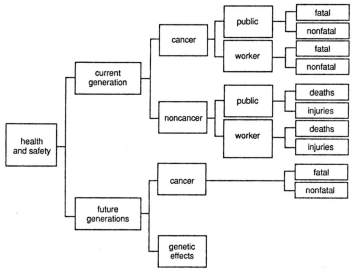

a. a fundamental objectives hierarchy

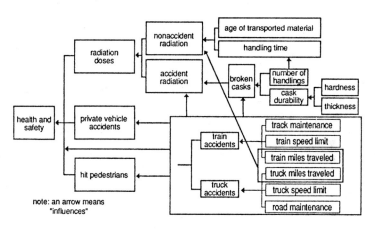

note: an arrow means "influences"

b. a means-ends objectives network

Figure 3.3. Objectives structures for the health and safety impacts of transporting nuclear waste

The means-ends objectives network in Figure 3.3b elaborates the means by which the impacts on health and safety occur. This case clearly indicates why means-ends relationships need a network rather than a hierarchy, since, as we see here, specific means can affect health and safety in more than one manner. For instance, one means objective is to minimize the number of truck miles involved in transporting spent nuclear fuel. As illustrated in Figure 3.3b, this could contribute to reducing both radiation exposure during transportation and truck accidents. The number of truck accidents, in turn, could directly affect the number of private vehicles and pedestrians involved, and both of these have implications for safety. Truck accidents can also lead to broken shipping casks, which can result in increased radiation doses and eventual adverse effects on health.

In relating the means-ends objectives network to the fundamental objectives hierarchy, note that the radiation doses are the means to the cancer cases and genetic effects. The number of private vehicles and the number of pedestrians involved in accidents are the immediate means to the noncancer effects on the public. Train and truck accidents have noncancer effects on the health and safety of workers. These means objectives can also be related to specific levels of the fundamental objectives hierarchy. For instance, if we wish to distinguish between cancer effects on the public and on workers in the current generation, we must separately specify the radiation doses to each group. We might specify the means objective "minimize radiation doses" as "minimize radiation doses to the public in the current generation" and "minimize radiation doses to workers in the current generation." Such a specification of a means objective directly relates it to more detailed levels of the fundamental objectives hierarchy. ∎

In these three illustrations, a more realistic structuring of objectives would include additional fundamental objectives addressing such issues as environmental and social impacts. These could be identified by expanding the fundamental objectives using the ideas introduced in Sections 3.1 and 3.2. The means objectives to these additional fundamental objectives would include many of the means objectives already discussed. For instance, in the transportation of nuclear waste, truck miles traveled, train accidents, and broken casks would also be means to detrimental environmental and social consequences. A single means objective can have implications for several fundamental objectives, and several means objectives can influence the achievement of a single fundamental objective.

3.4 How to Structure Objectives

In essentially all methods of analysis concerning multiple objectives, the objectives of the decision situation are structured (see, for example, Manheim and Hall, 1967; Miller, 1970; Keeney and Raiffa, 1976; Saaty 1980; von Winterfeldt, 1980; and Brownlow and Watson, 1987). Typically these structuring processes do not carefully distinguish between the items in the structure or the relationships between items. Often the objectives structures contain objectives, goals, constraints, and/or attributes mixed together in an unspecified fashion. They also do not distinguish between fundamental objectives and means objectives; they simply include both in the same structure.

Three critical issues arise in the structuring of either an objectives hierarchy or an objectives network. These are identifying the overall (highest-level) fundamental objective for the decision situation, relating objectives on different levels of a structure, and stopping the structuring process. Let us consider these in order.

Identifying the Overall Fundamental Objective

For a given decision situation, the overall objective is the same for both the fundamental and the means-ends objectives structures. It characterizes the reason for interest in the decision situation and defines the breadth of concern.

Fortunately, the essence of the overall fundamental objective for many decision contexts is relatively easy to identify. The essence of a financial investment situation is to make money. The essence of a medical treatment decision is to get well, and the essence of a negotiation is to reach a satisfactory agreement. Otherwise, the overall fundamental objective may be readily identified from perusal of the list of objectives.

The overall objective may be the combination of more specific fundamental objectives. For example, the overall objective for an air pollution problem may be "minimize health impacts, minimize environmental impacts, and minimize costs." Hence, it is useful to provide categories for those more specific fundamental objectives. These may be organized by type of impact, such as environmental, social, economic, and political, or by stakeholders affected. Once you have divided the list of fundamental objectives into several categories, you can identify the specific objectives in the list pertaining to each category. If the list of objectives in one particular category is large (say, more than four), it may be useful to divide them into subgroups and repeat the process. This should provide a basic structure for the top levels of an objectives hierarchy and a basis for defining the overall fundamental objective.

Relationships among Objectives

The fundamental objectives hierarchy specifies in detail the reasons for being interested in a given problem. For each of the fundamental objectives, the answer to the question "Why is it important?" is simply "It is important." With a means objective, the answer to the question "Why is it important?" is always an end that follows from that means. For instance, regarding the transport of nuclear fuel, the answer to the question "Why is the objective of minimizing radiation dosage important?" is that radiation doses can cause cancer and that cancer is important.

It should be clear that the types of relationships between adjacent levels in fundamental and means-ends objectives structures are distinct. In a fundamental objectives hierarchy, the lower-level objective is a part of the higher-level objective. The higher-level objective is defined by the set of lower-level objectives directly under it in the hierarchy. These lower-level objectives should be mutually exclusive and collectively should provide an exhaustive characterization of the higher-level objective. There should be at least two lower-level objectives connected to any higher-level objective.

In a means-ends objectives network, in contrast, the relationship between adjacent levels is causal. The lower-level objective is a means (that is, a causal factor) to the higher-level objective. Not all of the causal factors to a higher-level objective are included as lower-level objectives. For example, one causal factor affecting air pollution concentrations is the weather, but no objective concerning the weather should appear in a means-ends objectives network. This is one distinction between objectives networks and influence diagrams used in decision analysis (Howard and Matheson, 1984; Shachter, 1986). Thus, the means objectives are not in any sense a collectively exhaustive representation of the means to the higher-level ends. It may therefore be the case that a higher-level objective has only one lower-level means objective.

Fundamental objectives hierarchies have a clear and simple order. Each lower-level objective pertains only to the upper-level objective directly above it. The means-ends objective network, on the other hand, may have complex interrelationships, as illustrated in Figures 3.1–3.3. In Figure 3.2, for instance, the health impacts are part of the fundamental objectives hierarchy and are also a means to the cost implications in the means-ends objectives network. In Figure 3.3b, several of the means objectives are means to many other objectives. For instance, truck accidents can contribute to accident radiation directly; to broken casks, which lead to additional accident radiation; to the number of pedestrians hit; and to private vehicle accidents.

Both objectives hierarchies and objectives networks can be developed either from the top down or from the bottom up (see von Winterfeldt and Edwards, 1986). With fundamental objectives hierarchies, if you start at the top of the hierarchy and try to specify more precisely the meaning of the given objective, the specification addresses the question of what aspects of the higher-level objective are important. For instance, with regard to the health effects of transporting nuclear waste indicated in Figure 3.3a, you might ask for a specification of what cancers to the current generation are important. The answer is those pertaining to the public and to workers. The question of what cancers are important to workers is answered by the specification of nonfatal and fatal cancers. To structure the fundamental hierarchy from the bottom up, you ask the question "are specific cases of what?" Using the same example, the nonfatal and fatal cancers are specific cases of cancers affecting workers and the public. Then public cancers and worker cancers are specific cases of cancers affecting the current generation.

With a means-ends objectives network, top-down structuring answers the question of how better to achieve the stated objective. For instance, for carbon monoxide pollution in Figure 3.2, a means to minimize health impacts is to minimize doses. An answer to "How do we minimize health impacts?" is "Minimize doses." The answer to "How do we minimize doses?" includes "Minimize concentrations of the pollutant," and so on. Bottom-up structuring of the means-ends objectives network follows questioning of "Why is this important?" For instance, to the question of why the emissions of an air pollutant are important, the answer is that they lead to increased pollutant concentrations. And the answer to "Why are air pollutant concentrations important?" is that they lead to increased doses to individuals. The increased doses are important because they lead to health effects. And health effects are important because "They are important."

In a fundamental objectives hierarchy, we carefully investigate the specification for each stated objective to ascertain whether the immediate lower-level objectives completely specify what is meant by that higher-level objective. If the answer is no, we augment the hierarchy by filling in additional objectives. We also check for double-counting of the impacts. For example, if the environmental impacts include loss of wild-life habitat and loss of deer habitat, either the former should be rede-fined to exclude deer habitat or the separate category of impact on deer habitat should be omitted. Once you have worked from the top down through a fundamental objectives hierarchy, it is useful to reverse the process and work from the bottom up. Here, you ask what general concern is related to the specific objective at any given level. Again, a slight mismatch of lower-level and higher-level objectives may be identi-fied that will require an alteration.

With a means-ends objectives network, completeness is also an issue. For each objective, you attempt to specify all the means to achieve that objective. This process is particularly useful to stimulate thought about the range of alternatives that may influence the achievement of the fundamental objectives. You keep pursuing the question of whether there are additional means that influence each stated objective in the means-ends network.

Stopping the Structuring Process

The starting point for top-down structuring of both the fundamental objectives hierarchy and the means-ends objectives network is the over-all fundamental objective. But what is the ending point of these pro-cesses, or in other words, the starting point of bottom-up structuring?

In structuring the fundamental objectives hierarchy, always keep in mind the usefulness of identifying attributes to indicate the degree to which the objectives are achieved. These attributes will sharpen your definitions and understanding of the objectives. Hence the elaboration of the objectives hierarchy to lower levels continues until it reaches a level at which reasonable attributes can be found. The search for attri-butes pushes you to specify the objectives hierarchy further, as it is easier to find appropriate attributes at lower levels than at higher levels. For instance, it is easier to identify an attribute to measure loss of deer habitat than to measure environmental impact.

Balancing this push to specify objectives further is the fact that using fewer objectives makes it easier to get a feeling for the decision as a whole and limits the analysis required. This makes it desirable to identify reasonable attributes as high as possible in the fundamental objectives hierarchy. Once you have identified attributes, further speci-fication of objectives may help you better understand the implications of the attributes, but any analysis should proceed at the higher level. For instance, one objective in a problem might be to minimize the loss of forest, which could be measured by the attribute "acres of forest." Further specification of this objective might concern the loss of mature pine forest, the loss of virgin forest, the loss of young trees, and the loss of forest shrubbery. In making value judgments about forest losses and in collecting data about such losses, you would keep in mind that the forests of concern were composed of mature pine, virgin forest, young trees, and shrubbery.

If you continue to structure a means-ends objectives network to lower and lower levels, eventually you arrive at alternatives (see, for example, Ackoff, 1978). Hence, with a means-ends objectives network, the natural stopping point of specification is alternatives or classes of alternatives. These classes may not be listed on the objectives network, but they are implicit. For example, with the automobile safety problem in Figure 3.1, one lowest-level means objective is "enforce the law." One class of alternatives implied here is naturally the one that requires penalties for unsafe driving. One specific alternative is to set penalties to revoke driving licenses for certain reasons. This is directly a means to the lowest-level objective "enforce the law" in the means-ends network. Other possible alternatives include financial fines, jail sentences, community service, and required education about the reasons for safe driving.

Facts versus Values

It is important to recognize that the types of judgments necessary to structure fundamental objectives hierarchies and means-ends objectives networks are distinctly different. Value judgments are required to construct fundamental objectives hierarchies, and judgments about facts are required to construct means-ends networks. Quite simply, deciding what is important requires value judgments. Deciding how to achieve a higher-level objective requires factual knowledge. This difference means that for some decision situations it may be appropriate to have different individuals build the two types of objectives structures. For example, consider problems of public policy where solutions involve technical complexity. Either the public's values, or values expressed for the public by representatives (such as legislators or regulators), are those appropriate to construct the fundamental objectives hierarchy. But when it comes to constructing the means-ends objectives network, individuals with expertise about technical or factual aspects of the decision situation are often much better qualified than the public or its representatives.

3.5 Desirable Properties of Fundamental Objectives

The choice of fundamental objectives is a creative process that requires considerable judgment. It is possible to identify several different fundamental objectives hierarchies for the same decision problem (see Section 3.6). Some of these, of course, will be much better than others.

Fundamental objectives should be as useful as possible for creating and evaluating alternatives, identifying decision opportunities, and guiding the entire decisionmaking process. To be useful, the set of fundamental objectives should possess the nine important properties listed in Table 3.2. In simple terms, properties 1–3 pertain to framing the

Table 3.2.   Desired properties of the set of fundamental objectives

The set of fundamental objectives should be:
1. *Essential,* to indicate consequences in terms of the fundamental reasons for interest in the decision situation.

2. *Controllable,* to address consequences that are influenced only by the choice of alternatives in the decision context.

3. *Complete,* to include all fundamental aspects of the consequences of the decision alternatives.

4. *Measurable,* to define objectives precisely and to specify the degrees to which objectives may be achieved.

5. *Operational,* to render the collection of information required for an analysis reasonable considering the time and effort available.

6. *Decomposable,* to allow the separate treatment of different objectives in the analysis.

7. *Nonredundant,* to avoid double-counting of possible consequences.

8. *Concise,* to reduce the number of objectives needed for the analysis of a decision.

9. *Understandable,* to facilitate generation and communication of insights for guiding the decisionmaking process.

decision situation, properties 4–5 pertain to the quality of thinking and analysis, properties 6–8 pertain to the difficulty of such thinking and analysis, and property 9 pertains to the quality of insights from the thinking and analysis.

A fundamental objective is defined to be an objective that is both *essential* and *controllable,* as discussed in Section 3.2. A set of objectives is essential if each of the alternatives in the decision context can influence the degree to which the objectives are achieved. A set of objectives is controllable if all of the alternatives that can influence the consequences are included in the decision context. To be both essential and controllable requires a careful balancing that is worthy of elaboration.

Consider the specific decision situation framed within the strategic decision frame in Figure 3.4. As seen in Figure 3.4a, the fundamental objectives must lie somewhere between the decision context and the strategic objectives. Exactly where the fundamental objectives should lie is decided by a balancing of the requirements to be both essential and controllable. As indicated in Figure 3.4b, the requirement to be essential broadens the fundamental objectives by pushing them toward the strategic objectives, while the requirement to be controllable narrows the fundamental objectives by pushing them back toward the alternatives.

A set of fundamental objectives is *complete* if knowledge of the possible consequences with respect to each of the objectives provides a description of all the implications of interest when an alternative is selected in a decision problem. In terms of the diagram in Figure 3.4a, completeness refers to how large the set of fundamental objectives must be. To keep from including all possible objectives, the property of *conciseness* requires omitting any objectives that are not useful.

When you are first constructing an objectives hierarchy, there is little reason to omit any objective that seems important to the situation. But once you have identified alternatives and begun an evaluation phase, there are good reasons to omit stated objectives. An objective should be dropped from the list if the various alternatives cannot be differentiated in terms of that objective, so that its inclusion has no effect on the relative desirability of the alternatives. If an objective and an associated attribute are included in the evaluation, data on the possible impact of each alternative with respect to that objective must be gathered. Hence, an objective should be excluded if it is simply not worth the effort of including it. Another reason to omit certain objectives in the evaluation phase is that the scope of the problem is limited by those interested in the study. For instance, it is certainly appropriate

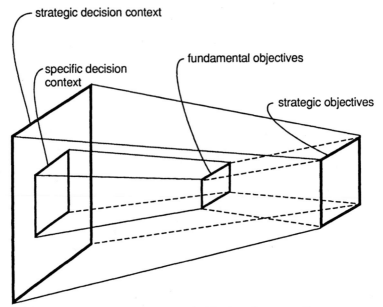

a. decision frame with fundamental objectives for a specific
   decision context

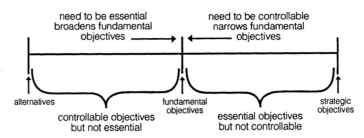

b. the effect of essential and controllable properties on the
   identification of fundamental objectives

*Figure 3.4. The need to balance requirements that fundamental objectives be both
essential and controllable in identifying the set of fundamental objectives*

to analyze the health effects of a particular air pollutant to assist in decisionmaking regarding emission standards. The analysis may or may not include socioeconomic effects, such as possible lost employment, and economic costs. If they are not included, the list of objectives will clearly not be complete. But in fact no analysis addresses everything. Therefore, in drawing implications from such analyses, it is critically important to be clear about what objectives have and have not been addressed.

The *measurable* and *operational* properties concern whether it is possible to obtain the information useful for thinking and analysis. Objectives are measured in terms of attributes that serve to define different levels of consequences of possible alternatives (see Chapter 4). Objectives are operational if it is possible to obtain the factual information necessary to relate the various alternatives to their possible consequences, and the value information to specify the relative desirability of these consequences in terms of a value model. This information can more easily be gathered when the objectives are *decomposable*. This means that the aspects of consequences relating to one attribute can be considered independently of the aspects of consequences relating to other attributes. Ideally, this will be the case both for describing the possible consequences of the various alternatives and for quantifying the desirability of those consequences.

It is desirable that the set of fundamental objectives be *nonredundant* to avoid double-counting in the evaluation of alternatives. This can be difficult, because double-counting can occur in two ways. One way involves double-counting the possible impacts of the alternatives, and the other involves double-counting the values of those impacts. Both types commonly occur when some means objectives are inadvertently included in the fundamental objectives hierarchy. Eliminating any redundancies naturally reduces the number of objectives that need to be considered. With other things equal, it is preferable that the final set of objectives be as concise as possible. This reduces the effort required to collect data and quantify values.

The reason to investigate any decision situation is to facilitate the eventual selection of better alternatives. The selection may be better because the known alternatives are more carefully evaluated, because better alternatives are created, or because better decision situations are chosen to be addressed. In all three cases, it is important that the insights provided by value-focused thinking be *understandable*, so that they can be adequately communicated to and understood by individuals in positions to make or influence decisions.

The requirements placed on the fundamental objectives for identifying decision opportunities, promoting the creation of alternatives, facilitating communication, and guiding the allocation of effort in a decision process are not as stringent as those for evaluating alternatives. In these situations, what is important is that the objectives be fundamental (essential and controllable), complete, and understandable. Indeed, for these processes, attributes need not be identified, data need not be collected, and a value model need not be constructed.

If individuals concerned with a given decision situation consider the objectives to be fundamental and complete and if they understand what is meant by each of them, productive communication should follow. Discussion of the pros and cons of various alternatives must be based on the set of objectives. The decision of what information is worth collecting should rest on what light the information would shed on the alternatives in terms of the objectives. The search for new alternatives should concentrate on those that are likely to measure up well in terms of the stated objectives. Objectives are also useful to stimulate thought that leads to the identification of decision opportunities. However, as discussed in Chapter 6, defining attributes, building models of the impacts of alternatives, and building models of values to evaluate alternatives may each substantially assist in these activities by uncovering hidden objectives.

Advantages of Structuring Fundamental Objectives

It is obvious why fundamental objectives are important, but it is not so obvious why it is worthwhile to structure these objectives into an objectives hierarchy. The general answer is that structuring improves our understanding of the values that matter, leads to a better value model, and enhances the quality of the value-focused thinking. The fundamental objectives hierarchy has several advantages that aid in the specification of values:

1. The higher levels of an objectives hierarchy relate to fairly general concerns, such as the environment, economics, health and safety, and flexibility. Consequently, they can be identified relatively easily.
2. Higher-level objectives provide a basis for specification of lower-level objectives.
3. A hierarchy helps identify missing objectives, since logical con-

cepts of the specification process can fairly easily identify holes in the hierarchy.

4. The distinctions between means objectives and fundamental objectives become clearer as the objectives hierarchy is structured.
5. Situations where redundancy or double-counting might occur can often be identifed with the logic of an objectives hierarchy.
6. It is easier to identify attributes to measure the achievement of more specific (lower-level) objectives than of more general (higher-level) objectives.
7. The attributes for lower-level objectives collectively indicate the degree to which the associated higher-level objective is achieved.
8. The complete set of lowest-level attributes for a fundamental objectives hierarchy provides a basis for describing the consequences in the decision problem and for assessing an objective function appropriate for the problem.

Chapter 4 discusses in detail issues raised by points 6–8.

3.6 Relating Objectives Hierarchies and Objectives Networks

There are several relationships between the fundamental objectives hierarchies and the means-ends objectives networks that are worth elaborating. This indicates how the two types of objectives structures are synergistically used to improve the thinking about and analysis of decisions.

Networks of Objectives Hierarchies

When the contexts of two decision problems are related, the fundamental objectives in one context may be means objectives in another context (see, for example, Ackoff, 1978). To illustrate this, consider the case of carbon monoxide (CO) air pollution discussed in Section 3.3. The context of one decision problem might be stated as reducing the concentrations of ambient CO. The overall fundamental objective would be "to minimize CO concentrations." More detailed fundamental objectives might involve minimizing CO concentrations at different locations of concern, say in industrial areas, urban areas, and rural areas. The means-ends objectives network would begin with the same overall fundamental objective. One means objective is to minimize CO emissions.

Lower-level means objectives that reduce emissions include minimizing the burning of certain fuels and maximizing the use of pollution control devices. These rather simple objectives structures are illustrated in Figure 3.5.

Compare this decision context with the more general decision context of setting an appropriate national ambient standard for carbon monoxide shown in Figure 3.2. It is obvious that the fundamental objectives in Figure 3.5 are means objectives in Figure 3.2. The means objectives in Figure 3.5 are of course also means in the broader decision context of Figure 3.2. This illustration should indicate that networks of

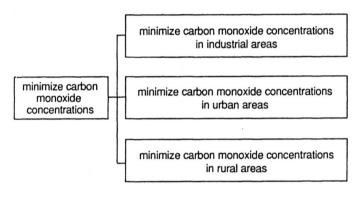

a. a fundamental objectives hierarchy

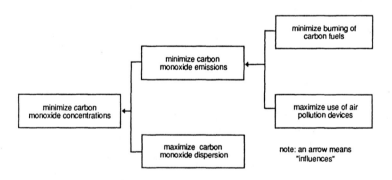

b. a means-ends objectives network

Figure 3.5. Objectives structures for reducing carbon monoxide concentrations

objectives hierarchies can be constructed to correspond to hierarchies of decision problems.

There are many personal and business contexts where networks of objectives hierarchies are natural. An individual may face a specific decision problem concerning work, in which, of course, the objectives pertain to that specific problem. A more general context facing that individual may concern the objectives of his or her professional career over the next five years. And an even more general objectives hierarchy concerns his or her life. To some degree, the more specific objectives hierarchies, such as for an aspect of one's career, should be means for career decisions to contribute to the more general objectives of life.

These same notions pertain to business situations facing firms or governmental organizations. There can be an objectives hierarchy for a specific decision situation. This may be a means to the division objectives in a private firm or to the objectives of a unit within a larger governmental body. And in both cases, there may also be an objectives hierarchy for the firm and for that larger governmental body. Chapter 4 returns to this issue and discusses the use of attributes to account for the implications that the choice of an alternative in a specific decision context may have on the achievement of the fundamental objectives in a more general context.

Both objectives hierarchies and objectives networks can be included in a single illustration to indicate their relationships and distinctions. Figure 3.6 does this using the decision concerning automobile safety from Figure 3.1. The means-ends objectives network is shown in Figure 3.6 with four separate objectives hierarchies that correspond to different decision contexts. These objectives hierarchies are not elaborated in great detail but are intended to illustrate the ideas. It would obviously be possible to construct a means-ends objectives network connecting all the objectives on the second levels of the four objectives hierarchies. If an extensive model were to be built to support analyses of automobile safety decisions, such a network would be appropriate.

Connecting Objectives Hierarchies and Objectives Networks

When an analysis of alternatives for a decision situation is to be conducted, the fundamental objectives hierarchy and the means-ends objectives network for the decision must be connected. The possible consequences in terms of the achievement of fundamental objectives are

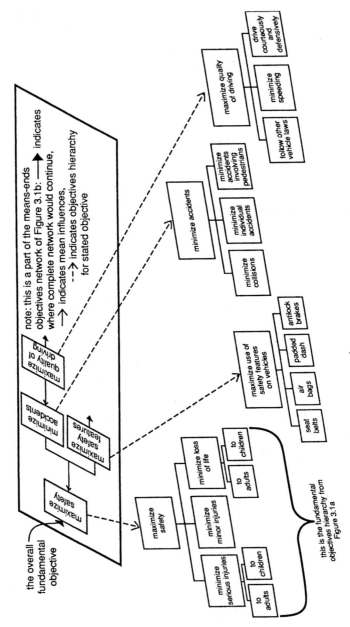

Figure 3.6. Relationships between several objectives hierarchies and an objectives network for automobile safety

90

calculated based on the objectives network. To illustrate this point, re-consider the decision context of transporting nuclear waste shown in Figure 3.3. The way the means objectives influence the consequences for the fundamental objectives is illustrated in Figure 3.7. Only selected means objectives are shown, and the lowest level of the fundamental objectives is omitted to avoid cluttering the figure. In some sense, the original means-ends objectives network in Figure 3.3b also connects the means-ends network to the fundamental objectives hierarchy. It just makes this connection at the highest level of the objectives hierarchy. For the model of consequences in Figure 3.7 to be operational, the relationships between connected means objectives and between the means objectives and the fundamental objectives must be quantified based on available factual data and judgment.

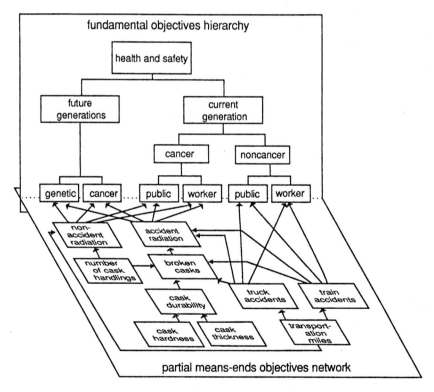

Figure 3.7. Connecting fundamental objectives hierarchies and means-ends objectives networks

Hybrid Objectives Hierarchies

It is possible to structure objectives so that some adjacent levels are related causally and others are related through specification. Such hybrids could be considered as a third type of objectives structure, but to facilitate clear thinking it is preferable to keep objectives hierarchies and objectives networks distinct.

Sometimes in a means-ends objectives network a specification relationship may be added immediately after the overall objective to indicate the level of the fundamental objectives hierarchy to which the means are connected or to suggest how impacts might be modeled. For instance, in Figure 3.2b, the overall objective is first divided into the two fundamental components, health and costs, before the means-ends structuring is begun. This simply indicates that fundamental impacts will be categorized as impacts on health and on costs, something we know directly from the fundamental objectives hierarchy. Also, this indicates that many components in the means-ends network for costs will be different from those in the means-ends network for health effects.

As another example, consider Figure 3.3b, where under the objective of minimizing radiation doses we could have listed objectives of minimizing radiation emitted during transport and of minimizing radiation emitted during handling operations. As lower-level objectives under these, we might have listed minimizing radiation emitted during normal operations and minimizing radiation due to accidents. This specification would help define what radiation emissions are important. It would basically suggest how we would tabulate radiation emissions in a model and would not alter the basic means-ends structure of the objectives network.

3.7 Incomplete Objectives Hierarchies and Networks

Both a fundamental objectives hierarchy and a means-ends objectives network can be very useful for addressing a complex decision situation. Without both, or when either is incomplete, the framing of the decision situation and any analysis done in the situation can suffer.

Framing a Decision Situation

The fundamental objectives hierarchy indicates why there is an interest in a problem, and the means-ends objectives network suggests how something can be done to improve matters. Both are crucial to facilitate communication among stakeholders interested in the problem. At the stage when an analysis is structured, there is no attempt to weight any of the fundamental objectives according to some index of importance. Indeed, as the analysis proceeds, any objective can be given a zero weight if a stakeholder considers the objective inappropriate. Hence, it should be relatively easy for diverse groups to reach agreement that the fundamental objectives are appropriate. Agreeing on a fundamental objectives hierarchy is tantamount to agreeing on the decision context. Given such an agreement, any future disagreements must be within this context.

Any necessary agreements on a means-ends objectives network should also be much easier to reach than agreement on specific functional relationships among different means objectives. Such relationships are considered later, in the analysis. Although individuals with a factual knowledge of a problem area are required to construct both the means-ends network and the functional relationships used in the analysis, interested laypeople should be able to understand and constructively comment on the network. This is not likely to be the case with the functional relationships. Hence, using distinct steps—first creating the means-ends network and then constructing an impact model—aids both communication and participation in a decision problem and its analysis.

As indicated in Part Three, both the fundamental objectives hierarchy and the means-ends objectives network can be useful to facilitate the creation of alternatives and the identification of decision opportunities. To the extent that either objectives structure is missing or incomplete, this usefulness is reduced.

Analyzing the Decision

Distinguishing clearly between means objectives and fundamental objectives enhances the separation of fact and value judgments in the analysis. This has several advantages. When disagreements do occur, it is easier to determine whether they are based on different facts, different judgments about facts, different values, different expressions of value judgments, or a combination of these.

With facts and values clearly separated, individuals with knowledge of the facts can build the impact model consistent with the means-ends objectives network, while those whose values are relevant to the problem can provide them for the fundamental objectives hierarchy. As a result, the individuals with technical or factual knowledge are not required to make inappropriate value judgments, and lay people need not speculate about complex factual relationships. An example will clarify this point.

■ Acid Rain

The damage to forests and lakes caused by acid rain is acknowledged as an important problem. One means to such damage is the amount of sulfur dioxide and nitrogen oxides emitted from burning fossil fuels. Because of the very complex relationships between the amounts of such emissions and the eventual impacts on lakes and forests, much of the discussion of decision alternatives has focused on the reduction of the emissions—that is, on better achievement of means objectives. Because an understanding of those complex relationships requires expertise in, at a minimum, long-range meteorological patterns, atmospheric chemistry, and the biological impacts of different doses of acid rain, few people are adequately informed to participate constructively in discussions about the problem. Those with such expertise, if there are any for this particular situation, are technical professionals, and it can be argued that they should have neither the right nor the responsibility to make the value judgments on behalf of the public for the acid rain problem. If decisions about alternatives focus on emissions, many value judgments must de facto be left either to the technical community or to the lay public with less than the desired technical knowledge. ■

When the value model used in an analysis is assessed over attributes that measure means objectives, inappropriate weighting or, more generally, an inappropriate value model can easily result. Such a value model will combine value judgments about the fundamental objectives with factual judgments about the implications of the means objectives for these fundamental objectives. Aside from the point that different individuals should make these judgments, it is easy to make errors in such complex tasks. Double-counting or undercounting can result. For instance, in Figure 3.2b, the carbon monoxide doses can cause health impacts, which can cause increased costs. If an attribute measuring the number of people receiving a high (appropriately defined) dose is meant to be used to evaluate the health impacts alone, there is a chance that double-counting will occur. Specifically, this attribute may be inadvertently weighted to account for both health impacts and costs, but the value model may also include an attribute measuring costs in millions of dollars. Whether double-counting results depends on how well the facilitator can help the person expressing value judgments to understand and separate the relationships of health impacts to their costs and of dose to both of these.

3.8 Objectives Hierarchies for Groups

Up to now I have focused on decision situations in which the objectives hierarchy is developed by an individual or a single entity (such as an organization). There is another type of situation in which an objectives hierarchy should be constructed for several distinct individuals or entities, often referred to as stakeholders. A classic example concerns important governmental decisions that affect many different interest groups (see Edwards and von Winterfeldt, 1987; and Sections 11.2 and 11.4). When multiple stakeholders are involved, it is essential to have a facilitator guide the elicitation of objectives from each stakeholder, structure each set of objectives into an objectives hierarchy, and aggregate the hierarchies into a single fundamental objectives hierarchy. The facilitator is typically an independent analyst hired by the decision-maker—typically a government organization—because of his or her skills and impartiality to work on the specific decision being considered.

The discussion so far has indicated how to elicit objectives and construct objectives hierarchies. Aggregation brings up only a few additional issues. These concern the selection of participant stakeholders whose objectives should be elicited, interaction between the facilitator and the stakeholders, and the combining of objectives hierarchies to obtain one overall hierarchy.

Selection of Stakeholders

Stakeholders should be selected jointly by the decisionmaker and the facilitator so that the desirable properties of an objectives hierarchy can be met. Specifically, a comprehensive listing of all objectives should be generated, including organized structures of means objectives and of fundamental objectives. Thus, a broad range of stakeholder groups should be involved to provide a broad range of suggested objectives. Selecting groups and individuals to represent these groups (for example, choosing which environmentalists to invite to participate) involves balancing many concerns such as the time and cost of the process, the quality of the resulting set of objectives, and the stakeholders' contribution to legitimacy of the process.

In selecting participants, it is important to take into account both the fairness and the *perceived* fairness with which different groups are treated. The desire to be comprehensive suggests that many groups should participate. Somewhat counteracting this is the need to limit the effort of the process to a reasonable level. In practice, the careful selection of from three to five groups representing different perspectives in a decision problem is likely to provide a comprehensive list of objectives. The number of participating groups necessary to provide fair treatment is more problem-dependent.

Interaction with Stakeholders

Stakeholders should be involved early in a decision process. This increases their willingness to cooperate, since it lets them see that the decision has not already been made. Also, the objectives should be elicited early to provide guidance for data-collection efforts. Since a problem of public interest is supposedly to make a decision "for the public," early involvement of stakeholders, as representatives of the public, may lead to creative alternatives and a deeper understanding of the "real problem."

It is sometimes desirable to have the initial meeting between the facilitator and all stakeholders be a common meeting. Then the stakeholders receive the same information at the same time, which puts them on equal footing and suggests that the process is a legitimate effort rather than simply window dressing. There are several important topics to review in this general meeting. You, the facilitator, should outline the problem as it is currently understood. Then clarify the purposes of involving the stakeholders, how they were selected, and the uses of their results. Next, discuss the principles that will be used to elicit their objectives and to combine them. It is also useful to discuss issues such as gaming, meaning the intentional biasing of objectives to enhance the eventual selection of a preferred alternative. Gaming is always a consideration, but at this stage the purpose is try to list all possible objectives. Indeed, one purpose of gaming is to ensure that one's own objectives are listed, but this is precisely why the stakeholders should be involved. The perhaps more crucial step of weighing the objectives may or may not be done with separate stakeholders. In any case, you should clearly point out to participants that any weighing of the importance of objectives will occur later, after a comprehensive list of fundamental objectives has been developed.

Combining Objectives Hierarchies

Once you have structured the fundamental hierarchies of each of the stakeholder groups using a common overall fundamental objective, it is necessary to combine them. The basic principle for this is one of union. The combined fundamental objectives hierarchy should include all of the objectives in any individual hierarchy. One way to begin is to list all the top-level objectives (those immediately under the overall objective) in each hierarchy. Objectives in this list that are essentially the same should be aggregated. The aggregation procedures of different groups differ. For instance, one group may consider the socioeconomic implications of a decision to be a part of environmental impacts. Another group may define environmental impacts as only those on species other than humans. The list of top-level objectives should be adjusted to account for such differences. The result of this aggregation process is a set of top-level objectives for the combined fundamental objectives hierarchy.

The next step is to go through each individual hierarchy and list all of the lower-level objectives directly associated with each of the top-level objectives in the combined hierarchy. Then, under each of the top-level objectives, repeat the process of aggregating similar terms and making logical adjustments. The result is the second level of the combined hierarchy. The process repeats until all of the objectives in the individual hierarchies have been accounted for.

At this stage, the combined fundamental objectives hierarchy should be considered a draft. It should be appraised in terms of the desired properties of objectives hierarchies discussed in Section 3.5, and appropriate revisions should be made. (For a case study involving the construction of an overall objectives hierarchy from the individual hierarchies of several interest groups for the energy supply alternatives for the Federal Republic of Germany, see Keeney, Renn, and von Winterfeldt, 1987.)

Because comprehensiveness is important and the equitable treatment of the various groups is also important, the last appraisal of the draft of the combined objectives hierarchy should include separate consideration of each objective in the individual hierarchies. The purpose is to determine where and how each of the objectives is addressed in the combined objectives hierarchy. Once any omissions have been rectified, the draft is ready to send out to participants. You should tell the groups how the combined hierarchy was constructed and how it should be interpreted, so that they can determine if their concerns are appropriately included. Ask them for any suggestions to improve the combined objectives hierarchy. Once you have incorporated these suggestions, the resulting objectives hierarchy should be useful for the purposes of focusing effort on a problem, defining creative alternatives to achieve the objectives, and evaluating those alternatives.

With groups, another crucial role of the objectives hierarchy is to provide a constructive mechanism for communication between groups about significant aspects of the problem. By approving the combined fundamental objectives hierarchy, each group in effect states that the objectives in the hierarchy characterize all that is fundamentally important in the problem area being addressed.

CHAPTER 4

Measuring the Achievement of Objectives

A clear listing and structuring of the fundamental objectives provides considerable insights. If your intention is to use these insights in creating alternatives, identifying decision opportunities, and systematically appraising alternatives without quantitative analysis, there is no requirement to measure the achievement of any objectives (see Chapters 7–10). However, measuring the achievement of the fundamental objectives and developing a value model (see Chapter 5) using these objectives can enhance the process and benefits of value-focused thinking. Also, when means objectives are identified, the measurement of their achievement can provide useful insights. Specifically, the measurement of objectives clarifies their meaning, and this may lead to the creation of desirable alternatives—perhaps even an obvious "solution" to a problem. It should also improve communication. In addition, when an explicit model of the possible consequences is built to aid analysis of alternative decisions, measurement of the means objectives is necessary.

It is worthwhile to keep in mind the iterative nature of value-focused thinking. When you are identifying objectives, there is no need to know for sure whether you will take the next step and measure those objectives. Once you have identified the objectives and are using them to guide your thinking, you can appraise whether it is worth the effort to measure objectives.[1]

---

1. Readers mainly interested in the insights available from the qualitative use of value-focused thinking may wish to skip Chapters 4, 5 and 6. The quantitative material of these chapters is mainly to clarify the objectives that have been qualitatively expressed. Beginning in Chapter 7, the objectives are used to create alternatives, identify decision opportunities, and provide guidance for decision processes.

4.1 The Concept of an Attribute

The degree to which an objective is achieved is measured by what I refer to as an attribute. This definition of *attribute* is not universally used. Others have used terms such as *measure of effectiveness, measure of performance,* and *criterion* to define what I call an attribute.

As an illustration of the notion of an attribute, consider a simple example. The objective of a firm to maximize profit can be measured by the attribute "annual profit in millions of dollars." Although in this case it is easy to specify an attribute, often the process is difficult.

Suppose the objective of a governmental health program is to minimize the loss of life. In this case, an obvious attribute is "the annual number of fatalities" due to the cause of concern. This may be reasonable, but let us understand the value judgments implicit in this attribute. It implies that each death is evaluated equally, so the death of a 10-year-old is equivalent to the death of an 80-year-old. Is this value judgment appropriate for the decision context? Whether it is or not, the issue is important to identify and understand. Clearly, the 10-year-old loses much more expected future life than the 80-year-old. Hence, "total expected years of life lost" may be a better attribute for the objective "minimize loss of life." With a life expectancy of 76, the 10-year-old loses 66 expected years, whereas with a life expectancy of 86, the 80-year-old loses 6 expected years. The implicit value judgment setting one year of life equivalent to any other year of life implies that the death of the 10-year-old is eleven times as significant as the death of the 80-year-old.

This example indicates that it is not possible to avoid placing a value judgment on the relative importance of death to different individuals— even saying that all deaths are equal is a value judgment. It also suggests that any weighting scheme that indicates the relative importance of death at different ages is a possible attribute. If additional complexities are introduced, such as the health status of the individuals at risk due to the cause of concern, identifying a reasonable attribute is by no means a simple or insignificant task (see Raiffa, Schwartz, and Weinstein, 1978). The important point is that the assignment of attributes to measure objectives always requires value judgments. These value judgments, like all other value judgments, can lead to important insights from value-focused thinking.

4.2 The Types of Attributes

There are essentially three types of attributes. I refer to these as natural attributes, constructed attributes, and proxy attributes. AltHough the designation of a particular attribute as one of these three types is not always obvious, the trichotomy is useful to point out distinguishing features of the attributes.

Natural Attributes

Natural attributes are those in general use that have a common interpretation to everyone. If an objective is to minimize cost, the attribute "cost measured in dollars" is a natural attribute. For the objective "minimize loss of pine forest," a natural attribute is "acres of pine forest lost." In a risk management context, the objective of minimizing fatalities can be measured by the natural attribute "number of fatalities."

Even though the selection of a natural attribute may appear to be completely obvious, it is still the case that the selection involves value judgments. For the acres of pine forest attribute, there is the value judgment that all acres should be evaluated equally. But is this a good value judgment if the density of the forest is much different on different acres? Another possible natural attribute for the same situation that partially addresses density is the "number of pine trees lost." This exact issue was important in evaluating proposed sites for a dam and reservoir associated with an electric power plant in New Mexico (see Keeney, 1979).

If a natural attribute does not exist or if it seems to have inappropriate built-in value judgments, there are two other possibilities. One is to construct an attribute to measure the associated objective directly. The other is to measure the achievement of the objective indirectly using a proxy attribute.

Constructed Attributes

It is difficult, if not impossible, to come up with natural attributes for many important objectives. Examples of such objectives include "improve the image of the corporation" in a business context, "minimize facial disfigurement" in a medical context, and "increase the international prestige of the country" in a governmental context. For objectives such as these, the attribute plays a doubly important role, as it essentially defines what is meant by the objective.

For important objectives, development of a constructed attribute may be a very satisfactory approach. Unlike natural attributes, which are relevant in numerous decision contexts, a constructed attribute is developed specifically for a given decision context. Table 4.1 presents one constructed attribute that has been used to evaluate public attitudes toward various power plant sites (Keeney and Sicherman, 1983). It was necessary to construct such an attribute because no natural attribute existed to measure the objective "maximize public receptivity to the proposed power plant site." This attribute is made up of verbal descriptions of five different levels of impact. For convenience in designating impacts, a numerical indicator is assigned to each impact level. For example, action-oriented opposition is designated as level -2. In general, constructed attributes involve the description of several distinct levels of impact that directly indicate the degree to which the associated objective is achieved. It is essential that the descriptions of those impact levels be unambiguous to all individuals concerned about a given decision.

With time and use, some constructed attributes tend to take on the features of natural attributes. Examples include the gross national product (GNP), the Dow Jones industrial average, and the Richter scale for earthquake magnitudes. The GNP was constructed to aggregate sev-

Table 4.1. A constructed attribute for public attitudes

Attribute level	Description of attribute level
1	*Support:* No groups are opposed to the facility and at least one group has organized support for the facility.
0	*Neutrality:* All groups are indifferent or uninterested.
-1	*Controversy:* One or more groups have organized opposition, although no groups have action-oriented opposition. Other groups may either be neutral or support the facility.
-2	*Action-oriented opposition:* Exactly one group has action-oriented opposition. The other groups have organized support, indifference or organized opposition.
-3	*Strong action-oriented opposition:* Two or more groups have action-oriented opposition.

eral factors to indicate the economic health of a country. After years of use, implications of GNP levels and changes in those levels are understood and are interpreted the same way by many individuals.

Proxy Attributes

If a natural attribute can be found or a constructed attribute created that will adequately measure the degree to which a fundamental objective is achieved, then this is probably the best way to proceed. But there are cases in which it is very difficult to identify either type of attribute for a given objective. In these cases, it may be necessary to utilize an indirect measure, or what I call a proxy attribute. A proxy (indirect) attribute for a fundamental objective may also be a natural (direct) measure for a means objective. There is, however, an important distinction. When an attribute is used as a proxy attribute for a fundamental objective, levels of that attribute are valued only for their perceived relationship to the achievement of that fundamental objective. When the attribute is used as a natural measure for the means objective, levels of the attribute are valued for their perceived (or calculated) relationships to *all* the fundamental objectives.

As a simple example, consider decisions involving the control of the effects of sulphur dioxide. One fundamental objective in cities is to minimize the damage to stone statues and historic buildings caused by the acid formed by water and sulphur dioxide (acid rain). However, it may be difficult to identify either a natural attribute or a constructed attribute to measure "stone disfiguration." In this case, a proxy attribute defined as the sulphur dioxide concentration measured by parts per million in the vicinity of those statues and buildings may be appropriate. This indirectly indicates the impacts on statue and building disfiguration. It also directly measures the achievement of a means objective, namely, "minimize sulphur dioxide concentrations." However, this objective is a means to health effects and environmental impacts as well as building disfiguration.

4.3 Developing Constructed Attributes

The term *constructed attribute* is not universally used for the concept that it refers to in this book. Many studies (for example, Huber, Sahney, and Ford, 1969; Gustafson and Holloway, 1975; and Keefer and Kirkwood,

1978), use terms such as *subjective scale* or *subjective index* for what I call a constructed attribute. My reasoning for eliminating the term *subjective* is that the use of any attribute, even a natural attribute, requires subjective judgment. The careful development of a constructed attribute, with the clarification of the value judgments that are essential to that attribute, may promote thinking and describe the consequences in a decision situation much better than the "subjective" choice to use a readily available natural attribute.

Value Judgments in Constructed Attributes

Most constructed attributes are meant to measure more than one facet of a complex problem. As a result, in addition to all the considerations necessary in the selection of natural attributes, additional value judgments are made. As an illustration, consider a constructed attribute that measured the objective "minimize the biological impact" in the evaluation of sites for a proposed nuclear power plant (Keeney and Robilliard, 1977). This attribute, illustrated in Table 4.2, was meant to describe possible impacts on productive wetlands, migratory and endangered species, and virgin and mature second-growth timber stands. Level 0 is defined as the least biological impact, since agricultural and urban land are already completely biologically disturbed. Higher-numbered levels indicate increasing disturbance.

Note that many value judgments are necessarily built into the attribute. With levels 3, 4, and 5, the loss of the land used by an endangered species and loss of productive wetlands are implied to be equally important. For level 4, an area of native second-growth forest is deemed equal in value to the same area of other (nonforest) undisturbed communities. Such value judgments are difficult to make and context-dependent. In the case illustrated, the judgments were made by experienced biologists who had visited the proposed sites and were familiar with the biological resources of the area.

The use of such a constructed attribute does not eliminate the possibility of including other biological factors in the evaluation. For instance, some of the proposed power plant sites were in semidesert areas. A major biological impact at these sites was the loss of mature sagebrush communities and their associated small animal communities. In estimating the biological impact at such a site, the biologists were required to specify the likelihood that the impact would be between levels 2 and 3, 3 and 4, and so on. This required professional judgments about the

Table 4.2. A constructed attribute for biological impacts at proposed power plant sites

Attribute level	Description of attribute level
0	Complete loss of 1.0 sq. mile of land which is entirely in agricultural use or is entirely urbanized; no loss of any "native" biological communities.
1	Complete loss of 1.0 sq. mile of primarily (75%) agricultural habitat with loss of 25% of second-growth forest; no measurable loss of wetlands or endangered species habitat.
2	Complete loss of 1.0 sq. mile of land which is 50% farmed and 50% disturbed in some other way (e.g., logged or new second-growth); no measurable loss of wetlands or endangered species habitat.
3	Complete loss of 1.0 sq. mile of recently disturbed (e.g., logged, plowed) habitat plus disturbance to surrounding previously disturbed habitat within 1.0 mile of site border; or 15% loss of wetlands or endangered species habitat.
4	Complete loss of 1.0 sq. mile of land which is 50% farmed (or otherwise disturbed) and 50% mature second-growth forest or other undisturbed community; 15% loss of wetlands or endangered species habitat.
5	Complete loss of 1.0 sq. mile of land which is primarily (75%) undisturbed mature "desert" community; 15% loss of wetlands or endangered species habitat.
6	Complete loss of 1.0 sq. mile of mature second-growth (but not virgin) forest community; or 50% loss of big game and upland game birds; or 50% loss of wetlands and endangered species habitat.
7	Complete loss of 1.0 sq. mile of mature community or 90% loss of productive wetlands and endangered species habitat.
8	Complete loss of 1.0 sq. mile of mature virgin forest and/or wetlands and/or endangered species habitat.

value of the sagebrush habitat relative to the defined impacts of levels 0–8. Regardless of the difficulty of making such judgments, they are an inherent part of the problem and must be either implicitly or explicitly addressed.

    To gain some insight into the judgmental process of developing a constructed attribute, consider a simplification of the siting problem in which the only concerns are the loss of productive wetlands and the loss of rare species habitat. Suppose it is reasonable to use two natural attributes of this biological impact: X_1, acres of productive wetlands, and X_2, acres of rare species habitat. If we let these range from 0 to 640 acres and from 0 to 50 acres, respectively, the possible consequence space is as illustrated in Figure 4.1.

    Clearly, the best biological consequence is no impact, described by $(x_1 = 0, x_2 = 0)$, which is 0 acres of productive wetlands and 0 acres of rare species habitat. The worst consequence is $(x_1 = 640, x_2 = 50)$. Other possible consequences fall between these bounds. Suppose questioning of biologists and ecologists elicits the indifference curves illustrated in Figure 4.1. From this, the constructed attribute called Y in

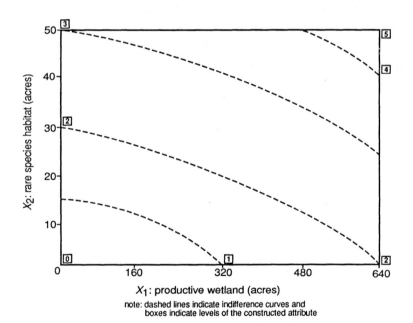

Figure 4.1. Value judgments necessary to construct an attribute for biological impact

Table 4.3.   A constructed attribute Y of site biological impact

Attribute level	Description of attribute level
0	No loss of productive wetlands or rare species habitat.
1	Loss of 320 acres of productive wetlands and no loss of rare species habitat.
2	Loss of 640 acres of productive wetlands and no loss of rare species habitat or loss of 30 acres of rare species habitat and no loss of productive wetlands.
3	No loss of productive wetlands and loss of 50 acres of rare species habitat.
4	Loss of 640 acres of productive wetlands and loss of 40 acres of rare species habitat.
5	Loss of 640 acres of productive wetlands and loss of 50 acres of rare species habitat.

Table 4.3 can be developed. Note that the attribute level is defined to increase with increasing seriousness of consequences.

Several value judgments are indicated in Table 4.3. At level 2, the loss of 640 acres of productive wetlands with no loss of rare species habitat is equated with no loss of productive wetlands and loss of 30 acres of rare species habitat. Figure 4.1 indicates that both of these consequences are equivalent to the loss of 320 acres of productive wetland plus 20 acres of rare species habitat. For simplicity, it is often convenient to use reference attribute levels with only one kind of detrimental impact.

To develop more formally a constructed scale Y, one could assess a value model v over the (x_1, x_2) consequences. This would provide a complete set of indifference curves over the consequence space in Figure 4.1. Then a specific attribute level y could be defined as $v(x_1, x_2)$, which would serve to define the constructed attribute Y. This is in essence the process used to generate all constructed attributes. The distinction is the degree of formality or informality with which the value model is determined and whether the entire attribute scale or only specific points are clearly defined.

If clearly identifiable natural attributes X_1 and X_2 existed, there would be no need for a constructed attribute. But when no such natural attributes exist, the judgments formally indicated above must be made informally to create a constructed attribute. First the major concerns of losses of productive wetlands and habitat must be identified. Then several distinct attribute levels need to be defined, as indicated in Table 4.3. It may be necessary to describe the loss of wetlands or habitat with words or examples; the natural attribute of acres may not be appropriate since, for instance, it implies that all acres of productive wetlands are equally valuable. Since only a few levels of the constructed attribute are clearly described, it is not possible to create indifference curves, as in Figure 4.1, or to construct a complete value model over possible consequences. The value judgments analogous to those necessary for indifference curves and value models must be made when biologists assess that the values of impacts at the site are, say, between levels 3 and 4 or at approximately level 2 of the constructed attribute.

For a simple example of a constructed attribute based on explicit value judgments, suppose one fundamental objective of an automobile safety program is to maximize safety. And suppose this objective is specified with the component objectives "minimize fatalities" and "minimize serious injuries." Single natural attributes for these lower-level objectives may be "number of fatalities" and "number of injuries requiring inpatient hospitalization." Collectively, these two attributes are used to measure the degree to which the higher-level objective "maximize safety" is achieved. In other words, the two-dimensional vector indicating fatalities and injuries can be thought of as a vector attribute for "maximize safety."

It is possible to construct a single scalar attribute for the objective "maximize safety" using the two components of the vector. Creating a scalar attribute for the higher-level objective requires explicit value judgments to combine fatalities and serious injuries. This will indicate, for example, how a consequence (6, 12), meaning 6 fatalities and 12 serious injuries, compares to the consequence (8, 3). Suppose it is determined that 1 fatality is equivalently as bad as 6 serious injuries. Then (6, 12) is equivalent to (8, 0), whereas (8, 3) is equivalent to (8.5, 0). This is effectively a constructed scalar attribute of "equivalent number of fatalities" to measure the objective "maximize safety."

Types of Constructed Attributes

It is worth mentioning three specific types of constructed attributes to indicate the breadth of usefulness of such attributes. Two of these types

were used by Krischer (1976) to evaluate different treatments for children with the common congenital problem of cleft lip and palate. The
objectives of such treatment included "minimize the degradation of
hearing" and "minimize facial physical disfiguration." The former objective was measured with a simple constructed attribute of whether or not
a hearing aid would be required. Such dichotomous yes-no attributes are
often useful. In another evaluation (see Section 11.5), one constructed
attribute of a very large scale integrated circuit tester was whether or
not the tester had data analysis software associated with it.

The objective of "minimize facial disfiguration" raises a general issue. For medical problems or environmental problems, how can visual
effects be adequately accounted for with attributes? One might contemplate the need for an attribute and think "What words can describe a
whole picture?" The answer is that you do not need words; pictures can
be used for such an attribute. Krischer had facial pictures of several
children approximately 10 years old. The faces showed different
amounts of disfiguration from the treatment of cleft lip and palate.
These were used as the basis for a constructed attribute. However, since
the hair, eyes, cheeks, and chin are not affected by treatments, they
were not used on the faces for the constructed attribute. A professional
artist drew those features, which were then common to all faces. A part
of the photos showing the nose and mouth areas was superimposed on
this sketch. The superimposed part was a triangle from the top of the
nose to both sides of the lower jaw and connected with a line cutting
off the chin. Both parents of children with cleft lip and palate and
professionals concerned with their treatment found the attribute very
useful.

Creation of such an attribute is itself the result of a bit of value-
focused thinking. An attribute is necessary because the objective of minimizing physical disfigurement is part of an important decision. The
alternatives for attributes that naturally come to mind are attributes
described with text. But this is only one alternative, albeit the most
common one, to describe attribute levels. Broadening the search for
attributes can lead to the visual attribute. To broaden the search, think
about the objectives for the decision situation of choosing an attribute.
These objectives are the desirable properties of attributes discussed in
Section 4.5.

A constructed attribute can be created directly from the alternatives
available or hypothetical alternatives or both. With respect to a given
objective, you rank alternatives in terms of the degree to which they

achieve that objective alone. The result is a value function (that is, an ordinal value function) for contributions of alternatives on that objective. If you develop the constructed scale using questions similar to those used to develop a measurable value function or a utility function, then the resulting constructed scale has the corresponding cardinal properties of that function as discussed in Chapter 5. Such a constructed attribute was used in an evaluation for the Baltimore Gas and Electric Company of different coal technologies for a large power plant (Keeney, Lathrop, and Sicherman, 1986). The objective was to minimize the decision difficulty, which involved the nonproductive use of executives' time, in the entire decision process. As the decision difficulty associated with previous decision processes involving power plants was well known to executives in the company, the constructed scale used some of these past processes as levels of the constructed attribute.

4.4 Use of Proxy Attributes

A major difficulty in many decision situations is that attributes are not easy to identify. For evaluating hazardous waste sites, two objectives are to minimize the detrimental socioeconomic and environmental impacts. But what obvious measures are there for these socioeconomic or environmental impacts? The best way to measure such impacts may be with proxy attributes.

Consider a simple problem, illustrated in Figure 4.2, involving one fundamental objective and one proxy attribute. Suppose there is a fundamental objective O for which no natural attribute X exists. Hence, a proxy attribute Y, with specific levels represented by y, is selected to evaluate the consequences of alternatives. The use of Y requires special consideration in the evaluation phase of analysis. To indicate this, assume that both the natural attribute X and the proxy attribute Y have been identified. To specify the objective function, which for this discussion we will assume is a von Neumann-Morgenstern utility function $u^*(y)$ over attribute Y, one should think about two considerations: the likelihood of various levels of attribute X, denoted by x, being associated with a particular level y of attribute Y, and the preference for various levels of x. The first consideration could be quantified by the probability distribution $p(x|y)$, which indicates the probabilities of various levels of x given that the level of Y is y. The second consideration could be quantified by the utility function $u(x)$. The utility function $u^*(y)$ could then be derived from

$$u^*(y) = \int u(x)p(x|y), \tag{4.1}$$

where $\int$ represents summation or integration, whichever is appropriate. However, the use of the proxy attribute Y was necessary in the first place either because no obvious natural attribute X exists or because impacts over X cannot be reasonably estimated. Hence the process just outlined must be done informally by directly assessing $u^*(y)$.

Now to evaluate an alternative A_j, it is necessary to specify the possible y levels that may result from choosing A_j. This can be represented by the probability distribution $p_j^*(y)$ so the expected utility of alternative A_j is

$$Eu^*(A_j) = \int u^*(y)p_j^*(y). \tag{4.2}$$

As long as there is a one-to-one relationship between any lowest-level fundamental objective and a proxy attribute, the situation is reasonably manageable. However, in many cases there may be several means objectives interacting in a complex way to affect the achievement of several lowest-level fundamental objectives. This implies that there

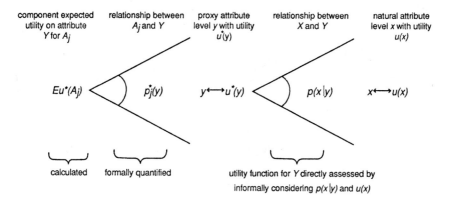

Figure 4.2. Relationship between a proxy attribute and a natural attribute

are interdependencies among the proxy attributes necessary to measure the degrees to which the corresponding set of lowest-level fundamental objectives are achieved. The situation is even more complex when natural or constructed attributes can be specified for some of those lowest-level fundamental objectives.

As an example, consider the decision situation related to acid rain. Two means objectives, of the many related to acid rain, are to minimize the concentration of sulphur dioxide and to minimize the concentration of nitrogen oxides in ambient air. Fundamental objectives include minimizing the degradation of lakes, minimizing the degradation of forests, minimizing control costs, and minimizing negative impacts on employment. Suppose we identify natural attributes for control costs as millions of dollars spent annually and for impacts on employment as the number of lost jobs. In addition, suppose we identify no natural or constructed attributes for lake and forest degradation. We might select the concentrations of sulphur dioxide and of the nitrogen oxides as proxy attributes for these. However, the relationship between the proxy attributes and the environmental degradation is very complex. It is nevertheless precisely this relationship that is necessary in order to evaluate the relative desirability of alternatives intended to reduce the pollutant concentrations.

4.5 Desirable Properties of Attributes

All of the desirable properties of attributes are directly related to the desirable properties of fundamental objectives discussed in Section 3.5. If the set of fundamental objectives is carefully identified and structured, there are three main properties desired of the respective attributes. Namely, the attributes should be measurable, operational, and understandable. Attributes that have these three properties will clarify the respective objectives and facilitate value-focused thinking.

A critical issue affecting whether an attribute is measurable, operational, and understandable is ambiguity. Each attribute should be unambiguous. This means that every level of achievement indicated by the attribute should have a clear meaning. For an attribute "annual profit in millions of dollars," a $3 million profit in a year is unambiguous. Before the year begins, there may be large uncertainties about whether profits will be $3 million, $1 million, −$1 million, or something more like $1.536 million. This, however, is not the issue of ambiguity, it is the different issue of uncertainty.

Measurability

An attribute that is measurable defines the associated objective in more detail than that provided by the objective alone. To do this, the attribute must embody implicit value judgments that are appropriate and avoid those that are inappropriate.

In the introduction to this chapter, one objective of a health program was to "minimize the loss of life." Attributes considered for this objective included "annual number of fatalities" and "total years of expected life lost." As discussed, the value judgments implicit in these attributes are very different. In a given context, one attribute may measure the objective better than the other.

For a more complex example, suppose a hazardous waste facility is to be located somewhere in a state. One objective for evaluating possible sites is to minimize local social disruption. An attribute to measure this might be the "annual number of deliveries to a site." But what counts as a delivery, and should all deliveries count the same for social disruption? If two potential sites have very different population densities on the routes to the sites, is the social disruption the same at each site for the identical set of deliveries? Probably not, so the annual number of deliveries would not clearly describe the level of social disruption. The basic problem with this proposed attribute is that number of deliveries relates to, but does not directly measure, social disruption.

In such situations, an attribute called something like "level of local social disruption" is often constructed to rate disruption on, say, a scale of 1 to 5. Alternatively, levels of this attribute are qualitatively defined with terms like *none, low, medium,* and *high.* In both cases, the levels are often not clearly defined, so there is significant ambiguity with their use.

Problems of measurability can occur with constructed or proxy attributes. Consider the objective "maximize the economic well-being of the United States." This might be measured using the constructed attribute known as the gross national product (GNP). Whether this is appropriate will depend on the specific decision context. GNP does not take into account individual purchasing power or the distribution of purchasing power, which could be considered important parts of economic well-being. In such circumstances, it is perhaps useful to decompose the

objective concerning economic well-being into components using specification. More on this follows in Section 4.6.

Operationality

An attribute is operational if it is reasonable for two purposes: to describe the possible consequences with respect to the associated objective
and to provide a sound basis for value judgments about the desirability
of the various degrees to which the objective might be achieved. Let me
consider these in order.

The actual consequences of any alternative with respect to a given
objective should be describable by one level, and one level only, of the
attribute associated with that objective. Before an alternative is selected
or after its selection but before the occurrence of its actual consequences, the possible consequences should be describable by a probability distribution over the attribute. A special case of a probability distribution is a point estimate in the case where there is no uncertainty. Ways
to determine the probability distribution involve collecting and synthe-
sizing data, modeling the processes leading to the consequences using
the means-ends objectives network to help develop the model, directly
assessing professional judgments, or a combination of these approaches
(see Keeney, 1980).

Suppose an objective of an air pollution program in a metropolitan
area is to minimize sulfur dioxide pollution. And suppose the attribute
selected is "parts per million of sulfur dioxide." Without further clarification, this attribute is not operational, because it is not clear where the
pollution is measured, how often it is measured, or how multiple measures over time and/or space are aggregated. In addition, with many
scientific measurements, it is helpful to know how they will be measured.

As indicated in detail in Chapter 5, attributes are essential to the
building of a value model over the consequences. For attributes to be
operational, it must be possible to express relative preferences for different levels of achievement of an objective as indicated by attribute levels.
Expressing preferences for proxy attributes is difficult, however, as
these preferences must intuitively combine facts and values as discussed
in Section 4.4. For example, suppose you are fundamentally concerned
about a particular health effect of a pollutant in water. If the proxy
attribute of parts per million of the pollutant in the water is used, the
value assessment must address the relative preferences of 1, 10, and 20
parts per million. The relative preferences will clearly be very different

depending on whether the lowest level of the pollutant thought to cause the health effect is 8, 15, or 50 parts per million. This information is of a factual nature and may be understood only by a small group of technical specialists. Yet a generalist program administrator may be expected to make decisions affecting the level of the pollutant.

There is also an issue of operationality regarding value tradeoffs between pairs of attributes. For example, two fundamental objectives in a study about Los Angeles air pollution (see Section 11.4) were to minimize cases of breathing impairment and to minimize cost. The health objective was measured by the annual number of people in the Los Angeles Basin experiencing a reduction of lung capacity of more than 20 percent, and the cost objective was measured in annual millions of dollars. It was easy to assess relative preferences for different numbers of people with lung impairment. Preferences were linear, meaning that 1000 cases were considered twice as bad as 500. Preferences were also linear in costs. But for many individuals the value tradeoff between the two attributes was very difficult to make. It strongly depended on how much a 20 percent reduction of lung capacity would restrict a person's activity. At one extreme, would it force one to lead a very sedentary life, or at the other extreme, would it simply mean one could no longer run marathons? Factual information about such matters needs to be obtained in order to render the attribute operational.

Attributes are more fully operational if assessments about possible consequences and values can be made individually for each attribute rather than jointly for sets of attributes. This means it is desirable for the possible consequences with respect to different attributes to be conditionally probabilistically independent given an alternative. It is also desirable for analogous independence conditions for values, discussed in Chapter 5, to be appropriate.

Independence conditions are often inappropriate, and hence operationality is adversely affected, when proxy attributes are used. Suppose two objectives of a developing country are to feed its populace and to export grains for hard currency. Say the local crops are wheat and rice. The proxy attributes selected for the two fundamental objectives may be "tons of wheat harvested" and "tons of rice harvested." Preferences for pairs of levels of these attributes are naturally intertwined, because both are means to both fundamental objectives (see Section 6.2). If the wheat crop is very good the importance of the level of the rice harvest may be diminished, and vice versa.

For this example, it is also likely that the rice harvest and the wheat harvest are not probabilistically independent, because both are dependent on the weather. However, given a specified level of both harvests, the implications for the achievement of the two fundamental objectives may be conditionally probabilistically independent. Or at least there may be some dependency that can readily be modeled.

Understandability

Each attribute should be understandable. This means there should be no ambiguity in describing consequences in terms of attributes and no ambiguity in interpreting consequences described in terms of attributes. Understandability implies that there should be no loss of information when one person assigns an attribute level to describe a consequence and another person interprets that attribute level. To illustrate these notions, consider the four different attributes for the objective "minimize fatalities" shown in Figure 4.3. All of these attributes purportedly measure the number of fatalities.

Here it will be useful to clarify one aspect of my definition of an attribute. I use the term *attribute* to include the conceptual part, fatalities in this case, with the measurement part, indicated by the scales in Figure 4.3. I do this because a measurement scale is always associated with a conceptual measure.

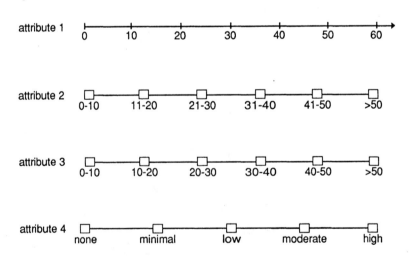

Figure 4.3. Four possible attributes for the objective "minimize fatalities" that measure number of fatalities

With attribute 1 in Figure 4.3, a consequence of 17 fatalities clearly fits on the scale, and another person seeing the attribute level of 17 would interpret it as 17 fatalities. The arrow at the upper end of the scale indicates that any number of fatalities greater than 60 can be distinctly indicated on attribute 1. If attribute 1 is used to describe the possible consequences of an alternative, this can be done with a probability distribution. This distribution might indicate, for example, a 0.03 chance of 10 fatalities, a 0.05 chance of 11 fatalities, and so forth. The issue of uncertainty does not affect ambiguity.

Attribute 2 does have some ambiguity associated with it. In this case 17 fatalities would obviously be assigned to the attribute level 11-20 fatalities, but another person would not be able to interpret that level to mean precisely 17 fatalities. The assignment of level 11-20 could obviously mean any number of fatalities from 11 to 20. The unnecessary shortcoming with attribute 2 is that information is lost from the description of a consequence to the interpretation of that consequence. This would not be a major shortcoming if the implications of all consequences described by a single attribute level were similar and if there were no easy improvement. In this case, however, 0 fatalities and 10 may not have the same implications and attribute 1 is a readily available improvement from attribute 2. Also, the category of more than 50 fatalities at the right of attribute 2 includes 50 and 500 fatalities, which do not at first glance appear to be equivalent in most decision contexts.

Attribute 3 is similar to attribute 2, with an additional deficiency. The adjacent attribute levels overlap so there is ambiguity about whether, for instance, 20 fatalities should be indicated as level 10–20 or level 20–30. The way to eliminate this deficiency is simply to select attribute 2, and yet many attributes like attribute 3 appear in reported analyses.

Attribute 4 is representative of a common and significant problem in the understandability of attributes. It is a vague and ambiguous attempt to scale possible fatalities. Numerous studies have indicated the ambiguity associated with interpreting attribute levels such as minimal, low, and high. Is 17 fatalities minimal, low, moderate, or high? It certainly depends on personal judgments and values exogenous to attribute 4. Similarly, if another person sees that low fatalities are indicated, what does this mean? Does it imply fewer than 2, at least a few but not 10, somewhere like 15, or what? A way to improve attribute 4 is to provide quantitative definitions of the meanings of the attribute levels. This in essence transforms attribute 4 into the same type as attribute 2.

If attribute 4 is so poor and if it is so easy to do much better in many cases, why do so many surveys and analyses use attributes as ambiguous as attribute 4? One possible explanation is that the uncertainty about what consequences might occur leads to the mistaken belief that the uncertainty should be included in the attribute. Then, for example, uncertainty about possible fatalities between 25 and 60 may simply be interpreted as moderate in a given context. This may simplify the assignment of consequences, but it definitely reduces understanding by confusing uncertainty and ambiguity. It is much better to use the unambiguous attribute 1 and to describe uncertainty over consequences with a probability distribution over the attribute levels.

4.6 The Decision of Selecting Attributes

Selecting attributes is an important part of fully expressing values. It is important for improving communication and for creating alternatives because of the insights it may provide about the values concerned. But selecting attributes is even more important, indeed essential, for quantifying a value model and subsequently evaluating alternatives.

It is useful to recognize that the selection of an attribute for a given objective is a decision problem facing the analyst (see Raisbeck, 1979). In the simplest terms, the choice is should one choose a natural, a constructed, or a proxy attribute. Clearly the answer depends on the circumstances. If a natural attribute is available, then it should generally be chosen. If no natural attribute is available, things become more complex. Either a constructed or a proxy attribute should be chosen or the objectives should be further decomposed into components, using the logic of specification discussed in Chapter 3, and attributes should be sought for each new lower level of objectives until attributes are found. The choice of an attribute should be evaluated in terms of the desirable properties of attributes discussed in Section 4.5. Let me mention some of the pros and cons of the three possibilities—constructed attributes, proxy attributes, and decomposition—for the difficult cases where no obvious natural attribute exists.

Constructed Attributes

Constructed attributes measure precisely what the fundamental objective is meant to address. Because of the way the attribute is constructed, it is a complete description of the associated objective. Furthermore, it is easier to separate judgments about consequences from value judgments when a constructed attribute is used rather than either a proxy attribute or further decomposition.

The potential shortcomings of constructed attributes concern whether they are understandable and operational. Constructed attributes do not have the common interpretation of attribute levels that is associated with natural and proxy attributes. Thus, it is more difficult to communicate about consequences using a constructed attribute. In the constructing of an attribute, care is taken to minimize this potential shortcoming, but this is still a complex issue. As a result of the difficulty of understanding the attribute, it may also be operationally difficult to quantify value judgments over levels of consequences. Again the issue boils down to how carefully the attribute is constructed.

Decomposition

Decomposition can be interpreted as a special procedure to construct an attribute for an objective. In this procedure, the objective is first specified into component objectives. Then attributes are found for those components and are integrated through the use of value judgments. The result of this integration is essentially a constructed attribute for the original objective. At the extreme, the value model is essentially nothing more than a constructed attribute for the overall fundamental objective in a decision situation.

The advantage of decomposition is that it may allow the identification of natural attributes for the new lower-level objectives created by the decomposition. These natural attributes are understandable and are likely to be relatively easy to use for describing consequences and quantifying a value model. The disadvantage is that more information needs to be gathered, because there are more attributes for each alternative and the value model requires more value judgments. There is also the possibility that the specification of a higher-level objective into component objectives may lead to holes in the objectives hierarchy, especially if the higher-level objective is both broad and a little vague. For example, with the objective "improve the morale of the organization," specification might easily miss important aspects of morale.

Proxy Attributes

The use of proxy attributes typically reduces the number of attributes necessary for a decision situation and simplifies the description of consequences. This reduces the effort required to gather factual information while increasing the effort necessary to specify the value model. It also confounds issues of fact with issues of value and consequently results in less insight than might otherwise be the case. Let me indicate some specific complexities of using proxy attributes.

The use of proxy attributes increases the likelihood of redundancy in evaluation, because it is equivalent to having some means objectives in the fundamental objectives hierarchy. To the degree that these means objectives are associated with more than one fundamental objective, the possibility of double-counting is increased. This double-counting may occur when the value model is assessed. In this assessment, weights are given to both the means objective and the related fundamental objective, where part of the weight on the former may be due to its impact on the latter. Empirically reducing the weight on the means objective to account for the fact that one end is also explicitly included in the value model is a difficult task.

A related complexity with proxy attributes involves possible inappropriate weighting. Fischer et al. (1987) discovered in an experimental context involving two objectives that many individuals tended to overweight a proxy attribute relative to a natural attribute in assessing utility functions. Two descriptions of an air pollution problem involving fundamental objectives concerned with cost and health effects were given. In the first description, the objectives were measured by natural attributes involving dollars and the number of health effects. The second had the natural cost attribute and a proxy attribute called control level for health effects. Respondents were given the probabilistic relationship between the proxy control attribute and the natural effects attribute (the p in Figure 4.2) and asked to express values for levels of the two attributes in both situations. The control attribute was weighted more than a consistent weighting with health effects implied. One hypothesis is that respondents tended to simplify their problem by using a worst-case scenario implying that the worst possible levels of the associated natural attribute would result from each specified level of the proxy attribute.

With proxy attributes, there must be an intermingling of facts and values. In assessing the utility function u^* in Figure 4.2, one needs to account for the relationship p, which is a question of facts, and the desirability of the various x levels, which is a question of values. This issue is crucial because it routinely leads to a situation in which the value judgments of individuals with factual knowledge about the possible p

relationship are used to specify the utility function u^*. Thus, those individuals with technical expertise are de facto put in the position of assigning the values appropriate for the achievement of the fundamental objectives, indicated by the x levels, in the decision situation. Unfortunately, the technical experts are often neither the parties responsible for the decision being addressed nor particularly knowledgeable about the value issues in that decision situation.

4.7 Connecting Decision Situations with Attributes

Most decisions are not made in a vacuum. The implications of one decision often influence the alternatives, the consequences, or the values in other decision situations. However, in any analysis of a specific decision, it is not reasonable to include the implications for all possible related decisions. The mind and the analysis would both completely bog down with such a massive problem structure. Thus, it is important to connect related decision situations in an efficient manner. The dual intent is to represent the relationship reasonably and to keep the analysis of the given decision manageable.

This section discusses several examples of how this can be done using specific attributes, each of which can be associated with a specific objective. It is invariably the case that this objective, which is a fundamental objective in the given decision context, is a means objective for the implications that decision may have for other decision situations.

Probability as an Attribute

In many decision situations it is reasonable to use an attribute defined as the probability of the occurrence of some event. A simple example involves medical decisions in which the only objective concerns whether or not death occurs soon after treatment (that is, whether or not the treatment was successful). A decision tree for this problem would contain all the alternatives and their uncertainties. The consequences at the end of the decision tree would be that a patient is dead or alive. A utility of 0 could be assigned to death and a utility of 1 to living. An analysis of this decision problem to maximize expected utility would be equivalent to an analysis to maximize the probability of living. Hence, one could simply define the attribute as "probability of survival" and assign linearly increasing utilities as the probability of survival increases.

A slightly more involved medical decision has two objectives: min-imizing the likelihood of death and maximizing the assets available after medical treatment. Consequences in this decision could be represented by (p, m), where attribute P is "probability of death" with level p and attribute M is "monetary assets after treatment" with level m. Utility functions assessed over these attributes often have the property that the probability of death is utility independent of the monetary assets after treatment, whereas the monetary assets after treatment are not utility independent of the probability of death (see Chapter 5). This is equiva-lent to having a state-dependent utility function, meaning that the utility for assets depends on the state of being alive or dead. If the patient lives, the monetary assets will be used for the patient and his or her family, and the earning power of the patient will be preserved. If the patient dies, the assets will be a legacy to the family, and the patient of course will have lost all earning power. It might, for instance, be the case that the utility function over assets given death would be more risk averse than the utility function given life, which would be one reason why assets would not be utility independent of the probability of death.

In many business contexts, the use of a "probability" attribute may connect related decision situations. The attribute "probability of bank-ruptcy" in important business decisions may be analogous to the proba-bility of death in personal decisions. In other business contexts, such as risk analyses involving hazardous materials, the probability of a major accident may be used as an attribute. In another situation, if approval (for example, licensing from governmental authorities, approval of ad-ditional financing) is important, the probability of forced project cancel-lation may be used as an attribute. In all of these situations, there is the implicit assumption that the event of concern, such as bankruptcy, an accident, or cancellation, does not come in degrees. In other words, use of the probability attribute implies that one bankruptcy is equally as bad as another bankruptcy. Whether such an assumption is appropriate in a given decision context must be explicitly appraised.

In the contexts above, suppose that a vector x represents the conse-quences of a decision situation and p represents the probability that the event (bankruptcy, an accident, or cancellation) will occur. Figure 4.4a illustrates this notation in part of a simplified decision tree. At uncer-tainty node A, there is a p chance that the event will occur and a $1 - p$ chance that it will not. In both situations, additional decisions, repre-sented by nodes B and C, and uncertainties, represented by nodes D and E, would affect the consequences represented by x. However, it may not be worth the effort to build a complete model of the situation in which the event occurs, especially when this probability is low.

A good example of this involves alternatives for building a large power plant where the event is that licenses are not received for the plant and the plan to build it is canceled. Then, of course, another decision process must follow to identify other sites for the plant, and the consequences of these alternative sites can be described in terms of x levels. To simplify the analysis of the problem at hand and yet to maintain the connecting link with the decision process when cancellation

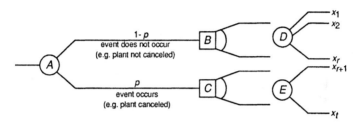

a. part of a decision tree with probability of plant canceled

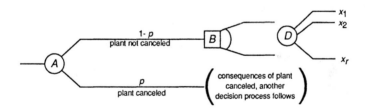

b. decision tree simplified to summarize implications of "plant canceled"

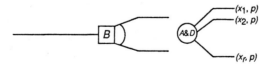

c. equivalent decision tree with probability of cancellation as a consequence

Figure 4.4. Use of probability as an attribute

of the chosen plant occurs, we simply summarize the consequences of the second decision process as the consequence "plant canceled," as shown in Figure 4.4b. To analyze the problem represented in Figure 4.4b directly, we would need to assess a utility for the consequence "plant canceled" that was consistent with the utility function assessed for x consequences.

Another equivalent representation of Figure 4.4a is given in Figure 4.4c, where the (x, p) consequences are illustrated. In this case node A is combined with node D, since the cancellation concern is included at the end of the decision tree.

There are restrictions on the form of the utility function involving the attribute "probability of cancellation." From Figure 4.4b, we can see that the expected utility $u(A)$ at node A is

$$u(A) = p\bar{u}_C + (1 - p)\bar{u}_X(x), \tag{4.3}$$

where $u_X(x)$ is scaled from 0 to 1 by

$$u_X(x^\circ) = 0 \text{ and } u_X(x^*) = 1, \tag{4.4}$$

x° and x^* are the least and most preferred consequences of building the facility, $\bar{u}_X$ is the expected utility given the facility is built, and $\bar{u}_C$ is the expected utility of "plant canceled" on the same scale as (4.4). In order to be consistent with (4.3), the utility function u over consequences (x, p) in Figure 4.4c must be

$$u(x, p) = p\bar{u}_C + (1 - p)u_X(x). \tag{4.5}$$

It is reasonable to use (4.5) when both the variability and the magnitude of the term $p\bar{u}_C$ are small relative to the magnitudes of the term $(1 - p)u_X(x)$. Then it makes sense to assess the utility $\bar{u}_C$ directly in a rather rough manner relative to the detail with which u_X is assessed. If $p\bar{u}_C$ is of the same order as $(1 - p)u_X$ or if $p\bar{u}_C$ is larger, then naturally more attention should be focused on the values that make up $\bar{u}_C$.

Suppose $\bar{u}_C < -10$ and $p < 0.02$, which is typical of the so-called low probability–high consequence events. Then the range of $p\bar{u}_C$ is less than 0.2. If the range on $(1 - p)u_X$ is approximately 1 since $(1 - p)$ is essentially 1 and u_X can range from 0 to 1, assessing $\bar{u}_C$ directly seems appropriate. Rearranging (4.5) yields

$$u(x, p) = u_X(x) + [\bar{u}_C - u_X(x)]p, \tag{4.6}$$

which clearly illustrates that the probability of cancellation can be considered an attribute. Also, when the variability of the term $[\bar{u}_C - u_X(x)]$ is small relative to its absolute magnitude, it can be approximated by $[\bar{u}_C - \bar{u}_X(x)]$, which is a constant. In this situation, which typically occurs whenever $\bar{u}_C$ should be directly assessed, (4.6) becomes the additive utility function

$$u(x, p) = u_X(x) + [\bar{u}_C - \bar{u}_X(x)]p \qquad (4.7)$$

over attributes X and P. This additive approximation has been utilized in several studies of technology options for utility companies (see for example, Keeney, Lathrop, and Sicherman, 1986).

In all of the uses of probability as an attribute discussed so far, the event of concern would occur only once. Thus, we could assume that the overall utility function was linear in the probability of its occurrence. In some situations, the probability of an event might be used as an attribute with the possibility of the event occurring more than once. One such situation concerned an evaluation of telephone networks. An aspect of the quality of service was summarized by the attribute "probability that the telephone line is blocked," which would cause the potential user to get a busy signal. That individual could hang up, try again in five minutes, and still find a blocked line. Getting a blocked line twice in succession might cause more inconvenience and be more irritating than getting a blocked line at two separate times with many successfully completed calls in between. Such a situation could result in the utility function over the attribute "probability of blockage" being nonlinear.

Timing of Consequences

The utility of any consequence in a decision situation may depend on when it occurs. For instance, one would usually prefer to receive income sooner than later because of what one could do with the money if owned. One would also prefer to have a major project (such as a power plant) completed on time rather than late to meet the needs that led to the project. If the project is late, additional decisions are required to fill in until the original project is finished.

The thorough way to address all the value aspects in such decision situations is to describe consequences as (x, t) where x is the actual consequence and t the time at which it occurs. There are several models that address this problem of preferences over time (see Koopmans, 1960, 1972; Meyer, 1976; and Bell, 1977b), but use of these models sometimes

greatly complicates the analysis. In some circumstances, one can limit
the analysis, but yet provide reasonable insights, by defining an attribute
to deal with timeliness or delay.

As an example, let attribute D be "delay in months" and let the
other impacts be described by attribute X. The consequences are of the
form (x, d). Assigning utilities $u(x, d)$ may proceed first by assessing
$u(x, 0)$, the utility of x consequences with no delay. Indeed it may be the
case that attribute X is utility independent of attribute D so

$$u(x, d) = f(d) + g(d)u(x, 0) \tag{4.8}$$

for some functions f and $g > 0$ (see Chapter 5). The specification of f
and g would follow from the assessment of two utility functions over d
given different x consequences. These assessments would need to account for two factors: (1) the impact of the delay on the utility of x, and
(2) the consequences that might occur in the interim from time 0 to d
as a result of some forced decision process due to delay. Factor 1 relates
to the issue of discounting to account for time preference. Factor 2
concerns the use of an additional attribute, namely delay, to connect
related decision problems in a manageable fashion. Indeed, in some
problems it may be reasonable to address factor 1 explicitly using time
preferences and factor 2 explicitly with a delay attribute. Note that (4.8)
does exactly this where function g addresses time preferences for x and
function f addresses additional consequences that occur because of the
delay.

Limiting the Time Horizon

In many decision processes, decisions are made over a long period of
time. However, it is clearly difficult to anticipate all of the circumstances
that may occur, for instance, in ten years or to identify all of the decision
alternatives that may be available in those circumstances. Hence a formal
analysis far into the future often will not be particularly fruitful. As an
alternative for thinking about problems or for analyzing them, a summary measure of the ability to deal with any situation that may occur
can be useful.

Consider a firm that is marketing a major product against several
competitors. It knows it will be in business for the long term and that
its fundamental objective is to maximize its profits over time. However,
the complexities mentioned above make it extremely difficult to forecast

either the implications of decisions in the present on profits more than five years in the future or decision opportunities that will be available in five years. Thus, in analyzing options now, the firm may utilize two attributes. One attribute may be "profits in the next five years" and a second may be "market share in five years." Maximizing future market share is a fundamental objective in the context of marketing the specific product now. It is of course a means objective for profits in years past the five-year period. Market share logically links the current decision with future, now even unforeseen, decisions. In the assessment of a utility function over near-term profits and market share at the end of a period, a greater focus on the long term is indicated by a greater relative weight on market share.

Flexibility

Flexibility is important in many decision situations (see Merkhofer, 1977; Evans, 1991). In these situations, it refers to the ability to adapt an alternative in light of circumstances different from those assumed when the alternative was selected. Rather than extend the model to include the probability of various changes in circumstances and reactions to these circumstances, an attribute referred to as "flexibility" can often be added to address such considerations. In an analysis to evaluate casks for the transportation and storage of spent nuclear fuel (see Section 11.2), it was assumed that it would not be necessary to retrieve casks from a permanent geologic repository. But because of the realization that, for reasons not known at present, it might become necessary to retrieve the casks at some time in the future, a flexibility objective was included in the analysis to address the ability to retrieve casks. This was measured by an attribute indicating whether or not the casks were self-shielded, as such casks would be much easier to retrieve. The relative importance of the two different levels of this attribute depended on the significance of the difference in flexibility afforded by those two levels and the likelihood that flexibility would ever be used (that is, that casks would be retrieved).

Another example of bridging interrelated decision situations was an evaluation of possible technologies for a coal-fired power plant at a site northeast of Baltimore. One important objective pertained to corporate image (see Keeney, Lathrop, and Sicherman, 1986). Clearly, a better corporate image was preferred to a worse one. A constructed attribute was developed to measure corporate image for the Baltimore Gas and Electric Company in this decision context. This attribute was important because of its implications for future relationships between BG&E and the financial organizations and regulatory agencies with which it dealt. Specifically, BG&E executives felt that a positive corporate image would provide flexibility for their dealings with such organizations on future decisions.

Learning Relevant to Future Decisions

It is often the case that an individual or an organization faces a number of decision problems over time that have a common feature. For instance, if one firm is considering choosing another organization to provide parts for a product, serious negotiations are likely to be involved. If negotiations may occur several times in the future, the learning that accrues in early negotiations may be important later. Including an attribute to account for this learning might affect the strategy used in early negotiation sessions. Simply stated, a strategy that might lead to a less desirable consequence (excluding learning) in the first negotiation might provide information that would lead to better consequences in other negotiations in the future. This is one way to link problems together without developing an enormous decision model. And even if attempted, such a decision model would probably be inadequate, as it is difficult to know all the related decisions to be faced in the future.

CHAPTER 5

Quantifying Objectives with a Value Model

There are several good reasons to quantify the objectives with a value model. Essentially they all boil down to the same thing. Quantifying objectives clarifies the meanings of the objectives, and this clarity uncovers hidden objectives and facilitates all aspects of decisionmaking. This chapter presents a brief summary of the art and science of developing a value model to quantify objectives. Chapter 6 discusses the usefulness of this quantification.[1]

The foundation for any value model (also called an objective function) is the set of objectives O_i, $i = 1, \ldots, N$ that defines a decision situation. These objectives may be the strategic objectives that describe all that a decisionmaker wishes to achieve, or they may be the fundamental objectives for a given decision context. A value model v assigns a number $v(x)$ to each consequence $x = (x_1, \ldots, x_N)$, where x_i is a level of attribute X_i measuring objective O_i, such that the numbers assigned both (1) indicate the relative desirability of the consequences and (2) can be used to derive preferences for alternatives. For example, these numbers are often assigned such that bigger numbers indicate preferred consequences. Thus, the model v may be thought of as a constructed attribute for the entire set of objectives.

A value model focuses on and clarifies many complex and intertwined issues about values. For example, it is usually not possible to achieve the best level with respect to all objectives in a decision situation. The question is, "How much should be given up with regard to one

---

1. This chapter is quantitative in nature. Readers not interested in this material may wish to go directly to Chapter 6.

objective to achieve a specified improvement in another?" This issue is one of value tradeoffs. For decisions with either single or multiple objectives, it is rarely the case that one alternative is guaranteed to yield the best available consequence. There are usually circumstances that could lead to relatively undesirable consequences with any given alternative. The question is, "Are the potential benefits of having things go right worth the risks of things going wrong?" This issue is about attitudes toward risk. Both value tradeoffs and risk attitudes are explicitly addressed in the development of a value model.

Before proceeding, it is worthwhile to mention one remarkable fact. In many complex decision situations, the consequences are significant, meaning in the hundreds of millions of dollars or involving potential fatalities or large-scale environmental degradation. The only reason for an interest in such problems is because some consequences may be much better than others, and some alternatives may be much better than others. And yet the amount of time devoted to careful study of the appropriate values is minuscule relative to the time used to address other aspects of the decision situation. The "objective function" may be chosen in an hour with very little thought, while several person-years of effort and millions of dollars may be used to model the relationships between the alternatives and the consequences and to gather information about those relationships. Since values are the entire reason for caring about the problem, it would seem reasonable to use a portion of those resources to structure, quantify, and understand the relevant values. Such an effort should be used to build a value model.

5.1 Building a Value Model

A value model is first of all a model with qualitative and quantitative relationships. The general procedure for building this model is essentially the same as for any model. Also, the motivation for building such a model is the same as for any model; namely, the intent is to have the model lend some insight into a complex situation to complement intuitive thinking.

A value model should be developed from first principles, sound logic, reasoned judgments, and carefully acquired, consistent data. Unfortunately, in practice most objective functions are hastily chosen from a rather superficial process that can accurately be described as arbitrary.

A value model is developed in a directed discussion between a trained analyst (the assessor) and an individual or group whose values are being quantified (the assessor). (Section 5.6 addresses the issue of whose values should be assessed.) The analyst focuses the discussion to elicit information about the value judgments necessary for quantifying a value model.

The first step in building a value model is to identify the set of objectives appropriate for the decision situation; the second is to define attributes for measuring the degree to which these objectives are met. (These topics were discussed in Chapters 3 and 4 respectively.) Next, there needs to be a general structure to combine the various attributes in some proper manner. This is analogous to the building of a model relating profits to sales, unit selling price, and the fixed and variable costs of producing a product. This general structure of the value model has a number of parameters that can be determined by specific value judgments. These value judgments are the "data" that we need to construct the model. Finally, once the first-cut version of the model is complete, it is necessary to check its reasonableness by examining how it performs in situations that are well understood, and to modify it if necessary.

The keys to building a value model are the sets of objectives and the attributes to measure them. For instance, if an objective is not included, the de facto weight on the objective is zero. If an objective is included, we have the option of weighting it with zero or a positive weight. To integrate the various attributes, we use independence concepts analogous to the concept of probabilistic independence in factual models. To structure relationships concerning different levels of a single attribute, we need concepts of attitudes toward risk. For instance, knowing that an individual is risk averse or risk neutral (see Section 5.3) says different things about the functional form of the value model.

The data needed for parameterizing a value model rest in the minds of decisionmakers or people knowledgeable about a given problem. The assessor gathers such data by eliciting judgments from these people. This situation is analogous to many scientific problems where the knowledge necessary for parameterizing a model is "out there," and individuals need to collect it. If the information is about geology, one digs holes in the ground to gather data. If the information is about values, one "digs holes" into someone's mind to collect the data.

Two Types of Objective Functions

The type of objective function needed depends on the particular characteristics of the decision situation. For instance, if there is no uncertainty relating the alternatives and the consequences, the value model need only assign higher numbers to preferred consequences. Still, we may be interested in the strength of preference of one consequence over another consequence. In this circumstance, the objective function should be a measurable value function constructed so that the differences in value derived for the consequences have a meaning in addition to the fact that larger numbers indicate preferred consequences (see Dyer and Sarin, 1979).

In most decision situations there are uncertainties about what consequences might result from any chosen alternative. In this case, the value model should be a utility function. This is constructed in a manner such that, if one accepts a set of logical principles (see, for instance, von Neumann and Morgenstern, 1947; Savage, 1954; and Pratt, Raiffa, and Schlaifer, 1964), the expected utility derived for each alternative is an indication of its relative desirability. An alternative with a higher expected utility should be preferred to one with a lower expected utility. However, the difference in these expected utilities has no meaning unless the utility function is also a measurable value function, which could be but need not be the case.

This chapter will mainly concentrate on utility functions, for three reasons. First, the concepts and procedures for utility functions and measurable value functions are analogous. Second, most complex decision situations involve significant uncertainties, and therefore attitudes toward risk are important. Risk attitudes are addressed by utility functions, but not by measurable value functions. Finally, concentrating on utility functions allows me to be more concise than if I also considered measurable value functions in detail.

5.2 Multiple-Objective Value Models

Our topic is now simple to state. We want to obtain a utility function u from an individual or group whose values are of interest (the assessee). The approach used is to subdivide the assessment of u into parts, work on these parts, and then integrate them. This requires that the general qualitative value judgments of the assessee be stated and then quantified. The mathematical implications on the form of u are then derived.

As a simple example, we may find

$$u(x_1, x_2) = k_1 u_1(x_1) + k_2 u_2(x_2) + k_3 u_1(x_1)u_2(x_2), \tag{5.1}$$

where the u_i are single-attribute utility functions, and the k_i are scaling constants that indicate the value tradeoffs. The attitude toward risk is embodied in each of the u_i by the nature of a utility function.

Experience has indicated that a few general value assumptions seem reasonable for essentially all decision situations. Furthermore, these assumptions imply a robust utility function that can be used to formalize widely different values. This section introduces these general assumptions and the particular forms of utility functions, such as (5.1), implied by their appropriateness.

The forms that follow from such assumptions require many value judgments to make them specific. These value judgments are the degrees of freedom, so to speak, that provide for the aforementioned robustness. Each focuses on one issue of value important to the problem, such as the value tradeoff between dollar costs and environmental impacts, the value of costs now versus those in the future, the significance of equity to various affected groups, and the risk attitude toward financial uncertainties. This in turn provides the means of properly including these crucial value judgments into a value model in a responsible, logical, and justifiable manner.

Independence Concepts

The main concepts of multiattribute utility theory concern independence conditions. There are four main independence conditions relevant to the issue of multiple objectives: they are preferential, weak-difference, utility, and additive independence.

Preferential Independence. The pair of attributes $\{X_1, X_2\}$ is preferentially independent of the other attributes $X_3, \ldots, X_N$, if the preference order for consequences involving only changes in the levels of X_1 and X_2 does not depend on the levels at which attributes $X_3, \ldots, X_N$ are fixed. ■

Preferential independence implies that the indifference curves over X_1 and X_2 do not depend on the other attributes. This independence condition involves preferences for consequences differing in terms of two attributes with no uncertainty involved.

The next assumption is also concerned with consequences when no uncertainty is involved. It addresses strength of preferences (that is, value differences) when changes occur in only one attribute level.

Weak-Difference Independence. Attribute X_1 is weak-difference independent of attributes $X_2, \ldots, X_N$ if the order of preference differences between pairs of X_1 levels does not depend on the levels at which attributes $X_2, \ldots, X_N$ are fixed. ∎

There are two important assumptions relating to situations that do involve uncertainty. As such, the conditions use preferences for lotteries rather than consequences. A lottery is specified by a mutually exclusive and collectively exhaustive set of possible consequences and the probabilities associated with the occurrence of each.

Utility Independence. Attribute X_1 is utility independent of attributes $X_2, \ldots, X_N$ if the preference order for lotteries involving only changes in the level of X_1 does not depend on the levels at which attributes $X_2, \ldots, X_N$ are fixed. ∎

The last independence condition concerns lotteries over more than one attribute.

Additive Independence. Attributes $X_1, \ldots, X_N$ are additive independent if the preference order for lotteries does not depend on the joint probability distributions of these lotteries, but depends only on their marginal probability distributions. ∎

To provide an intuitive feeling for these assumptions, I will illustrate them in simple cases. The substance of preferential independence can be indicated with a three-attribute consequence space, as shown in Figure 5.1.

To avoid subscripts, the attributes are denoted X, Y, and Z with corresponding levels x, y, and z. There are three X, Y planes shown in the figure. By definition, if $\{X, Y\}$ is preferentially independent of Z, then the preference order of consequences in each X, Y plane will be the same and not depend on the level of Z. For instance, suppose the consequences in the plane with Z set at z^o are ordered A, B, C, D, E, F, G, with H indifferent to G. Then, because of preferential independence, the consequences in the plane with Z set at z' must be A', B', C', D', E', F', G', with H' indifferent to G'. And also, with Z set at z^*, the order must be A^*, B^*, C^*, D^*, E^*, F^*, G^*, with H^* indifferent to G^*.

An implication of preferential independence is that the indifference curves in all X, Y planes must be the same. Several indifference curves are illustrated in each of the three planes in Figure 5.1, and it is easy to see that they are the same.

The usefulness of preferential independence is that it allows us to determine the preference order of consequences in only one X, Y plane and transfer this to all others. If $\{X, Y\}$ is preferentially independent of Z, it does not follow that any other pairs of the attributes are preferentially independent. However, if two pairs of attributes overlap, and are each preferentially independent, then, as proved by Gorman (1968a, 1968b), the pair of attributes involved in only one of the two given conditions (that is, not in the overlap) must also be preferentially independent. This means, for our example, that if $\{X, Y\}$ is preferentially independent of Z, and $\{X, Z\}$ is preferentially independent of Y, then $\{Y, Z\}$ must be preferentially independent of X.

The next two independence assumptions can be illustrated most easily with two attributes, as shown in Figure 5.2. Here the attributes are X and Y with levels x and y. Weak-difference independence introduces the notion of difference in value between two consequences. The purpose is to develop theories that allow us to make statements such as "The difference between consequences A and B is more important than the difference between consequences C and D." Weak-difference independence is illustrated by Figure 5.2 as follows. Suppose that, through a

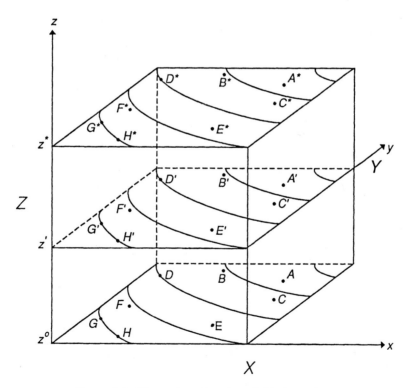

Figure 5.1. Illustration of preferential independence

series of questions, it has been established that the preference difference between consequences A and B is equal to the preference difference between B and C. Because the level of Y is fixed at y^0 for all three of these consequences, the preference difference relationship can be translated to all other levels of Y if X is weak-difference independent of Y. In this case, the preference difference between A' and B' must equal that between B' and C', and the preference difference between $A*$ and $B*$ must equal that between $B*$ and $C*$. With this condition, there is no requirement that the preference difference between A and B be equal to that between A' and B', although this may be the case.

Weak-difference independence is not a symmetrical relationship. That is, the fact that X is weak-difference independent of Y does not imply anything about whether Y is weak-difference independent of X. In terms of the example, suppose y' had been chosen such that the preference difference between A and A' equaled that between A' and $A*$. Then, even if X is weak-difference independent of Y, it may or may not be that the preference differences between B and B' and between B' and $B*$ are equal.

The last two independence conditions concern lotteries because we are interested in developing utility functions that can be combined with the probabilities to address the uncertainties present in decision situations. The notion of utility independence is very similar to that of weak-

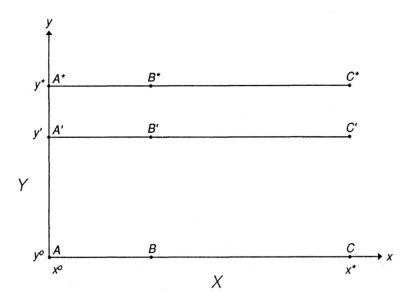

Figure 5.2. Illustration of weak-difference independence and utility independence

difference independence. In Figure 5.2, suppose that consequence B is indifferent to the lottery yielding either A or C, each with probability 0.5. Then if X is utility independent of Y, the same preference relationship can be translated to all levels of Y. This means, for instance, that B' must be indifferent to a lottery yielding either A' or C', each with probability 0.5, and that $B*$ must be indifferent to the 50–50 lottery yielding either $A*$ or $C*$.

The utility independence concept is also not symmetrical: X can be utility independent of Y, and Y need not be utility independent of X. However, suppose that Y is utility independent of X in Figure 5.2 and that A' is indifferent to a lottery yielding either $A*$ with probability 0.6 or A with probability 0.4. Then B' must be indifferent to a lottery yielding $B*$ with probability 0.6 or B with probability 0.4. The corresponding relationship holds for the C's.

The additive independence condition is illustrated in Figure 5.3.

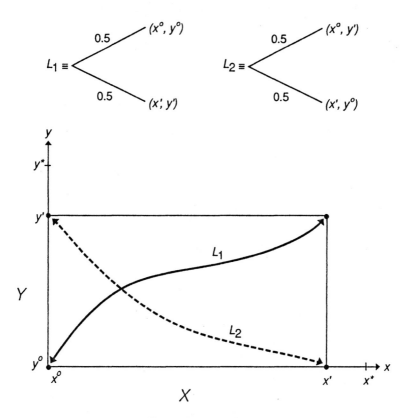

Figure 5.3. Illustration of additive independence

Consider the two lotteries L_1 and L_2 defined in the figure. Lottery L_1 yields equal 0.5 chances at the consequences (x^o, y^o) and (x', y') and lottery L_2 yields 0.5 chances at each of (x^o, y') and (x', y^o). Note that both lotteries have an equal (namely 0.5) chance at either x^o or x' and also that both have an equal 0.5 chance at y^o and y'. By definition, then, the marginal probability distributions on each of the attributes X and Y are the same in both lotteries. Thus, if X and Y are additive independent, the assessee must be indifferent between lotteries L_1 and L_2. This same indifference condition must hold if either or both of x' and y' are changed in Figure 5.3, because L_1 and L_2 will still have the same marginal probability distributions on the two attributes.

There is no meaning attached to the statement that X is additive independent of Y. Either X and Y are additive independent or they are not.

More extensive discussions of all of these independence conditions can be found in the technical literature. Some of the original sources are Debreu (1960), Luce and Tukey (1964), and Krantz (1964) for preferential independence; Krantz et al. (1971) and Dyer and Sarin (1979) for weak-difference independence; Keeney (1968), Raiffa (1969), and Meyer (1970) for utility independence; and Fishburn (1965, 1970) for additive independence. Keeney and Raiffa (1976) and von Winterfeldt and Edwards (1986) have detailed discussions of these conditions.

The Main Results

The main results for addressing multiple objectives are representation theorems stating conditions under which values can be represented in a convenient functional form. The following is a list of the main representation theorems for quantifying values using utility functions. Analogous results also hold for measurable value functions, but these will not be stated. The results will be presented without proof, although reference to sources with proofs will be made.

Result 1. Given attributes $X_1, \ldots, X_N$, $N \geq 2$, a multilinear utility function

$$u(x_1, \ldots, x_N) = \sum_{i=1}^{N} k_i u_i(x_i) + \sum_{i=1}^{N} \sum_{j>i}^{N} k_{ij} u_i(x_i) u_j(x_j) \qquad (5.2)$$

$$+ \sum_{i=1}^{N} \sum_{j>i}^{N} \sum_{h>j}^{N} k_{ijh} u_i(x_i) u_j(x_j) u_h(x_h)$$

$$+ \cdots + k_{1\ldots N} u_1(x_1) \cdots u_N(x_N)$$

exists if and only if $X_i, i = 1, \ldots, N$, is utility independent of the other attributes, where u_i is a utility function over X_i and the k's are scaling constants. ∎

To determine u in (5.2), we can assess the individual utility functions u_i on a zero-to-one scale and the scaling constants such that they sum to one. Result 1 is proved in Keeney (1972).

Result 2. Given attributes $X_1, \ldots, X_N, N \geq 2$, an additive utility function

$$u(x_1, \ldots, x_N) = \sum_{i=1}^{N} k_i u_i(x_i) \tag{5.3}$$

exists if and only if the attributes are additive independent, where u_i is a utility function over X_i and the k_i are scaling constants. ∎

Notice that (5.3) is a special case of (5.2) and u can be assessed accordingly. The original proof of (5.3) is found in Fishburn (1965).

Result 3. Given attributes $X_1, \ldots, X_N, N \geq 3$, the utility function

$$u(x_1, \ldots, x_N) = \sum_{i=1}^{N} k_i u_i(x_i) + k \sum_{i=1}^{N} \sum_{j>i}^{N} k_i k_j u_i(x_i) u_j(x_j) \tag{5.4}$$
$$+ k^2 \sum_{i=1}^{N} \sum_{j>i}^{N} \sum_{h>j}^{N} k_i k_j k_h u_i(x_i) u_j(x_j) u_h(x_h)$$
$$+ \cdots + k^{N-1} k_1 \cdots k_N u_1(x_1) \cdots u_N(x_N)$$

exists if and only if $\{X_1, X_i\}, i = 2, \ldots, N$, is preferentially independent of the other attributes and if X_1 is utility independent of the other attributes. ∎

As with the other utility functions, we can assess the u_i on a zero-to-one scale and determine the scaling constants k_i to specify u. The additional constant k is calculated from the $k_i, i = 1, \ldots, N$.

If $\Sigma k_i = 1$, then $k = 0$, and if $\Sigma k_i \neq 1$, then $k \neq 0$. If $k = 0$, then clearly (5.4) reduces to the additive utility function

$$u(x_1, \ldots, x_N) = \sum_{i=1}^{N} k_i u_i(x_i). \tag{5.5}$$

If $k \neq 0$, multiplying each side of (5.4) by k, adding 1, and factoring yields

$$ku(x_1, \ldots, x_N) + 1 = \prod_{i=1}^{N} [kk_i u_i(x_i) + 1], \tag{5.6}$$

which is referred to as the multiplicative utility function. The proof of Result 3 is found in Keeney (1974). Pollak (1967) and Meyer (1970) each use a set of related assumptions to derive the form (5.4). It is easy to see from (5.4) that it is a special case of the multilinear utility function (5.2). For the N-attribute case, the number of scaling factors required to specify (5.2) is $2^N - 1$, and to specify (5.4) is $N + 1$.

Because the assumptions for the multiplicative two-attribute utility function are slightly different from those in Result 3 and because I use it often for illustrations in Chapter 6, it is worthwhile to state it separately.

Result 4. Given attributes X_1 and X_2 are utility independent of each other, then

$$u(x_1, x_2) = k_1 u_1(x_1) + k_2 u_2(x_2) + (1 - k_1 - k_2) u_1(x_1) u_2(x_2) \qquad (5.7)$$

where u_i is a utility function over X_i and the k_i are scaling constants. ∎

There are several interesting properties of (5.7). It is first of all the two-attribute multilinear utility function (5.2). It is also the two-attribute analogy to the utility function (5.4). If $k_1 + k_2 = 1$, then clearly (5.7) becomes the additive utility function

$$u(x_1, x_2) = k_1 u_1(x_1) + k_2 u_2(x_2). \qquad (5.8)$$

If $k_1 + k_2 \neq 1$, we can define a constant k as $k = (1 - k_1 - k_2)/k_1 k_2$. By multiplying both sides of (5.7) by k, adding 1 to each, and factoring, we find

$$1 + ku(x_1, x_2) = [1 + kk_1 u_1(x_1)][1 + kk_2 u_2(x_2)], \qquad (5.9)$$

which is the two-attribute multiplicative utility function analogous to (5.6).

Verifying Independence Conditions

To examine the appropriateness of any independence condition, we consider specific cases with the assessee to see if violations of the independence condition are found. For instance, to examine whether the attribute pair X_1 and X_2 is preferentially independent of other attributes, we first identify pairs of attribute levels of X_1 and X_2, that is (x_1, x_2), that are indifferent to each other given that levels of the other attributes X_3 through X_N are fixed. If this indifference is maintained regardless of the levels of the other attributes, then the preferential independence condition holds.

To examine the appropriateness of utility independence, we set all attributes but one, say X_1, at a fixed level. Then suppose that $\hat{x}_1$ is indifferent to a lottery yielding either x_1' or x_1'' with probability 0.5. If this indifference holds when the levels of attributes X_2 through X_N are fixed at any other levels, then X_1 is probably utility independent of the other attributes. To verify this condition, the indifference between any level of X_1 and any lottery over X_1 must hold for all settings of the other attributes if it holds for one setting.

To examine the appropriateness of the additive independence condition, we present to the assessee several pairs of lotteries with identical marginal probability distributions, such as those illustrated in Figure 5.3. To make this simpler, all attributes but two can be fixed for all the consequences in both lotteries of a given pair. If the levels of the attributes that differ in the consequences cover the ranges of those attributes, and if the assessee is indifferent to each of the given pairs of lotteries, then it is probably appropriate to assume that $X_1, \ldots, X_N$ are additive independent.

If any of the independence conditions defined above are not appropriate, this is an indication that an objective other than those so far articulated for the problem is relevant. For instance, suppose additive independence did not hold and an assessee did care about how the levels of the different attributes were combined. This would suggest that the overall utility could not be determined by simply adding up the utility due to the components, appropriately weighted, of course, as indicated by (5.3). Thus, at least another term would have to be added to determine the overall utility. What this additional term is meant to capture is a hidden objective (see Section 6.2). Structuring value models in this way can lead to significant insights into what really should be examined in the decision situation.

5.3 Single-Objective Value Models

The components in a multiple-objective utility function are single-objective utility functions, or as they are more commonly called, single-attribute utility functions. Also, there are some decisions for which a single objective may be adequate. An example is the context of financial investments where the only objective is to maximize the financial return. In both cases, it is useful to specify the component single-attribute utility functions.

The procedures for determining utility functions for natural or proxy attributes are different from those for constructed attributes. The natural and proxy attributes include both continuous cases, such as costs in dollars, and discrete cases, such as number of fatalities. The constructed scales usually define clearly only a few points on the scale, such as the site biological impact index in Table 4.2. The utility functions for natural and proxy attributes are assessed using assumptions about risk attitudes that imply the functional form of the utility function. The utility functions for constructed indices are assessed directly for the defined points.

There are attributes, such as profits, for which preferences increase as the attribute level increases. The more profits, the more preferred the consequence is, assuming that all other factors are held fixed. In an analogous manner, preferences may decrease as attribute levels increase for attributes such as acres of forest destroyed. And sometimes, preferences may both increase and decrease depending on the domain of an attribute level. For example, up to a point of, say 15 percent annual growth, it may be desirable for the number of jobs in an area to increase. However, preferences for additional growth above that level may actually decrease because of the disruption that such growth would cause to the area. The point is that simple assumptions about the direction of increasing preferences can almost always be easily ascertained.

The important concepts about risk attitudes concern risk aversion, risk neutrality, and risk proneness. The following assumptions are mutually exclusive and collectively exhaustive when applied to any particular lottery.

Risk Aversion. One is risk averse if and only if the expected consequence of any lottery is preferred to that lottery. ∎

For example, consider the lottery yielding either a $1 billion or a $2 billion cost, each with a one-half chance. The expected consequence of the lottery is clearly $1.5 billion. If one is risk averse, then a cost of $1.5 billion must be preferred to the lottery.

Risk Neutrality. One is risk neutral if and only if the expected consequence of any lottery is indifferent to that lottery. ∎

Risk Proneness. One is risk prone if and only if the expected consequence of any lottery is less preferred than that lottery. ∎

A measure developed by Pratt (1964) indicates the degree of risk aversion of any single-attribute utility function. The measure may be positive, zero, or negative, indicating risk aversion, risk neutrality, and risk proneness, respectively. Pratt also introduced more sophisticated concepts of decreasing risk aversion, and so on, which will not be discussed here.

The Main Result for Quantifying Risk Attitudes

The general shape of the utility function is completely determined by the attitude toward risk. This can all be stated in one concise result.

Result 5. Risk aversion (neutrality, proneness) implies that the utility function is concave (linear, convex). ∎

These three cases are illustrated for both increasing and decreasing utility functions in Figure 5.4, where the assumptions are that the domain for attribute X ranges from a minimum x^o to a maximum x^* and that u is scaled from zero to one.

In theory, by using the more sophisticated risk attitudes, such as decreasing risk aversion, we can specify not only the general shape of the utility function but also an exact functional form. However, experience has indicated that such fine tuning is rarely required for the individual utility functions when they are part of a multiattribute formulation. It will almost always suffice to use a single-parameter utility function, where the single parameter quantifies the assessee's degree of risk aversion for the attribute in question. The exponential or linear utility functions are a fairly robust set of single forms for characterizing single-attribute utility functions. We can formalize this as follows.

Result 6. Classes of risk-averse, risk-neutral, and risk-prone utility functions are

$$u(x) = a + b(-e^{-cx}), \tag{5.10}$$

$$u(x) = a + b(cx), \tag{5.11}$$

and

$$u(x) = a + b(e^{cx}), \tag{5.12}$$

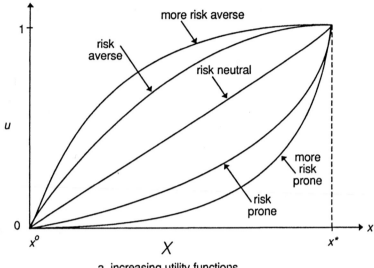

a. increasing utility functions

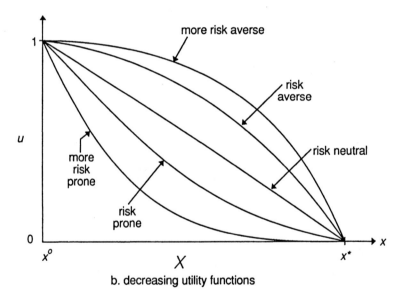

b. decreasing utility functions

Figure 5.4. Risk attitudes and utility functions

respectively, where a and $b > 0$ are constants to insure that u is scaled from zero to one (or on any scale desired) and c is positive for increasing utility functions and negative for decreasing ones. ■

The parameter c in (5.10) and (5.12) indicates the degree of the assessee's risk aversion. For the linear case (5.11), parameter c can be set at $+1$ or -1 for the increasing and decreasing cases, respectively.

Assessing the Value Judgments

Two types of value judgments are needed to determine an individual utility function. The first specifies the risk attitude and therefore determines the general shape of the utility function. The second identifies the specific utility function of that general shape.

Examining Risk Attitudes. Suppose we want $u(x)$ for attribute X for $x^o \leq x \leq x^*$. And since it is trivial to ascertain whether larger levels of X are preferred to smaller, let us assume larger levels are less preferred as in the case with costs. To begin examining risk attitudes, we take a 50–50 lottery at the extremes of X and compare it to the expected consequence. That is, we ask the assessee whether a 50–50 chance at each of x^o and x^* is preferred to, indifferent to, or less preferred than the sure consequence $\bar{x} \equiv (x^o + x^*)/2$. A preference for the sure consequence indicates that risk aversion may hold.

Next, the same line of questioning is repeated for the lower- and upper-half ranges of X. The lottery yielding equal chances at x^o and $\bar{x}$ is compared to the expected consequence $(x^o + x)/2$. Preference for the sure consequence again indicates risk aversion. Similarly, a preference for the sure consequence $(\bar{x} + x^*)/2$ to a 50–50 lottery yielding either $\bar{x}$ or x^* also indicates risk aversion. If assessments for the entire range plus the upper and lower halves are consistent in terms of their risk implications, risk aversion is probably a very good assumption to make. If different implications are found, and a reexamination indicates no errors in understanding, it is appropriate to divide the domain of X and search for sections exhibiting different risk attitudes. For instance, it may be that from x^o to x' the decisionmaker is risk averse, but from x' to x^*, risk neutrality is appropriate.

Selecting the Risk Parameter. Suppose that the risk attitude that implies one form in Result 6 is determined. If the form is (5.11), no additional assessments are necessary. Parameter c is set at $+1$ or -1 depending on whether the utility function is increasing or decreasing. Then the constants a and b are simply set to scale u from zero to one.

For the risk-averse and risk-prone cases, a little more effort is required. Suppose that preferences increase for greater levels of the attribute and that the assessee is risk averse. Then from Result 6, it follows that a reasonable utility function is

$$u(x) = a + b(-e^{-cx}), b > 0, c > 0. \tag{5.13}$$

If $u(x)$ is to be assessed for $x^o \le x \le x^*$, we might set

$$u(x^o) = 0 \quad \text{and} \quad u(x^*) = 1 \tag{5.14}$$

to scale u. Next, we need to assess the certainty equivalent for one lottery. In other words, we need to know a certainty equivalent $\hat{x}$ which the assessee finds indifferent to the lottery yielding either x' or x'', each with an equal chance, where x' and x'' are arbitrarily chosen. Then the utility assigned to the certainty equivalent must equal the expected utility of the lottery, so

$$u(\hat{x}) = 0.5u(x') + 0.5u(x''). \tag{5.15}$$

Substituting (5.13) into (5.14) and (5.15) yields three equations with the three unknown constants a, b, and c. Solving for the constants results in the desired utility function.

Preferences for Constructed Attributes. Now let us return to the case of a constructed index with clearly defined levels ordered $x^o, x^1, \ldots, x^6, x^*$, where x^o is least preferred and x^* is most preferred. Then we can again set our scale by (5.14) and assess $u(x^j)$, $j = 1, \ldots, 6$ accordingly. For each x^j, we want to find a probability p_j such that x^j for sure is indifferent to a lottery yielding either x^* with probability p_j or x^o with probability $(1 - p_j)$. Then, equating utilities,

$$u(x^j) = p_j u(x^*) + (1 - p_j)u(x^o) = p_j, j = 1, \ldots, 6. \tag{5.16}$$

For both the natural and constructed scales, once a utility function is assessed, there are many possible consistency checks to verify the appropriateness of the utility functions. We may compare two lotteries or a sure consequence and a lottery. The preferred situation should always correspond to the higher computed expected utility. If this is not the case, adjustments are necessary in the utility function or in the stated preferences. Such checking should continue until a consistent set of preferences is found.

5.4 Prioritizing Objectives

It is natural when thinking about objectives to think about their relative importance. In evaluating possible employment offers, you may naturally wish to maximize your salary and minimize your commuting time. Which of these objectives is more important? Suppose it is salary. Then is salary five times more important? As we will see below, it is not possible to answer such questions so that the response is unambiguous. When we quantify objectives by simply asking for their relative importance, considerable misinformation about values is produced and a substantial opportunity to understand values is lost.

The importance of an objective must depend on how much achievement of that objective we are talking about. Clearly a cost of $200 million is more important than a cost of $4 million. So if somebody asks whether the environmental risk at a hazardous waste site is more important than the cleanup cost, it should make a difference whether the cost is $4 million or $200 million. Let us examine this in more detail and then discuss how objectives should be prioritized.

The Most Common Critical Mistake

There is one mistake that is very commonly made in prioritizing objectives. Unfortunately, this mistake is sometimes the basis for poor decisionmaking. It is always a basis for poor information. As an illustration, consider an air pollution problem where the concerns are air pollution concentrations and the costs of regulating air pollution emissions. Administrators, regulators, and members of the public are asked questions such as "In this air pollution problem, which is more important, costs or pollutant concentrations?" Almost anyone will answer such a question. They will even answer when asked how much more important the stated "more important" objective is.

For instance, a respondent might state that pollutant concentrations are three times as important as costs. While the sentiment of this statement may make sense, it is completely useless for understanding values or for building a model of values. Does it mean, for example, that lowering pollutant concentrations in a metropolitan area by one part per billion would be worth the cost of $2 billion? The likely answer is "of course not." Indeed, this answer would probably come from the respondent who had just stated that pollutant concentrations were three times as important as costs. When asked to clarify the apparent discrepancy, he or she would naturally state that the decrease in air pollution was very small, only one part in a billion, and the cost was a very large $2 billion. The point should now be clear. It is necessary to know how much the change in air pollution concentrations will be and how much the costs of regulation will be in order to logically discuss and quantify the relative importance of the two objectives.

This error is significant for two reasons. First, it doesn't really afford the in-depth appraisal of values that should be done in important decision situations. If we are talking about the effects on public health of pollutant concentrations and billion-dollar expenditures, I personally don't want some administrator to give two minutes of thought to the matter and state that pollutant concentrations are three times as important as costs. Second, such judgments are often elicited from the public, concerned groups, or legislators. Then decisionmakers use these indications of relative importance in inappropriate ways.

The Clean Air Act of the United States provides an illustrative example. This law essentially says that the health of the public is of paramount importance and that costs of achieving air pollutant levels should not be considered in setting standards for those levels. Of course, this is not practical or possible or desirable in the real world. After spending hundreds of billions of dollars, we could still improve our air quality further with additional expenditures. This would be the case even if we could only further improve the "national health" by reducing by five the annual number of asthma attacks in the country. If the value tradeoffs are done properly and address the question of how much of one specific attribute is worth how much of another specific attribute, the insights from the analysis are greatly increased and the likelihood of misuse of those judgments is greatly decreased.

Assessing the Value Tradeoffs

The scaling constants, designated by the k's in (5.2) through (5.9), indicate the value tradeoffs between the various pairs of attributes. Given there are N attributes, there will be N scaling factors for the additive functions, $N + 1$ for the multiplicative functions, and $2^N - 1$ for the multilinear functions.

To assess the scaling constants, we construct equations with the k-parameters as unknowns and then determine them by solving the set of equations. To construct an equation, we need a pair of two consequences x and x' that the assessee finds indifferent. Then the utility of these consequences is set equal using whichever utility function (5.2) through (5.9) is appropriate. This creates one equation with the scaling constants as unknowns. Each pair of consequences that are indifferent can be equated in a similar manner creating another equation until the necessary number exist. Then they can be solved to yield numerical values of the scaling constants. A detailed dialogue used to assess value tradeoffs is presented in Keeney (1980).

In practice, it is usually best to set the levels of $N - 2$ attributes and vary just two to obtain a pair of indifferent consequences. If these two attributes are X_1 and X_2, then the question posed to the assessee directly concerns the value tradeoffs between X_1 and X_2. Operationally, if it turns out that some equations are redundant (that is, not independent), additional equations can be generated as indicated above.

5.5 The Art of Assessing Value Models

Assessing a value model from an individual or a group is an exercise of interpersonal communication. The assessor needs to be aware of the technical material pertaining to the assessment, but also needs to have good interpersonal interaction skills.

Perhaps a bit of personal philosophy is relevant here. Because I am interested in a prescriptive representation of the values, I am not overly concerned about biasing the people who are expressing the values. If I make suggestions that cause them to think deeper about their values and reach what they consider to be a better understanding, that "biasing" is part of what I am trying to do. On the other hand, if they sincerely believe that a particular representation of values is appropriate, forcing them to change would obviously be an inappropriate biasing. Clearly there is a continuum ranging from appropriate to inappropriate, and at some stage the distinction is indeed fine. However, the likelihood of not biasing is essentially nil. Some bias is inevitable.

Preparing the Assessee

At the beginning of any value assessment, it is important to make the assessee (for example, the decisionmaker, regulator, or stakeholder) feel comfortable and motivated to think hard about appropriate values for the problem. As part of this, a discussion of the viewpoint to be taken is necessary. For instance, if the problem involves impacts on the public, as is the case with air pollution problems, should the assessee take the point of view of the public or his or her own individual point of view? Should an assessee who is a manager in a corporation take the point of view of the overall corporation and try to represent the president's viewpoints, or should the point of view taken be that of the manager's division? The viewpoint needs to be made clear for such assessments.

You, the assessor, should explain that the values of interest are those expressed by the assessee, and that there are no right or wrong responses to the questions to be asked, although there are internally applied consistency criteria. In this regard, you should also point out that the value aspects of the problem at hand are very complex and that it is extremely difficult to express all these values consistently when one is doing this informally. Indeed, one of the major reasons to build a formal value model is to identify possible inconsistencies and insure that they are not included in the model. In almost every value elicitation that I have done, I have identified inconsistencies. It is important to point out ahead of time that identifying inconsistencies is one of the major reasons for the process. If the assessee could always make decisions in a manner consistent with a coherent set of values, there would be no need for the value model.

Delving Deep into Values

One of the most useful devices for quantifying values is simply to ask "why" questions. You and the assessee are jointly trying to build a value model. The assessee presumably has values somewhere in mind, even if not on a conscious level, and you have a generic framework to represent values. The essence is for you to help the assessee to articulate these values verbally or graphically so that you can represent them mathematically. Communication is essential. You want to get to the point where you almost know how the assessee will respond to any value question. It is crucial in this endeavor to ask many questions about the assessee's thinking and expressions. Why is A preferred to B? Why is attribute X

important at all? Why isn't an attribute Y included? Isn't the inclusion of separate attributes for water pollution and disrupted spawning grounds a double-counting? Why aren't preferences for costs linear? What are you thinking about when you are trying to decide whether consequence A is preferred to B? And the responses to each of these can be followed up by another "why" question. This process, if done skillfully, facilitates both communication and understanding.

It is useful in any assessment to ask redundant questions in different ways. The idea is to identify inconsistencies, reiterate, and eventually develop consistency within the model. The spirit is very similar to that of triangulation in surveying. Once you have enough different value judgments linked together in logical chains with interlocking checks, the overall value model must be quite reasonable.

Finally, if the assessee finds the assessment process interesting and informative, the quality of the value judgments is often much better. Hence you should point out interesting insights, contradictions, and implications throughout the process.

The Sensitivity of Values

One key element involved in the assessment of anybody's values is the realization that the responses may involve sensitive issues. For instance, many people recognize that it is necessary to make value tradeoffs between the costs of policies and the statistical numbers of lives that might be saved or lost by those policies. However, these same people may not want to go on record publicly as stating that an appropriate value tradeoff for a statistical life is, say, $5 million, meaning that only alternatives by which lives could be saved for less than $5 million per life should be selected. Their reasoning in making the value tradeoff may be that more lives could be saved with alternative investments for a cheaper price, but this may not be a convincing argument to certain members of the public or to adversaries.

To deal with these sensitive issues, you should realize that making value judgments public is a different question from whether or not those value judgments are important or should be used. In decision situations where making value judgments public is politically difficult or unwise, do not publicly communicate them, but use them to guide both thinking and a sensitivity analysis of the alternatives that can be made public. For instance, the value tradeoff between costs and statistical fatalities is represented in a value model by the scaling constants on the two attributes of costs and statistical fatalities. Thus, you can easily do a sensitivity analysis by varying those scaling constants over wide ranges that encompass any assessed values.

5.6 Issues to Consider in Value Assessments

There are, of course, many issues to consider in building any model. Here I discuss five specific ones that are important to any value assessment.

Whose Values Should Be Used

One key issue is whose values should be utilized in the problem. The simple response is that value models of any stakeholder interested in a particular decision context are appropriate. In some decision contexts, it is fruitful to construct multiple value models for the different stakeholders. After all, by definition, each of the stakeholders cares about the consequences, so finding out which consequences they care about and why may be useful.

When it is clear who the decisionmaker is in a given decision situation, it is desirable to quantify that decisionmaker's values. However, for complex decisions it often is not obvious who the decisionmaker is, and for other decisions there are multiple decisionmakers. For the most complex decisions, such as those involving education or immigration policy in the United States or disarmament or global warming in the world, it is not clear what the decision process is, what decisions will be made, or who will be involved in making them. It is clear, however, that decisions will be made, even if only by omission, and that the consequences of such decisions may matter a great deal. The moral is that it is useful, and sometimes necessary, to quantify values from interested and knowledgeable parties about a given decision context. Such a quantification, including the specification of objectives on which it is based, may be of considerable help to any of the parties eventually involved in the decision process. Indeed, it can help shape the decision process.

As the foundation for any value model is the set of objectives, it is here that I think the public should be involved in problems that affect the public. Simply put, the impacted public should be asked what set of objectives they want to be used for creating alternatives and for evaluating the alternatives. To do this, stakeholders and/or specifically created groups of the public to represent "the public" may be useful. Once a good set of objectives is determined, then governmental staffs or various interest groups can proceed with additional analysis.

Qualifications of the Assessee

I have found no relationship between the mathematical skills of the assessee and his or her ability to provide consistent value judgments. I also believe that there is no relationship between mathematical skills and the ability to represent values appropriate for the decision being addressed. The distinction between these two comments is that consistency is not identical to adequacy. What is relevant in the assessment process is that the assessee be willing to think hard about values and put forth effort to communicate clearly. Needless to say, the assessor can facilitate this process greatly.

It is interesting to note that the process of quantifying values seems much simpler with individuals higher up in an organization. The "real decisionmakers" seem to like structuring their values more than do middle-level managers. One explanation is that these executives know very well that they are always making decisions involving such values and feel somewhat relieved that there are some formal techniques that may assist them. A second possibility is that middle-level managers have not thought about the values as much as have executives. Third, managers must try to take the point of view of someone else, namely their superiors, when proceeding with structuring values.

Computer Support for Value Assessments

It is very useful to have a computer program to quantify the utility function given the value judgments expressed. Sicherman (1982) and Smith (1989) have developed programs that take the pairs of indifferent consequences and provide the parameters in a utility function of a specified form. For multiple attributes, that form may use combinations of multiplicative and additive utility functions as determined from the independence assumptions verified during the assessment process. Numerous functional forms are available for single-attribute utility functions.

The Distinction between Facts and Values

It is clearly not possible to distinguish perfectly between facts and values. For instance, when you try to determine a reasonable value tradeoff for costs versus statistical fatalities in a given problem context, you are presumably thinking, among other things, about possible other uses of the funds. Thinking about such other uses is factual and helps you select an appropriate value tradeoff. In some sense, the values are included in the given problem context to facilitate bounding of the problem and yet to relate the problem reasonably to other problems.

Are Value Models Scientific or Objective?

The final issue concerns the charge that value models are not scientific or objective. With that, I certainly agree in the narrow sense. Indeed, values are subjective, but they undeniably are a part of decision situations. Not modeling them does not make them go away. It is simply a question of whether these values get included implicitly and perhaps unknowingly in a decision process or whether there is an attempt to make them explicit and consistent and logical. In a broader sense, the systematic development of a model of values is definitely scientific and objective. It lays out the assumptions on which the model is based, the logic supporting these assumptions, and the basis for data (that is, specific value judgments). This makes it possible to appraise the implications of different value judgments. All of this is very much in the spirit of scientific analysis. It certainly seems more reasonable—even more scientific—to approach important decisions with the relevant values explicit and clarified rather than implicit and vague.

PART THREE

USES

CHAPTER 6

Uncovering Hidden Objectives

The process of obtaining objectives, attributes, and an objective function, as presented in Chapters 3 through 5, is a value assessment. Part of this process is qualitative in nature, namely identifying and structuring objectives, and part is quantitative, namely specifying attributes and determining the objective function (that is, the value model). Both parts are of considerable use in decisionmaking.

Many people think that the only reason to perform a value assessment is to obtain an objective function that can be used to evaluate alternatives. Used well, however, a value assessment provides much more. Because values are the reason for interest in a decision, value assessments can provide insights for every phase of the decision process. The insights are useful for characterizing the specific decision and for analyzing that situation. They help to identify implicit assumptions and hidden objectives of decisionmakers and others involved in the decision. The value assessment can guide the allocation of time and effort in the "problem solving" process, the determination of what data and information to collect, and the building of a model to aid the decision process. Most important, the value assessment enhances a thorough and systematic search for creative alternatives and for decision opportunities that may be improvements over those initially identified. In contrast to value assessments, simple procedures to obtain information to quantify an objective function "good enough" for evaluating alternatives do not provide the depth of understanding necessary for these more significant insights.

The qualitative statement of objectives and the quantitative representation of values are complementary in nature and offer complemen-

tary insights, as indicated in Figure 6.1. The main insights from carefully identifying and structuring objectives are directly useful for
stimulating thought about a decisionmaking process. This is of course
the intent of value-focused thinking. In addition, the statement of objectives indicates what values should be quantified. To be precise, it defines
the set of objectives for which values should be quantified.

The insights from specifying attributes and quantifying values are
mainly useful to help identify and understand the fundamental objectives for the decision situation. As indicated in Figure 6.1, quantifying
values also yields direct insights for the decisionmaking process.

This chapter discusses the usefulness of specifying attributes and
quantifying value judgments to better identify the "real" fundamental
objectives in a decision situation. The intent is to discover or uncover
hidden objectives, which are often referred to as hidden agendas. Those
that are obscured by the complexity of the decision situation are discov-

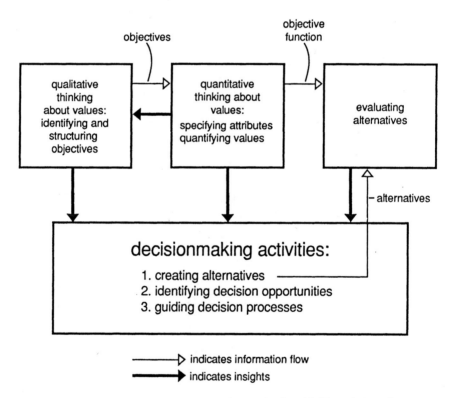

Figure 6.1. Roles of qualitative and quantitative thinking about values
in value-focused thinking

ered, and those that are intentionally obscured by a party to the decision are uncovered.[1]

Let me briefly summarize what I mean by a value assessment and introduce a minimum of notation. Suppose that the identification and structuring of objectives have led to N fundamental objectives of concern in a decision context. These can be designated $O_i, i = 1, \ldots, N$. For each objective O_i, we determine an appropriate attribute X_i. A specific level of achievement measured on X_i will be x_i. Consequences in the decision situation can now be represented by $x = (x_1, \ldots, x_N)$. Either a utility function u or a value function v is then assessed that assigns numbers $u(x)$ or $v(x)$ to possible consequences. These utilities and value numbers are measures of the desirability of the consequences. The elicitation of the objectives O_i, the attributes X_i, and u or v or both makes up a complete value assessment.

6.1. Insights from Attributes

The careful choice of attributes to measure objectives makes those objectives much clearer. This clarification often indicates that there is more than one aspect to a stated objective. Sometimes the original objective needs to be further specified into components. In all cases, each aspect of an objective may suggest potential alternatives or decision opportunities.

Objectives with Multiple Meanings

A stated objective may represent different things to different people or multiple things to a single person. The distinctions are frequently subtle so that they are not recognized when objectives are being stated. Only during the task of specifying attributes to measure objectives do the important clarifications occur.

■ *Loans in Default*
One objective of a major lending organization, agreed upon by all, may be to minimize defaulting on loans. But different individuals may suggest different attributes for this objective that mean rather distinct

1. The material in this chapter is technical, though not too quantitative. Readers interested mainly in the uses of value-focused thinking for creating alternatives and identifying decision opportunities may wish to skip ahead to Chapter 7.

things. Three potential attributes are the percentage of loans in default, the monetary amount of the loans in default, and the monetary amount of interest not paid on time. With percentage of loans in default, a $100,000 loan and a $1 million loan count the same. With monetary amount in default, the $1 million loan is 10 times as significant. With the third attribute, assuming the same interest rate, if the $1 million loan is ten months late and the $100,000 loan is one month late, the former is now 100 times as significant as the latter. The different implications of these attributes are significant for creating alternatives. Minimizing the percentage of loans defaulting suggests policies to better appraise prospective borrowers. Using the second attribute suggests alternatives that concentrate more time and effort on awarding larger loans. Minimizing the amount of unpaid interest may lead to alternatives that concentrate on working with borrowers in default to help them bring their loans into compliance. It should be clear that these three attributes measure somewhat different aspects of loan defaults. It may be that each attribute and its corresponding objective should be included in the decision problem. ■

The case above indicates a simple but important fact. People may honestly say they are in complete agreement on the objectives and then find they are mistaken. Phrases such as "minimize defaulting on loans" afford a considerable range of interpretation that facilitates agreement. At the same time, these objectives set bounds on how distinct values can be. For example, people who preferred more defaults would probably not agree with the objective of minimizing defaulting on loans. But who would possibly prefer more defaults? Well, if only 0.1 percent of loans were in default, easing access to loans might increase defaults to 0.2 percent but also increase profits on lending activities. Some people would definitely prefer more defaults, up to a point, as a negative by-product of a policy that increased achievement of the objective of increasing profits (see the Loan Management example in Section 6.4).

■ *Pinyon-Juniper Forest*
In evaluating sites for a pumped storage facility (a type of hydroelectric power plant) one objective was originally defined as minimizing the loss of pinyon-juniper forest (see Keeney, 1979). The attribute selected to measure the objective was acres of forest, but this led to a discussion about what is a forest. As it happened, some areas under consideration had less than 5 percent tree cover and others had more than 15 percent. These were very different in terms of their value, since the latter pro-

vided habitat for large animals such as deer. It became clear that protecting animal habitat was another problem objective. Hence, forest was operationally defined as an area with more than 15 percent tree cover, and its loss was significant because of both tree loss and habitat loss. ∎

∎ *Airport Operations*

In a study of alternative strategies to develop the airport facilities of Mexico City (see Keeney and Raiffa, 1976), one objective was stated as "to provide adequate capacity to meet air traffic demands." A key question here was what demands were of concern. One might think of measuring this objective in terms of operations per hour or operations per day. Should only limitations in capacity due to airport design be considered, or should weather factors also be taken into account?

Taking hourly capacity as the standard would indicate more emphasis on a fundamental objective concerning travelers' convenience than on one concerning travelers' necessity, which would be just as well served by daily capacity. Choosing to exclude limitations on capacity caused by weather might indicate that the fundamental objective was to please the planners of the airport, whereas the inclusion of weather considerations would indicate that the objective was to please the operators and users of the airport. Understanding such subtleties in a complex decision situation may have an important effect on how one deals with it. ∎

When Both Quality and Quantity Matter

In many situations, both the quality and the quantity of a consequence are important to consider in measuring an objective. Although one objective is initially stated, at least two objectives are really implied. Many examples involve either loss of or use of resources, such as the loss of agricultural resources, the loss of recreational resources, the use of parents' time with children, the use of formal education opportunities, and the use of vacations. Often the first attribute that comes to mind measures quantity, such as acres of agricultural land put out of production or time spent with children, but the notion of quality quickly follows when it becomes clear that the value of one unit of the attribute does not necessarily equal the value of another unit.

∎ *Loss of Salmon*

In an evaluation of possible sites for a power plant in Washington state, minimizing the loss of salmon was identified as an important objective (see Keeney and Robilliard, 1977). But two proposed attributes both seemed inadequate, namely the number of salmon killed and the percentage of salmon in a stream killed. Further reflection with knowledgeable biologists indicated that these attributes measured different aspects of the overall objective. In a given stream, more salmon loss is obviously worse because it is depleting a biological resource. But an equal number of salmon lost is more significant in a smaller stream (that is, a stream with fewer salmon) because salmon return to spawn in the stream in which they hatch. The bigger the percentage of salmon lost, the greater the disruption of a unique, irreplaceable biological process. ▪

▪ *Right to Die*

A particularly interesting problem involving concern for both quality and quantity has become important with the ability of modern medicine to keep people legally alive but at a severely limited quality of life. Historically, living meant "being alive," and the assumption that all "being alive" was more or less equivalent was often reasonable. Now, the single attribute for medical problems indicating only if the patient lives or dies is not sufficient. The wider range of what might be called living, has created a need for explicit consideration of the quality of life in medical problems. ▪

▪ *Vital Services*

With any of the vital services, such as electricity, gas, or telephone, the provider wishes to minimize outages. The provider is concerned about inconvenience to customers, but its main way to control this is to minimize outages, so this is one of its fundamental objectives. The quality-quantity issue is crucial in these cases, where the magnitude of the outage (the number of customers without service) corresponds to quantity and the duration of the outage corresponds to quality. There is a very strong synergy of values for achieving the two component objectives of minimizing both magnitude and duration of outages (see Section 6.2). If either the magnitude of the outage is very small or the duration is very short, the overall impact of the outage will not be too significant. ▪

Appraising Implicit Value Assumptions

The specification of attributes introduces implicit assumptions about values that need to be checked. For example, two consequences represented by the same level of a proposed attribute might not be of equal value to a decisionmaker. In such situations, either the attribute must be changed or the objective itself requires clarification. An example is mentioned above, the case of salmon loss where the loss of 100 salmon was not always equivalent but depended on the number of salmon in the stream. There are many other cases.

■ *Public Risks*

One objective often stated in decisions involving risks to the public is to minimize deaths. Number of fatalities is sometimes selected as an attribute. This carries the big assumption that the death of one person is equivalently as bad as the death of another. Indeed, to the question "Should all people be treated equally?" the overwhelming response is yes. But scrutiny suggests that this principle may not be appropriate in many contexts. For instance, is the death of a healthy 15-year-old equivalent to the death of a suffering 85-year-old? There is no "objective" answer, but many suggest that the life of the 15-year-old is more important to save. Perhaps the principle of treating all people equally should mean that a year of life to one individual is equivalent to a year of life to another. An attribute that measures this is "years of life lost," where the death of a 30-year-old with an expected lifetime to 75 would mean a loss of 45 years. If state of health is also included, maybe there should be additional adjustments to make the attribute "healthy years of life lost" (see Raiffa, Schwartz, and Weinstein, 1978). Indeed, Slovic, Fischhoff, and Lichtenstein (1979) suggest numerous additional factors that may influence an appropriate evaluation of potential fatalities. ■

■ *Financial Consequences*

Certainly a dollar is a dollar, but one dollar does not always have the same implications as another dollar. As discussed by Bell (1982, 1985), the desirability of receiving $1,000 may depend on (1) whether you learn that by choosing a different alternative you could have had $10,000 or that in fact the $1,000 was the best dollar consequence under the circumstances, and (2) whether you had expected to receive about $10,000 or about nothing. Failure to recognize such features can lead to perceived dilemmas because of the inadequate statement of objectives. In this example, psychological concerns such as regret and disappointment may be relevant in addition to the financial implications. Once such concerns are identified, objectives can be defined to address them. ■

■ *Net Present Value*

An assumption often made in financial situations where the returns occur over time is that net present value, say, of profits, is a good attribute for the objective of maximizing profits. It is possible to argue over an appropriate discount rate, but the point to be made here is not influenced by the discount rate. Suppose you were the new president of a firm and could choose one of two five-year profit streams: $A = (1, 2, 3, 5, 8)$ or $B = (8, 5, 3, 2, 1)$, where profits are in millions. With any discount rate, stream B must be preferred. However, many individuals might prefer stream A, and this would suggest that they had additional objectives. One objective might be to increase the financial value of the firm, and a firm with stream A appears to be much more valuable at the end of the five years than a firm with stream B. The second objective could be more personal to the president. He or she might wish both to manage successfully and to be perceived as managing successfully. Again, profit stream A looks better in these regards.

The point is that the unexamined use of the net present value of a profit stream to evaluate financial performance can have major shortcomings. Investigating the implicit value judgments of this attribute can often indicate its inadequacy and thereby suggest additional fundamental objectives. ■

■ *Evacuation Policy*

In emergencies that can threaten a geographical area, it is common to have a fundamental objective that is to minimize loss of life. As in other cases, issues about how to count lives and what lives to count are difficult.

After an accident at the Three Mile Island nuclear power plant in Pennsylvania, hydrogen began accumulating in the reactor containment building. This increased pressure in the containment building, and there was concern that the pressure might cause a leak, releasing radioactive materials into the atmosphere. People exposed to this radiation might later in life get cancer and perhaps die from it. One alternative considered to reduce this risk was to evacuate approximately 100,000 people living in the vicinity of the plant.

But evacuation itself could be dangerous. For example, many people would leave the area in cars, and some people's judgment for driving might be impaired by the stress of the situation. Should the potential loss of life due to evacuation be included with the potential loss of life due to radiation in the appraisal of alternatives? Clarification of this would better define the fundamental objective. ■

A final insight concerning the choice of attributes is that logically equivalent but operationally different attributes often influence an individual's stated preferences. As Tversky and Kahneman (1981) state, choices of alternatives involving gains relative to a reference point are often consistent with risk aversion, whereas choices involving losses are consistent with risk taking. One of their examples involves the risk of a disease that may kill up to 600 people. The attribute "number of the 600 who die" and the attribute "number of the 600 who survive" are obviously logically equivalent. It follows that it is useful to use both attributes simultaneously to measure an objective. For example, one might refer to the consequence where 200 people die and 400 are saved rather than to the consequence where 200 of the 600 die.

This same idea has been used on decision problems involving the siting of power plants. One attribute may refer to the cost per kilowatt-hour of electricity generated and another to the monthly impact on an average residential customer's bill. Levels of each are simultaneously used to interpret cost consequences with the necessary interrelating assumptions (such as electricity use by an average customer) made clear.

6.2 Insights from Violations of Independence Assumptions

In assessing any multiattribute objective function, one examines the appropriateness of assumptions that relate the relative desirabilities of different levels of some attributes to stated levels of other attributes. After developing a set of reasonable assumptions one chooses a functional form of the objective function consistent with them. Both the act of assessing the objective function and its resulting functional form yield insights.

Each independence assumption examined is either appropriate or not. If any assumption is not appropriate, either a fundamental objective has been overlooked or means objectives are being used as fundamental objectives. A clearer picture of both fundamental and means objectives in the problem emerges.

Violation of Additive Independence

There are many situations for which additive independence is not an appropriate assumption. These situations can be illustrated with two-attribute examples.

■ *The National Harvest*

Suppose that a country's major agricultural products are wheat and rice. In any year, the country may wish to maximize the production of each crop. Let us define attributes W and R to be wheat and rice production with w^* and r^* representing great harvests and w^o and r^o representing poor harvests. For this situation it may be found that W and R are not additive independent because lottery L_1 yielding a 50–50 chance at either (w^*, r^*) or (w^o, r^o) is much less preferred than (not indifferent to as required by additive independence) lottery L_2 yielding either (w^*, r^o) or (w^o, r^*) with equal probability. Pursuing the reasoning, it may be that it is possible to feed the country's population and generate some foreign income with both consequences of lottery L_2. With lottery L_1, the consequence (w^*, r^*) results in a banner year but consequence (w^o, r^o) implies devastation. In this case, the objectives of minimizing hunger and maximizing foreign income are fundamental and the wheat and rice harvests are means to achieve them.

To illustrate an important point, assume that attributes W and R are utility independent of each other. Then, from Result 4 in Chapter 5, we know that the utility function u for levels of wheat and rice harvests must be

$$u(w, r) = k_W u_W(w) + k_R u_R(r) + k u_W(w) u_R(r), \tag{6.1}$$

where u_W and u_R are the component utility functions for the wheat and rice harvests respectively scaled from 0 to 1, k_W and k_R are positive scaling constants indicating the relative importance of the two crops, and k is another constant assigned so

$$k_W + k_R + k = 1. \tag{6.2}$$

For this situation, k will probably be negative because W and R are substitutes for each other in that either a large wheat harvest or a large rice harvest would have many of the same implications for the fundamental objectives.

Continuing with this problem, suppose we define attributes H and I to measure hunger and foreign income. Attribute H might be the percentage of the nation that is well fed, and attribute I might be foreign income in millions of dollars. We will define h^o and i^o to be the worst levels of H and I and h^* and i^* to be the best levels. It may be very reasonable for attributes H and I to be additive independent. In this case, Result 2 from Chapter 5 says the utility function u' over H and I is

$$u'(h, i) = k_H u_H(h) + k_I u_I(i), \tag{6.3}$$

where u_H and u_I are scaled 0 to 1 and $k_H + k_I = 1$ so u' is also scaled from 0 to 1.

There is an important subtle point to be made concerning additive independence in this case. Someone might argue that H and I should not be additive independent because the lottery L_3 yielding (h^*, i^o) or (h^o, i^*) with equal chances is definitely preferred to lottery L_4 yielding either (h^*, i^*) or (h^o, i^o) with a 0.5 chance. This reasoning, when pursued (and it should always be pursued) might be that hunger is more important than income and that with consequence (h^o, i^*) from lottery L_3 the high income level could be used to purchase food to increase the percentage of well-fed citizens from its worst level h^o. This may be true, but it is an exchange that should have been included before we determined the consequences. By stating there is a 0.5 chance of (h^o, i^*), we mean that this is the consequence to be evaluated. Reducing income by amount x to increase the well-fed percentage by amount y would change the consequence to $(h^o + y, i^* - x)$. This would confound the facts, namely that food leading to y can be purchased for x, with the values for (h, i) consequences. This would also be treating increased income as a means to the reduction of hunger. ∎

The implications of this example are simple to state and quite powerful for clarifying objectives. If additive independence is violated, you probably do not have the appropriate set of fundamental objectives. The reverse is just as important and as accurate. If you do have an appropriate set of fundamental objectives for the context of a decision, additive independence is probably a very reasonable assumption.

■ Public Risk Equity

Consider a two-person society with objectives to minimize the likelihood of death to individuals I_1 and I_2. Let attributes D_1 and D_2 take on levels 0 and 1 to represent respectively whether I_1 and I_2 are alive or dead. Then the consequence (1, 0) is that where I_1 dies and I_2 lives. As indicated in Diamond (1967) and Broome (1982), the desirability of lottery L_1, yielding either (1, 1) or (0, 0) with an equal chance, may be preferred to L_2, yielding equal chances of either (1, 0) or (0, 1). If so, additive independence is violated. In the first lottery the consequences are in some sense equitable, whereas in the latter they are definitely not equitable. Thus D_1 and D_2 are complements because the better the achievement is on one objective, the more significant it is to improve achievement on the other objective. ∎

In this decision situation, the attributes D_1 and D_2 represent the fundamental concerns of whether each individual lives. Additive independence is violated not because the attributes represent means objectives but because a third fundamental objective, namely equity, was not originally identified. Numerous papers have examined objective functions in this general decision context, including Fishburn (1984), Sarin (1985), Keeney and Winkler (1985), and Fishburn and Sarin (1991).

■ *The Politician's Dilemma*
As a third decision context, consider a hierarchical decision where a politician with utility function u is trying to please two groups whose utilities are scaled by utility functions u_i, $i = 1,2$, from 0 to 1. We can consider that these utilities are levels of attributes U_i, $i = 1,2$, respectively. Suppose that both u_1 and u_2 are utility independent, so from Result 4 in Chapter 5

$$u(u_1, u_2) = k_1 u_1 + k_2 u_2 + k u_1 u_2,$$
(6.4)

where we have assumed that u is linear in both u_1 and u_2 and $k_1 + k_2 + k = 1$. The linear assumption is equivalent to saying that only the one group's preferences matter if the other group is indifferent. In this context $(u_1 = 1, u_2 = 1)$ is clearly the best consequence and $(0, 0)$ is often chosen as the worst. However, McClelland and Rohrbaugh (1978) discuss cases where $(0, 0)$ is actually preferred to $(1, 0)$ or $(0, 1)$ because the latter two are so unfair. For our illustration, we take $(0, 0)$ to be the worst and suggest logic where u_1 and u_2 may be either complements or substitutes or the additive form will hold. All three cases can be visualized in Figure 6.2.

Let L_1 be the lottery yielding $(0, 0)$ or $(1, 1)$ with equal chances and L_2 yield $(1, 0)$ or $(0, 1)$ with equal chances. A politician may prefer L_1 to L_2, implying that u_1 and u_2 are complements, if equitable treatment of the two groups is also a fundamental attribute. In this case, k in (6.4) must be positive.

On the other hand, the attributes may be substitutes consistent with

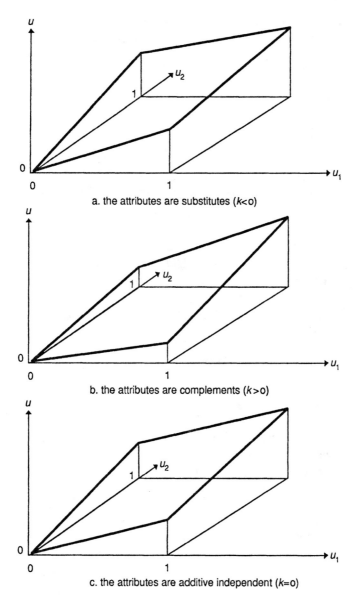

a. the attributes are substitutes (*k*<o)

b. the attributes are complements (*k*>o)

c. the attributes are additive independent (*k*=o)

Figure 6.2. Implications of dependent attributes

L_2 being preferred to L_1. Then, of course, k in (6.4) will be negative. This can occur when the (u_1, u_2) consequences are partially (or entirely) means to a more fundamental objective. A politician may not want to risk a one-half chance of a (0, 0) consequence that may lead to a political defeat whereas political victory would be rather secure with either (0, 1) or (1, 0).

There are two circumstances where $k = 0$ in (6.4), implying the additive form of the utility function. The first is when the equity argument and the political victory argument both apply and cancel each other out. One could even think of this situation as having four fundamental attributes: pleasing each of the two groups, equity, and promoting political victory. The first two would be measured by the first two terms in (6.4) and the last two each by terms $k_3 u_1 u_2$ and $k_4 u_1 u_2$ where $k_3 = -k_4$. The other circumstance where the additive case holds is where the objectives of pleasing each of the two groups are the only fundamental objectives in the problem. ∎

It may be useful to mention that a preference for L_1 and L_2 in the context above is consistent with a choice to take a "big risk" of all or nothing relative to the range $u(0, 0)$ to $u(1, 1)$, whereas a preference for L_2 definitely results in an in-between consequence $u(1, 0)$ or $u(0, 1)$. This led Meyer (1970) and Richard (1975) to recognize that the substitute-complement issue could also be interpreted as one of multiattribute risk attitudes. Multiattribute risk proneness (that is, accepting the big risk) is consistent with complementary attributes, multiattribute risk aversion is consistent with attributes that are substitutes, and multiattribute risk neutrality corresponds to additivity.

∎ Blood Bank Inventory

In an examination of the preferences of a nurse ordering whole blood for a hospital blood bank (see Keeney and Raiffa, 1976), the attributes X_1 and X_2 were shortage of blood and outdating of blood measured from 0 to 10 percent in each case. Shortage was defined as blood requested by the hospital but not filled from available inventory, and outdating was blood that had been in inventory for 21 days and hence "degraded" to a quality that could not legally be used in transfusions.

Both X_1 and X_2 were verified by the nurse who managed the blood inventory as being utility independent, but additive independence did not hold. Specifically, a lottery yielding equal chances at either (0, 0) or (10, 10) was preferred to the lottery yielding either (10, 0) or (0, 10).

In other words, the attributes were complements and the nurse was multiattribute risk prone. Pursuing her reasoning, the nurse noted that with both (10, 0) and (0, 10) there was a rather clear implication that the inventory-ordering policy was not particularly appropriate. With (10, 0), ordering more units of blood should result in less shortage with perhaps no increase in outdating. With (0, 10), ordering less would reduce outdating and might not result in any shortage. On the other hand, of course (0, 0) is great, but (10, 10), while being relatively bad, also indicates that the dynamics of the demand for blood cause any reasonable ordering policy to have some shortage and outdating. The additional objective indicated by the violation of additive independence was the nurse's desire to be an effective manager. ■

Violation of Preferential Independence

Any violation of preferential independence, like violations of additive independence, should lead to a better understanding of the fundamental objectives in the problem. Quantitatively, the multilinear utility function (5.2) has a form similar to the utility function (5.4), which is equivalent to either the multiplicative or the additive form. The difference is that there are $2^N - 2$ independent scaling constants in (5.2) and only N independent scaling constants in (5.4). In both cases, each attribute X_i is utility independent of the others. In rough terms, the N constants in (5.4) capture the relative weights between $N - 1$ pairs of attributes with one additional constant to capture a synergistic effect analogous to the notion of multiattribute risk aversion introduced above. With the $2^N - 2$ constants in (5.2), each pair of attributes, each trio of attributes, and so on, is allowed to have its own special synergy. Cases where some pairs of attributes are preferentially independent result in some restrictions on the scaling constants in (5.2). Let us consider some examples.

■ Operating a Consulting Firm
In one decision problem involving the operation of a consulting firm, three of the objectives were to maximize retained earnings and to maximize salary increases to two classes (exempt and nonexempt) of employees (see Keeney and Raiffa, 1976). These objectives were measured by X_1, the percentage of earnings retained in the firm, and X_2 and X_3, salary raises to the employee classes. Assessments indicated that X_2 and X_3 were preferentially independent of X_1, but that neither X_1 and X_2 nor X_1 and X_3 were preferentially independent of the remaining attribute. Consider

the case of why X_1 and X_2 were not preferentially independent of X_3. If the raise X_3 was low, the value assessments indicated that less of X_1 should be given up to make X_2 high than was the case when the raise X_3 was high. In addition to helping the class of employees represented by X_2 in both cases, the former also produced an inequitable situation, whereas the latter produced an equitable one. The violation of preferential independence indicated an equity objective concerning the salary raises to the two groups of employees. ∎

■ Unemployment and Inflation

Another example concerns the preferences for unemployment levels measured by percentage unemployed annually and the annual inflation rate measured by percentage. Suppose that governmental policies are being examined that may affect both of these attributes in each of the next two years. So let the attributes be E_i for unemployment and I_i for inflation rate in year i, $i = 1,2$. The pair E_2 and I_2 may not be preferentially independent of E_1 and I_1 because the indifference curves over E_2 and I_2 may depend on what the levels (e_1, i_1) of E_1 and I_1 were. Figure 6.3 illustrates possible indifference curves given (e_1, i_1) is (6, 3) and (8, 5) respectively. The basis for such curves could come from different reasoning.

In the case of Figure 6.3a, any increase in unemployment could be important both because people lose their jobs and because they have no jobs. A decrease in unemployment may be important only because fewer people are out of work. This may, for instance, imply that $(e_2 = 6, i_2 = 5)$ is preferred to $(e_2 = 8, i_2 = 2)$ if $(e_1 = 6, i_1 = 3)$, whereas the reverse preference will occur if $(e_1 = 8, i_1 = 5)$. In this situation, another fundamental objective is to minimize the number of jobs lost.

A second reason for the violation of preferential independence may be due to fundamental political objectives related to the improvement and worsening of unemployment and inflation. The annual increase or decrease of one percent in either index may have far greater proportional political consequences than an increase or decrease of 2 or 3 percent. Hence, as illustrated in Figure 6.3b, $(e_2 = 7, i_2 = 4)$ is less preferred than either $(e_2 = 5, i_2 = 6)$ or $(e_2 = 9, i_2 = 2)$ if $(e_1 = 6, i_1 = 3)$ occurs. On the other hand, just the reverse preference holds if $(e_1 = 8, i_1 = 5)$ occurs. ∎

There is a general principle related to this example. Many important decision problems have impacts that are important over time. The preferences at any given time may be dependent on what consequences recently have occurred. When this dependence is modeled in value assessments, the preferences in time period t depend on what consequence occurred in time period $t - 1$. Specifically, attributes measuring impacts in time period t are not preferentially independent of those measuring impacts in time period $t - 1$. The general reason is that the level of impacts in time t and the change from $t - 1$ are concerned with different fundamental objects. Bell (1977a) analyzed preferences over time for profit and employment in the logging industry, measured respectively by dollars and the percentage of mill capacity in use, in the context of evaluating policies for treating a forest pest. The assessments indi-

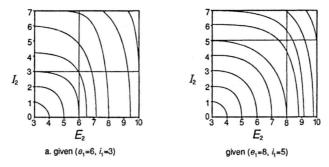

a. indifference curves indicating a heavy weight to lost jobs

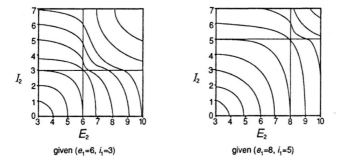

b. indifference curves indicating a significance of fundamental political objectives

Fig 6.3. Violations of preferential independence

cated violations of preferential independence for the reason suggested above.

■ *Salmon Management*
In a problem involving salmon fishing policy on the Skeena River in Canada (see Section 8.1), the fundamental objectives were to please groups of stakeholders. Each objective was measured by an attribute representing the utility that would accrue to the associated group. Specifically, objectives included pleasing net fishermen, lure fishermen, and sports fishermen, measured by attributes U_N, U_L, and U_S, respectively. It was determined that the pair of attributes (U_N, U_L) representing commercial fishermen and U_S were utility independent of each other. Furthermore, (U_N, U_L) and U_S were complements because of the desire for equity between commercial and sports fishermen—a fundamental objective. Attributes U_N and U_L were also utility independent of each other and identified as partial substitutes because of the desire to have some successful commercial fishing activity—another fundamental objective.

The above conditions imply that U_S paired with either U_N or U_L cannot be preferentially independent of the other. If, for instance, U_N is high, meaning that net fishermen are having good catches, it is not as important that lure fishermen have good catches than is the case when net fishermen are having poor catches. One would be willing to give up more of the lure fishermen's catch to increase sports fishermen's catch in the former case than in the latter case. The former "exchange" would both help sports fishermen and promote equity between them and commercial fishermen (since they would still be doing well owing to the net fishermen's good catch). The second "exchange" would also help sports fishermen but would not promote equity. ■

Violation of Utility Independence

Violations of utility independence yield insights into the fundamental objectives for the problem and the thought processes of the person whose value judgments are being assessed (the assessee). Two important examples can be drawn from medical contexts.

■ *Medical Treatment*
Suppose you are examining alternatives for a crucial medical operation. There is a chance that you may not survive the operation, but if you do

survive, your health should not be impaired. You evaluate alternatives in terms of the attributes P and A representing probability of survival and assets after treatment. Then P may well be utility independent of A. Indeed, given a specific asset level, the conditional utility function over P may be linear, which is equivalent to maximizing the probability of survival. On the other hand, attribute A may not be utility independent of P. If $p = 1$, you survive and the assets are available for you and your family and you can still "directly" contribute and participate in the family. If $p = 0$, you do not survive and the assets represent your legacy. Your risk attitudes, and hence your utility function, may be different in the two cases; that is, A is not utility independent of P. This may be viewed as a state-dependent utility function, where the state is alive or dead. The violation of utility independence occurs because A is an attribute for a means objective that is concerned with the fundamental objective of supporting your family as well as possible. The contribution and relative significance of money to this support may be viewed differently in the two states. ■

■ *Quality of Life*
Related to this medical problem is one in which both your length of survival and your quality of life are potentially influenced by medical options. You could use the attribute Y for years of survival and attribute Q for an index of quality of life. Notwithstanding the fact that Q may be difficult to define or measure, it may be the case that Q is not utility independent of Y. For a short survival period such as a month, you may be willing to "gamble" to achieve a high quality of life because this would allow you to take care of the more fundamental objectives that you wish to fulfill before dying. If the survival period is more than a year, you may not "gamble" for a high quality of life, because a lower quality of life would still allow you to fulfill those fundamental objectives at a slower pace.

It may also be the case that Y is not utility independent of Q. Indeed, if quality of life is at a level judged intolerably low, many people may prefer shorter lives, whereas longer lives are preferred in most instances. This would suggest that the fundamental objective is to live a humane life, not simply to live. Even for quality levels above any intolerable level, the utility function over Y may have different shapes. At poorer quality levels, the length of survival is again a means to fulfill the fundamental objectives before dying. At higher quality levels, these objectives can certainly be fulfilled and additional length of life becomes

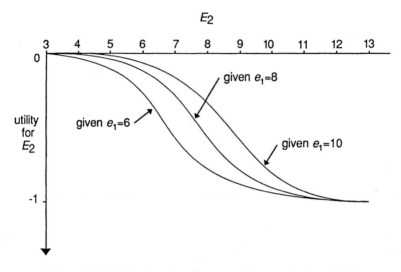

*Figure 6.4. Utility functions for unemployment E_2 in period 2
given unemployment E_1 in period 1*

a means to pursuing all the enjoyable and worthwhile activities of
living. ∎

∎ *Aspiration Levels*
Utility independence is routinely violated when individuals have aspiration levels for achievement in terms of some attribute (see, for example,
Bell, 1977b). This occurs because of the tendency to be risk averse for
gains and risk prone for losses (Tversky and Kahneman, 1981). As an
example, if you are evaluating preferences over unemployment levels
in two successive years, measured by attributes E_1 and E_2 respectively,
then E_2 may not be utility independent of E_1. Over the range from 3 to
13 percent for E_2, the utility functions may be as shown in Figure 6.4
for $e_1 = 6$, 8, and 10. The reason is that the absolute value of e_2 and
the change from e_1 to e_2 capture different fundamental objectives respectively concerned with the number unemployed and the number
losing their jobs. ∎

Functional Form of the Objective Function

Two short abstract examples concisely indicate how both the violation
of any independence assumption and the form of the utility function

have important implications for understanding and fundamental objectives of any decision situation.

■ Example One
Suppose that attributes Y_1, Y_2, Y_3, and Y_4 are initially chosen for a problem and no conditions of additive independence, utility independence, or preferential independence can be verified. This leads to a search for why, and three fundamental objectives are found, so attributes X_1, X_2, and X_3 replace the Y's, which are now recognized to represent means objectives. All possible independence conditions hold among the X attributes, and indeed the utility function u has the simplest possible additive form

$$u(x_1, x_2, x_3) = x_1 + x_2 + x_3. \tag{6.5}$$

Examining the problem further, it is found precisely how the fundamental x levels depend on the means y levels. Specifically,

$$x_1 = y_1 y_2, \qquad x_2 = y_1^3 y_3^{0.5}, \qquad x_3 = (y_2 y_3)^2 (\log y_3). \tag{6.6}$$

Thus, substituting (6.6) into (6.5), the implied utility function u_Y over $Y_1, \ldots, Y_4$ needs to be

$$u_Y(y_1, y_2, y_3, y_4) = y_1 y_2 + y_1^3 y_3^{0.5} + (y_2 y_3)^2 (\log y_3), \tag{6.7}$$

from which it can be checked that no independence conditions hold over the Y attributes. ■

■ Example Two
Let W_1 and W_2 be the originally chosen attributes. No utility independence or additive independence is found to be appropriate. Searching for the fundamental objectives leads to attributes Z_1 and Z_2, defined as the mean and difference of the W's, specifically $Z_1 = W_1 + W_2$ and $Z_2 = W_1 - W_2$. Then Z_1 and Z_2 are found to be additive independent, and therefore utility independent, and the utility function is assessed to be

$$u(z_1, z_2) = z_1^2 + z_2. \tag{6.8}$$

It follows that a utility function u_W over W_1 and W_2 would necessarily be

$$u_W(w_1, w_2) = u(w_1 + w_2, w_1 - w_2) \qquad (6.9)$$
$$= w_1^2 + w_1 + w_2^2 - w_2 + 2w_1w_2.$$

The Z's then measure more fundamental objectives than the means measured by the W's. It should be noted that many real problems have the characteristic just discussed. If W_1 and W_2 represent profits in two divisions of a company, total profit Z_1 and difference in profit Z_2 may be the fundamental concerns. ∎

6.3 Insights from Value Tradeoffs

In a value assessment, once the objectives and attributes are identified and perhaps modified as a result of the development of an appropriate form for the objective function, the next steps are to assess the scaling constants (the k's) and the component objective functions in (5.2) through (5.9) for whatever objective function is selected. The scaling constants are determined from the assessment of value tradeoffs. The assessee is asked to specify pairs of consequences that are indifferent. This indicates exactly how much achievement with respect to one objective the assessee is willing to forgo in order to improve the achievement of another objective by a specified amount. It is important to recognize that value tradeoffs do (and often should) depend on both the starting consequence and the range of consequences.

Difficulties in Expressing Value Tradeoffs

The attempt to assess value tradeoffs often indicates shortcomings in the fundamental objectives. When the assessee realizes that he or she has "no idea" what the value tradeoffs between two attributes should be, then either the attributes are poorly defined or clarification of the underlying objectives is needed.

∎ *Transporting Nuclear Waste*
In an assessment of preferences over potential health effects of the radiation emitted during the transporting of nuclear waste (see Section 11.2), two health attributes considered cancer cases to the current gener-

ation and genetic effects to future generations. Both were measured by the number of cases. In assessments with three different individuals, none had any difficulty addressing the relative undesirability of different numbers of genetic effects. Whatever they were or however they were defined, 5 cases was indifferent to an equal chance at either 0 or 10 cases. However, each assessee had difficulty selecting an appropriate value tradeoff between cancer cases and genetic effects. They were not clear about whether a genetic effect was less important than a case of cancer to the current generation or more important than several cases. The information that was lacking dealt with the definition of, and specifically the implications of, a genetic effect in this decision context. The insight was that a clear understanding of a fundamental objective, namely to minimize genetic effects, was needed. ∎

∎ Acid Rain
A similar example concerned preferences for impacts of different alternatives to address acid rain. Two of the attributes were acres of lakes acidified and acres of forest acidified. Assessing value tradeoffs yielded an understanding that both attributes needed to be better defined. What was lacking was a clear understanding of the importance of either an acre of forest or an acre of lake being acidified.

Additional insights were gained about the fundamental objectives. In some value assessments, the importance of acres of forest relative to acres of lakes, was difficult to determine, because of the unknown impact that forest acidification would have on the lumber industry. Key objectives concerned lumber industry employment and regional economic vitality in addition to the biological asset of the forest. Recognizing this was clearly relevant for guiding the creation of reasonable alternatives. ∎

In many instances when the value tradeoffs are difficult for a respondent, the attributes may be partially proxies for more fundamental objectives. In the above example, acres of forest acidified was partly a proxy for lumber industry jobs and regional vitality. These fundamental objectives, once identified, should often be separately analyzed in the decision model, and the relationships between the proxy attribute and levels of the newly identified fundamental objectives should be clarified.

∎ Salmon Management
In the study of salmon fishing policy on the Skeena River in Canada (see Section 8.1), one fundamental objective was to please the lure fish-

ermen as much as possible. Two component objectives were to maximize annual income from fishing and to maximize annual days of fishing time. An implication of this was that a lure fisherman should be willing to accept a somewhat lower annual salary to increase the fishing time from, say, 40 to 70 days. This led to a big discussion about whether fishing time was important only as a means to higher income or whether it was also a fundamental objective. The latter was decided to be the case up to at least 80 days a year. If fishing time were only a means to income, any weighting of this objective in an objective function that gave the appropriate weight to fishing income would necessarily be double-counting. ■

Combining Value Tradeoffs and Factual Tradeoffs

In dealing with value tradeoffs, it is not uncommon to recognize that a respondent is mixing up the concepts of a value tradeoff and what I will refer to as a "factual tradeoff."

■ *Stock Portfolio*

To illustrate this idea, suppose a decisionmaker is interested in evaluating various portfolios of two stocks, company C and company D. Then from the assessment of the utility function, the complete set of indifference curves can be constructed. These curves, which for our example are shown in Figure 6.5a, provide a complete representation of all value tradeoffs. That is, for each consequence (x_1, x_2) representing the amount of shares of companies C and D respectively, they indicate the maximum number of shares of one stock that one would be willing to give up to obtain any specified number of shares of the other stock. The indifference curves are illustrated as convex because of a preference for diversity.

The prices of these stocks may be well known, and it is easy to trade them on the open market. Thus, if the price of a share of stock of company C is twice that of company D, the factual tradeoff curves between the shares of stock are shown in Figure 6.5b. This indicates the number of shares of one stock that must be given up to obtain any specified number of shares of the other stock. Putting the information in Figures 6.5a and 6.5b together, we see that the appropriate combination of shares for any level of stock holdings is where the value tradeoff curves (that is, indifference curves) and the factual tradeoff curves are tangent, as illustrated in Figure 6.5c. ∎

In many value assessments, respondents mistakenly state the factual tradeoff as the value tradeoff. The former concerns the "facts": how much of one attribute must I give up to get a specified amount of another attribute. The latter concerns values: how much of one attribute would I be willing to give up to get a specified amount of another attribute. When these are mixed up, it is usually easy to recognize that the assessee is doing calculations to respond to value tradeoff questions.

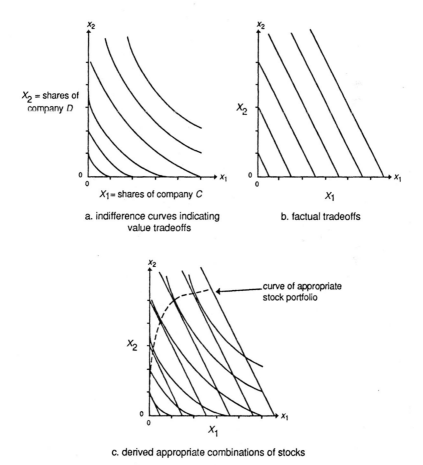

Figure 6.5. The difference between value tradeoffs and factual tradeoffs

This may suggest that some of the stated attributes represent means objectives. The appropriate way to handle these means objectives is to use the factual tradeoffs to determine their implications on the fundamental objectives.

■ *Private Electricity Generation*

A large, publicly held electricity company in California was concerned that a medium-sized industrial customer planned to construct a facility to generate some of its own electricity. This concern stemmed from the potential loss of electricity sales to that customer and from the fact that, if the project succeeded, other customers would be likely to construct such facilities. Also, because of regulations of the California Public Utilities Commission, the electricity company would have costs associated with the proposed private generation. It would be required to purchase any excess electricity generated and to build transmission lines to the facility to carry that electricity.

The electricity company had options ranging from fighting the facility to cooperating, including the option to do nothing. The initial stated objectives for the problem were to minimize cost concerning this facility, to minimize loss of electricity sales, and to minimize the number of other companies that would construct such facilities. The attributes were respectively lost revenue, number of megawatt-hours not supplied, and number of similar units constructed. In the assessment of value tradeoffs, it became obvious that the respondents were using factual tradeoffs to convert impacts of the last two attributes into financial impact on the firm. Megawatts could be easily converted using the cost of electricity, and number of units could be converted using additional assumptions about the capacity of the units in megawatts. With this new insight, a single fundamental objective concerned with annual revenue lost to the company was utilized, and the impacts of the means objectives were translated into that fundamental objective as part of the impact model. ■

6.4 Insights from Single-Attribute Objective Functions

The assessment of single-attribute utility functions provides much insight about the fundamental objectives in a problem. I will present several examples. The first two concern implicit constraints and "rational" risk-averse gamblers, and the others focus on the insights from types of utility functions: nonlinear, S-shaped, and nonmonotonic.

Implicit Constraints

Either for reasons externally imposed or because of internally generated aspirations, implicit constraints are a part of many decision problems. They can often be recognized by either an S-shaped utility function or a "bump" in an otherwise smooth utility function, as illustrated in Figure 6.6. However, not all utility functions of this form indicate constraints.

■ *Bonuses*

One common case in which the extreme S-shaped utility function indicates an implicit constraint concerns bonuses offered by many organizations. Suppose the head of a division of a firm receives a significant bonus if the profits of that division meet a goal x^+ measured in terms of a profits attribute X. Then, for the division head, the levels of X are proxies for the bonus, so all amounts less than x^+ are more or less equivalent. Being less than x^+, but close, may still indicate a "good try," so the utility function may not be a step function. Above x^+, three general possibilities exist, indicated by curves A, B and C in Figure 6.6a.

With curve A, more profits above x^+ are still better, since the firm makes more money. This indicates that profit is itself a fundamental objective to the division head, as well as the bonus. With curve B, only the bonus matters or the opposing effects of curves A and C are both relevant and cancel each other. Curve C indicates an insight about how bonuses in future years may be established. Namely, if profits are "too high," perhaps representing extraordinary effort by the division head, next year's bonus goal will be substantially increased. Another fundamental objective is to keep next year's bonus goal as low as possible. ■

The same general insights are available from a utility function when the bonus amount is a function of profits above a threshold x' up to x'', as illustrated in Figure 6.6b. If utility assessments show that the bonus structure is not promoting the desired behavior to maximize profits for the firm, changes may be necessary.

With a bonus goal, the utility function increases rapidly near x^+ because of a positive event that will follow if the goal is met. Similar utility functions may result when negative events are possible if x^+ is

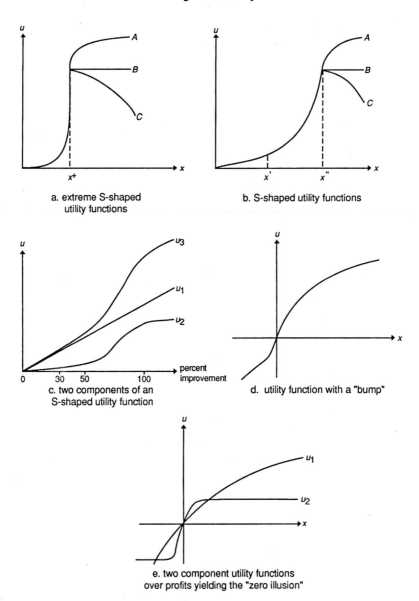

a. extreme S-shaped
utility functions

b. S-shaped utility functions

c. two components of an
S-shaped utility function

d. utility function with a "bump"

e. two component utility functions
over profits yielding the "zero illusion"

Figure 6.6. Utility functions consistent with constraints

not met. Several years ago I assessed some utility functions of managers of organizations in countries with central planning. Goals were set for these managers that "had to be met." Illustrative utility assessments for the attribute "percentage of increase in annual electricity production" for representatives of the German Democratic Republic (formerly East Germany) indicated exactly this phenomenon. Their fundamental objective was clearly to meet the stated goal.

■ *Telecommunications Research*

Another case that yielded a utility function similar to curve A in Figure 6.6b involved the selection of research projects in a telecommunications research laboratory. One attribute for selecting projects was the "percentage of improvement in handling capacity" of existing equipment afforded by a technological development of the type searched for in the proposed projects. Improvements up to 30 percent were not particularly desirable, as the director felt these improvements were not the main concern of this laboratory. Hence the 30 percent acted somewhat as an internally generated constraint. The director was interested in "revolutionary breakthroughs" in the range of 50 to 100 percent improvement. Above 100 percent improvement the utility function would flatten out a bit, as all "realistic" breakthrough intentions would have been met.

With this understanding of the director's values, we could identify two fundamental objectives. One was to improve the handling capacity of the existing equipment. This was the stated objective. The other more subtle fundamental objective was to make a revolutionary breakthrough of major significance.

To illustrate, let the curve u_1 in Figure 6.6c represent the utility of the first objective of improving handling capacity. It may be close to linear, as indicated. Curve u_2 represents the utility of meeting the breakthrough objective. The third curve u_3 is the sum of u_1 and u_2 that results from an additive utility function over the two fundamental objectives. Note that u_3 has the same shape as curve A in Figure 6.6b, where we have defined x' and x'' to be 30 percent and 100 percent improvement respectively. ■

■ *The Zero Illusion*

The so-called zero illusion illustrated by the bump in the utility function in Figure 6.6d has long been discussed in the literature (see Hammond, 1967). The bump occurs near an aspiration level, so when the attribute is profits, the bump occurs around zero. This usually indicates that profits are of concern for more than one reason. Specifically, one objective concerns the contribution to assets by profits and the other concerns whether one is a loser (unprofitable) or a winner (profitable). The latter has its greatest effect near zero profits. Figure 6.6e illustrates two component utility functions over profits, u_1 for contribution to assets that is risk averse and u_2 for being a winner or loser; u_2 is S-shaped because of the implicit aspiration level of zero. An additive combination of these two utility functions yields the utility function in 6.6d. The implication is that the bumps in utility functions may indicate hidden objectives. ∎

Rational Risk-Averse Gamblers

It is sometimes stated that utility theory must be wrong because clearly many people who consider themselves risk averse gamble in casinos, where the odds are against them. On one level, this can be dismissed by saying that people's behavior is not always consistent with their values and information. In other words, utility theory is generally a poor model of descriptive behavior and a good model for prescriptive behavior.

On another level, it may be quite rational to gamble when one is risk averse. It is naturally accepted as reasonable that many rational risk-averse individuals go to a movie at times. And yet they lose money every time they go. Movies are a guaranteed financial loser to a customer. Entertainment, which is the obvious objective of seeing movies, may also be an objective of gambling. Specifically, if X is the change in assets from gambling, separate utility functions, illustrated in u_1 and u_2 in Figure 6.7, may represent the financial implications and the entertain-

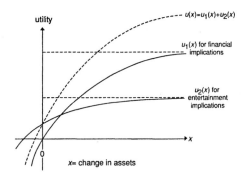

Figure 6.7. Illustration of rational risk-averse gamblers

ment implications of various consequences of gambling. The additive combination represented by u is the utility function for changes in assets and entertainment from gambling; it is not just the utility function for changes in assets, which is represented by u_1.

This circumstance may lend some insight into why assessed utility functions and measurable value functions are not necessarily the same (see Keller, 1985). An assessee responding to preferences about lotteries to obtain a utility function for change in assets may necessarily be providing answers appropriate for constructing u, since the entertainment of the gamble is involved. If a measurable value function is assessed, the responses do not involve gambles. Hence, a measurable value function may be assessed that is identical to u_1. The reverse implication should be clear. If one assesses both a utility function and a measurable value function over the same attribute, different resulting functions may indicate that the same attribute does not represent the same consequences in both cases. Further probing may identify an additional objective.

Nonlinear Utility Functions

As argued in Keeney (1981), any utility function that is not linear must be important partially as a means to other objectives. A utility function that is extremely risk-averse around the zero level and relatively risk-neutral elsewhere often indicates a hidden objective. Two examples illustrate the idea.

▪ Electricity Generation

One attribute considered in all studies concerning the siting of power plants or the choice of technologies for electricity-generating facilities is cost. This may be measured by an annualized cost of construction and operation, by mills per kilowatt-hour, or by monthly impact on customer bills. In many cases, the utility function is somewhat risk averse, meaning for example, that a $4 increase in the monthly bill is preferred to a 50–50 chance at either a $2 or a $6 increase. The fundamental objective is to minimize economic impact to customers by the necessary price increases, and there is no clear measure for this. One is risk averse for costs because of the perceived increasing hardship induced by each additional dollar increase.

One assessment of a cost utility function in the context of siting a facility yielded a very risk-averse curve (see Keeney, 1979). This appeared to be more risk averse than the implied hardship to customers would merit. In inquiring about why this curve was so risk averse, it was recognized that cost was also being used as a proxy attribute for the difficulty of acquiring the necessary construction funds in the bond markets. This suggested including two objectives, addressing economic impact to customers and difficulty of obtaining funds for construction, and explicitly investigating the perceived relationship between facility cost and the difficulty of obtaining necessary funding. ■

■ Infant Mortality

Suppose a governmental agency has responsibility for reducing infant mortality in the country. One reasonable attribute to use in evaluating available alternatives is the number of cases of infant mortality avoided. Value assessments with the directors of the agency may indicate a preference for one alternative with a guaranteed 50 fatalities avoided to another alternative that would result in either 0 or 1000 fatalities avoided with equal likelihood. Most people may feel the lottery should be preferred. However, from the viewpoint of the director, saving 50 infants would likely justify continued program funding and job security. The insight from such assessments is that the director is using infant mortality as a proxy for two additional fundamental objectives as well as that of saving infant lives. The reason may be that the evaluation of the director and her agency is inappropriately based on the actual consequences of chosen alternatives rather than on quality of chosen alternatives. If the alternative with the uncertainty is selected and if 0 infants are saved, a consequence that has a 50 percent chance, the director and her agency should not be penalized for making a poor decision. It was a good decision with an unfortunate consequence. ■

Reward structures are too often based on the consequences of decisions rather than on the quality of the decisions. Perhaps this partially explains a finding by Swalm (1966) that many American managers were strongly averse to accepting financial risks based on their utility functions for company profits. Such reward structures may also have been part of the reason for findings of MacCrimmon and Wehrung (1986) that most managers think they are greater risk takers than they actually are. Their perception about risk attitudes directly for financial implications may be reasonably accurate, but because reward implications must also be accounted for, they behave in a more risk-averse fashion.

S-Shaped Utility Functions

Whenever an elicited utility function is S-shaped, the function is either measuring more than one objective or at least partially measuring a means for some other objective. Some examples concerning constraints appeared earlier in this section. Let us consider some others.

■ Unemployment

In Section 6.2 I introduced a decision situation with the objective of minimizing unemployment. If this is measured by the attribute X defined as the annual percentage unemployed, a utility function may look like that in Figure 6.8a, where x' is defined as last year's unemployment level. This curve suggests that changes in unemployment as well as the level are important. Changes may reflect either an objective of minimizing additional layoffs or an objective concerning the political implications of an improving or worsening unemployment picture. Further inquiry might indicate whether either of these or both are in fact relevant in addition to the hardship of being unemployed. ■

■ Preventing Accidents

Several objectives have been analyzed with respect to the number of fatalities that may result from rare public accidents. Three fundamental objectives are to minimize loss of life, to minimize the inequity of the consequences of the risks, and to avoid catastrophes. As shown in Keeney (1982), these imply, respectively, risk-neutral, risk-prone, and risk-averse utility functions over fatalities. When all three objectives are relevant, a utility function like that in Figure 6.8b may result. Recognizing this, it may be much easier in this situation to assess three utility functions over the same attribute and then to combine them logically with a functional form using appropriate weighting. Separately analyzing the component parts (that is, the separate objectives) often provides a better assessment and always provides a consistency check for any direct assessment. Another insight from the utility function in 6.8b, or any other nonlinear utility function for fatalities, is that one is willing to risk additional deaths either to avoid catastrophes or to promote equitable consequences. ■

■ Oil Wildcatters

Some of the first empirical work on the assessment of utility functions involved the monetary consequences to oil wildcatters of drilling exploratory oil wells (Grayson, 1960; Kaufman, 1963). Several of the resulting utility functions were S-shaped like those in Figure 6.8c. This made very clear the point that money, although fundamental in many problem contexts, is almost always important as a means to fundamental objectives in other contexts. Money is important for what you can do with it. For the wildcatters, changes in assets Z less than z' meant life would go on as usual, meaning more wildcatting somewhere else. For asset changes above z', there was the opportunity for a new style of life as one essentially "hit it big." The fact that the utility function in Figure

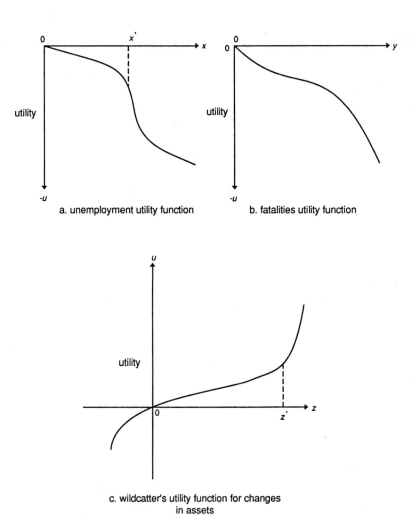

a. unemployment utility function   b. fatalities utility function

c. wildcatter's utility function for changes
in assets

Figure 6.8. S-shaped utility functions representing more than one objective

6.8c does not take a step jump at z' is simply due to the realization that there is no precise threshold for this change of lifestyle. ■

Nonmonotonic Utility Functions

In many contexts, single-attribute utility functions can be nonmonotonic. The basis for this is almost always either the balancing of two or more objectives or the anticipation of the actions of others (see Coombs and Avrunin, 1977).

■ *Automobile Speed Limits*
There have been serious discussions in both Germany and the United States about speed limits for automobiles, but the decisions reached in the two countries have been very different: Germany has no speed limit on freeways and the United States has a 65-mile-per-hour maximum. For such cases, one of the attributes to use in evaluating options is the actual speed of travel, call it X. A reasonable utility curve for actual speed might be shaped like that in Figure 6.9a, where x' could be thought of as an ideal speed. The utility might decrease at speeds above x' because of the increasing accident hazards, because of increased fuel consumption, or because of increased pollution. Below x', the utility might decrease because of inconvenience to drivers, safety considerations, or a tendency to discourage automobile travel, which would have a negative effect on a major industry. Indeed, all of these aspects might be acting at once. Examining which aspects are relevant is important, and building a model to interrelate them and to relate each to the speed limit would be extremely helpful. ■

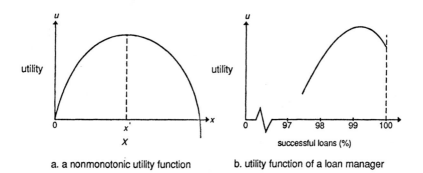

a. a nonmonotonic utility function   b. utility function of a loan manager

Figure 6.9. Nonmonotonic utility functions

■ *A New Product*

Another reason for a utility function like that in Figure 6.9a may be potential action by competitors. Suppose a company is trying to evaluate actions that will create a market for their new product. The tendency is to think that a larger potential market is better. But if at some level, represented by x' in Figure 6.9a, a major competitor is likely to enter the market, the company may have decreasing preferences for the market size. Such a utility function might suggest that the attribute be changed from total market size to market size for the company or to company profits, and that the competitors' possible actions be included in a model of consequences. ■

■ *Loan Management*

Sometimes a nonmonotonic utility function may indicate an evaluation structure to account for the appropriate balancing of a series of repeated actions. For example, a major objective of a loan manager in a bank is to contribute to the bank's profits. A common attribute used to measure this is the percentage of loans paid back on time. Although 100 percent might appear to be best, such a record might indicate that a loan manager has been too conservative. Taking a little more risk might have resulted in a few failed loans, but also in more loans, so that the contribution to the fundamental objective of profits would be larger. A utility function over the attribute defined as the percentage of successful loans that is consistent with this idea is shown in Figure 6.9b. ■

■ *Writing a Book*

There is an interesting, somewhat counterintuitive implication about the appropriate weight that should be given to nonmonotonic utility functions in multiattribute contexts. Consider the options of a writer who needs to finish the final draft of a book (see Section 11.6). Several objectives can be identified: maximizing the quality of the book; minimizing time spent working on it that could be allocated elsewhere; maximizing the productive and enjoyable time working on the book; minimizing time spent on routine tasks (such as checking references); and minimizing the time until the book is completed. The important point is that the proxy attribute time, measured in full weeks of effort, is potentially an attribute for each of these. More time spent working on the book is better for some objectives, such as quality, and worse for others, such as other unrelated activities.

Suppose the work time attribute Y is a proxy for both quality of the book and time taken away from other activities, measured by u_1 and u_2 respectively. As illustrated in Figure 6.10a, preferences increase in Y for u_1 and decrease for u_2. For this problem, an appropriate utility function u combining u_1 and u_2 may be

$$u(y) = 0.4u_1(y) + 0.6u_2(y),$$

which is shown in Figure 6.10b ranging from 0.4 to 0.7. On this common scale, the respective ranges of u, u_1, and u_2 are 0.3, 0.4, and 0.6. Thus, both components of u are more "important" than u itself because the increasing and decreasing implications tend to cancel each other out to some degree. This is important to recognize to avoid the overweighting of Y. Because it is measuring two significant objectives, changes in Y seem particularly important, but the competing implications suggest that they are less important as a whole than as either of the parts. ■

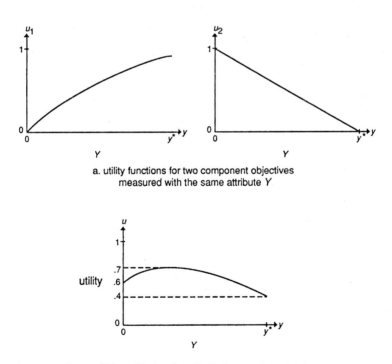

a. utility functions for two component objectives
measured with the same attribute Y

b. an additive utility function with the two components above

Figure 6.10. Nonmonotonic utility function derived from components

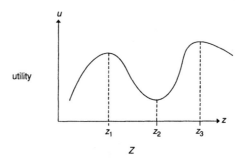

Figure 6.11. Utility function for quality of local school system

■ *Quality Schools*

Finally, a utility function can be even more involved. Suppose you are selecting a town near a major metropolitan area in which to live. A major concern is the quality of your children's education, so one attribute Z to use for evaluating towns is the quality of the local public school system. Such a utility function may be as illustrated in Figure 6.11. Below quality z_1, you feel there would have to be a good private school in the area, so the main concern around this level of Z is for educating other people's children. As the school system improves beyond z_1, there is an increasing chance that the private school could not compete for students and hence that you might be forced to send your children to "poor" public schools. Between z_2 and z_3, the increase in utility is due to a much higher quality of education for your children at the public school. And beyond z_3, you may feel that the school is simply too good and too challenging and therefore even intimidating for students. The point is that significant insight can be obtained about people's thought processes and fundamental objectives from their assessed utility functions. ■

6.5 Insights from Multiple Value Assessments

Multiple value assessments, meaning value assessments conducted with more than one assessee, are useful in a wide variety of decision situations. Examples include public decisions where a set of different stakeholders are interested in the consequences of the decision, organizational decisions where one level of the organization recommends action to a higher level, and bargaining and negotiation contexts. Each value assessment may potentially yield many insights about objectives. Additional insights may result from comparison of the assessed values. Let us discuss some examples.

In several recent studies, objectives hierarchies have been elicited from a number of stakeholders. The contexts include the guidance of German energy policy (Keeney, Renn, and von Winterfeldt, 1987), the leasing of offshore tracts for oil exploration in California (von Winterfeldt, 1987), and the shipping of spent nuclear fuel to a geologic repository (see Section 11.2).

Individual stakeholders often have an elaborate and sound objectives hierarchy with respect to their main concerns and a sparse hierarchy with respect to other obvious concerns. For a slightly exaggerated example, an environmental group concerned with energy policy may have a three-level objectives hierarchy addressing environmental consequences, with thirteen lowest-level objectives, and then state that energy should also be inexpensive. In the same context, an industry organization may have detailed economic objectives concerning use of materials, different types of costs, market implications, and ability of the national industry to compete internationally, and then add the single objective of minimizing environmental degradation. Hence the combination of objectives hierarchies from stakeholders with different viewpoints yields both a broader and a deeper perspective on the problem (see Section 3.8). The distinctions also make it possible to construct an overall objectives hierarchy that closely resembles the individual hierarchies in the areas of greatest concern to those individuals. As a result, the process lends legitimacy to the resulting set of objectives.

■ Small Hydroelectric Projects

Some apparently significant disagreements between stakeholders whose values are being assessed dissolve when the "real" fundamental objective is clearly understood. Yet without careful value assessments, this objective would have been less likely to be uncovered. An example involved the possible development of small hydroelectric projects by Seattle City Light, the municipal utility of Seattle. One objective concerned minimizing impact on salmon, since many streams and rivers in the vicinity contain salmon. The objective was initially measured by the attribute "number of salmon lost."

Two officials in Seattle government concerned with energy had extremely different value tradeoffs for salmon lost and financial cost. Essentially, one evaluated the loss of a salmon at approximately $100 and the other at greater than $1 million. We then quickly discovered that the former considered hatchery-bred salmon in the stream and the latter salmon indigenous to the stream. This suggested an important specification of the fundamental objective of minimizing impact on salmon. These lower-level fundamental objectives were to minimize impact on indigenous salmon and to minimize impact on hatchery-bred salmon. Although not identical, the two officials' values converged significantly for the two types of salmon after this clarification. ∎

Expressing Values of Other Stakeholders

In many decision situations, preliminary expressions of values are developed by some individuals representing the viewpoints of others. Examples include subordinates representing management, regulators representing the public, and analysts representing clients. In all of these cases, the former individuals have some knowledge about the latter's values. Multiple assessments with members of the former group have the potential to identify areas where clarification of the value structure would be useful. Two examples from the analysis of salmon policy for the Skeena River (see Section 8.1) are interesting.

∎ Salmon Management Revisited

In the Skeena case, two complete utility functions were assessed using the judgments of two experienced analysts, Ray Hilborn and Carl Walters. Hilborn and Walters had worked together on this and several other problems and interacted with the various stakeholders. They agreed that the general objectives concerned net, lure, and sport fishermen, regional development, impact on native Indians, and governmental costs (see Section 8.1). However, their values indicated some areas of disagreement. (For a complete comparison of their two utility functions, see Keeney, 1977a.)

For net and lure fishermen, there were three attributes, concerning annual income, days of fishing, and diversity of salmon in the river. Hilborn thought that the net and lure fishermen would have similar values, and provided identical utility functions. Walters thought they would be different. He thought lure fishermen would be more risk averse for income since they fish over the entire year and have little chance to subsidize their income with other activities. Hilborn thought that the only positive aspect of more fishing time was additional income. Since this was accounted for in the income attribute, less fishing time was preferred to more fishing time. Walters felt that up to a point (50 and 80 days annually for net and lure fishermen, respectively) more fishing time was preferred to less in addition to the income it generated. The difference was that lure fishermen mainly worked in the daytime in pleasant weather, whereas net fishermen fished at night in all kinds of weather. These differences remained even after thorough discussion. The key points are that value assessments conducted with the lure and net fishermen should resolve such issues and that such resolution is important. The multiple value assessments indicated that these issues should be resolved in order to obtain an appropriate set of fundamental objectives. Subsequently, Hilborn and Walters (1977) clarified these value issues in discussions with the stakeholders. ∎

CHAPTER **7**

Creating Alternatives for a Single Decisionmaker

. The mind is the sole source of alternatives. Either the alternatives are somewhere in the mind waiting to be found, or they can be created from what is in the mind. But in this regard a person's mind is like a vast unexplored space. With such a vast area to search for alternatives, intuitive and informal search strategies are often inadequate. Natural cognitive processes tend to guide our thoughts away from the areas of the mind that hold keys to creative alternatives. And with few guidelines for facilitating thought to generate alternatives (Ackoff and Vergara, 1981), the task is very difficult. What is needed are systematic and efficient ways to search through the mind that negate the natural tendency to think as we have thought before.

This chapter suggests numerous guidelines to aid the search for alternatives, or more precisely, the search for good alternatives. The principle is that alternatives should be created that best achieve the values specified for the decision situation. This implies that the order of thinking is first on what is desired and then on alternatives to obtain it. The initial thinking should focus on values to identify and structure objectives, to specify attributes to measure the degree to which the objectives are achieved, and to assess a composite objective function (that is, a utility function or a measurable value function).

Once you have obtained a full expression of values for a decision situation, it is time to use this knowledge to create alternatives. Both the qualitative and the quantitative statements of values should be systematically probed to initiate creative thought. Ideally, you would create the best possible alternative using the least amount of time, effort, and resources. But realistically, in complex decision situations, you may not recognize the best possible alternative even if it has been identified. Indeed, for most decisions you can only hope to find the best alternative that is possible given the time, effort, and resources allocated for this purpose (see Simon, 1969, 1982). Although it may be easy to differentiate the "good" from the "bad" alternatives informally, often only after a careful formal evaluation can the best in a set be identified. Hence the practical aim in creating alternatives is to generate a set of very promising ones.

Whether one set of alternatives is better than another is difficult to determine. This difficulty arises from the fact that the goodness of the set of alternatives should be evaluated prior to the careful evaluation of each alternative in the set. If the definitive evaluations of the individual alternatives were available, the goodness of a set of alternatives could be measured by the desirability of the best alternative in the set. Lacking this information, it is imperative to recognize that a smaller set of alternatives can never result in a better "best alternative" than a larger set of alternatives in which the smaller set is included. Many books on creative thinking and problem solving emphasize the importance of this simple fact (see, for example, Ackoff, 1978; and Adams, 1979).

The set of ideas I present for stimulating the creation of alternatives is relevant to all decision opportunities or problems. You should proceed through the set and use any that may be helpful. Even though the ideas may overlap in the ways they stimulate thought processes, redundancy is never a shortcoming in this regard. More alternatives cannot be worse. All of the ideas are applicable to individual or organizational problems with one value structure. Chapter 8 describes additional procedures for generating alternatives when the values of more than one stakeholder are relevant.

7.1 Counteracting Cognitive Biases

The way people think and process information has a strong influence on the way they address decision situations. Part of the extensive literature on this topic concerns cognitive biases, meaning errors or oversimplifications in thinking that repeatedly occur in decision situations with similar characteristics (see Edwards, 1968; Tversky and Kahneman, 1974, 1981; Slovic, Fischhoff, and Lichtenstein, 1977; Kahneman, Slovic, and Tversky, 1982; Hogarth, 1987; and Dawes, 1988). As a result of such biases, decisions are often not made as wisely as they could and should be. Although many of the experiments about cognitive biases concern estimates of either quantities (for example, probabilities) or values, the same types of biases tend to limit the ability to create alternatives. Let us consider some of these limitations.

When someone makes several estimates of related quantities, the first estimate often becomes an anchor for the others, so that subsequent estimates are more similar to the first one than they should be. For instance, in estimating the probability distribution of a variable (such as sales of a new product), one often begins with the median. The median then serves as an anchor for estimates of fractiles (for example, the 0.95 fractile is the amount of the variable that is felt to have only a 0.05 probability of being exceeded). As a result, the assessed probability distribution is typically much tighter than is appropriate (see Alpert and Raiffa, 1981).

Anchoring can also occur in the creation of alternatives. Once a first alternative is suggested, others often tend to be more similar to it than a full range of alternatives would suggest (Russo and Schoemaker, 1989). People tend to anchor on the first alternative to create the second. I was recently involved in a negotiation process over a long-term commercial rental contract. One party initially suggested specific levels for the yearly price per square foot, the annual rental increase, and dollar allowances to make interior improvements. The other party countered, but used the same variables with only slightly revised numbers. The range of alternatives could have considered flexibility in the lease, whether rents should increase annually, and caps on the maximum annual increase, to name just a few additional rental variables. However, the alternatives became anchored in a narrow range.

Thinking can also be anchored on a part of the value structure. For example, a means objective for a division of a company may be to sell as many units of its product as possible, supposedly to achieve the fundamental end of maximizing company profits. However, an all-out effort to sell the product might result in less profit because the effort required to make the last sales might be greater than for the first and because of misallocation of company resources. Such shortcomings are sometimes classified as cases of suboptimization. The search for the best alternative in these cases is actually only the search for the best of a set of inferior alternatives.

Events that have more recently occurred or that have some other memorable feature are easier to bring to mind than others. The cognitive process that causes this phenomenon is referred to as availability.

Because of availability, decisionmakers tend to anchor their thoughts on the types of alternatives used on recent problems. Big successes or big failures are also likely to stand out in memory. This causes a tendency to create alternatives similar to those used in recent successes. People also tend to categorize problems into types and to identify alternatives based on the type of problem. In all of these cases, the effect is to anchor thought and stifle innovation, limiting the range of alternatives considered.

Recognizing that an anchor may exist is the first step toward counteracting it. Most of the ideas in this chapter counteract anchoring on existing alternatives. Here, it is worthwhile to mention some general suggestions that help avoid anchoring.

Major anchors occur because of tendencies to follow past practice (Walker, 1988) and to take the party line of an organization (Miser and Quade, 1985). Hence, it is useful to develop some alternatives that are contrary to past practice. For example, put yourself in the position of other parties (such as your competitors) and create alternatives that they might consider. Another way to avoid the narrow focus on "business as usual" is to generate several distinct scenarios that may describe the future state of affairs, then to create desirable alternatives for each scenario (Keller and Ho, 1988).

It is often easier to be complete in identifying alternatives if you are accountable for the decisionmaking process. Consequently, it is useful to find ways, even if they have to be self-administered, to increase accountability and document the process. Accountability also promotes learning over time about how you can best help yourself in creating alternatives.

7.2 Use of Objectives

It is obvious that thinking about how to achieve your objectives may help you create alternatives. It is less obvious how to think about how to achieve your objectives. This section indicates how each of the aspects of a value assessment can suggest creative alternatives.

Fundamental Objectives

The objectives in the fundamental objectives hierarchy list all aspects of consequences that are important in the context of a decision. The relative desirability of contending alternatives is measured solely by the degree of achievement of these objectives. Hence, thinking about how to better achieve these objectives can suggest alternatives.

One way to begin is to focus on one objective at a time and think of alternatives that might be very desirable if that were the only objective. You should consider every objective, regardless of its level in the hierarchy. This exercise is likely to generate many alternatives, most of which would evaluate rather poorly on some objectives other than the one for which they were invented. If this is not the case, you have not been very creative in generating the alternatives. This process should provide a broad range of potential alternatives.

The next step is to consider objectives two at a time and try to generate alternatives that would be good for both. The alternatives you create now are likely to be either refinements or combinations of those you created using single objectives. Then take three objectives at a time, and so on, until all objectives are considered together.

Next, examine the alternatives you have generated to see if it is possible to combine any of them into a single alternative. For instance, suppose you have a month off from your job and your objectives for using the time include having fun and learning something useful. The alternatives you generated for having fun and those for learning something useful may not have much in common. But having fun and learning need not come from the same alternative in a narrow sense; they can come from different alternatives simultaneously pursued in the same time period. And in a larger sense this is just a single alternative composed of two distinct elements.

Not specifying the fundamental objectives in sufficient detail may inhibit the creation of alternatives. Consider a decision situation where the fundamental objective is to reduce the deaths and injuries that occur in automobile travel. Alternatives such as reducing speed limits, installing dividers on highways, and installing airbags in vehicles come to mind. Alternatives such as requiring safety seats or special helmets for small children may be overlooked unless the fundamental objectives hierarchy includes separate categories for deaths and injuries to infants, children, and adults. Specifying the objectives by asking, for each objective, "To whom does this matter?" or "In what circumstances does this matter?" can open the mind to many new alternatives.

A good objectives hierarchy helps to remove inappropriately narrow anchors for creating alternatives by increasing the breadth of concern. Focusing creative thought on different objectives provides multiple anchors over the range that should be searched for alternatives.

This statement is supported by some empirical evidence. An experiment by Pitz, Sachs, and Heerboth (1980) suggests that more alternatives are created when objectives are considered one at a time as opposed to jointly. Jungermann, von Ulardt, and Hausmann (1983) find that more alternatives are generated when the level of specification of a fundamental objectives hierarchy is increased. Keller and Ho (1988) summarize recent research on using objectives in generating alternatives.

Attributes

The attribute specified for a given objective defines its meaning more precisely. For example, in problems involving employment, almost everyone would agree that one objective is to minimize unemployment. But what exactly does this mean? One attribute to measure the achievement of the objective might be the percentage of workers who are unemployed; another might be the number of workers losing their jobs. Clearly, the same alternatives with the same data could be ranked in reverse order depending on which of these attributes was chosen. With the number of workers losing jobs as an attribute, alternatives that would preserve existing jobs, perhaps even at the expense of creating fewer jobs, would be preferable. With the unemployment rate as an attribute, alternatives that would let "dying industries" pass away and retrain workers for new and growing fields would be preferable.

Because the attributes used to evaluate alternatives have such a strong influence on the creation of alternatives, they should be selected carefully. In fact, it is useful to consider alternate attributes for the same objective while creating alternatives.

Tversky and Kahnemann (1981) have shown that, even though two attributes have a clear deterministic relationship, the attribute selected to describe consequences can affect the choice of alternatives. An important illustration is presented by McNeil, Pauker, and Tversky (1988), who asked both patients and doctors whether they would prefer surgery or radiation therapy for lung cancer. For one group of respondents, the attribute in which consequences were expressed was survival time after treatment (that is, the probability of surviving more than x years). For other respondents, the attribute was time until death after treatment (the probability of dying within x years). The percentage of respondents preferring one treatment over the other depended strongly on the attribute selected. When the survival time attribute was used, 18 percent of the respondents preferred radiation therapy over surgery; when time until death was used, 47 percent preferred radiation therapy. This finding suggests that viewing the "same" attribute from different perspectives may lead to the creation of alternatives that might otherwise be overlooked.

The Objective Function

Both a utility function and a value function provide much information about values. This information can be used to identify potentially desirable alternatives. The objective function or insights gathered from it can be used directly or in conjunction with the fundamental objectives and attributes.

Any objective function indicates which objectives are most important in a decision situation given the range of possible consequences. Other things being equal, spending time thinking of alternatives that better achieve an objective accounting for 50 percent of the combined weights of the objectives will be more worthwhile than spending time focusing on an objective with 10 percent of the weight. Roughly speaking, a 50 percent improvement on an objective with 10 percent of the weight is better than a 5 percent improvement on an objective with 40 percent of the weight if each is anticipated to take the same effort. However, a 30 percent improvement on a specified objective may or may not be better than a 15 percent improvement requiring only half the effort. The preference in this case should depend on the specific circumstances of the problem.

The form of every objective function provides an improved understanding of the fundamental objectives in a problem (see Chapter 6). For instance, suppose the two attributes for a problem concern the degrees to which two stakeholders are pleased with the consequences. The presence in the utility function of a multiplicative term of the two attributes with a positive weight indicates that equity considerations between the two stakeholders are important. The absence of a multiplicative term suggests that equity is not important. In the former case, the realization that equity is a de facto objective may stimulate creative thought for types of alternatives that would be overlooked if the focus were only on pleasing the two individuals separately.

Means Objectives

The means-ends objectives network is a fruitful grounds to stimulate thinking about alternatives. Essentially any alternative that influences one of the means objectives should influence at least some of the associated fundamental objectives. More complicated decision situations will tend to have more complicated means-ends objectives networks, which should suggest more alternatives.

Consider a rather simple fundamental objective of a firm to maximize profits from the sale of a product. Means objectives, in this case, might address sales volume, price of the product, cost of manufacturing the product, cost of distributing the product, and overhead cost. Alternatives could be created that influence each of these. For example, advertising and marketing programs would presumably boost sales but increase overhead costs. Pricing strategies might include cheaper introductory offers and regional experimentation with pricing. If one sophisticated machine used in the manufacturing process was prone to breakdown, event-tree and fault-tree analyses might suggest the causes of breakdowns. Then of course means objectives to maximizing profits would include reducing the likelihood of each of these causes. Reviewing these causes may suggest useful alternatives.

▪ *Transporting Nuclear Waste*

For a more detailed example of using means objectives to create alternatives, consider the problem of transporting spent nuclear fuel. Part of a simple decision tree to describe this problem is illustrated in Figure 7.1. The first decision, at node 1, involves selecting the type of cask in which to place the fuel for shipment. At node 2 a transportation route is selected, and at node 3 the number of casks in a shipment is chosen. Nodes 4 and 5 concern whether an accident will occur during shipment and the amount of radiation released. Node 6 indicates whether there is an efficient plan for evacuation if necessary. The fundamental health and safety and cost implications, as well as others, are then related to each value node (here, nodes 7 and 8) at the end of the decision tree. Means objectives from the means-ends objectives network can be related to branches at any stage of the decision tree. For instance, at node 1, a means objective might be to select a zircon cask, if zircon casks are believed to be particularly sturdy or safe. Means objectives related to the selection of the route at node 2 might be to reduce the transportation miles or to select a route with few people along it. For node 3, one means objective might be to use large shipments as much as possible, since this would reduce exposure times and costs associated with emergency teams following each shipment. A means objective related to node 4 would be to minimize the likelihood of accidents. At node 5, a means objective would be to minimize the likelihood of radiation release or to

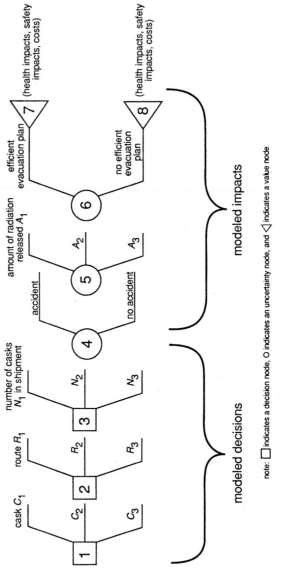

Figure 7.1. Partial decision tree to evaluate alternatives
for transporting nuclear waste

minimize the amount of radiation released. Regarding node 6, a means objective might be to develop a good emergency response system.

Focusing on how to better achieve each of the means objectives fosters the creation of alternatives. At node 1 in the figure, for the objective of selecting a zircon cask, specific design options concerning thickness or size might come to mind. At node 2, the means objective of reducing the number of people along the transportation route would suggest particular routes. There would be obvious alternatives regarding the number of casks per shipment at node 3. At node 4, the means objective of minimizing the likelihood of an accident would suggest potential special transportation rules (such as lower speed limits, daytime driving only, or use of special vehicles in transportation). At node 5, minimizing the probability of a radiation release would suggest making casks more durable. At node 6, the desire of an efficient evacuation response would suggest special training of emergency response teams and alternatives that would improve communication in times of crisis. As mentioned above, fault trees may be used to estimate probabilities required at any of the uncertainty nodes (nodes 4, 5, and 6 in Figure 7.1). Any of the components in these fault trees should directly suggest alternatives, or parts of alternatives, that might increase the chances of better consequences. ▪

7.3 Use of Strategic Objectives

A decisionmaker's broadest objectives are the strategic objectives. These provide the foundation for creating any alternatives or identifying any decision opportunities based on values. Sometimes the wide open question of what can be done to contribute to the achievement of each strategic objective is worth pondering. For example, published strategic objectives (goals, in their terminology) of Southern California Edison (SCE) include providing reliable low-cost electricity service, developing renewable sources of energy, improving productivity, developing and rewarding good employees, and contributing to the improvement of social and economic conditions in communities served (Southern California Edison, 1983). Applying the ideas in Section 7.2 to these strategic objectives should suggest some worthwhile alternatives. Using the strategic objectives in this way, without a decision context, is closely related to identifying decision opportunities using strategic objectives as described in Section 9.1.

Now, consider a decision context where a division of a large organization is trying to create alternatives to best achieve its fundamental objectives. It may use each of the firm's strategic objectives to suggest alternatives. For instance, one unit of Southern California Edison may have the responsibility to operate certain power plants as efficiently as possible. Asking what the division can do to contribute to each of SCE's strategic objectives while pursuing its own fundamental objectives may yield some useful alternatives. If the division identifies potentially worthwhile alternatives that do not fall under its own responsibility, it can communicate them to the appropriate parties. One advantage of a broad approach to thinking about alternatives is that it makes alternatives that do not fit neatly within some unit's jurisdiction less likely to be overlooked.

Broadening the Decision Context

It is often useful to broaden the fundamental objectives used for a particular decision context, but not to broaden them all the way to the strategic objectives. Too often, the objectives used as the fundamental objectives in a decision situation should in fact be means objectives in a more appropriate decision frame involving a broader context.

Numerous risk analyses have been done in recent years to decide how to make something safer. These include studies of power plants, industrial facilities, ambient air quality, proposed or existing foods and drugs, consumer products, and automobiles. In many cases the stated objective of the analysis is to find ways to minimize the probability of the occurrence of some unfortunate event. These events may be an accident at a nuclear plant, an unhealthy concentration of a pollutant in the air, or a fatality in a particular type of accident. Reducing such probabilities may be worthwhile given all the other implications that the alternatives may have, but the characterization of the problem is unnecessarily narrow because of the objectives. It concentrates on one means (the probability of an event) rather than on the more fundamental end (the consequences of the event). It limits the search for alternatives to those that strive toward fail-safe and omits consideration of those that concern safe-fail.

■ *Nuclear Plant Safety*
Suppose that a utility company is required to spend $1 billion to reduce the probability of a major accident at a nuclear plant in the event of a

large earthquake. The main reason is to minimize the radiation danger to the residents of a nearby town. But suppose there is evidence that such an earthquake would probably destroy the town. Indeed, it may be the case that parts of the town would be destroyed by earthquakes or other events that would not damage the nuclear plant with its current protection standards. An alternative that used $200 million from the utility to improve safety in town and the town's ability to respond to disasters might be much better for the town's residents than the $1 billion spent on the plant. It would also lead to lower utility rates for the company's customers. ■

7.4 Focus on High-Value Alternatives

Alternatives themselves can trigger thought processes that generate new alternatives. The original alternatives may be actual or hypothetical. They may be described by actions to be taken or by possible consequences. By stimulating thought about what is particularly good or particularly bad, they can help us to develop better options.

Focusing Thinking on Desirable Consequences

Often in decision situations, there is an alternative such as the status quo or the "do nothing" option that readily comes to mind. If no better alternatives are found, this one is likely to be followed, even if not explicitly chosen. As discussed above, the decision process may anchor on such an alternative, thus limiting the search to similar alternatives. The anchor may even include the attributes chosen to be sufficient to describe the existing obvious alternatives.

To counteract this tendency, you can create a new anchor representing a much more desirable consequence than the existing ones. For instance, suppose the fundamental objectives hierarchy has been established and attributes X_i, $i = 1, \ldots, N$ identified with respective ranges x_i^o to x_i^* are thought to be possible. Then the consequence $x^* = (x_1^*, \ldots, x_N^*)$ would be the best possible consequence with utility $u^* = u(x^*)$, where u is the utility function over the consequences. We want to stimulate thinking about how to achieve x^*, or more generally a consequence of utility close to u^*. If some thought does not create any alternatives, aspirations can be slightly lowered from u^* and the process repeated. In simple terms, we begin with a description of the consequences of the hypothetically best alternative and degrade the minimal amount to reach a feasible alternative, rather than begin with a minimal "acceptable" alternative and improve it some.

Obviously, the selection of x^* is important. Each element of x^*, that is each x_i^*, may be defined by selecting an alternative that is particularly good in terms of attribute X_i. If there is uncertainty regarding the implications with respect to X_i, a favorable resolution of the uncertainty should be assumed.

Two other points are worth noting. First, several different desirable anchors in terms of consequences can be used in a given problem. Each should anchor thought differently in an attempt to search "different places in the mind" for alternatives. Second, it is useful to create the feeling that x^* is definitely feasible. Experience suggests that it is much easier to figure out how x^* can be reached than to figure out *if* and how x^* can be reached.

The concept of using desirable descriptions of the consequences of decisions to promote constructive thinking about possible alternatives has been suggested and applied in various forms. In one sense, any objective function with a broad range of possible consequences indicates consequences to strive toward. The best such consequence is sometimes called the ideal, and one should attempt to create alternatives that lead to consequences as similar to the ideal as possible. Zeleny (1982) develops one procedure to create alternatives that is based on this general concept. As made clear by Ackoff (1978), the role of an ideal is not so much to be reached, but to focus the allocated time and effort toward achieving it. If indeed an ideal is achieved, a new "improved" ideal should take its place to guide thought and action.

Common Properties of Good Alternatives

Focusing on properties that good alternatives (those evaluated as among the best) have in common may also stimulate useful thinking. Ackoff (1978) discusses a visual example of this. A manufacturer of kitchen appliances had introduced several new products in recent years, some of which had succeeded and some of which had failed. Placing the successful products on one side of a room and the failures on the other made one trait immediately obvious. All the successful products had the property that users could operate them without bending over, and all the failures lacked this property. Such clear evidence, whether provided by an analysis or a visual evaluation as in this example, has strong implications for the types of alternatives that should and should not be created.

7.5 Use of Evaluated Alternatives

It is important to attempt to create desirable alternatives throughout the decision process. After a set of alternatives has been completely evaluated for the first time, significantly more information is available than before the evaluation. Any of this information may stimulate creative thought to generate new or improved alternatives.

Improving Good Alternatives

After the initial evaluation of alternatives, you may examine the good alternatives to identify why their consequences are less desirable than necessary. For instance, if firm profits appear lower than necessary because of high inventory costs with one product, focusing on alternatives to reduce these may be fruitful.

■ *LNG Facility Risk*
An analysis of a proposed liquified natural gas (LNG) facility for receiving LNG from large ships was performed to examine potential risks to the public (see Keeney, Kulkarni, and Nair, 1979). The proposed operation of the facility included 143 incoming shipments of LNG spread out rather evenly over the year. The analysis indicated that 76 percent of the resulting risk to the public was attributable to tourist weekends, which were defined as weekends from May through October. Hence, over three-fourths of the risk occurred in one-seventh of the time. This suggested that an alternative that excluded shipments during tourist weekends should be considered. Prior to the analysis, such an alternative had not been obvious. ■

Almost any alternative, including of course the one identified as best, will have some negative implications. In some sense, you are by definition willing to accept these implications if you select the alternative. But especially when these negative implications turn out to be more significant than originally thought, reflection to create new alternatives may be useful. You should reframe the decision and ask whether, given the specified negative implications, other alternatives are likely to yield either more "good implications" for the price of the bad ones or fewer "bad implications" for the price of the same good ones.

Consider a high technology firm that is searching for a reliable supplier of parts for its product. The initial focus is on potential suppliers within the country. After a careful appraisal of the alternatives, it is clear that the best alternative involves approximately an eight week delay from ordering time to delivery. This is a means that could negatively affect both profits (through sales) and service. Once the firm recognizes that such a delay may be necessary, alternatives of foreign supply may appear reasonable. Perhaps they were not initially considered because they could not deliver within four weeks, the maximum delay the firm originally saw as acceptable. At this stage in the decision process, more careful development of some foreign supply alternatives may be very appropriate.

■ *Pumped Storage Site*
In an analysis of sites in New Mexico for a potential pumped storage facility (a hydroelectric power plant consisting of two large connected reservoirs of water), the initial analysis of ten sites identified one as having particularly desirable economic implications, but its lower reservoir would have had an unfortunate environmental impact (Keeney, 1979). Overall, the site ranked ninth because of this situation. Given this additional knowledge, a new alternative was created that kept the same economic advantages but eliminated the specific environmental impact. A careful study of the immediate area resulted in a design that used a similar upper reservoir on the same site and utilized a different valley around the mesa for the lower reservoir. ■

Hindsight

How often has each of us said "I shouldn't have chosen that alternative; I should have picked a different one." Usually this occurs quite a while after the decision had to be made and during the time when consequences are accruing. Our hindsight now is better than our foresight was. We have presumably learned something that should help us with our decisions. But it will not help with the decision in question, as that one has been made and implemented. Still, it is useful to reconsider the decision using hindsight and decide what we should have done and why and then store the knowledge for future use. We want to turn today's hindsight into tomorrow's foresight.

The Alternative of a Decision Opportunity

Readers of this book have had and will have many small professional opportunities offered them "out of the blue." These offers may include invitations to present a talk, prepare an article for publication, or participate in a seminar. The way such offers are presented implies that the alternatives are yes and no, as well as maybe "maybe yes" and "maybe no." Hindsight has taught me that another alternative is often realistic and better than any on the table. The alternative is to change the offer by recognizing it as a decision opportunity. This is a good alternative even if you would gladly say yes to the offer—in fact, especially when you would say yes to the offer. This merely indicates that in some sense the offer is win-win for you and the offerer.

A simple example may be helpful. Suppose you are asked to participate in a large three-day meeting and this appeals to you because the meeting organizer is someone you would like to get to know better. You might suggest the alternative of spending three days working with the organizer at some time other than the meeting. By recognizing this alternative, you are essentially examining the decision opportunity of how you and the organizer may productively "do something" together. Your fundamental objectives for this decision context may guide you to a much more desirable alternative for both you and the organizer.

7.6 Generic Alternatives

A generic alternative refers to an entire set of related specific alternatives. The generic alternatives are defined by certain features of all alternatives in the set, but details are not specified. These generic alternatives can be developed by a variety of procedures. One is to search through the fundamental objectives hierarchy and ask what types of general changes in alternatives might change impacts with respect to a single objective. For example, in the context of sulfur dioxide emissions from power plants and industrial facilities, a fundamental cost objective is to minimize the costs of enforcing emission standards. An obvious generic alternative is to monitor emissions automatically using a to-be-invented technological device. This is a generic alternative because details about the device are not now known. Indeed, competing devices might be developed having different costs and accuracy levels. It may be possible to do rough but reasonable evaluations of generic alternatives to indicate where effort may be worthwhile. Such a preliminary evaluation may take place higher in the fundamental objectives hierarchy than any definitive evaluation, or it may take place using proxy attributes with readily available data.

As another example, say a large grocery chain is searching for a site for a new central warehouse facility. Generic alternatives may specify general regions of the chain's retail area as possible locations. These regions may be more than 1000 times the size of the required land for the site, but the general characteristics will be fairly similar for all possible sites within a region. An appraisal of regions may suggest three or four as the most promising for a detailed search for alternative sites. This process is directly related to screening, which is discussed in Section 7.11.

Sometimes generic alternatives are suggested by elements in a means-ends objectives network. For instance, a means to producing a better-quality product and to more profits might be improved quality control. Generic alternatives might postulate a 10 percent, a 25 percent, and a 50 percent improvement in both rejecting "unfit" products and not rejecting acceptable products. Such generic alternatives could be roughly evaluated in terms of their possible costs and contribution to profits to see if it would be worthwhile considering precisely how to achieve such improvements.

Defining Generic Alternatives by Resources Allocated

A natural way to define generic alternatives is by varying the amount of resources allocated to those alternatives. The following example, which is analogous to situations that have occurred while working on several R&D allocation problems, illustrates the idea.

■ *Research Projects*
Members of a research staff propose a research project, which has an associated cost and a specific research objective. The objective may be to "increase the telephone-call-carrying capacity of fiber optic lines." Management must decide whether to fund this project. Some proposed projects will not be funded and others will get only partial funding, as requests for research funds always exceed funds available.

It would be possible to define specific research alternatives on fiber optic lines for each possible funding level, but that would take a great deal of effort, perhaps too much effort for this stage. It is often useful to take the resource, research funds in this case, and define generic alternatives that invest in the project, say, 0, 25, 50, 75, and 100 percent of the funds requested. Details about exactly what research would be done at the different resource levels is not specified. The generic alternatives can then be appraised in terms of their cost and their likely contribution toward the stated objective. If it turns out that 50 percent funding looks better than other possibilities, two or three specific alternatives using between 40 and 60 percent of the requested funding should be defined and evaluated. ∎

∎ *Mexico City Airport*

A slightly more involved case using generic alternatives was an appraisal of alternatives to improve Mexico City's airport facilities (see de Neufville and Keeney, 1972; and Keeney and Raiffa, 1976). Two possible sites, the present Texcoco airport or a new Zumpango site, could have been developed as the single metropolitan airport, or a two-airport strategy could have been followed. The main resource to be allocated that distinguished alternatives was the funding levels at each of the two sites. For each site, funding was categorized into four levels. The implications of these funding levels for airport development in terms of land reserved, facilities constructed, equipment purchased, and maintenance was spelled out to better define the alternatives. The resulting 16 generic alternatives, illustrated in Figure 7.2, were evaluated in a preliminary analysis that led to a focus on four generic types of alternatives. Five specific alternatives that were consistent with these four generic alternatives were defined and evaluated in a more detailed analysis. ∎

Defining Generic Alternatives by Analogy

Generic alternatives can sometimes be created using analogy. Suppose Harbourne Solar, an established consumer products firm, was considering ways to market its first product to industrial firms. Using its considerable experience in marketing products to individual consumers, Harbourne could make a list of all the elements involved in marketing consumer goods (for example, primary purchaser, primary user, different modes of communication, support services, marketing organization structures). It could try to match these by analogy to the elements to market industrial products. Then each well-tried alternative for con-

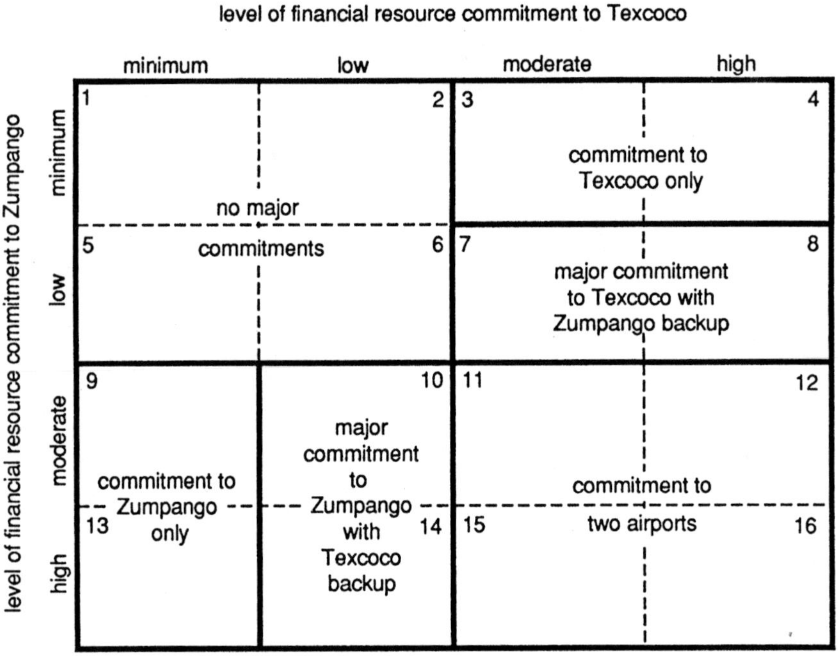
level of financial resource commitment to Texcoco
minimum
low
moderate
high
level of financial resource commitment to Zumpango
minimum
low
moderate
high
1
2
3
4
commitment to Texcoco only
no major commitments
5
6
7
8
major commitment to Texcoco with Zumpango backup
9
10
11
12
major commitment to Zumpango with Texcoco backup
commitment to Zumpango only
13
14
15
16
commitment to two airports

Figure 7.2. Sixteen generic alternatives for airport development in Mexico City in 1971

sumer products would have a natural analogue in the new context. Each one might or might not appear to be worthwhile, but those that did should suggest a focus for creative thought about specific alternatives.

7.7 Coordinated Alternatives

It is unimportant whether the achievement of the fundamental objectives is produced by a single alternative or by several alternatives integrated in a coordinated fashion. Value-focused thinking makes it easier to identify coordinated alternatives than it is with alternative-focused thinking. Using the objectives singly and then in pairs or groups naturally turns up alternatives that individually satisfy single objectives, but collectively satisfy more. Had the initial focus been on alternatives, there would more likely have been an attempt to satisfy all the objectives with a single alternative.

■ *Condominium Purchase*

Professor Buehring was about to retire after a distinguished career at the University of Michigan. He indicated an interest in spending about two months each winter pursuing nonprofessional activities in a warm climate while minimizing both the cost and hassle of such pursuit. He had framed his problem as purchasing a condominium in a sunny location with many recreational and leisure activities. This generic purchase alternative (generic since specific alternatives, such as location, were not yet defined) had two clear variants: to rent or not to rent out the condominium when he was not using it. Another generic alternative, leasing a condominium each year, was not included in Buehring's decision frame although it seemed potentially desirable given his objectives.

A rough analysis suggested that both purchasing a condominium without renting it to others and leasing were expensive, whereas purchasing and renting to others would involve a lot of hassle. Fortunately, considering the disadvantages of the first two alternatives suggested a coordinated alternative to improve them significantly. Namely, with a minimum consulting involvement scheduled over the two-month period, the net costs (that is, actual costs minus consulting revenue) of either leasing or purchasing a condominium for personal use only could be reduced to near zero. And of course, hassles would be significantly less than renting to others. Indeed, the consulting could probably be developed to be both enjoyable and interesting. ■

Add-On Alternatives

After you choose an alternative but before you implement it, you have a useful opportunity to search for add-on alternatives. In simple terms, you ask yourself if you could "solve" another problem by slightly altering or embellishing the alternative. For example, if you have to make a business trip to Washington, D.C., for one purpose, ask yourself whether other purposes could also be addressed on the trip.

■ *Temporary Workers*

Suppose your firm has just received a contract requiring that you hire several temporary workers. The typical way to address this problem might be through contracting with a temporary employee agency for, say, ten workers. Also, suppose you know that in two or three months you will need to hire two full-time employees with skills that are similar to those required for the temporary assignments. You might create the alternative of hiring six workers from the temporary agency and four workers individually. Then you could consider these four workers for the full-time positions after the temporary assignments are completed. ■

To identify possible decision situations for add-on alternatives, you need to peruse the decisions you are working on and review your strategic objectives. Just ask whether the chosen alternative can be modified to help out on a given decision or objective.

7.8 Process Alternatives

In many complex decision problems, the decision process takes place over time. In the course of a decision process, either by taking specific action or by simply remaining alert, you may pick up information that is useful for either evaluating or creating alternatives. Of particular importance is the ability to include as a part of an alternative the possibility of collecting sample information. The sample information may be about facts, such as the relationship between any means objective and some of its ends objectives (including the fundamental objectives), or it may be about values, such as sampling public values in problems. Indeed, there are standard ways to calculate the value of sample information that will suggest which alternatives to gather sample information are worth considering (see, for example, LaValle, 1968; Raiffa, 1968; and Merkhofer, 1977).

In complex decisions, there are many uncertainties about which sample information can be collected. The best you could theoretically do would be to resolve an uncertainty completely. This would be equivalent to knowing for sure what would happen in the future. It can be useful to consider your decision situation exactly as it is but imagine that you know one "uncertainty" for certain, then create alternatives for this different state of knowledge. Repeat the process assuming different uncertainties are known. The resulting set of alternatives should be less anchored in conventional wisdom.

Using Objectives Influenced by Process

In many decision problems, the consequences of the alternatives are partly due either to the process by which alternatives are chosen or to the process that occurs as a result of the alternative chosen. Examples of both situations can be given when equity considerations are important.

■ *Land Management*
The U.S. Bureau of Reclamation is responsible for management plans for many large tracts of land in the western United States. For any tract, the Bureau strives to find a decision that pleases all stakeholders: ranchers, farmers, the tourism industry, environmentalists, local communities, and energy developers, to name some. Among other objectives, all the stakeholders are concerned about the fairness with which they are treated relative to other stakeholders and with the "reasonableness" of the decision process. Both of these objectives can be influenced significantly by the process by which a decision is made. This observation naturally suggests the consideration of different processes as part of the alternatives. Ways in which process alternatives can differ include who is involved, how they are involved, when they are involved, and how their input is used in the decision process. Alternatives selected through a process that constructively involves the stakeholders are likely to be seen as fairer and more reasonable than those same alternatives would be if selected by the Bureau with little stakeholder involvement. ■

■ *Public Risk Equity*
Decision problems involving the potential loss of human life are obviously important. Agencies of governments and organizations make many such decisions concerning worker safety, drugs, road repair, air pollution, and so on. Equity in such decisions is important to many individuals, but as discussed in Section 6.2, it is difficult to include in an evaluation.

In a two-person society, many would argue that alternative A resulting in the death of individual I_1 and the survival of individual I_2 is equivalently as undesirable as alternative B that results in the death of individual I_2 and the survival of individual I_1. The consequence of each alternative is one death, and in each case that individual "never had a chance." However, if a third alternative C is proposed that involves flipping a coin to choose either A or B, many people prefer C to either A or B. With C, too, one person dies and one person survives, but both people have a fair chance of survival. The consequence of "having a fair chance" results from the process of the decision and not just from whether alternative A or B is eventually chosen. Hence, it is important to describe the process of decisionmaking as part of any alternative definition. This means that the alternatives should be decision strategies that suggest which decision will be taken in any situation that may occur (see Sarin, 1985; and Keeney and Winkler, 1985). ∎

Improved Communication

Others can be of significant assistance to anyone facing complex problems. Almost everyone has a guru whose advice they seek and respect. Before lending advice, the guru needs to understand the objectives of the person or organization facing the decision. A qualitative list of well-thought-out objectives provides considerable guidance to one whose insights you are soliciting. Going further, a clearly articulated value structure, including objectives, attributes, and an objective function, should be very helpful to the guru.

It may be more important to articulate values clearly when seeking advice than when making decisions yourself without external advice. Presumably you know your values better than others do, so making them explicit should provide more new knowledge to others. Simply stated, with a better understanding of where you wish to go, others can make more suggestions and *better* suggestions to help you get there. Your value structure is the key, because it is a complete description of where you want to go.

7.9 Removing Constraints

Constraints limit thinking about possible alternatives and are another kind of anchor that stifles innovation. The removal of any constraint, therefore, has the potential to result in a much improved alternative.

Removing Constraints on Alternatives

Constraints on alternatives occur because of restrictions on resources available or because of restricted thought about possible alternatives. An example of the former is a constraint that an alternative be implemented in less than eight weeks. An example of the latter is a decision between performing surgery and releasing the patient when other treatments and tests to acquire additional information are also available.

Resource constraints such as the eight-week deadline, are easy to recognize since they must be stated. The hope is that removing the constraint will create desirable alternatives that may take more than eight weeks to implement. If the constraint turns out to have been justified, an evaluation in terms of the fundamental objectives will reveal that alternatives that take more than eight weeks are less desirable than at least one alternative that could be implemented within the eight weeks.

Restrictions on the types of alternatives considered are more difficult to identify because they are not explicitly stated. They occur because of issues related to bounded rationality, cognitive biases, and the complexity of the decision situation (see Kleindorfer, Kunreuther, and Schoemaker, 1992). In this regard, many of the suggestions listed earlier in this chapter serve to broaden the thought processes. Specifically, focusing on the fundamental objectives to facilitate thought should lessen the constraints on the alternatives, which are only means.

It is perhaps useful to mention one simple idea to remove constraints. You just assume that a constraint doesn't apply. You say, for instance, something like, "If cost were of no concern, what additional alternatives would there be?" On decisions that you are handling by yourself, you may ask yourself these questions to stimulate thought. But this idea is of even more significance when the alternatives are essentially provided by an advisor. Your doctor suggests alternative treatments for your disease. Your investment advisor lists alternatives for investing your funds. Your employer tries to convince you that there is only one possibility—no choice. They may be applying constraints that are completely inappropriate for your decisions.

There are always choices. If you keep in mind that there are always alternatives and that there are always alternatives in addition to those on your list, you have a better chance of identifying them. After identifying them, you can evaluate them and compare them to other alternatives.

Removing Constraints on Consequences

Constraints on consequences may be either explicit or implicit. If profit is a fundamental objective, a constraint (or goal) that annual profit should exceed $50 million may inhibit the suggestion of innovative alternatives with a chance, even a small chance, of bringing in less than that level of profit. A utility function over profits is a logical and effective way to handle such issues, and such a constraint can be shown to be inconsistent with this logic. Specifically, an alternative resulting in a one percent chance of $49 million profit and a 99 percent chance of $200 million profit is likely to be preferred to an alternative with a sure $50 million profit even though the latter alternative definitely satisfies the constraint and the former alternative may not.

Consequences can be implicitly constrained by a failure to use the complete set of fundamental objectives or by the use of means objectives in place of fundamental objectives. Quite obviously, if a fundamental objective is not articulated (is missing), then it will be less likely that an alternative that achieves that objective well will be identified. The main way to minimize this effect is to make an explicit effort to construct a fundamental objectives hierarchy. All objectives should be carefully appraised as to whether they are means objectives or fundamental objectives in the context of the decision.

7.10 Better Utilization of Resources

It is important to recognize that the implementation of any alternative takes resources such as time, money, and effort. Also, descriptive research on decisionmaking has made it clear that processes to arrive at decisions are often not as logical or systematic as the decisionmakers might like them to be (see, for example, Edwards, 1968; and Einhorn and Hogarth, 1981). Thus, at the end of a decision process when you are about to choose an alternative, you should reconsider it from a different perspective. Ask what resources are necessary to implement the alternative, and then consider whether the fundamental objectives can be better achieved by using those resources in a different way.

■ *Hawaiian Vacation*
The summary of a case presented in Chapter 1 illustrates the idea. Recall that the Lees are planning a two-week vacation to Hawaii and have considered several options, tentatively selecting one. Then the travel agent suggests a two-week extension to the South Pacific for an attractive price. The Lees decide to go there also, a plan that necessitates asking for additional time away from work. Then, since they are using four weeks for a once-in-a-lifetime vacation, they decide to go first class and "not worry about the cost." At this point, the alternative they are about to choose is significantly different from the two-week trips to Hawaii they originally appraised. Now they are planning to utilize four

weeks of time, additional work leave, and, say, $8,000. At this stage they should ask themselves, "Given that we are going to spend four weeks and $8,000, what is the best use?" The question may even change the context from vacation. And in the vacation context, alternatives such as an African picture safari, a tour of China, or an Amazon cruise may appear as very reasonable alternatives, although they would not have been considered in the context of two-week Hawaiian vacations. ■

■ *Radioactive Waste Disposal*

Another important example can be seen in the context of disposing of radioactive waste from nuclear power plants. The alternative currently being pursued is to place the waste in a geologic repository to be built approximately half a mile underground in Nevada. The cost of this repository is estimated at well above $25 billion. One reason for the expense is to protect future generations for up to 10,000 years. The concern is that at some future time radioactive particles may escape from the repository because, for example, of earthquakes or corrosion of the storage casks. The particles may enter the water supply, and people may drink the water. With enough exposure, drinking water with radioactive particles may cause cancer. The financial resources being allocated to reducing this possibility are enormous. Are they being well spent?

To appraise this question, consider that the radioactivity would be much more likely to reach a water supply 500 or more years from now than in the next 500 years. Also, existing technology, allows us to detect any radioactive material in water. But what is the chance that cancer will be a disease of major concern in 500 years? It wasn't a major concern even 100 years ago, when diphtheria, smallpox, whooping cough, and tuberculosis took millions of lives annually, more than cancer takes today.

If we simply put $1 billion of the projected cost of the repository in a bank to be invested to save lives of future generations, it would grow to about $20,000 billion (in current dollars) in 500 years even at only 2 percent real interest. With such funds, it should be possible to make many significant contributions to the health and well-being of future generations. If it happens that there is a leak of radioactive particles into some water supply, these funds should be sufficient to rectify the problem.

There are other possible uses of the resources that might be reasonable. The $1 billion might be used to endow a research laboratory that would investigate cures and treatments for cancer. The impact of 500 years of research could be significant for any local population possibly exposed to water contaminated with radioactivity. The same research would also be helpful to the rest of the human race. ∎

7.11 Screening to Identify Good Alternatives

There are certain classes of decision problems for which, because of physical or legal circumstances, all possible alternatives can be identified. Regarding physical circumstances, if a company is considering building a coal-fired plant in Montana and if such a facility requires one square mile, then, ignoring the possibility of overlapping sites, the number of alternatives is 147,046, the number of square miles in Montana. Regarding legal circumstances, if the law requires that an air quality standard be established for carbon monoxide in terms of parts per million (ppm) in the air, the alternatives presumably can range from 0 ppm to a level at which many people would die. When a realistically complete set of alternatives can be easily stated, as in these cases, the search for good alternatives for careful comparison may be facilitated by screening to eliminate obviously inferior alternatives.

To screen alternatives effectively, you use subsets of either means objectives or fundamental objectives for which data on the potential alternatives is relatively easy to collect. In decisions about power plant sites, one means objective affecting costs and environmental damage is the distance over which cooling water needs to be pumped to the facility. If a distance of 25 miles would add 20 percent to the cost of any power plant, you may initially screen out such sites. This is essentially imposing a constraint. Then later, after evaluating "good" sites, you should verify the reasonableness of this screening. For instance, if a site that is perfect in terms of other attributes but is 25 miles from the water source is evaluated and found to be less desirable than the identified best sites, the screening is verified.

More sophisticated procedures to verify the appropriateness of screening criteria are found in Keeney (1980). If a given criterion is not verified, then it should be relaxed, allowing the search for additional alternatives. Suppose the "perfect" hypothetical site 25 miles from the water source is better than the best evaluated alternative, but that if it is 35 miles away it is worse than the best alternative. Then you should consider additional sites in the 25-to-35-mile range.

7.12 Alternatives for a Series of Similar Decisions

There are numerous situations in which many decisions concerning the same general problem will be made over time. For an individual, examples include obtaining useful information from medical experts, paying taxes and interpreting tax codes and regulations, purchasing automobiles or houses, and "bargaining" with the boss. For firms, examples include dealing with the loan departments of banks, introducing new products, negotiating with potential suppliers, and hiring key employees. For each case of a given general problem, the fundamental objectives are likely to be similar. For instance, each time that you purchase a home, you may want the deal to be as much of a bargain as possible, to be done efficiently and honestly, and to meet your needs for "comfortable" shelter. Your fundamental objectives for the entire process of buying houses over a lifetime will be the same. However, an important additional fundamental objective in a specific case may concern what you can learn that will help you make better decisions in other problems of the same class. The objective of learning is a means objective to the future set of similar problems.

Because the learning objective is so distinct in nature from the others in such a situation, specifically trying to create alternatives to achieve that objective may lead you in entirely new directions. As a simple personal example, suppose that you expect your tax returns to be audited by the IRS approximately every five years. In any given audit (a case), the most reasonable alternative to you may be to accept whatever the IRS concludes and accept any refund or pay any additional taxes if necessary (unless extreme). This alternative saves both time and inconvenience. However, learning about how time consuming it is to question the IRS findings may be worthwhile since this information may have value in future cases. By challenging one audit, you may learn enough to save money and to reduce the probability of a future audit, thus saving additional time and inconvenience in the future.

CHAPTER 8

Creating Alternatives for Multiple Decisionmakers

In many decision situations, more than one party is interested in the consequences of a decision or in the process by which the decision is made. Such parties, whether they are individuals, groups, or organizations, are referred to as stakeholders. In decision situations involving multiple stakeholders, systematically focusing additional time and effort on the creation of alternatives is likely to pay big dividends. This systematic focusing should be based on the values of the stakeholders, since their values are the reason for their interest in the decision.

Different stakeholders may have different values, and these may be reflected in differences in their lists of objectives, objectives hierarchies, attributes, and objective functions. Hence, in structuring the values for a problem with multiple stakeholders, you should structure values separately for each one. In addition, it is often useful to develop a combined value structure, as described in Section 3.8.

This chapter considers two different classes of decision situations. One class involves multiple decisionmakers that must collectively agree on a course of action. Most bargaining and negotiation problems and so-called group decisions fall within this class. In the second class, one stakeholder is the main decisionmaker, but it wishes to account for the values of other stakeholders. Each stakeholder's values may be treated equally, or a main decisionmaker may place less weight on the values of other stakeholders.

Two general observations are useful here. First, all of the suggestions of Chapter 7 can be used with the value structures of each stakeholder to identify desirable alternatives. Second, with multiple stakeholders, the process by which the decision is made is likely to be

important. A clear example involves decisions about alternatives to reduce risks to the public. Even if none of the risks eventually cause fatalities, a decision that placed much more risk on one group than on others
would probably be considered inferior to one that "balanced" risks to
the groups.

8.1 Pleasing Other Stakeholders

In many decision situations one of the objectives of a decisionmaker is
to please another stakeholder as much as possible. This desire may be
altruistic because of the impact on the stakeholder, or it may be self-
interested, because of what the stakeholder may do for the decisionmaker. An example of the former is a governmental agency trying
to best solve some public problem, and an example of the latter is an
employee trying to please the boss in hope of getting a promotion. In
such decisions, the decisionmaker has the authority to make the decision
and the other stakeholder has only indirect influence.

In such situations it is helpful to make explicit the values of the
stakeholder or stakeholders to be pleased. From this, alternatives should
be generated. The decision context framed by the decisionmaker is of
crucial importance, as illustrated by a story described in Ackoff (1978).
A Mexican governmental agency wished to help farmers in a certain
region increase agricultural production. They built a dam, but production did not increase. Rather, the farmers achieved the same level of
production, with less work and used the additional time for leisure activities. In a context defined by the alternatives of having a dam or not, a
dam was definitively preferred. But for the supposed means objective
of pleasing the farmers, alternatives increasing leisure time might have
been better than a dam. For the agency's fundamental objective of increasing agricultural production, alternatives other than a dam would
also probably have been more effective.

A case dealing with salmon management on the Skeena River in
Canada illustrates the usefulness of explicating the values of the multiple stakeholders in a complex decision situation. I developed this case
jointly with Ray Hilborn and Carl Walters, who were faculty members
at the University of British Columbia and colleagues of mine at the
International Institute for Applied Systems Analysis. Although the work
took place several years ago, today's environmental management problems are similar.

■ *Salmon Management*

The Skeena River and its tributaries in British Columbia are an important salmon fishing area. Salmon fishing is the basis of the area's economy, currently providing about 5,000 jobs. This includes the fishermen themselves, cannery workers, and people who earn a living from tourism attracted by recreational fishing. Policy decisions indicating, for example, (1) who can fish, (2) what they can fish (types or size of salmon), (3) where they can fish, (4) which methods they can use, and (5) when they can fish, affect, directly or indirectly, everyone living in the Skeena area. Generic alternatives such as the development of artificial spawning grounds are also possible. Such alternatives have many parameters (size, construction type, cost). If one should decide to construct spawning grounds, how should they be designed?

The decisionmaker for this policy problem is the Canadian Department of the Environment (DOE). There are five stakeholders whose values are important to DOE. Four of these—lure fishermen, net fishermen, sport fishermen, and Indians—are directly involved in fishing. The fifth stakeholder includes all other individuals whose welfare is linked to fishing, such as cannery employees and motel operators.

The lure and net fishermen fish for a livelihood, the lure fishermen near the mouth of the Skeena and the net fishermen a little farther upstream in a controlled area. Upstream from them are the sport fishermen and still farther upstream the Indians. These two groups fish mainly for pleasure and food.

The objectives hierarchy for this problem is illustrated in Figure 8.1. As decisionmaker, DOE has two major objectives: to satisfy each of the five stakeholders as much as possible and to minimize its own (government) expenses. The degree to which the net fishermen are satisfied depends, of course, on how well their own objectives are satisfied. As indicated in Figure 8.1, their main interests are to maximize the income per net fisherman, to optimize their fishing time (that is, to have neither too much nor too little work), and to maximize the diversity of the catch. The last objective addresses future well-being. Knowing that the river is healthy (supporting many species) provides both future flexibility and future security. The lure fishermen have analogous objectives. The Indians and sport fishermen are interested in maximizing their catch. The region wants to maximize economic benefits from employment and recreational sources as well as to have an abundance of fresh fish to eat.

Let me elaborate on the complexity inherent in such a problem.

Suppose DOE is considering changing its licensing policy. The new policy may result in a small increase in the number of salmon that return to the Skeena to spawn, or the increase may be large. The change in licensing policy may increase administrative (government) costs. It may lead to better harvests for the lure and net fishermen, but this may leave fewer fish for the sport fishermen and the Indians. The latter

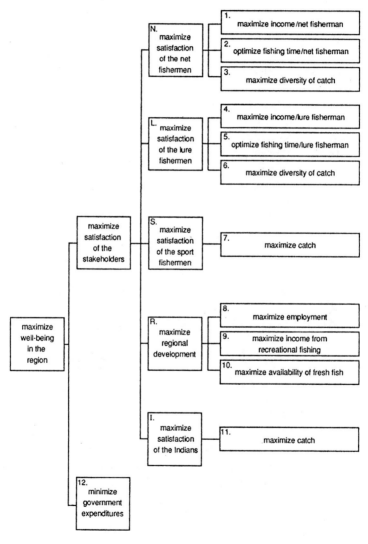

Figure 8.1. The objectives for salmon management on the Skeena River

stakeholders will then be displeased. The overall impact on the region may be more employment in canneries, and so on, but less recreational income. With these conflicting objectives, each with significant uncertainties, what should the DOE do? Somehow it must measure each of the possible impacts, balance these in some fair way, consider all pros and cons, and decide whether to implement the new licensing rules or not.

As with all decisions of this type, it is extremely important to create good alternatives. Many generic alternatives are suggested above. The objectives suggest other possibilities, most of which are dynamic in nature. If the annual catch is disappointing, the season may be extended or the river may be stocked with hatchery-bred salmon. If the lure and net fishermen are doing well but the sport fishermen and Indians are having poor catches, the commercial fishing time may be limited. If the income from recreation is poor, alternatives may be developed to attract more visitors.

There are also decision opportunities that are suggested by the objectives stated. It would be worthwhile to clarify what is meant by optimizing fishing time for the net and the lure fishermen. This issue, which concerns the value tradeoffs between income and fishing time, is discussed in Section 6.5. Hilborn and Walters (1977) and Keeney (1977a) go into much more detail on the stakeholder values that should guide much of DOE's effort to address the salmon management problem. ∎

8.2 Stakeholder Influence on Your Consequences

There are many situations in which the actions of other stakeholders can influence the consequences that are eventually felt by you. Some of these situations are naturally competitive, in that the better the other stakeholders do the worse you will tend to do. Examples include businesses competing in a market and cities competing for major conventions. Another common example is where the other "stakeholder" is the public. Bargaining and negotiation situations, which fall into this general class of problems, are considered separately in Section 8.4.

Uses of Stakeholder Actions

As a single stakeholder in these situations, you would like to know the possible actions of others in response to your actions. To help predict your competitors' potential actions, you need an understanding of their value structures. It helps to view the situation from their perspectives in both prescriptive and descriptive fashions.

It is useful to recognize that many alternatives of interest in such a situation are strategies. Your strategy includes an initial action (or reaction) on your part, waiting for the competitor's action, reaction again, and so forth. The question of how many moves to think through for each stakeholder in creating alternatives needs to be addressed separately in each decision context. At a minimum, one action of the competitor is very important to consider. The significance of other stakeholders' actions can be illustrated with the following case.

■ *Hot Instant Breakfast*
Real Cereal, a small firm, was considering whether to introduce a hot instant breakfast. It commissioned a market survey and planned to choose one of two alternatives: to produce the product if the market appeared large enough, and not to produce it if the market was too small. However, an analysis that included the actions of competitors made a third alternative seem reasonable. This alternative was not to produce the product if potential sales looked too high. At first, this seemed counterintuitive. But if sales were too high major competitors would soon enter the market, cutting into Real Cereal's profits before the fixed costs of beginning operations were covered.

This analysis suggested a decision opportunity. How could Real Cereal profit if the hot instant breakfast looked like it would be a big winner? Alternatives included how to position Real Cereal to be acquired by a major company, how to control patents, and how to enhance the desirability of possible mergers. ■

Use of Possible Consequences

It is often useful to think of the possible consequences in a decision context and then focus on alternatives that might decrease the likelihood or the severity of the worst of those consequences. You begin with a bad consequence and ask what must happen for that consequence to occur. With the answers to this and similar questions, you can work backwards from the consequences using means-ends relationships. The process is somewhat analogous to fault-tree analyses of technological risks. For every means identified as a potential contributor to the bad consequence, you should create alternatives using the ideas in Chapter 7. The distinction is that several of these means may occur as the result of actions of others.

▪ *Exxon Valdez Oil Spill*

An important example of such a problem is communication about risk in crisis situations. In 1989, the *Exxon Valdez* ran aground in Prince William Sound, Alaska, and spilled massive amounts of oil in pristine environmental areas. The Exxon Corporation immediately had several important decision problems to face. One of these was how to communicate about the crisis to the nation. By almost all accounts, Exxon management handled this communication poorly. They might have approached the problem more effectively if they had thought about the values of all stakeholders and created alternatives that addressed those values.

Stakeholders included Alaskans, the fishing industry, environmentalists, other oil companies, several government agencies, and the entire public. All of these groups could affect the consequences to Exxon. The ultimate consequences probably pertained to Exxon's profits and corporate image. As means to these, the company's communication about the disaster should have been credible, timely, open, and accurate. Management should have considered accepting full responsibility and supporting the best cleanup possible. They should have studied how their communication about risks could help them or hurt them. Consequences affected by the quality of communication included whether the public would turn in Exxon credit cards (as many did) and avoid stopping at Exxon stations, whether acts of sabotage would be taken against Exxon, whether stockholders would attack management's competence, whether government agencies would file suits and on what grounds, and whether other oil companies would consider Exxon the industry's pariah.

From thinking about stakeholder values, Exxon might have considered several avenues. It might have established direct lines of communication to executives of other oil companies about the crisis. It might have established a panel of respected environmental authorities to be sure the information it offered was accurate. It should have realized that communication about the crisis would occur over time, so that initial statements should be used to build credibility and foster an image of responsibility.

It might also have been worthwhile to consider the desirability of certain communications in conjunction with actions. What would happen if the company announced that one cent of every gallon of Exxon gas sold would be dedicated to the cleanup, or that the price per gallon would increase by one cent and two cents from each gallon would be used for the cleanup? Should a percentage of each stock dividend be forgone and allocated to the cleanup? How would the stockholders perceive and react to such actions? How would these reactions affect Exxon? There were many questions that needed answers, but the problem was a monumental one. Answering these questions or even thinking about them might have suggested alternative risk communication strategies for Exxon that would have improved matters for all stakeholders. ■

8.3 Clarifying Stakeholder Values for Group Decisions

By group decisions, I mean all those in which an alternative must be collectively chosen by more than one stakeholder. Typical situations include decisions made by friends, partners, and syndicates, as well as public decisions affecting many stakeholders. In the latter case, a governmental agency may finally make the decision, but stakeholder groups significantly influence this choice by their actions and potential actions.

In the creation of alternatives for such situations, the separate value structures of the stakeholders provide distinct decision frames that can be of significant assistance. All the suggestions of Chapter 7 can be used in conjunction with each of these decision frames. A combined value structure may also be developed for creating alternatives.

Ask Stakeholders for Alternatives

A very elementary idea that is too often not tried is to ask stakeholders to suggest alternatives. It may also be worthwhile to work with the individual stakeholders to help them express their values and use these values to suggest additional alternatives. For an interesting example, consider a decision problem about prostitution in a major city.

■ *Prostitution in Boston*
In Boston, as in most metropolitan U.S. cities, prostitution is illegal but the law is not stringently enforced. In the decision problem of what to do about prostitution in Boston, who are the stakeholders? They certainly include the workers in the criminal justice system, the police, prostitutes and their employers, businesses and residents in the areas where prosti-

tution occurs, the hotel industry, city government, and citizen groups (of which there are many).

Just thinking of these groups' likely values can suggest alternatives. Courts, jails, and police may not like using their time on "unimportant" cases. They may prefer some form of legalization. Prostitutes may want some form of legalization, too, although from their point of view it may be worthwhile to have a significant stigma attached to the profession to keep out competition. Business may want to minimize hassle to customers and therefore prefer that the prostitutes go elsewhere. The hotel industry and city government may recognize both pluses and minuses to the status quo and legalization. Certainly city government would be pleased to have the taxes that legalization would bring. Citizen groups obviously vary. Conservative religious groups are likely to call for absolute enforcement of the law, whereas libertarians may support legalization with no governmental control.

These thoughts suggest at least five generic alternatives: (1) *enforcement,* meaning enforce the existing laws; (2) *status quo,* meaning rarely enforce the existing law but keep it on the books; (3) *licensing,* meaning legalize prostitution but require licenses to practice; (4) *decriminalization,* meaning legalize prostitution with essentially no control; and (5) *brothel zones,* meaning legalize prostitution in certain controlled areas only. Within each of these generic alternatives are several components to define specific alternatives. How much would licensing fees be, what would happen to offenders given enforcement, what zones would be proposed for brothels, and so forth.

In a class on decision analysis that I taught at M.I.T., the class project was to analyze these five generic alternatives for Boston. We attempted to take a perspective that balanced the values of several stakeholder groups. This produced a stable ranking of generic alternatives that went from best to worst as follows: brothel zones, licensing, enforcement, decriminalization, and the status quo. ■

Decisions Involving Interdependent Values

In a common class of group decisions, two or more stakeholders are jointly responsible for taking a coordinated action and each stakeholder wishes, among other objectives, to please the other stakeholders. This can be illustrated for two stakeholders (Keeney, 1981). Let stakeholders S_1 and S_2 have values for impacts on themselves represented by the utility functions u_1 and u_2 respectively. Collectively, suppose consequences x represent all those of value to either S_1 or S_2, and finally let U_1

and U_2 be the "social" utility functions for the respective stakeholders, considering all impacts of relevance to both stockholders. Then, for the problem class, we know $U_1(x, u_2)$ and $U_2(x, u_1)$. The creation of alternatives in this situation can sometimes be very poorly handled because each stakeholder is trying to decide what the other would like.

■ *French Restaurant*
A classic example might involve two people selecting a restaurant for dinner. Each is polite and limits suggestions to those expected to please the other, but each interprets the suggestions of the other to represent the other's preferences. Somehow a French restaurant is chosen, and over dinner a more relaxed conversation begins. Soon, each finds out that the other would have preferred a Chinese restaurant but accepted the French, thinking the other preferred it. ■

Better alternatives can probably be created if each person first structures his own values, leading to u_1 and u_2. Presumably, these are matters for which S_1 is most informed about u_1 and S_2 is most informed about u_2. Then stakeholder values are discussed so u_1 becomes factual information to S_2, and u_2 becomes factual information to S_1. Alternatives should then be generated using the objectives and utility functions u_i for the individual stakeholders. Once the facts and value structures are clear, the social utility functions U_1 and U_2 can be used to evaluate and select an appropriate alternative. At this stage, choice of an action may be readily apparent.

The same general ideas can be utilized using direct evaluations of the alternatives. A simple example illustrates this.

■ *No Smoking Please*
Four people, one of whom was a smoker, were eating dinner together on a business trip. The smoker asked if it was all right to smoke. The other three looked at one another as if to say "If it is all right with the others, I guess it is all right with me, since the vote is three to zero, not including mine." But then one member of the party suggested that each should state his preference thinking of himself only. Three no's came forward immediately, and the choice was obvious. ■

Improving Alternatives for Potential Losers

In many situations involving groups, it is rather easy to find an alternative that most stakeholders prefer to the status quo, but a few stakeholders will lose if that alternative is chosen. In such problems, a natural base point influencing stakeholder aspirations and actions is the status quo that will continue if no agreed upon action is found.

■ Joint Investments

A simple but elegant example was developed by Raiffa (1968). Suppose two people can act alone or together to accept a business proposition that will return \$1 million if successful or lose \$0.5 million if unsuccessful, the chance of each consequence being equal at one-half. Suppose also that each person has the single objective of maximizing economic return.

By analyzing reasonable utility functions u_1 and u_2 for the two people over their respective returns and losses, Raiffa identified creative alternatives for two generic situations where neither person would accept the business proposition alone and where there was no way to divide the proposition proportionally so that both people would prefer their share to the status quo.

In one situation, it is possible to alter the proportional sharing of the proposition with a side payment from one person to the other such that both will accept their parts of the proposition. In the second situation, it is impossible to divide the proposition in any way, even with side payments, that will improve each person's utility over the status quo. However, in this case, it is sometimes possible to devise two such unacceptable divisions, call them A and B, and use them to create an alternative C that each person prefers to the status quo. For example, alternative C might be to flip a coin to choose between A and B. How could alternative C be acceptable to both parties if neither A nor B is? If A is very attractive to the first party and slightly unattractive to the second, and B is very attractive to the second party and slightly unattractive to the first, then alternative C offers to each party an equal chance at a very attractive offer and a slightly unattractive offer, and this chance is preferable to the status quo for both parties. ■

Dynamic alternatives and concepts analogous to nonproportional sharing when attributes are not identical for each stakeholder are obviously relevant to multiple-stakeholder cases. Suppose there are M stakeholders S_m, $m = 1, \ldots, M$, with utility functions u_m, $m = 1, \ldots, M$, and let $u^\circ = (u_1^\circ, \ldots, u_M^\circ)$ be the status quo level. You wish to find an alternative A where $u_m(A) > u_m^\circ$ for all m. If, for example, some initial alternative D is very good for most stakeholders except say for S_1, then a careful review of the components of $u_1(D)$ may indicate that attributes

X_1 and X_2 are mainly responsible for the poor evaluation. Furthermore, attribute X_3 may have little or no link to objectives of other stakeholders. The former observation should suggest that effort to create alternatives could initially focus on ways to modify alternative D to do better on X_1 and X_2 from the perspective of S_1 without reducing the desirability of D to other stakeholders. The latter observation suggests finding devices to improve matters in terms of X_3 for S_1. These devices, being at most weakly linked to the objectives of other stakeholders, should not make them much worse off. The idea is then to combine the identified device with alternative D. This general approach has been used in seeking the agreement of stakeholders for energy development proposals (see Gardiner and Edwards, 1975; Ford, 1979; and Ford and Gardiner, 1979).

8.4 Creating Alternatives for Negotiations

Negotiations are an obvious class of important decisions in which more than one stakeholder must agree on an alternative for it to be chosen. In such cases it is naturally still important to create alternatives for consideration by the stakeholders. However, it is particularly important to create alternatives that are desirable to all of the stakeholders in the negotiation (Fisher and Ury, 1981). The class of negotiations considered here involves multiple issues. In these cases, each stakeholder must address the vexing value tradeoffs of how much to give up in terms of one issue in order to gain a specified amount on another issue. Focusing on values can contribute much in such situations (see Keeney and Raiffa, 1991).

If you are one of the stakeholders, you should do several things to prepare for the negotiation. As discussed in detail in Raiffa (1982), you want to structure completely your values and the other stakeholders' values. This structuring should definitely include identification of the fundamental objectives and should probably include specification of the value tradeoffs. If time permits, it may be worthwhile to quantify these objectives by specifying your complete utility function and an estimate of the others' utility functions.

Next, it will be worthwhile to identify potential issues for the negotiation and possible resolutions of each. Issues and fundamental objectives have a natural relationship, as the resolution of issues is the means by which a negotiated agreement affects the achievement of fundamental objectives. Thus, thinking about how an approaching negotiation can influence the achievement of objectives is one way to identify issues. Once a single issue is defined, possible resolutions are often not difficult to suggest.

Finally, before any negotiation, it is important to understand the desirability to you of your BATNA—*best alternative to a negotiated agreement*. This alternative indicates your power in a negotiation, as there is no reason to consider alternatives less desirable than your BATNA. It will of course be useful to understand the BATNA values of the other stakeholders, because this will indicate their relative power and "willingness to negotiate." The alternatives that are most desirable to create are those that are better than the BATNA alternatives for all of the stakeholders.

■ *Labor versus Management*

Consider a negotiation between labor and management over a work contract, where the fundamental objectives of both labor and management have been carefully identified. Suppose, for example, that labor has fundamental objectives concerning the economic well-being of its members, the stability of their lives, and the safety of the workplace. Issues may include the term of the contract, the beginning salary for new workers, the base pay of journeymen, pay increases over the lifetime of the contract, the health benefits package, time off for maternity leave, the safety of some equipment, and so forth. Clearly, many of the issues affect each of the three fundamental objectives. As an example, the reason to care about the health care package is that a better package (1) covers more medical expenses and therefore improves economic well-being, (2) makes a significant illness or injury less likely to bankrupt a family and produce instability, and (3) allows workers more time to recover from injuries and thus reduces the likelihood of reinjury upon return to work.

Suppose that utility functions u_L and u_M are assessed for labor and management respectively, scaled each from 0 to 100. The expected utility of an alternative A to labor and management can be denoted as $u_L(A)$ and $u_M(A)$. Finally, suppose that the BATNA values for each party have been calculated as

$$u_L(\text{BATNA}) = 20 \quad \text{and} \quad u_M(\text{BATNA}) = 30. \quad (8.1)$$

As indicated in Figure 8.2, there are presumably alternatives such as D,

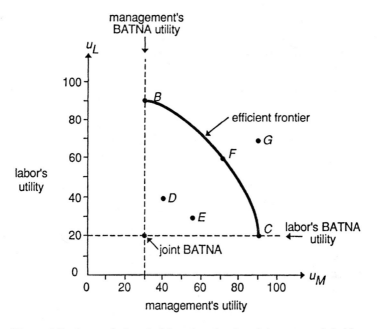

Figure 8.2. A negotiation decision situation involving two stakeholders

E, F, and G that would be preferable to both labor and management relative to their respective BATNAs. The trick is to find them. ∎

Using Other Stakeholders' Issues

It is important to identify potential issues for the other stakeholders in a negotiation based on their fundamental objectives. There is likely to be less uncertainty about their fundamental objectives, which are relatively stable over time, than about the issues they will raise. From their value structure, you may be able to infer the value they assign to different resolutions of the issues.

Even if you do not care directly about the resolution of an issue that concerns another stakeholder, you should care indirectly. If an issue matters to another stakeholder, you should be able to negotiate a gain with respect to an issue that you do care about when you yield on the issue in question. In short, an issue of relevance to another stakeholder should be of relevance to you. Giving up something that is not important to you in exchange for something else that is important is naturally a desirable trade. The identification of such alternatives is akin to the notion of empathetic negotiation discussed in Section 9.6.

Issues of style may be as important as those of substance. Being gracious on issues of style may in fact yield significant benefits on issues of substance. For example, a fundamental objective of many negotiators may be to be treated with decency and respect. You may give up little to conform to this objective and, as a quid pro quo, you may gain on the substantive issues. And in addition, treating others with decency and respect may be one of your own fundamental objectives.

Using the Efficient Frontier

Experience indicates that in negotiations stakeholders often end up agreeing on alternatives that are inferior to others in the range of possibilities. That is, other alternatives exist, but are apparently not found, that are preferable for all of the stakeholders. For example, the stakeholders may fail to reach an agreement and end up with the joint BATNA consequence in Figure 8.2 rather than agree on an alternative D, or they may end up with D when an alternative F was possible. To help create alternatives in this situation, analysis as outlined in Raiffa (1982) can be used to construct what is called the efficient frontier in Figure 8.2. Each consequence on this frontier is reachable by some negotiated agreement, and each consequence is such that within the decision context of the negotiations the value to one stakeholder cannot be improved without adversely affecting the value to some other stakeholder. Such analysis may be used before any negotiated agreement or in possible postsettlement negotiations (see Raiffa, 1985).

It may be possible to go beyond the efficient frontier, as illustrated by alternative G in Figure 8.2, but this is likely to require an expansion of the decision context for the negotiations. The ideas for expanding the decision context may be found in the stakeholders' fundamental objectives or strategic objectives. Any stakeholder may be able to identify such a situation as a decision opportunity; this is the topic of Chapter 9.

CHAPTER 9

Identifying Decision Opportunities

Decisionmakers usually think of decision situations as problems to be solved, not as opportunities to be taken advantage of. It is perhaps not surprising that decisionmakers do not systematically hunt for decision situations. Who needs yet another problem? One of the main ideas of this book is that perhaps you do need another "problem"; that a decision problem may not be a problem at all but an opportunity. A decision opportunity may alleviate some decision problems or perhaps allow you to avoid many future problems. In this sense, recognizing and following up on decision opportunities is analogous to prevention, whereas dealing with decision problems is analogous to cure.

There are at least two reasons why decision opportunities are not routinely identified. One reason is that many decisionmakers are not aware that identifying decision opportunities is an activity to which time should be allocated. If you are from the school that says the squeaky wheel gets oiled, you spend your time on decision problems; they squeak. Decision opportunities do not squeak. If you spend your time fighting fires, you fight decision problems. Decision opportunities require no fighting. In order to find decision opportunities, you must first realize that you should be looking for them.

The second reason decision opportunities are not readily pursued is that there are few, if any, guidelines for identifying them. Whereas decision problems are often thrust upon you by situations beyond your control, you must identify and explore your decision opportunities. One of the big differences between decision problems and decision opportunities is that you always know when you face a decision problem but you do not necessarily know when a significant decision opportunity exists.

Actions initiated by others will not inform you of a decision opportunity. Identifying a decision opportunity requires your own effort.

The identification of decision opportunities and the creation of alternatives for them are complementary activities. They often occur simultaneously because they involve the same type of thought process. The initial thought is often "I wish that . . ." or "We should . . ." The wishes focus on consequences and the shoulds focus on alternatives, but both clearly suggest that a decision opportunity should be formulated. One another relationship is worth noting: one generic alternative in a specific decision situation is to recognize a decision opportunity to change to a more advantageous decision context.

9.1 Use of Strategic Objectives

The strategic objectives of an organization or an individual are the foundation from which decision opportunities can be identified. But how many individuals or organizations have written down their strategic objectives? How many have even carefully thought about them? In how many organizations do the employees know and understand the organization's strategic objectives? The answer to all three questions is "very few." The chance to state and clarify these strategic objectives is itself a decision opportunity. One case where this decision opportunity was exploited involved the British Columbia Hydro and Power Authority (see Chapter 12).

It may seem as if, once you decide to express your strategic objectives, then you just do it. But in fact there are numerous alternatives for expressing strategic objectives. For an individual or organization, you have choices about how thoroughly to search your values. You certainly want to list the objectives. The next decision is whether to develop attributes for these objectives or specify their meaning in more detail. If you do specify in more detail (and such specification is usually worthwhile), you must decide how far to specify. And at each lower level in the objectives hierarchy you again need to decide whether to develop attributes.

There are also several decisions about quantifying the objectives. A prioritization of the objectives may be a first-cut quantification that yields useful value information but does not overburden those supplying the values. For such a prioritization, it is necessary to know ranges for the achievement of the objectives, but attributes need not be specified.

It may be appropriate to construct a complete value model that integrates all the strategic objectives. This is particularly helpful in an organization where over time a large number of people will make decisions affecting achievement of objectives. The value model indicates all that is of ultimate interest in the organization.

In the construction of a value model for an organization, alternatives concern who should be involved in the construction process. It may be useful to have broad participation in the first step, the identification of the strategic objectives. A working group may integrate all the suggested objectives into a preliminary strategic objectives hierarchy. Many of the objectives suggested may not show up in the preliminary hierarchy; these are likely to be means objectives to the achievement of the strategic objectives. The working group may also be responsible for developing preliminary attributes for each of the strategic objectives.

At this stage, the structure of the value model should be reviewed by upper management as well as a broad cross-section of employees. After appropriate revisions, upper management may prioritize the objectives and express the value tradeoffs and risk attitudes necessary to completely quantify the objectives. Finally, there may be a period of review and revision.

Using a Strategic Objective

The decisionmaker should develop specific procedures to initiate the search for decision opportunities. Some of these procedures should be independent of decision situations currently being addressed. For example, it may be useful to set up a procedure of seeking potential decision opportunities on the first day of every month. To put this procedure into operation the decisionmaker should initially identify and structure its strategic objectives. Then each month the decisionmaker should verify that the strategic objectives are appropriate and make any necessary changes. There should usually be no changes. Then the decisionmaker should use each strategic objective to help think of decision opportunities to do things better.

▪ *Recreational Opportunities*
Suppose that one strategic objective of the California Parks Department is to provide outdoor recreational areas. These areas are meant to serve both current residents and future generations. Looking toward the future, a decision opportunity may be to identify properties that should be reserved now for future use and mechanisms to reserve them. Parts

of alternatives to consider may include developing an inventory of all possible park lands in the state, listing obstacles to reserving each of these for park use, and ranking the value of each property for recreational use. ■

The general idea is very simple. For each stated strategic objective, such as "provide outdoor recreational areas for future generations," ask if decision opportunities should be pursued either to achieve the objective or to achieve it better.

Using a Means Objective

Once strategic objectives are specified, it may be desirable to think of means for achieving them. An important case can be illustrated by the following situation.

■ *Reentering the Workforce*
Victoria Nabors is a 36-year-old woman who has not worked outside her home since soon after she graduated from college. Her two children are now 10 and 12 years old, and she wishes to do something different. This wish naturally suggests the question of what to do. Victoria has spent some time structuring her strategic objectives. One of these objectives is to improve her self-esteem and another is to use and improve her knowledge. A means objective to each of these is to develop and pursue enjoyable relationships with adults. Spending time working as a professional would help. With a college degree in sociology, she believes she could work in advertising, marketing, or public relations. Thinking further, she realizes that a means objective to working as a professional is to improve her education.

This means objective triggers a decision opportunity. What alternatives should Victoria consider to improve her education, and what are her objectives in that pursuit? Objectives may be learning useful tools for a job, gaining information about what jobs to go after, and increasing her attractiveness to prospective employers. The cost and time of getting that additional education are also relevant. Alternatives include various night school options, working in a voluntary organization to gain experience, accepting a lower-level position in a field with advancement opportunities, and entering a master's degree program. ■

Each means objective to achieve one or more of the strategic objectives defines a decision opportunity. The decision context is essentially framed by the means objective. Alternatives are identified by answers to the question of how this means objective can be achieved. The strategic objectives are the fundamental objectives of the decision context.

Using Value Tradeoffs

Major service organizations have strategic objectives concerning both service and profits, if they are a private organization, or costs, if they are a governmental organization. Each organization must make tradeoffs between these objectives. Many individuals have strategic objectives that concern both their physical well-being and their economic well-being. One manifestation of this is that they sometimes must make decisions that involve tradeoffs between risks to their lives and economic costs. The value tradeoffs necessary in such decision situations may suggest other decision opportunities.

▪ *Bank Teller Machines*

Southwest Bank has strategic objectives concerning service and profitability. It specifies its service objectives into categories, one of which deals with service at automatic teller machines. This objective is measured by the attribute defined as the average wait for service at an automatic teller. In assessing the value tradeoff between waiting time at automatic tellers and profits, Louise Nance, the Director of Customer Service at Southwest Bank, evaluates a one-minute average reduction of waiting time per customer over the period of a year as worth $12 million. If each of 3,000 automatic tellers serves 100 people a day, a minute saved per transaction saves 1.8 million customer hours per year, which evaluates an hour of customer time at about $6.70.

This tradeoff suggests that decision opportunities may exist to improve service. Several things first need to be done. One is to collect data on current waiting times. Obviously, this should concentrate on busy machines. Alternatives ranging from adding more machines with full features, adding machines with some "fast" features such as cash withdrawal, speeding up transaction time, and spreading transactions over time may be fruitful. Regarding the last set of alternatives, suppose the most serious delays occurred between 11 A.M. and 6 P.M. To encourage customers to use the machines at other times of day, the bank might offer a lottery for off-peak transactions that would add, say, $1000 to the winner's account. ▪

9.2 Use of Resources Available

Decisions involve making a commitment of resources to achieve a purpose. These resources are typically money, time, skills (mental, physical, artistic), and others such as land, forests, and water rights. The availability of these resources to commit to a decision is a basis for developing decision opportunities.

The general question you ask to develop a decision opportunity from resources is what you might do with these resources to achieve some of your objectives. These objectives may be strategic objectives, means objectives, or fundamental objectives in a specified context.

The Resource Inventory

Suppose you are pondering what you might do that would really make a difference in achieving some of your important objectives. One useful place to start would be to make a resource inventory—a complete list of all resources that could be committed. You could follow this by asking how you might use each of those resources to support alternatives. These activities would provide the basic information to characterize a decision opportunity. Let me suggest a simple example.

■ *Summer Employment*
At the end of the first semester of her junior year as a geology major at the University of California at Los Angeles, Tina Eastman started thinking about how she could earn some money over the summer for her senior year. The jobs she had held the past two summers, as a lifeguard at a swimming pool and as an aide in an insurance office, did not seem exciting or worthwhile. Tina recognized that she might end up with such a job, but she wanted at least to think about more interesting possibilities. To help her think, she decided to inventory her resources.

The time and money resources were easy. She had three months of time and essentially no money. But she checked with the UCLA financial office and found that she qualified for a scholarship for her senior year. Next, she thought about her skills. She had done very well in her classes and felt that she knew more about geology than most of her classmates. She was particularly interested in geology in the field, and had taken two elective courses in such work. Also, she had affiliated herself with the Los Angeles chapter of the American Geological Society and had attended many of their monthly meetings. She was one of only three students who regularly attended.

It seemed a little more difficult to tally up her "personal" resources, but she was well-liked by others, found it easy to work as part of a team, and was physically strong. She also spoke Spanish well. With these resources, how could she create a desirable offer of summer employment in geology?

Tina knew faculty members in geology at UCLA, many professionals who regularly attended the local geological society meetings, and some of the people who had presented seminars at those meetings. She decided to talk with the professors about summer opportunities early, before other students started thinking of summer, and to talk to people at the next geological society meeting. Then a thought hit. Perhaps she could give a short presentation at the meeting; then she could talk to everyone there. She had never heard a student talk at such a meeting, but people there always seemed interested in her opinions about the UCLA program and in a student's perspective on a career in geology. So she called the chairperson of the local society and asked if she could give a ten-minute presentation at the next meeting after the main speaker was finished, for anyone who would like to stay. The chairperson said "Absolutely not." Instead, he suggested that Tina speak for ten minutes *before* the main speaker.

Tina was delighted, excited, and a little scared. She prepared and practiced that talk and delivered it to approximately fifty people in late January. She mentioned at the end of her presentation that she hoped to spend the summer working on an important geological problem or problems. By mid-February, five people had contacted her about summer jobs in geology and she already had three offers. One involved a month at a geological field site not far from Quito, Ecuador, with good pay. You know what Tina chose. ■

Check before You Commit

Just before making a decision, you have a good idea of what resources will be needed to implement the alternative you are about to choose. At this stage, it is useful to reflect on whether there are better ways to use the same resources to achieve either the same objectives or broader objectives.

■ *Retail Development*
Consider a problem faced by Mirchandanis, the largest retail store in downtown Tucson, Arizona. Tucson had expanded rapidly in the past two decades and shopping malls had spread around the area as rapidly.

Mirchandanis had opened two anchor stores in malls, but still seemed to be losing some of its customers and market share to a smaller local rival and a major national chain. They had studied the Tucson area carefully for a location for a fourth store that was to become their flagship store. The study was completed and the best alternative, among those they had considered, was clear. The new store should be built in a rapidly growing affluent area of Tucson. The alternative appeared to be a good one, but Mirchandanis executives suspected that something else might be better, especially since so many of the company's resources would have to be committed to make the new store, as proposed, a reality.

This is precisely where decision opportunities should be identified. What types of decision situations should be considered? To pursue the same objectives of regaining customers and market share, other possible alternatives might involve upgrading existing stores, building additional stores in the Tucson area that would not be flagship stores, and changing products or methods of doing business. For the broader objective of maximizing profit, other alternatives might be opening a store in the Phoenix area, negotiating with manufacturers to create a store brand, or acquiring some small manufacturing businesses that might complement the existing stores. ▪

The general idea here is simple. At some time in considering serious decisions, you need to focus on an existing set of alternatives. You are not sure exactly how good these alternatives are, although in selecting them you made many implicit judgments about how good they are. After careful appraisal, you have a much better idea about how good the best alternative is and about the resources needed to implement it. With this additional knowledge, ask the question of whether there is a better way to use the resources before you allocate them to the best of the already-identified alternatives.

Add-on Decision Opportunities

Once you have decided to use certain resources to pursue a specific alternative, you may be able to identify an add-on decision opportunity. Ask yourself whether any additional unrelated alternative is worth pursuing for a small increase in the resources required. The idea is that the unrelated alternative may be able to share the resources necessary to implement the first alternative. As a simple illustration, if you are using time and money for a business trip with a specific purpose, ask yourself whether there are other things you can accomplish on the trip for very little additional time or money.

Many people naturally think about add-on decision opportunities in situations like the one of the business trip. It is like following the old adage of trying to kill two birds with one stone. It is worthwhile to think explicitly of decision opportunities that might be added to *any* commitment of resources, because some of these opportunities may not come to mind so naturally. If the housing authority in a metropolitan area is spending millions of dollars trying to make public housing projects safe and available for homeless American families, should they consider spending thousands to catch and convict drug dealers operating in those projects and to evict illegal aliens living there? With every commitment of resources, there may be add-on decision opportunities that allow the decisionmaker to take additional advantage of those resources.

9.3 A Broader Decision Context

A decision opportunity can come to mind as a result of thinking about a particular decision problem. Much of the thought about decision problems focuses on the evaluation of existing alternatives. Sometimes that thinking may be about creating alternatives in the given decision context. Exploring whether a broader decision context is appropriate can open up decision opportunities.

I have already given several examples in which broadening the decision context suggested decision opportunities. In Section 9.2, Mirchandanis was considering alternatives in the decision context of regaining customers and market share. Broadening the decision context to the maximization of company profits suggested decision opportunities that had not previously been considered.

Air pollution problems are often framed as a need to reduce air pollutant emissions. In 1989 the Los Angeles Air Pollution Control District passed regulations requiring emission reductions the implementation of which cost approximately $9 billion annually (see Section 11.4). A broader decision context for air pollution is to reduce pollutant concentrations. Decisions that affect the time and location of pollutant emissions are additional candidates in the new context of this decision opportunity. A still broader decision context is to minimize health effects from air pollution. In the context of this decision opportunity, alternatives that change people's exercise habits during episodes of high pollution are legitimate candidates along with all alternatives that affect either pollutant emissions or concentrations. More exotic alternatives might be to develop an air pollutant vaccine that would make people immune to air pollution, to develop better cures for diseases aggravated by air pollution, or to address the health implications of indoor air pollution, which seems to be responsible for more than half of the health effects due to air pollution.

To develop a broader decision context from a given decision problem, you first need to identify the fundamental objectives that characterize the decision context. Then you try to move from these fundamental objectives toward the strategic objectives using a means-ends logic. Independent of the current decision context, you ask why each of the stated fundamental objectives is important. Usually the responses do not require difficult thinking. Pollution emissions lead to pollutant concentrations which lead to exposure for individuals and environments and to health and environmental consequences. In the Mirchandanis retail business, greater market share and more customers lead to greater profits. Pushing this means-ends logic is a worthwhile endeavor.

■ *Fulfilling Responsibilities*

Many people in research and development organizations frame one of their decisions as how to fulfill responsibilities to the organization. Suppose your boss suggests tasks and you have the responsibility to accept "enough of them." Some of the tasks are uninteresting and unrewarding, and you would rather not do them. This defines your decision opportunity: how to contribute and yet avoid getting stuck with the undesirable work and even avoid being asked to do it.

You are probably able to develop a long list of potential work useful to your organization. Now, proactively, take your pick of this work. Discuss your choices and reasons for them with your boss. Indicate what the boss and the organization will get out of agreeing to your choices. You will probably get credit for being proactive, knowledgeable, and willing to contribute. Someone else will end up with the undesirable work. ■

9.4 Monitoring Achievement

Monitoring the level of achievement of objectives, or monitoring performance as others might prefer to say, is a common activity of sophisticated decisionmakers. In some sense, the decisions made steer the decisionmaker through life and the consequences, with their associated value, accrue along the way. Monitoring the level of achievement over time can be a key to identifying a decision opportunity. This monitoring to identify decision opportunities is analogous in spirit to monitoring physical health to identify potential medical problems.

Use of Indices

Many organizations use indices as measures of achievement. We find out about unemployment and inflation from the federal government, budget status (deficit or surplus) and backlog of court cases from state and local governments, mortality rates from the Center for Disease Control, and achievement test score averages from schools. With each of these indices, we have a concept of what is good performance and what is bad. Annual inflation of 2 percent is good and 12 percent is bad; a billion-dollar deficit in Massachusetts is bad and a small surplus is good. There are also, not surprisingly, in-betweens.

The level of performance on indices can suggest decision opportunities. If performance is bad, clearly you should define a decision opportunity and figure out what to do to improve matters. But, if performance is so-so or good, you still may want to define a decision opportunity to see if you could do better.

Firms also have many indices that can be used in the same way. Firms often track sales, profits, market share, annual changes in profit levels, price of their stock, and so forth. Performance with respect to any of these indices can be used to suggest a decision opportunity.

Individuals and families typically do not have personal indices to track. Perhaps they should. Maybe they should investigate the decision opportunity to create and track personal indices or not, and if so, what indices. It is an issue worthy of thought.

Avoiding the Waste of Resources

We have all put resources into activities that did not turn out to be worth it. Almost by definition, we wish to avoid decisions that are not worth the resources they require. It is worth remarking, though, that if every decision you ever make turns out to be worth it, then probably you are not pursuing challenging enough or risky enough decisions. But that is not the main point here, let me return to resources wasted.

How many times have you made a commitment of your time and

resources to someone asking for them over the telephone, and then hung up with "Why did I do that" echoing in your mind? You agreed to do something and then wished you had not. Many busy people feel they say yes to too many requests.

▪ *Saying No*

There are nice people in all fields of expertise who have a hard time saying no. After all, the causes are all good. The main resource being wasted is time, and the implications are that more useful things get delayed or even missed. If you are one of these people, you need to address the decision opportunity of "how to say no." If you think hard about this, you will no doubt come up with your own suggestions. Some alternatives include asking why the particular activity is occurring. Also, if the organizers of a conference want you to speak, why do they need you? Ask who else is coming. Ask what the product of the activity is to be. Ask what the person asking you to attend will contribute. All of these questions serve multiple purposes. The responses may help you decide whether you wish to say yes or no. Often, you get "I don't know" or "I'm not sure" responses. If you are being asked to provide, say, one to ten days of your time, shouldn't the requester have thought a little more about it? Keeping this in mind makes it easier to say "I'd need to know more about it before I could make a commitment." The questions also buy you time to think about whether you want to say yes. ▪

Decision Opportunities for Repeated Decisions

In some circumstances, it is generally understood that the appropriate decision when you are doing something just once is different from the decision you should make if you do this thing many times. The best-known cases concern decisions involving financial risks. An insurance company can reasonably choose to insure thousands of similar risks, whereas the individual policy-holders should not insure themselves. It may be reasonable for a gambler to bet one or even several times at a roulette table, but it does not follow that to play a million times is reasonable. It is often worthwhile to explicitly address the policy decision in such situations.

▪ *Airline Check-In*

Consider a trivial example. Suppose you have never missed a scheduled airline flight in over 1,000 flights. Then you have probably waited more than 1000 hours in the real exciting environments of airport terminals.

If you had arrived an average of half an hour later for each flight you would have spent only 500 hours in these terminals, and perhaps you would have missed one flight. Saving three solid weeks of time in return for missing one flight seems like a bargain, especially when missing a flight typically means a delay of only one to six hours.

Monitoring the performance of the repeated decisions to arrive at an airport on time suggests that it is worthwhile to define a decision opportunity of deciding on a policy for leaving to the airport. Simple alternatives would be to leave a fixed time before the scheduled departure. More involved alternatives would consider expected travel time to the airport and the seriousness of being late for the plane. Policy alternatives might also depend on the importance of what else you could do with the time if you did not leave for the airport at a given interval before the scheduled flight time. ■

■ *Responding to Proposals*

Many technical consulting firms spend a great deal of professionals' time and firm resources writing proposals to get work. These proposals may go to branches of government or to other firms. Often, decisions about whether to bid on a request for proposal (RFP) are made in a decentralized fashion throughout the firm. At higher levels in the firm, there are objectives concerning profitability. A means objective that contributes to profitability concerns the "billable time" of the professional staff. Writing proposals does not produce billable time, although winning the bid with the proposal does.

Management should monitor the time spent on writing proposals. If it gets too high, there is a decision opportunity to examine the situation. Perhaps a policy is needed to help select RFPs on which to bid. The firm might gather data on the features of the RFPs and the proposals that would make future proposals more likely to be accepted. Management might ask those making proposals to assess the resources likely to be needed to write the proposal, the likelihood of acceptance, and the funds likely to be associated with receiving the bid. This information might be useful for setting policy guidelines for whether or not to bid on specific RFPs in the future. ■

Using Expectations

By definition, all decision situations eventually have at least two alternatives. At the time you decide to commit resources to what you consider to be the best alternative, you have both an expectation of how good that alternative is and some idea of how good the next best alternative is. At a minimum, you have a sense of how good some alternative like the status quo or the "do nothing" alternative is. Your expectations about how good the various alternatives are can help you identify decision opportunities. As you begin pursuing the alternative initially chosen, you understand its implications better and better. If your expectations drop sufficiently, this may signal the need to look at decision opportunities.

■ *Animal Vaccine*

Suppose that Animal Biotech, Inc., of Calgary, Alberta, has discovered and developed a vaccine that will eliminate the problem of *Trichinella* in pigs and swine. The product is in the final stages of regulatory approval in both Canada and the United States. Rob Daniels, the founder and main shareholder of Animal Biotech, wants to have access to the European market. He commissions a study to identify European firms that might market ABI's product in the countries of the European Community (EC). A French firm in Lyon is chosen as the best candidate. The second-best candidate is located in the Danish city of Odense.

Negotiations begin with the French firm. ABI's interests include the time needed to get regulatory approval to use the product in the EC, the level of sales expected after one year and five years, the final arrangements of any agreement, and ABI's freedom to pursue other options if performance turns out to be poor. All of these concerns are related to the bottom line of profits. Daniels believes that the introduction to the European market should take no more than one year, profits one year later should be $1 million Canadian, and profits five years later should be about $25 million.

After three months of rather intense interaction, the negotiations are not progressing well, and Daniels's perception of the benefits of continuing to negotiate with the French firm has dropped considerably. Indeed, they are now far below his original expectations of benefits from negotiating with the Danish firm, even delaying those benefits by three months. In fact, they are only marginally better than what Daniels has calculated that ABI could achieve without a European partner.

These circumstances clearly suggest a decision opportunity. What should Animal Biotech do to take advantage of the European market? Going it alone and negotiating with the Danish firm are clearly candidates. Others include affiliating with either a Canadian or a U.S. firm with good access to the European market. Another alternative is to create a new firm, perhaps with venture capital funds, to be primarily registered in an EC country, to sell ABI's products and related products. Finally, looking for European partners outside the EC countries may be fruitful. Sweden, Switzerland, Austria, and Hungary, for example, may be useful places to look for partners. ∎

9.5 Establishing a Process

You do not need to create all of your decision opportunities for yourself. Rather, you can establish processes by which others will create decision opportunities for you. As a simple example, you may ask someone whose judgment you respect something like "What should I be achieving or doing that I am not?" This may be totally open or constrained. For example, you may add "with respect to my career" or "in my personal life" to the question. Often, it takes some prodding to get revealing responses, so do the prodding.

∎ *Environmental Issues*
Suppose Chuck Brown is the director of environmental affairs for the Intermountain Utility Company, headquartered in Denver. He is attending the annual conference for those concerned with utility companies and the environment. His peers from other utilities are there, as well as representatives of environmental groups such as the Sierra Club and Friends of the Earth. Chuck may ask them what issues utility companies should be addressing that they are not currently considering. Responses of people from Florida about their current problems may be directly relevant or have analogues in the Rocky Mountains. The perspectives of environmentalists may be different from Chuck's perspectives, but their thoughts may help define decision opportunities. ∎

The indirect use of process requires that you position yourself so that you will be more likely to discover decision opportunities. That is perhaps part of why job-seekers migrate to the city, first-rate universities have an abundance of applicants, and companies locate near potential customers.

∎ *Independent Consultant*
Consider the case of Ted Winter, an independent consultant. Although Winter was known to a few people for his ability to perform difficult tasks, his skills were not generally known. Consequently, he was not

getting as many opportunities to do things and contribute as he hoped for. Somehow, Winter needed to find ways to create decision opportunities. What he decided to do was to publish his ideas in the technical literature. This required that he improve his ability to express himself in writing. This process took considerable time and effort, but is paying off. Now, more people are familiar with Winter's ideas through his publications than through direct contact. Opportunities have come from many organizations, both private and public, for lecturing and consultation. Each such opportunity is a decision opportunity to say yes or no. ∎

9.6 Negotiating for Your Side and for the Other Side

In a common class of decision opportunities, a stakeholder wishes to have a certain alternative selected, but a different stakeholder has the power to make the decision. An employee wants a boss to agree to a leave of absence, a firm wants its proposal to supply a product to another firm accepted, a government wants another government to sign an agreement, and so on.

Suppose you are the stakeholder who wants a particular alternative selected by another stakeholder. You should recognize your decision opportunity to take control of the decision situation. Rather than simply allow the other stakeholder to make a choice that may not be the one you desire, you should create alternatives that modify your desired alternative so that it maintains its essential features for you and is better than the current situation for the stakeholder whose decision is required.

∎ Leave of Absence

Suppose you want a two-month leave of absence which can only be granted by your boss. For granting this absence, your boss is the decisionmaker and you are the stakeholder. When you first think of a leave, your boss is probably not even aware that this decision is one she may face. You are the decisionmaker in a different decision situation, namely the decision opportunity concerning how to increase the chances that your leave will be granted. Your boss is the stakeholder in this decision. What you want to do is create a deal, including a leave for you, that your boss cannot possibly refuse.

One alternative is just to ask for a leave. Your boss may approve it or not. To improve your chances of getting the leave, you should consider what reasons the boss may have for refusing your request. Your absence would load more work on her, might cause hassle for her with her boss (who might object to her approval of your leave), and would probably cause some temporary disarray in the department. Studying these reasons, you may recognize your boss's more fundamental objectives, such as increased sales, increased profits, and a need to make an important go/no-go decision on a proposed product next year. The latter may be key to your boss's promotion and to her boss's status too. You now need to create some alternatives that will have positive effects on these three fundamental objectives that outweigh the negative influence of your desired leave. For example, you might volunteer to head a special task force to reduce production costs when you return, in addition to your normal duties, or to accept a temporary assignment to analyze the go/no-go options. Such a suggestion may make your leave sound like a bargain to your boss and one she could clearly justify to her boss. ■

The essential features of this class of decisions are illustrated in Figure 9.1. Let $U_Y(A)$ indicate the utility to you of any alternative A,

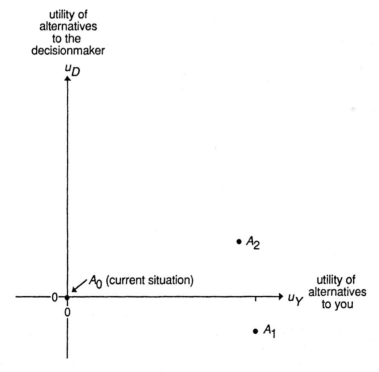

Figure 9.1. A representation of empathetic win-win negotiations

and let $U_D(A)$ indicate the utility of that alternative to the original decisionmaker. For convenience, let us set the utilities of the current situation, represented by A_0, as

$$U_Y(A_0) = 0 \quad \text{and} \quad U_D(A_0) = 0. \tag{9.1}$$

You think of an alternative A_1 that is much better for you than A_0. We indicate this by

$$U_Y(A_1) >> 0. \tag{9.2}$$

The problem is that A_1 is not as desirable as A_0 to the decisionmaker, so

$$U_D(A_1) < 0. \tag{9.3}$$

Consequently, the decisionmaker will not be inclined to choose A_1 over the current situation A_0. You understand the relative desirabilities of A_0 and A_1 to yourself and to the decisionmaker. The decisionmaker does not yet realize that you are thinking about A_1. What you need to do is create an alternative, such as A_2 in Figure 9.1, that keeps the very desirable features of A_1 for yourself and is more desirable than A_0 to the decisionmaker. Then you present A_2 to the decisionmaker. Upon comparing A_2 to her status quo A_0, the decisionmaker should select A_2, which essentially provides you with what you want. Both parties win.

The key to "solving" a problem of this nature is to view it from the perspective of the other stakeholder, meaning the decisionmaker. First structure her values as much as possible. Indeed, she should have little objection to your efforts in this regard, as she may end up better off as a result. In this process, begin by identifying the negative impacts of your desired alternative relative to the status quo in terms of her values. These impacts probably affect the means objectives. Follow their implications through a means-ends objectives network to the fundamental objectives of the stakeholder. Now you should be able to create modified alternatives that can at least improve matters in terms of these objectives while maintaining the key consequences desired by you. And in many cases the improvement can render the modified alternatives better than the status quo to the other stakeholder. It is worth noting that the strategic objectives of a stakeholder whose decision is needed are likely to be much broader than the set of fundamental objectives influenced by your desired alternative. Thus, an alternative distinct from the original alternative may be used to "satisfy" a stakeholder when used in conjunction with the original alternative.

From your perspective, the decision alternatives include the status quo and any others you can create. From the perspective of the other stakeholder, the alternatives are the status quo and the alternative that you are suggesting. The problem may be characterized as an *empathetic negotiation*. You negotiate for the other side and make sure the other stakeholder gets enough to be willing to support your desired alternative, and you negotiate for your side as well. This situation may also be viewed as removing constraints to action. The interplay between the descriptive and prescriptive aspects of decisionmaking in empathetic negotiations is interesting. You are essentially using your description of another stakeholder's values as a basis for negotiating that stakeholder's position prescriptively. Also, you are trying to balance overall impacts to the other stakeholder and overall impacts to you in a manner that is prescriptively reasonable to you, and that the other stakeholder will view as descriptively fair and responsible. In simple terms, your goal is to create a win-win alternative.

▪ Data Transmission

Innerbelt Data Transmission was a new firm in the Washington, D.C., area that specialized in high-quality data transmission via fiber optic cables within the capital area. The CEO, Fred Meyer, had the idea of installing a transmission system within the Washington Metro. The lines could presumably be placed in service much more rapidly at a much cheaper cost than if the company had to build separate underground conduits. Furthermore, maintenance costs would be much lower. To implement this alternative, Meyer had to get the approval of the Metro Authority.

As a public agency, the Metro Authority had rather complex and political objectives. Naturally, one fundamental objective of interest was the revenue it would receive from Innerbelt. Another objective had to do with impacts on service. Specifically, Metro did not wish to allow anything that would have a negative impact on transportation service. Preliminary discussions also suggested two other fundamental objectives. It was important to Metro management to appear to be in control of the situation, and there could be no appearance that any shady backroom deals were a part of the agreement.

This information about objectives suggested several alternatives that Meyer felt would be acceptable. He had previously determined by a rather detailed study that his firm could save approximately $10 million of construction cost and $2 million annually of operating cost by using the Metro tunnels. In addition, they could begin operating the system much earlier. This indicated the range of revenues that could be paid to Metro that would be acceptable to Innerbelt. Regarding the disruption of service, Meyer was willing to construct the lines between 10 P.M. and 6 A.M., when there would essentially be no disruption. This would increase construction costs only by approximately 10 percent.

Regarding the need to be in control and avoid any hint of shady deals, Meyer had three suggestions. His preference was an agreement that the Metro Authority would be given a detailed timetable of proposed activities and a weekly one-page status report. If this was not enough to alleviate any political fears, a member of the Metro Authority management could sit in on all meetings with the contractor to look out for Metro's interests. Finally, as his third option but still acceptable, Meyer was willing to have the Metro Authority select an independent third party, at Innerbelt's expense, to monitor all of Innerbelt's progress.

Meyer contacted the Metro Authority to initiate formal discussions. In two short months, the contract giving Innerbelt access to the Metro tunnels was signed. There was a joint announcement at the Metro offices that stressed this was part of a new Metro effort to obtain revenue from external sources in order to maintain a high-quality transit service at reasonable cost. Both the Metro Authority and Innerbelt got a very good deal, as Meyer had designed. ■

In creating alternatives to get others to accept your desired decisions, it is useful to recognize that different stakeholders often have quite distinct lists of objectives. This means that you should be able to develop alternatives that better achieve the other stakeholders' objectives without hurting the achievement of yours by much. For instance, the Metro Authority in the previous example had the objective of minimizing disruption of transit service. Innerbelt did not have an "opposite" objective to maximize disruption of service. Therefore, minimizing transit disruption did not directly hurt Innerbelt. There were indirect implications in the form of increased construction costs, but they were not large in this case.

It is fair to note that sometimes there are also objectives on which better achievement by one stakeholder will definitely mean lesser achievement by another. Innerbelt wants to maximize profits and Metro Authority wants to maximize revenue from granting authority to use their tunnels. Even with naturally conflicting objectives, there is still plenty of potential for the stakeholder to gain the decisionmaker's cooperative decision by varying levels of achievement of these objectives. An increase in annual revenue paid to Metro from $1 million to $1.5 million would still be less than Innerbelt's annual savings from using the tunnels, and might be what would create a win-win situation.

Influencing the Other Stakeholder's Values

All of the discussion in this section has assumed that the stakeholders' values remain constant. Thus, a stakeholder must search for various alternatives in order to influence the value that will accrue to the other stakeholder. In some cases, it may be possible to frame a decision opportunity to change another stakeholder's values so that stakeholder will view a previously unacceptable alternative as acceptable.

■ *House Purchase*
Suppose you are prepared to buy a house for a price x that is less than the owner's asking price. The owner can accept this offer, refuse it, or make a counter-offer at price y, which may be the asking price. Suppose the owner refuses or counters with a price higher than x. You may feel that x is as much as you are willing to pay and that it is a fair price to the owner. You may also believe the owner will be better off accepting your offer. Maybe you can change his perceptions of the relative utilities of selling for x now and not selling. Issues that may influence his values may include the prices of comparable houses, the costs of owning a vacant house, and potential downturns in the housing market. From your perspective, you are trying to identify what you consider to be erroneous assumptions in the owner's thinking that have made him conclude that not selling for x is more desirable than selling for x. ■

You are not likely to be able to change the underlying strategic values of another stakeholder. But the values used by another in any specific decision context can be changed. These values should be based on the other's fundamental objectives for that decision context or, inappropriately, on more limited means objectives. In either case, the values will necessarily be based on the stakeholder's strategic values and on the stakeholder's understanding of the facts relating the objectives used in the specific decision context to the achievement of the strategic objectives. What you can influence is the stakeholder's understanding of the facts, which affects the values he or she uses in the specific decision context.

9.7 Being in the Right Place at the Right Time

A small company beat out several larger competitors for a lucrative contract. An attorney just made partner in a prestigious law firm at a record early age. A young professional moved to Atlanta four months ago and already has a few good friends. An obvious question to each is "No one else seems to do it, how did you?" The response is often "By being in the right place at the right time." At first glance, this doesn't seem like a useful answer. It is, though. It contains very sound advice for identifying decision opportunities. The implications are that (1) you should figure out the right place and be there instead of in the wrong place, and (2) you should be in the right place more often. Both increase your chances of finding good alternatives. Both points can be followed simultaneously.

Usually, of course, there is no single right place. There is a continuum, and some places are much better than others. If you are trying to meet interesting women, an aerobics class is probably better than a library reading room, which is probably better than a winter tour to Greenland. If you are trying to meet interesting men, a current events organization is probably better than a singles bar, which is probably better than solitary reading at home. It is also useful to recognize that you cannot control the right time; there is some randomness about it. Some times are better than others, though. Singles bars are not usually hopping at 10 A.M. and ski slopes are deserted at 11 P.M.

Creating the Right Place

Sometimes there doesn't seem to be a right place. This suggests the decision opportunity to create one.

■ *Advertising Council*
Strategic Advertising, a small, successful advertising firm in the San Francisco Bay area, had several clients and a staff of eighteen. What they did not have was a major corporate account. They knew they were

good at advertising. What they wanted was chances to pitch their services to major clients. From discussions with other small advertising firms, Strategic's founder, Alan Rosenstein, realized that none of these firms were getting such chances. They all essentially said "If we just had the chance, we would surely impress them and win some accounts."

This suggested a decision opportunity. The smaller firms needed to create their own chances. Rosenstein thought through the objectives of major corporations with respect to selecting advertising agencies. These objectives concerned good-quality advertising, timely service, and efficiency in the process of selecting agencies. Rosenstein felt that Strategic, as well as some of their same-sized competitors, could provide good-quality advertising and timely service. However, he had to admit it was not convenient for a major corporation to interview several small agencies in addition to larger ones.

After a little informal marketing research about how big corporations might respond to a new advertising institution and about what were considered the top small agencies in the Bay Area, Rosenstein invited executive officers of a few small agencies to a meeting. He proposed forming an organization that might be called the Bay Council of Small Advertising Agencies. This council would be composed of six firms. Its purposes would be to increase the opportunities of member firms to pitch their services to major businesses and to improve their likelihood of winning those accounts. Details were to be worked out over the first year of operation. At the beginning, the council would hope to receive an offer to send one member to bid for any large account. The council would help make the process efficient for the potential customer by screening its members to see who would present. It would enhance the likelihood of acceptance by sometimes assisting in presentation preparation and by forming possible joint efforts. ∎

Selecting the Right Time

We have all heard the adages "timing is essential" and "there is a time and a place for everything." In situations where timing matters, there is a decision opportunity to select or influence appropriate timing.

∎ *Graduate Research Support*

In graduate schools for technical education, many of the doctoral students are supported as research assistants. In the spring of each year there is a flurry to solidify the arrangements for the next fall. Faculty members push this because they wish to get the best available students if they know they will have funds to support them. Students push this because they do not want to be stuck without support. Because of this process, the better students tend to be committed for the next school year by the end of the spring term. Only the lesser-qualified students are still looking for fall support in the summer.

How can you, as a first-rate student, take advantage of this? It is rather easy: do not commit until late summer. The risk is not too great. First, being first-rate, you will certainly get *some* support. And making the best of a not-particularly-good situation is often better than accepting a good situation as defined by others. Many research assistants have the leeway to create alternatives using value-focused thinking as discussed in Chapter 7. More important, it is typically the case that many faculty members receive new or renewed research grants over the summer. Early in the fall, they will be looking for the best available assistants from a small pool that does not include most of the best. Your ability to pick an exciting research opportunity and mold it to match your interests will be greatly enhanced. It is a simple matter of demand and supply. A spring market with 100 positions and 140 students, 90 of whom are very good, is a much tougher situation than a fall market with 40 positions and 40 students of just acceptable quality. ■

Sometimes you have what you consider to be a great alternative (such as an idea or a product), but its time has not yet come. Your decision opportunity is to set up procedures to identify the right time when it does come. In addition, you can prepare the alternative so that you will be able to implement it quickly when the right time comes, and you can improve it while you wait, so that the right time will effectively be lengthened.

Being in the Right Place More Often

You can significantly increase your chances of having good things happen by more often being in the right place for such things to happen. First, however, you must recognize the decision opportunity and then create the alternatives to do this.

■ Meeting a Potential Mate

So you are interested in meeting someone. This is not an uncommon desire. What decisions can you make about it? There are plenty, all of them process alternatives. You could just wait for that special person to walk up and say "Here I am." It could happen, but the chances aren't good. Staying home and reading might work, but then you would only have contact with telephone callers and people who knocked at the door. And most of these people you would probably already know. You need to increase your chances.

You should probably consider doing things you like to do in places where other people, specifically potential mates, might go. Whether your interests take you to concerts, ski slopes, or professional meetings, those may be some of the right places. At least the other people there will share one of your interests. ▪

The more time you spend in a right place, the more likely it is that a good consequence will occur. Although the chances are usually low for any given time in the right place, you compound your chances by return visits. Consider a simple numerical example. If you like concerts, there may be a 2 percent chance of meeting someone special at any single concert. If this chance is the same for each concert, your chances increase to 65 percent by attending two concerts per week for a six-month period.

After you meet that special person, friends will ask, "How were you so lucky?" The answer will be obvious: "Just being in the right place at the right time."

9.8 When You Have No Idea about What to Do

When you have no idea what to do about some decision problem, you are in an ideal situation for identifying decision opportunities. This kind of situation is tailor-made for value-focused thinking. You can not possibly use alternative-focused thinking if you do not see any alternatives. At such a time you should identify and structure your objectives to define the decision opportunity and then create alternatives in the decision context of that opportunity.

▪ *Dissertation Topic*
One of the major hurdles for any doctoral student is selecting a dissertation topic. Many students search for a topic for a year or more and still find themselves in the position of having no good alternatives, but plenty of bad ones. If you are in such a situation, the decision problem is clear.

You need to identify and select a topic. The decision opportunity is perhaps not so clear. You can identify and develop alternatives to help you find a topic.

You may begin by writing down what you hope to achieve by completing your dissertation. One objective is to get the Ph.D., but since all dissertations contribute equally to this objective, it does not help you distinguish among topics. Other objectives may have to do with what opportunities the dissertation opens up for you. What jobs might it lead to? Will it facilitate an academic career? Will you be able to publish it? Will it make you a recognized authority on something that society values?

There are also objectives related to the process. Will the research be interesting? Do you wish to work with people (as subjects) or not? Do you want to do a lot of calculations? Should the dissertation be theoretical or applied? How long will it take to finish?

Collectively, these objectives should give you some insight about types of alternatives to follow to help find a dissertation topic. These alternatives include how you spend your time, to whom you talk, and what you read. You may consider working outside the university for a year and returning. In the course of pursuing these activities, you should identify candidate dissertation topics. The same objectives that assisted the search for possible topics should help you appraise those topics. ∎

■ *Unmanageable Risks*
Many executives feel that business is much riskier today than it used to be. They worry about rapid technological innovation, global competition, and many "nonbusiness" risks. Lawrence Winkler, the CEO of International Plastics, thought of the nonbusiness risks as unmanageable. They were less tangible and less understood than so-called business risks. Examples included possible sabotage, industrial espionage, political risks (such as expropriation of physical assets), loss of key personnel (because of kidnapping, drug use, or improper conduct), and implications of environmental risks such as global warming or a yet-to-be-discovered health risk of the manufacturing process. Winkler was stymied: What could be done to make some sense out of this mess and to make responsible decisions?

This situation clearly characterizes a decision opportunity: not just what to do about particular risks but how to identify risks of possible concern. For risks of such magnitude, the characterization of the decision context should begin with strategic objectives. Many means objectives should also be identified.

To identify potential risks, Winkler might request that a risk audit be performed. This would carefully appraise each of International's objectives and ask what events might affect the achievement of each. The risk audit would also go through lists of generic risks (such as political risks, obsolescence, curtailment of raw materials, changes in public tastes) that might affect performance. The intent would be to develop a comprehensive list of possible threatening risks. Next, it would be appropriate to screen those risks to identify the set that seemed to matter the most, and then to prioritize their significance to International Plastics. At this stage, Winkler's situation would be better framed. It may not be simple to decide how to manage particular risks, but it is a much better defined problem than trying to decide what risks should be considered for management. ∎

The general principle here is simple and important. Whenever you are in a very messy situation and do not know what to do or even what might be done, thinking about your values will definitely be effort well spent. By starting with values, you can identify decision opportunities where you should consider something to do. Then you can create alternatives for what to do, and finally you can evaluate the alternatives and act. Focusing first on your values, which are your reasons for caring what happens in the situation, will facilitate the creation of alternatives—and good ones—that make it much more likely that you will eventually get what you want.

CHAPTER **10**

Insights for the Decisionmaking Process

A deep and thorough understanding of the values inherent in a decision situation can provide important insights for all aspects of decisionmaking, and these insights make it possible to achieve much better consequences from the decisions we face. Better consequences occur because we create better alternatives and because we identify decision opportunities. This chapter focuses on how value-focused thinking can improve the process of decisionmaking. As indicated in Figure 10.1, improving the process has synergistic effects on the creation of alternatives and the identification of decision opportunities as well as direct effects for better consequences.

Value-focused thinking contributes to the decisionmaking process in the following ways:

guiding information collection;
evaluating alternatives;
interconnecting decisions;
improving communication;
facilitating involvement in multiple-stakeholder decisions;
guiding strategic thinking.

There is a significant amount of synergy among these aspects of decisionmaking. Better communication leads to better information collection, better evaluation of alternatives, and better involvement in multiple-stakeholder decisions. Better information leads to better evaluation of alternatives and better interconnection of decisions, as well as better

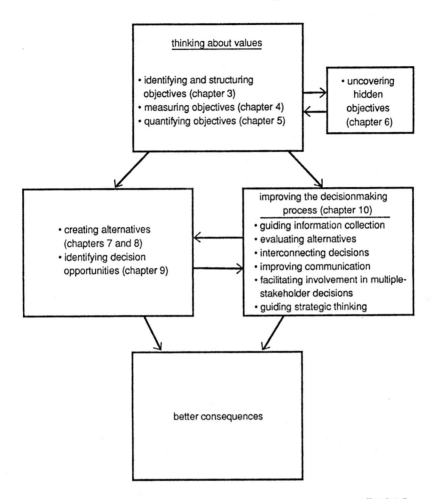

note: an arrow means "leads to"

*Figure 10.1. The influence of value-focused thinking
on the processes of decisionmaking*

recognition of decision opportunities. The recognition of decision opportunities helps guide strategic thinking. The desire to interconnect
decision problems guides strategic thinking, which in turn suggests better ways to interconnect decision problems. In short, when some of these
aspects of decisionmaking are managed well, it is easier to manage the
others well.

10.1 Guiding Information Collection

Information about values relevant to a given decision situation should be obtained early and thoroughly. At a minimum, you should carefully identify the fundamental objectives, structure them into a hierarchy, and develop a means-ends objectives network. It is also often useful to quantify the fundamental objectives with a value model, as discussed in Chapter 5.

An early effort to structure values is a very effective allocation of resources. For a given decision situation, you need to specify only one value model. But there are at least two alternatives and probably many more, so information about consequences is required for many alternatives. Collecting this information can be time-consuming and expensive. So can modeling the consequences of each alternative in terms of the fundamental objectives. A clear understanding of values helps you limit both of these tasks and allows a better allocation of effort.

An awareness of the significance of values to any decision situation can be of considerable use. Sometimes even a very cursory examination of values can produce key insights, as the following example indicates.

■ Air Quality Standards

The Environmental Protection Agency (EPA) has the responsibility for setting an ambient air quality standard for carbon monoxide (CO). Initial discussions with the EPA indicated that the key health effect thought to be related to CO exposure was heart attacks (see Keeney and Ozernoy, 1982). However, essentially all the data on the impacts of CO pertained to angina attacks and other health effects deemed to be less significant. Judgments obtained in a few minutes made it apparent that some individuals at EPA believed that the heart attack rate would be in the neighborhood of 5 percent of the angina attack rate and also that one heart attack was 1,000 times more important than one angina attack. Roughly speaking, this suggested that heart attacks were 50 times (5 percent of 1,000) more important than angina attacks for any proposed policy decision. Hence it seemed appropriate to seek out the best professional judgments available about the relationship of CO exposure to heart attack rates. There would naturally be uncertainties about this relationship, but not addressing the relationship would be tantamount to skipping the problem. A subsequent analysis quantified the judgments of several medical experts about the relationship between carbon monoxide exposure and heart attacks (Keeney, Sarin, and Winkler, 1984). ∎

The fundamental objectives and their associated attributes tell you exactly what information you want in order to analyze any alternative. You would like to know the likely impacts of the alternatives in terms of these attributes. In technical terms, you want a probability distribution for each alternative describing the possible impacts. Going further and quantifying values may be of additional help.

Once you have calculated the scaling constants for any utility function from the value tradeoffs, additional insights are available. For the ranges of the attributes thought to be reasonable for the problem, the scaling constants indicate where you should allocate the most effort. In simple terms, if the scaling constant for attribute X_1 is ten times as large as the scaling constant for attribute X_2 and if consequences probably go over the full range of each attribute, you should expend more effort on addressing attribute X_1.

When there are many alternatives, you can use value judgments to eliminate several of them before putting in too much time and effort collecting information. Suppose there are seven attributes and the combined weight of the first four scaling constants is 0.9 of the 1.0 of all seven scaling constants with an additive utility function. After collecting data for all alternatives on those four higher-weighted attributes, calculate their contribution to the utility of each alternative. Call the result the partial utility of the alternative. Now, suppose that alternative A has the highest partial utility which will be denoted $u'(A)$. Then any alternative with a partial utility less than $u'(A) - 0.1$ can be eliminated, since its total utility cannot be as high as that of A. In practice, since any model is not the real world, perhaps the cutoff should be 0.2 below the partial utility of alternative A. Additional data on eliminated alternatives need not be collected. As illustrated in Keeney (1980), this general principle can be useful in screening alternatives and can be used sequentially as data are collected for each attribute.

Sometimes the insights from the scaling constants indicate information that should be gathered rather than information that need not be. Consider the following example:

∎ *Plutonium Theft*
In a preliminary evaluation of different options to minimize the possible theft and misuse of plutonium, one attribute of six was the amount of

plutonium successfully stolen (see Keeney, 1977b). This attribute was a proxy attribute for the objective of minimizing the physical damage that might be done with such plutonium. The other problem attributes dealt more with the social and political implications of the policies aimed at reducing the likelihood of and the amount of any such theft. The initial utility assessments assigned more than 50 percent of the weight to the plutonium attribute given its perceived possible range. This indicated that a key part of the problem concerned what might be done with stolen plutonium. Hence it was appropriate to address this issue directly rather than simply include it as a big weight on the proxy attribute indicating the amount of plutonium stolen. ■

If you quantify the objectives with a utility function, then it is straightforward to calculate the value of obtaining any information in a given decision context (see Raiffa, 1968). If some information can be gathered for $70,000 and it is worth $240,000, then it will seem reasonable to collect it. In other situations, it may be difficult to determine the value of information, but insights about that value can still be obtained by using the value model, as the following example indicates.

■ *Salvage Rights*
New England Electric (NEE) was deciding whether to bid, and if so how much, for the salvage rights to a sunken ship, the S.S. *Kuniang* (Bell, 1984), in order to refurbish it and use it for hauling coal from Virginia to New England. The usefulness of the *Kuniang* depended on whether it was American made, as American ships had priority in docking at Virginia coal ports. Without this priority, the *Kuniang* would be practically useless to NEE.

The *Kuniang* had been built in Britain, but an 1852 law specified how to convert the ship to "American built": if repairs made in the United States were worth at least three times the salvage value of the ship, the *Kuniang* would be deemed American made. The U.S. Coast Guard had the responsibility for setting the salvage value. A major uncertainty was whether the salvage value would be set at the scrap value of the ship, which was less than $5 million, or at the value of the winning bid. The Coast Guard had announced that it would not specify the salvage value of the *Kuniang* until after the bids were submitted. Calculations indicated that NEE could bid up to $20 million and still get a fair return if the salvage value was set equal to the scrap value, whereas any bid over $8.75 million would not allow a fair return if the salvage value was set at the bid price. This difference was significant enough to suggest that some direct inquiry into what the Coast Guard might do would be worthwhile. ∎

10.2 Evaluating Alternatives

Value-focused thinking can lead to better models and to better analysis with those models. The fundamental objectives hierarchy defines the line to separate facts from values in an analysis and provides the foundation for a value model. The means-ends objectives network provides the elements and structure for a model to relate alternatives to their possible consequences.

∎ *Railroad Maintenance*
If the objectives of a railroad company for its track maintenance policies are to minimize train accidents and to minimize maintenance costs, how should the company decide whether over ten years one expected accident and a $30 million maintenance cost would be better than two expected accidents and a $15 million cost? The company executives would have to consider whether the damage of one additional accident would be worth $15 million. This indicates that the fundamental concern is not train accidents but "damage." Value-focused thinking would define the meaning of damage and promote modeling of the relationship between train accidents and damage however defined. ∎

A careful definition of fundamental objectives often indicates the relevance of indirect effects on consequences. Suppose it is discovered that some automobiles of a particular model and year have a defective part that can cause accidents. Should the automobiles in question be recalled to dealers to have the parts checked and any faulty ones replaced? Many people consider the "most important" objective in this decision is whether people will die as a result of the defective part. The obvious attribute might be the number of deaths caused by the defective part.

∎ *Automobile Recall*
Just such a decision problem occurred some years ago when there were about 5.3 million vehicles of a particular model on the road. Alerted to a possible defect in the rear axle, the National Highway Transportation Safety Administration (NHTSA) was considering a recall for inspection

and replacement if necessary. Careful analysis indicated that without a recall the expected number of future injuries due to the defect was at most 16. Some people concluded that the automobiles should obviously be recalled: 16 injuries due to the defect were 16 too many and 16 more than would occur if the recall went ahead. An insightful analysis by Lave (1983) showed that in the case of a recall more than 1.3 expected fatalities and 131 injuries were likely to occur while the 5.3 million cars were being driven to the dealers to have their rear axles examined. The NHTSA did not order a recall. ■

In this case it was important to sort out the issue of whether the objective should be to minimize deaths and injuries due to the axle defect or more generally to minimize deaths and injuries involving the particular model of automobile. If I owned the automobile, I would not want a recall; my chances of living would be better without it. I would, however, want the NHTSA to consider other alternatives such as communicating with owners and having dealers examine the axle the next time the car is in for servicing.

Thinking about the fundamental values relevant to decisions concerning automobile recall indicates the appropriateness of expanding the scope of consequences to include indirect effects. On the other hand, the means objectives indicate ways in which the scope of a problem could be limited if necessary for budget or time considerations or if appropriate on other logical grounds.

■ Global Warming

It may be extremely difficult to model the relationship between concentrations of greenhouse gases and resulting global climate changes. Even a substantial expenditure of both money and effort may not clarify this relationship sufficiently in the near future to make it useful in analysis. Thus, we might analyze only the part of the decision relating given alternatives to concentrations of greenhouse gases. Then, in any evaluation of alternatives we would need to address the relative desirability of the various greenhouse gas concentrations, and to do this would require an implicit consideration of the relationship between those concentrations and climate change. If this relationship is too difficult to model explicitly, it will also be very difficult to do implicitly in one's head, although if this could be done it would save considerable cost and effort. That tradeoff of cost and effort versus the quality of the resulting information and insight helps define an appropriate scope for any analysis. ■

The value model indicates which objectives are most important in a decision context. If there is an additive utility function over seven attributes and if scaling constants for three of these sum to 0.8, it is reasonable to conduct most of the sensitivity analysis over those three attributes. Factual judgments concerning relationships between different levels of the means objectives and their implications for the achievement of the fundamental objectives are also important. Sensitivity analysis may consider changes in any of these judgments to examine their effect on the relative desirability of the given alternatives.

After analysis and sensitivity analysis, it is worthwhile to consider a decision opportunity. Do not assume that the next step is to select the best alternative and implement it. Ask what alternatives are available other than selecting the best alternative and implementing it. Others include trying to create additional alternatives and gathering more information. If it is best to choose and implement an alternative, then give some thought to the decision opportunity of how to implement it. There may even be a subtle interplay here. How you implement an alternative may affect whether you should implement it at all.

10.3 Interconnecting Decisions

Value-focused thinking facilitates the logical and consistent linking of interconnected decisions in several ways. One is by guidance from the strategic objectives, a second is by the use of common fundamental objectives, a third is by attributes, and a fourth is by value tradeoffs. I will elaborate a bit on each of these.

Any decisionmaker wishes to make decisions in a consistent manner. It seems useless to have some alternatives cancel out the effects of others. The strategic objectives provide common guidance to all of the decisions of a decisionmaker. The strategic objectives help suggest fundamental objectives for different decision contexts so these fundamental objectives have the same foundation. If the decisionmaker is an organization, then different decisions are likely to be taken by different individuals. The common guidance of the strategic objectives, if they are clearly and unambiguously stated, can be of considerable help in ensuring consistency across decisions. If the various decisionmakers of the organization have taken part in defining those strategic objectives, then the likelihood that all the organizational decisions will be oriented in a consistent manner is greatly enhanced.

In many circumstances, numerous decisions are made that are directed at the same purpose. Making this purpose explicit by expressing the fundamental objectives and possibly also developing a value model enhances the ability to coordinate decisions. The manager of a major project (such as reconstructing an area of a city or producing a report) may have fundamental objectives concerning the time and cost to finish the project and its resulting quality. Over the course of the project, the manager will face decisions about personnel, resources, details of what should be done, when and how to do it, and changes in the project, to name a few. Common fundamental objectives should facilitate the coordination of all these decisions.

An important fundamental objective in a given problem context may be a means of achieving other fundamental objectives in a broader decision context (see Ackoff, 1978, 1981). This is significant because any given decision can relate to many other decisions. However, one cannot analyze all decisions at once, nor would this seem fruitful if it were possible.

■ Marketing Decisions

Suppose a firm is considering various marketing alternatives for one of its products. The fundamental objective of the firm is to maximize its profits this year, next year, and each year thereafter. These profits, however, will be influenced by many decisions in addition to the marketing problem under consideration. In the context of the specific problem, two fundamental objectives may be "maximize this year's profits from the current product" and "maximize the year-end market share." The former is a direct contribution to the firm's annual profit and the latter is a means to future profits. The logic is that greater market share will lead to more appealing decisions to be faced in the future (that is, decisions that should result in higher profits than the decisions that would be faced given a smaller market share). ■

■ Siting a Prison

In the evaluation of potential sites for a prison, fundamental objectives may concern the receptivity of the local community, impacts on the work force, health and safety, and economic costs. If a site is chosen and a prison is built, implications in terms of these fundamental objectives will occur. If the prison is not built there, then another decision process must begin, using different sites or different alternatives for handling prisoners. Of course this alternative too may fail, resulting in another decision problem. Eventually, either a prison will be sited somewhere or another alternative for dealing with prisoners (for example, early releases from prison or shorter sentences for crimes) will be chosen. At that time, it will be possible to characterize the consequences of the series of decisions in terms of the receptiveness of the local community, impacts on the work force, health and safety, and economic costs.

In the evaluation of initial sites, it is reasonable to focus on the specific siting problem at hand, but the possibility that any chosen site may fall through because of political or financial circumstances must be addressed. Rather than explicitly address the possible series of decisions, it may be worthwhile to summarize this implication by the objective "minimize the probability that the prison will not be completed." The relative (un)desirability of not being able to complete the facility can then be evaluated in terms of the possible implications of all future decisions that would follow in such a case. This simplification should logically link related decisions and yet not distort the evaluation of the given sites for the specific problem being considered (see Section 4.7). ∎

Value tradeoffs offer an opportunity to ensure consistency in decisions that have an overlapping concern. One set of decisions that currently lacks consistency is regulatory decisions involving among other things the potential for loss of life.

■ *Statistical Lives*
The Environmental Protection Agency (EPA) has numerous programs that are intended to reduce the loss of life. This is a common objective. Another common objective concerns the cost of the programs. Each program also has additional fundamental objectives that are not common to all. Would it be reasonable to spend $40 million to save one statistical life from pollutant A and not spend $1 million to save a statistical life from pollutant B? As Graham and Vaupel (1981) point out, decisions are made in the EPA and other federal agencies that in fact evaluate statistical fatalities at very different costs. You do not need to be particularly perceptive to realize that transferring $40 million from the program saving one statistical life to the other program will save 40 statistical lives for a net saving of 39 statistical lives. These lives might be yours or mine. The use of a common value tradeoff between statistical lives saved and costs could guide consistency in such decisions. ∎

■ *Product Quality*

Suppose an organization is considering ways to improve the quality of its product for a cost. In one decision problem the alternatives involve changing the fabrication process. In the other decision problem, the alternatives involve changes in the materials used in the product. It is reasonable that the value tradeoffs for both decisions be the same. In specific terms, the value tradeoffs between dollars spent to improve the product and the degree of improvement should be the same. If a given improvement via the change in the fabrication process is worth $1.2 million, it would be unreasonable to reject a materials change costing $0.7 million for the same improvement. Additional objectives in these problems should naturally affect choices, but to interconnect the decisions logically, the value tradeoffs should be the same. ■

10.4 Improving Communication

Value-focused thinking provides important insights for communicating about decisions in general and about specific decision situations. The insights concern not only what should be communicated but also to whom it should be communicated. Delving deeply into values also often helps to clarify one's own thinking. If you are an analyst trying to help a decisionmaker faced with a tough decision, you certainly will be better able to help if you thoroughly understand the decisionmaker's values.

People care about decisions because of their impact on the achievement of fundamental objectives. Thus, these objectives tell you what is important to communicate. In an analysis of alternatives, it may be that alternative A is better than alternative B. If you pursue why this is the case, the answer must lie in both the value judgments and the possible impacts. The framework of value-focused thinking should help clarify the contributions of each. When means objectives are used in place of fundamental objectives, the clarification of the relative roles of facts and values in an evaluation is more difficult.

No specialized training or knowledge is usually needed to understand implications in terms of the fundamental objectives. Everyone understands the relevance of a specified environmental impact (such as loss of species habitat), but few understand the relevance of a pH of 5.9 in a lake. The fundamental objectives therefore provide the basis for a common language for discussing the issues in a decision situation. This common language facilitates the involvement of stakeholders. It also provides a logical and responsible way to involve the public in major problems that concern them. Namely, the public can be involved in identifying the fundamental objectives for a decision situation.

One of the most important general insights of value-focused thinking for communication is that prioritizing objectives is both difficult and subtle (see Section 5.4). It makes no sense to say that one objective is more important than another without saying how much of each you are talking about.

▪ *Prioritizing Objectives*

Over the past few years, I have presented seminars on risk issues to members of the press. At the beginning of the seminar, I ask partici-pants to fill out a small questionnaire that includes the following question:

In considering the cleanup of old hazardous waste sites, rank the following in order of importance:

economic costs of the cleanup;
potential human life loss or sickness due to the hazard;
potential damage to the natural environment (flora and fauna).

I have asked more than 50 members of the press to respond to this question; all have obliged. Essentially all have ranked loss of life and sickness first, environmental damage second, and cost third. When I ask them what their ranking means, they either don't know or are ambiguous (that is, they don't know that they don't know). When I ask them if $2 billion is less important than the aggravation of breathing difficulties to six people or the death of two acres of pine trees, they get irritated. When I point out what useful things this country or its citizens could do with $2 billion, the press members realize their response to the question is at best superficial, but they are not sure why. By now, they will listen to the explanation in Section 5.4 about why the range of impacts being considered is absolutely essential in any weighing of the importance of objectives. Of course the press is composed of more than 50 reporters. Many keep asking for and reporting meaningless judgments such as "the public strongly feels that objective X is much more important than objective Y" in some decision context. ▪

Even when the ranges of possible impacts are addressed properly, it may be that one objective is important only for its relationships to other objectives in the problem. Failure to recognize this can lead to significant misinterpretation about the importance of objectives.

■ *Water Resources Development*

In an appraisal of water resource plans for the Tisza river basin of Hungary (see Keeney and Wood, 1977), one of the initial twelve objectives concerned Hungary's ability to control its own water resources. Discussions with water resource planners in Hungary indicated that this objective was "very important." When we pursued their reasoning, responses indicated that such control was important to (among other things) reduce the likelihood of floods and the resulting impacts of floods. But, in fact, flood consequences were included in the problem under other objectives. Another reason for the control objective was to improve the country's agricultural and industrial output. But, again, objectives pertaining to these concerns were also in the hierarchy. We eventually determined that almost all of the more fundamental consequences related to the control objective were also included in the objectives hierarchy. Only a concern about the prestige of national control over water resources was not accounted for elsewhere. The objective of control remained, but its relative importance in the assessment of the utility function was much lower. It had become a proxy for prestige alone, and the interdependencies with the other objectives had thereby been eliminated. ■

■ *Coal-Fired Power Plants*

Another example of the thought processes illuminated by value tradeoffs occurred in an assessment of preferences for various coal-fired power plant developments for the Baltimore Gas and Electric Company (Keeney, Lathrop, and Sicherman, 1986). Two of the economic attributes were customer cost, measured by the monthly change in the electricity bill, and shareholder return, measured in annual percentage. For these two attributes, a utility function with the form of (5.7) was appropriate because of an additional fundamental objective concerning equity between customers and shareholders. But difficulties in assessing the value tradeoffs over the two attributes led to the clarification that although each was a fundamental objective in the decision context, each was also a means to the other. Higher prices to consumers would anger the regulatory commission, who would "penalize" the electricity company with lower allowable returns to shareholders. On the other hand, lower returns to shareholders would make investment in the company less attractive, so the bond rating of the company might fall, and the interest rate they must pay to borrow money would necessarily rise. This increase in costs would have to be passed on to the customers.

Having recognized the dynamics of the problem, the analyst has at least two choices. One is to try to model the dynamics and not include the means implications of each objective in the value tradeoffs, and the other is to assess the value tradeoffs more carefully to indicate, roughly speaking, how much of the weight for each of the two attributes is due to the direct fundamental impact and to the indirect means impact. The latter is difficult to do precisely because A affects B, which affects A, and so on. But at least recognizing and understanding what is occurring and why can be useful. ∎

10.5 Facilitating Involvement in Multiple-Stakeholder Decisions

When multiple stakeholders are involved in a decision, there are naturally multiple value structures, one for each stakeholder, that are relevant. If the values are assessed for each of these stakeholders, the insights available from improved communication can multiply too.

In decisions where you need to negotiate both for yourself and for others, the framework of value-focused thinking provides a way to spell out what may be important to the other parties. This is essential as you try to create alternatives that would be desirable to those other parties.

In bargaining and negotiation situations, especially for positive-sum cases, it may not be difficult to have the stakeholders jointly develop a common list of fundamental objectives. This allows the stakeholders to ensure that their stake in the decision will be addressed and possibly broadens their perspective on the decision.

A general insight from value-focused thinking is that it is not necessary to quantify values to obtain ideas for creating alternatives or identifying decision opportunities. A careful qualitative statement of objectives often fosters such ideas. This is significant for several reasons. First, listing objectives and differentiating between fundamental objectives and means objectives require less skill, though perhaps more originality, than quantifying values. Second, it is likely that many of the fundamental objectives of various stakeholders will not conflict. The Republican and Democratic parties both want lower unemployment, lower inflation, and lower interest rates. Finally, perhaps as a consequence of the first two properties, it is often not difficult to get stakeholders involved in structuring objectives for decision situations that concern them if they believe that their values will be used appropriately and can make a difference.

■ Energy Policy for West Germany

An important case demonstrating the role of qualitatively structuring values in significant decisions concerned the objectives of West Germany's energy policies. As discussed in Keeney, Renn, and von Winterfeldt (1987), West Germany (now Germany) faces a myriad of energy decisions in the next 50 years. Such decisions concern the demand and supply of energy, impacts of energy use, public opposition to technology, and political implications of energy policies. To develop a comprehensive and politically acceptable list of objectives to appraise energy policy, we conducted interviews with leading representatives of nine major political, social, and technical organizations: the Association of German Industries, the German Society for Nature Protection, the German Catholic Church, the German Lutheran Church, the Society of German Engineers, a large electricity company, a major power plant supplier, the Federation of German Labor Unions, and the Ecological Research Institutes.

As a result of structuring each organization's objectives hierarchy and then combining hierarchies as discussed in Chapter 3, we identified eight major fundamental objectives that were specified into approximately 100 detailed objectives. The breadth of legitimate concern can be seen in the focus of the eight major fundamental objectives: security of energy supplies, national economic impact, resources utilized, environmental impact, health and safety, social impact, political impact, and international impact. ■

Many of the insights in multiple-stakeholder decisions concern the assumptions, reasoning, and understanding of the different stakeholders. When you quantify the values of each stakeholder over a common set of objectives, it is possible to identify points of agreement and points of disagreement. This facilitates communication and suggests information that may help to reconcile the disagreement.

In many situations when utility functions are assessed from more than one stakeholder, there will be differences. Having the differences clearly articulated will be an advantage in the search for why the differences occur.

■ *Corporate Objectives*

One multiple value assessment in which I was involved concerned the objectives of Woodward-Clyde Consultants (see Keeney and Raiffa, 1976). The stakeholders whose values were assessed were company executives. The decision situation concerned different possible organizational arrangements for the firm. Fundamental objectives addressed personal, professional, and financial implications to the employees. Individuals had either an additive or a multiplicative utility function over these objectives. With an additive form, one would be willing to make lots of money with minimum personal "enjoyment"; and with a multiplicative utility function, some of both would be required to be at all desirable. The former type of executive felt the purpose of work was mainly for money that could be used to pursue personal interests outside of work. The latter type preferred their work and pleasure to be more integrated.

In this same study, there were major differences in the value tradeoffs between attributes of earnings retained in the firm and salary increases. Some executives thought that retaining 8 percent of the earnings in the firm for growth was much more important than giving 20 percent salary increases, assuming no salary increases occurred in the first case and no earnings were retained in the second. Others had exactly the opposite opinion. Forced reflection on the basis for these differences uncovered two main causes, one that could easily be eliminated and one that could not. The former concerned "facts" and the latter "values."

In the value assessments, the time period of concern was not made clear. Some of the executives assumed the value tradeoff concerned a one-year situation and could be changed annually. Others thought it was the value tradeoff to be used each year. After clarification, most felt that the 8 percent retained earnings was more significant for one year but that repeated annual 20 percent increases in salary were more important. From the one-year viewpoint, retained earnings is a means to future salary increases and firm viability. From the multiple-year viewpoint, viability is effectively assumed (otherwise how could there be multiple years) and the salary increases are more relevant.

Once the time issue was clarified, the other issue that had a big influence on the value tradeoff between retained earnings and salary increase was the age of the respondent. If the respondent was near retirement, the salary increase would be directly useful, but the retained earnings would have no personal impact. Younger executives, on the other hand, could expect to benefit from retained earnings in future years. Recognizing this feature, of course, did not bring agreement, but it did provide a better understanding for creating alternatives or compromise. ■

10.6 Guiding Strategic Thinking

It is easy to recognize that if the strategic objectives of a decisionmaker, whether an individual or organization, are clearly stated and quantified, then this representation of values should guide all decisionmaking activity. The strategic objectives completely specify what the decisionmaker cares about and consequently why it should ever bother to make decisions. What is not so easy to recognize is the contribution of value-focused thinking for guiding strategic thought.

Value-focused thinking stresses the identification of decision opportunities. The intent is to identify decisions, not forced upon you by others, where the investment of resources to identify alternatives and pursue one will lead to consequences worth the effort. Recognizing the decision opportunity to identify and understand your strategic objectives is useful. Following through on that opportunity can bring substantial rewards over a long period of time.

The techniques and thought processes used in value-focused thinking can provide the tools necessary to identify and quantify strategic objectives. Once this is done, the language to communicate and use these objectives is also provided.

Devoting time, effort, and perhaps money to the development of a clearly articulated set of strategic objectives is an extremely effective use of resources. The simple reason is that by definition there is only one set of strategic objectives for a decisionmaker. There is only one value model that appropriately quantifies these objectives. These strategic objectives will not change very much over time. Over years there may be some changes, but over months changes should almost always be minimal. What changes much more rapidly is the status of the decisionmaker with respect to achieving the strategic objectives and the decision situations that the decisionmaker is considering that can influence the achievement of these strategic objectives.

Many people state that their overall strategic objective is to have a high quality of life. Specifying the precise meaning of quality of life is difficult (but see Section 13.1 for one attempt). However you define quality of life, two means objectives might be to maximize funds and to maximize time available to pursue that quality of life. Over time, your value tradeoffs between funds and time available change drastically. In short, many of us go from leading what I call money-constrained lives in high school and college to time-constrained lives later. The strategic objectives will remain more constant. If two components of a quality of life are to help others and to enjoy life oneself, the value tradeoffs here may be almost the same in college and later in life.

The strategic objectives are the basis for developing fundamental objectives for any specific decision context. Having these values articulated "ahead of time" allows you to more rapidly respond to specific decision situations as they occur. You then have more time to spend creating alternatives and identifying decision opportunities because you spend less time identifying the relevant fundamental objectives. This aspect of value-focused thinking is of particular importance when decision situations are quickly evolving, such as in the case in high technology fields and intense negotiations.

So why is it so worthwhile to articulate strategic objectives? Over time, a decisionmaker will either identify or miss many decision opportunities and will face many important decisions. Each of these will have fundamental objectives and alternatives. The decisionmaker will need to gather information for all the alternatives in each of the decisions. The set of strategic objectives is the same for every one of those decisions. You get to use the same strategic objectives over and over. It is a phenomenal bargain!

PART FOUR

APPLICATIONS

CHAPTER 11

Selected Applications

This chapter presents several applications of value-focused thinking. There are two purposes: to indicate ways in which value-focused thinking can be implemented and to indicate ways in which it can be useful. The only common component of the applications is the identification of fundamental objectives. Some applications include the development of an objectives network, and in some attributes are explicitly specified. Others include quantification of values. In some applications alternatives are introduced and even evaluated, whereas in others they are not discussed. Several of the applications involve multiple stakeholders. Each of the nine uses of value-focused thinking outlined in Section 1.5 and discussed in detail in Chapters 7–10 is illustrated in at least one application.

11.1 NASA Leadership in Space

A difficult problem for the National Aeronautics and Space Administration (NASA), and one of concern to many members of Congress and citizens, is what future space missions the U.S. civilian space program should pursue. The potential consequences of this decision are obviously significant. These consequences include effects on national pride, international prestige, scientific advancement, and technological progress, as well as large social and economic costs and benefits. The difference in the desirability of consequences resulting from different proposed missions can be enormous.

The choice of a space mission is also extremely complex. Multiple objectives, uncertainties, and numerous stakeholders with potentially distinct values contribute to the complexity. In addition, to obtain funding from Congress and support from the public, NASA must justify its proposed missions in many public forums.

A careful analysis of possible mission alternatives has a high potential payoff for NASA and the country. The cost and effort are very small relative to the billions of dollars that will be spent on future space missions. At stake are U.S. leadership in space and the economic, technological, and social advantages of such a position.

The foundation on which analysis of NASA missions should rest is the objectives, which are also often referred to as goals. As stated by Ride (1987) in a document addressing America's future in space, "if there are no goals, or if the goals are too diffuse, then there is no focus to the program and no framework for decisions." It is clearly essential to have a precise specification of the objectives for NASA in space.

As part of a small effort to examine the desirability of a systematic analysis of NASA mission alternatives, in collaboration with Ray Hook of the NASA Langley Research Center, I spent a couple of days identifying and prioritizing NASA mission objectives. The purpose of this section is to show that even such a minuscule effort focused on values can lend some important insights. Although a thorough and deep investigation of values concerning NASA is obviously needed, a tiny effort can make a contribution on such a complex problem.

Identifying and Prioritizing Objectives

On the basis of Ride (1987), the White House (1988) fact sheet on National Space Policy, and discussions with a few people with current and past involvement with NASA, we identified the fundamental mission objectives in Table 11.1.

The discussions probed the meanings of the objectives. National pride referred to the feelings of the citizenry about the country. International prestige had to do with other nations' opinions of the United States, with emphasis on the technologically advanced nations. Scientific knowledge referred to content, whereas education and excellence referred to spirit. The former concerned advanced knowledge, whereas the education objective addressed schoolchildren and university undergraduates. The excitement and drama objective was there to contribute to making life interesting.

As discussed in Section 5.4, a meaningful setting of priorities must

Table 11.1.   A preliminary list of NASA mission objectives and their relative importance

Objective	Ranked priority	Relative importance
Enhance national pride	1	100
Aid national defense	9	20
Promote international prestige	8	35
Foster international cooperation	7	40
Create economic benefits	5	50
Advance scientific knowledge	4	60
Promote education and excellence	6	45
Provide excitement and drama	2	90
Maintain fiscal responsibility	3	70

account for the possible ranges of consequences for the various objectives. To determine these ranges, we created a constructed attribute as discussed in Section 4.3 using the four possible NASA mission alternatives specified in Ride (1987):

1. mission to planet Earth,
2. explore the solar system,
3. outpost on the moon,
4. humans to Mars.

To construct attributes for the objectives, we asked someone knowledgeable about NASA objectives and missions to rank the four alternative missions in terms of each of the objectives. In terms of national pride, the highest-ranked mission was humans to Mars, next was outpost on the moon, then explore the solar system, and then mission to planet Earth. With regard to national defense, outpost on the moon was ranked the highest and explore the solar system was ranked lowest. The rankings with respect to all of the objectives are indicated in Table 11.2, with a rank of 1 indicating the highest achievement of that objective.

The prioritizing of objectives began with paired comparisons. With respect to the first two listed objectives, national pride and national defense, we asked our respondent to imagine a mission with consequences for national pride and national defense corresponding to the worst rankings for those attributes in Table 11.2. If he could improve the mission by changing the consequences of just one of these objectives to the consequence corresponding to the best ranking, which one would he change? Note that this question is asking whether the difference in desirability of the consequences on national pride between mission to planet Earth and humans to Mars is greater than the difference in desirability of the consequences on national defense between explore the solar system and outpost on the moon. The respondent, who was a NASA employee providing "reasonable" but illustrative answers, stated that the change in national pride was preferred. This response indicated that the priority of national pride was greater than the priority of national defense given the ranges of consequences involved.

Next, we compared national pride with international prestige. In this case, according to our respondent's judgments, the changes in desirability from the worst-ranked to the best-ranked consequence both pertained to the differences between mission to planet Earth and humans to Mars. He designated the change with respect to national pride as more significant than that with respect to international prestige. This

Table 11.2.   Ranking of NASA missions in terms of their consequences for each NASA objective

Attribute	Mission to planet Earth	Explore the solar system	Outpost on the moon	Humans to Mars
National pride	4	3	2	1
National defense	2	4	1	3
International prestige	4	3	2	1
International cooperation	1	2	4	3
Economic benefits	1	4	2	3
Scientific knowledge	2	1	3	4
Education and excellence	3	2	4	1
Excitement and drama	4	3	2	1
Fiscal responsibility	1	2	3	4

implied that given the ranges of consequences involved, national pride was of higher priority than international prestige. By comparing the ranges of desirability for national pride to the ranges for the other objectives, we found that national pride had the highest priority.

Similar use of paired comparisons showed excitement and drama to be the second most important objective. Proceeding through the list of objectives in this manner produced the ranking of priorities shown in Table 11.1.

In a very preliminary effort to quantify the relative importance of the objectives, I arbitrarily set the importance of national pride equal to 100 and assessed the other objectives relative to this. To gauge the relative importance of excitement and drama, I asked the respondent how important was an increase in the desirability of consequences from the worst to the best with respect to excitement and drama compared to such an increase for national pride. He answered that increasing the desirability with respect to excitement and drama was 90 percent as important. Hence, I set the relative importance of excitement and drama at 90.

Another question compared the difference in the desirability of the range of consequences from worst to best with respect to economic benefits with that for national pride. The respondent considered improving economic benefits from worst to best over the range of consequences to be half as important as doing so for national pride, so the relative importance for economic benefits was set at 50. The relative importance of all the objectives determined from this illustrative assessment is indicated in Table 11.1.

Insights for Decision Opportunities, Alternatives, and Process

This preliminary work points up an obvious decision opportunity to determine and even quantify NASA's strategic objectives. Mission alternatives that cost in the range from $40 to $200 billion, as the four listed do, are the means to achieve those strategic objectives. The priorities indicate that national pride, as influenced by NASA missions, can be more significant than the $160 billion range of the cost objective. Even if this is an order of magnitude off, it seems worthwhile to define and understand what is meant by national pride. For the same reason, namely that the range of possible consequences appears to be worth the equivalent of tens of billions of dollars, a thorough understanding of the meaning of each of the other objectives would be desirable.

The process to identify NASA objectives should involve a broad spectrum of people knowledgeable about and interested in the space program, including people from both inside and outside NASA, members of Congress or their staffs, any stakeholders who can be identified, and the public. Since the purpose is to end up with a comprehensive list of objectives to cover all the concerns, it makes sense to base the list on a broad range of viewpoints.

Since the intent of any alternative is to achieve the objectives, searching through the objectives may suggest changes to alternatives, supplements to alternatives, or completely new alternatives that may be desirable. For instance, since national pride and international prestige are important objectives of NASA missions, research on how proposed missions contribute to those objectives would be very useful. It might be found that much of the impact occurs not only from the missions in themselves but also from the way the missions are interpreted to the public. This might suggest supplements to given mission alternatives that would involve changes in the education and communication campaigns associated with the missions. Such changes might cost much less than changes in the missions, and yet the impacts in terms of the desired objectives could be relatively large.

Evaluating proposed missions in terms of the objectives may make it possible to suggest other missions that incorporate the best aspects of the proposed missions. For example, suppose we better understood the objectives on which humans to Mars and mission to planet Earth rank high and the reasons for these rankings. Then we might be able to create hybrid alternatives that would rank high on more of the objectives than did either of the original proposals alone.

Several insights for the decisionmaking process are available from even such a limited effort. The objectives can be the basis for constructively involving stakeholders in NASA decisions. This involvement need not take away any decisionmaking authority from NASA. In fact, NASA's decisions will have more authority if analysis indicates that the missions NASA proposes are the best way to achieve a legitimate, broadly supported set of strategic objectives.

The listing of objectives also facilitates communication and indicates some fundamental information that would be useful to gather. That information pertains to how particular missions have positive or negative effects on the achievement of NASA's objectives. If NASA establishes an outpost on the moon, how does this foster international cooperation and promote education and excellence? Even more important, such knowledge might help us figure out how better to foster international cooperation and promote education and excellence.

11.2 Transporting Nuclear Waste

Fuel for nuclear power plants is contained in rods that are inserted into the reactor. After use, these rods, then referred to as spent fuel rods, are withdrawn and stored in pools of water to allow their radioactivity to decrease through radioactive decay. After some years, they are taken from the pool and placed in a cask for shipping to either a temporary "monitored retrievable storage facility" or a permanent "geologic repository." If temporary storage is utilized, the spent fuel will later be shipped to a geologic repository.

As part of the Department of Energy's program to evaluate alternatives for managing spent fuel, a study was commissioned to evaluate metal cask systems for shipping spent nuclear fuel from power plants to storage locations (see Westinghouse, 1986). To evaluate metal cask systems, one must specify a set of objectives. If this set is judged to be inadequate by industry executives, governmental regulators, legislators, or public interest groups, the credibility of the evaluation will suffer. Recognizing this, the study included the involvement of stakeholder groups to develop a comprehensive set of objectives (see Keeney, 1988).

This study illustrates several aspects of value-focused thinking. One is how multiple stakeholders can be legitimately involved in decisions. A second is the integration of stakeholder objectives hierarchies into a combined objectives hierarchy. The third is the identification of classes of means objectives representative of those typically identified in the elicitation of objectives.

Identifying Stakeholder Objectives

During a two-day meeting, objectives for the shipment of spent nuclear fuel were elicited from three panels, each of 10 to 15 members. These panels were referred to as the technical, governmental, and public interest panels. The technical panel was composed of people from utility companies and other firms in the nuclear industry. The governmental panel included representatives of state governments and federal agencies. The public interest panel included people from environmental groups, consumer groups, and universities.

The initial meeting with stakeholders was a common meeting. This let the stakeholders know that they received the same information at the same time, putting them on equal footing and suggesting that the process was a legitimate effort rather than simply window dressing. Several important topics were reviewed in the general meeting. First the waste shipment problem was outlined. Then the purposes of involving the stakeholders, how they were selected, and the uses of their results were clarified. This set the stage for the identification of objectives using the techniques discussed in Section 3.1, which was carried out in a separate ninety-minute session with each panel.

Using the results of these sessions, my colleague Detlof von Winterfeldt and I structured preliminary objectives hierarchies for each panel. These provided the basis for integrating the three sets into one overall objectives hierarchy. We then analyzed and modified this overall hierarchy to distinguish ends from means and to ensure that important points brought out in the panel discussions had not been omitted. To save space, tables that follow present only the objects corresponding to the associated objectives (for example, "economic cost" rather than "minimize economic cost").

Value Structure of the Technical Panel. The hierarchy of objectives resulting from the technical panel discussion is presented in Table 11.3. Most of the categories of objectives (health and safety, economic, social, and political) are commonly found in public interest problems. Two additional categories, namely scheduling impact and system flexibility, were distinct.

Scheduling impact concerned consequences that would occur if a spent fuel management system were not available at the appropriate time and with the necessary capacity. In such a case, spent fuel would continue to increase at reactor sites and/or certain reactors would have to shut down. Either situation might have health and safety, economic, political, and social consequences.

System flexibility objectives had a similar role. Many decisions about the spent fuel management system would not be made by the time the metal cask systems were evaluated, and yet it would be appropriate to evaluate metal cask systems in light of all of the contingencies. Since there are so many possible scenarios (for example, different rock types for the repository and future regulations), it would be impractical to evaluate the metal cask alternatives for all cases. The alternatives could be evaluated in terms of the direct consequences (on, for instance, health

Table 11.3.   Objectives hierarchy of the technical panel

Economic costs
  Government costs
  Utilities costs

Health and safety impacts
  Radiation effects
    To the public
    To the workers
  Transportation effects
    To the public
    To the workers

Political impacts
  Political acceptability
  Public confidence
  Local and state attitudes

Social impacts
  Impacts on transportation system
  Aesthetics

Scheduling impact
  Timely availability of system
  Ability to handle required quantities of spent fuel

System flexibility toward
  Consolidation of spent fuel
  Regulatory changes
  Plant types
  Repository media
  Changes in transportation requirements

and safety and economics) assuming certain likely future scenarios and in terms of their flexibility to adapt to different future scenarios. Thus, the objectives under system flexibility might be thought of as means to avoid economic, health and safety, political, and social consequences due to scenarios other than those directly evaluated.

Value Structure of the Government Panel. The objectives hierarchy of the government panel is shown in Table 11.4. Several features are noteworthy.

Cost objectives specified that indirect, as well as direct, economic

Table 11.4. Objectives hierarchy of the government panel

System flexibility
  Institutional
      Timely licensability
      Adaptability to regulatory changes
  Technical
      Retrievability (e.g., from the monitored retrievable storage facility)
      Durability of cask
      Handleability (easy to lift, etc.)
      Independence of type of repository

Costs
  Direct economic costs
      State government costs
      Federal government costs
      Utility company costs
  Cost impacts on other parts of the system
  Indirect economic costs
      Costs for state and local responses to system
      Court costs, regulatory costs, etc.
      Road maintenance costs

Health and safety impacts
  Radiation exposure
      To the workers
      To the public
  Transportation accidents
      To the workers
      To the public
  Other accidents
      To the workers
      To the public

Environmental impacts
  Groundwater contamination
  Roadbed damage
  Visual impacts from storage
  Land resources for plants

Political impacts
  Public confidence in
      Government
      Nuclear industry

Table 11.4.   (continued)

Fulfill government commitments
Public acceptability

Equity of risks
Among groups (public, transportation workers, industry workers)
Geographical

---

costs should be accounted for in evaluating alternatives. Indirect economic costs include, for instance, the costs of court proceedings concerning chosen alternatives and the costs of road repair due to damage caused by the heavy vehicles transporting spent nuclear fuel. Also, one metal cask might be more expensive than another, but might allow significant economic savings in other parts of the spent fuel management system. In such a case, the more expensive cask should get this economic credit. Finally, it was important to indicate who was responsible for direct costs, since these might be borne by state governments, the federal government, and utility companies. It was recognized that all the costs would eventually be passed on to the general public, although the distribution of costs to the public might be different in the three cases.

Under political impacts, the public's confidence in government and in the nuclear industry were deemed important. There were several means by which these would be affected, including the credibility of studies, the openness of communication with the public, and the trustworthiness of individuals and institutions communicating to the public. It was also considered important that the government fulfill its commitment to deal with the spent fuel waste problem.

An interesting category of objectives identified by the government panel concerned the equity of risks resulting from the spent fuel management system. It was important that the risks not fall in an unbalanced manner upon the public, transportation workers, or industry workers. It was also desired that these risks be shared geographically across the country rather than by residents of one area.

Value Structure of the Public Interest Panel. The objectives hierarchy of the public interest panel is presented in Table 11.5. As with the previous panels, some aspects of this value structure are unique.

The health and safety objectives of the public interest panel speci-

Table 11.5. Objectives hierarchy of the public interest panel

---

Health and safety impacts
  Radiation exposure
    To the public
    To the workers
  Transportation accidents
    To the public
    To the workers
  Future generations
    Genetic effects
    Cancer

Environmental impacts
  Land use impacts (e.g., storage facilities)
  Impacts on biosphere (from radiation release)

Political and institutional impacts
  Resilience against
    Regulatory changes
    Major political changes
  Reduce need for regulation/inspection
  Political acceptability
    Increase trust and credibility
    Practical implementation

Fairness and equity
  Equity between risk bearers and beneficiaries of nuclear power
  Equity between present and future generations
  Liability and compensation

Psychological concerns
  Fears and anxieties
  Assurance of a compensation system

Costs

---

fied two features common to all of the panels. Health and safety impacts distinguished between those caused by radiation exposure and by transportation accidents and between effects on members of the public and on workers in the spent fuel management system. However, the panel specified a separate category of health and safety impacts on future generations. This included possible genetic changes and cancer caused by radiation.

In common with the government panel, the public interest panel showed a strong desire for fairness and equity. But, the specific issues were different. There was concern for the equity between impacts on present and future generations. There was also a belief that those who were benefiting from nuclear power should bear the risk associated with spent fuel management. A separate objective concerned appropriate liability and compensation for people who were adversely affected by the spent fuel management system.

The public interest group was also concerned about the psychological impacts of the alternatives. Specifically, they felt that the fears and anxieties that might be induced by the system should be considered in the evaluation of alternatives for spent fuel management. They also considered it important to assure the public of the adequacy of the compensation system. Such assurance addresses the public's psychological concerns, whereas the actual existence of an adequate compensation system falls under the fairness category. Discussion indicated that it was not clear whether the different metal cask systems could be differentiated with respect to these psychological objectives, but that such differentiation might be possible. Thus, it was important to include these objectives in the value structure.

Structuring the Combined Objectives Hierarchy

The next step was to combine the objectives hierarchies of the three panels. The result is presented in Table 11.6, where the letters P, G, and T stand for the public interest, government, and technical panels, respectively. When a letter follows a major objective, it indicates that the corresponding panel had a more elaborate value structure than the other panels with regard to that objective. Thus, for instance, the flexibility objective was mainly specified by the technical panel, whereas the fairness objective resulted from values expressed by both the public interest and government panels. When placed after a specific objective, a letter indicates that the corresponding panel specified that objective.

The first step in creating the combined objectives hierarchy was simply to list the nine distinctive major objectives from the three objectives hierarchies and put the appropriate objectives within each category under them. Then we began to modify the value structure using the means-ends and specification concepts discussed in Chapter 3. Thus, for instance, the psychological objectives of the public interest panel were included as follows: fears and anxieties are part of the social impacts, and assurance of a compensation system is one of the means to public confidence in the technical system and in government, both political concerns. Interpreting the fundamental objectives included in the combined objectives hierarchy and discussing the means objectives excluded should clarify the detailed reasoning.

The Fundamental Objectives. The meanings of many of the objectives in Table 11.6 are obvious. However, some elaboration is appropriate. Public health and safety implications due to radiation exposure may result from normal operations of the spent fuel management system, from vehicle accidents in which broken casks release radiation, or from casks stored in a repository eventually leaking radioactive material into the groundwater system. Worker health and safety impacts due to radiation exposure may also result from either normal operations or accidents.

The economic objectives address both direct and indirect costs, which include such things as repairing road damage, court costs, costs of emergency response, and costs or benefits accruing in other parts of the overall waste management system due to the specific metal cask alternative.

The environmental impacts exclude, by definition, health and safety. There may be visual impacts of having, for instance, aboveground monitored retrievable storage systems. There is also the use of land resources for such facilities or the possible loss of the use of land as a result of a major accident. The political objectives might be stated in several different manners. We chose to categorize them into public confidence and local and state attitudes. Public confidence may depend on such features as cask durability, the understanding of the system,

Table 11.6.   Combined fundamental objectives hierarchy

1. Health and safety impacts (P)
     Radiation exposure
        To the public (PGT)
        To the workers (PGT)
     Transportation accidents
        To the public (PGT)
        To the workers (PGT)
     Future generations
        Genetic effects (P)
        Cancer (P)

Table 11.6.   (continued)

2. Economic costs (G)
     State government costs (G)
     Federal government costs (PGT)
     Utility company costs (PGT)

3. Environmental impacts (G)
     Visual (G)
     Land use (PG)

4. Political impacts (G)
     Public confidence in the technical system (PG)
     Public confidence in government (G)
     Local and state attitudes (GT)

5. Social impacts (PT)
     Fears and anxieties (P)
     Transportation system inconvenience (PT)

6. Fairness (PG)
     Equity
         Transportation workers, industry workers, public (G)
         Geographical (G)
         Beneficiaries of nuclear power (P)
         Intergenerational (P)
     Liability (P)

7. Scheduling (T)
     Timely availability of system (GT)
     Ability to handle appropriate quantities of spent fuel (T)

8. Flexibility (T)
     Technical with respect to
         Consolidation of spent fuel (T)
         Reprocessing (T)
         Plant types (T)
         Retrievability (G)
         Repository media (GT)
     Institutional with respect to
         Transport regulation changes (T)
         Regulation changes (PGT)
         Political changes (P)

Note: P, G, and T stand for the public interest, government, and technical panels, respectively.

and so forth. It may also depend on other objectives concerning, for instance, the liability system (represented under fairness) and fears and anxieties (a social impact), both of which are directly important in themselves as well as a means to public confidence. The social impact on the transportation system is mainly the inconvenience due to special rules (for example, road closures to accommodate shipments) and possible road damage caused by heavy vehicles.

The fairness objectives might have been placed within other categories: the equity objectives in the social category, and the liability objective in the economic category. Because of the prominence with which fairness concerns were mentioned by both the public and the government panels, we considered it appropriate to distinguish them in the objectives hierarchy.

The first six major objectives reasonably represent the fundamental consequences from metal cask waste management systems. On the other hand, scheduling and flexibility do not explicitly address fundamental consequences that occur when the spent fuel management system is either late or of inadequate capacity, or when the scenarios that evolve are different from those used in evaluation. The fundamental consequences of either of these situations would also be categorized using objectives 1 through 6. However, to model the multitude of mechanisms by which those more fundamental consequences could occur would require more from an analysis than could be adequately offered. Thus, scheduling and flexibility are fundamental objectives for selecting a metal cask system now, but they are means objectives for more fundamental consequences that may occur due to necessary future decisions.

Means Objectives

Numerous objectives proposed by the panels are not explicitly shown in the fundamental objectives hierarchy of Table 11.6. That is not because they are unimportant, but because they are means to objectives that do appear in the table. Let me list some of these means and indicate how they are addressed.

Transportation and handling. One stated objective was to reduce both transportation and handling as much as possible. The reasons were that with less transportation and handling there would be fewer accidents, and hence better health and safety, that operations and transportation are costly and hence fewer operations would reduce costs, that operations and transportation increase visibility of the system and thus induce fears and anxieties, and so forth.

Catastrophes. There were suggestions that a separate objective should be to reduce catastrophes. The consequences of catastrophes are the negative effects with respect to objectives 1 through 6, and all of these should be explicitly considered if the possibility of a catastrophe is deemed sufficiently probable.

Transportation accidents. Clearly, reducing transportation accidents reduces costs and improves health and safety as well as environmental impacts.

Sabotage. It would be desirable to reduce the vulnerability of a system to sabotage, but this is important for the political impacts in terms of confidence as well as for the health and safety, economic, environmental, and social impacts that might accrue if successful sabotage occurred.

Cask durability. One proposed objective was cask durability: that the cask should be able to withstand a severe crash. But this is simply important for reducing the consequences of any accident involving a cask and for increasing the political confidence in the system.

Governmental strain and the need for regulatory inspections or hearings. The basic concern with these is the costs of the associated hearings or inspections as well as the effect on public confidence in government and in the technical system.

Meeting regulations. There is, of course, a need to meet the regulations that apply to a spent fuel management system. To some extent, these regulations limit the alternatives that should be evaluated using the stated objectives. Meeting regulations is one means to the public's confidence in government and to reducing fears and anxieties. Meeting regulations is also a means to "acceptable" health, safety, and environmental impacts and to the timely availability of the system.

Communication. A proposed objective was to have open, honest, and clear communication from the government and industry authorities to the public. This was felt to be a means to all of the political objectives as well as those concerning fears and anxieties.

Insights for Decision Opportunities, Alternatives, and Process

Many of the proposed objectives suggest features that might make the alternative metal cask systems more desirable. For instance, it might be possible to enact laws or regulations to improve the liability provisions associated with metal cask systems. There might be ways to label the casks that would over time have positive political effects as well as alleviate some of the public's fears and anxieties about the system.

Because of the indirect costs that the need to respond to emergencies would impose on the states, it was suggested that a federal emergency management team might be formed and that a team member might accompany all shipments of spent fuel. These individuals should insure that all transportation rules are observed and should be knowledgeable about what to do in case of an accident. In a similar vein, it would be unreasonable to select a specific metal cask system that would create a need for greater expense in other parts of the spent fuel management system. Regulations to address these indirect costs, so that the utility companies or cask owners could benefit from actions that reduce such costs, may be useful.

An important decision opportunity is to identify attributes to indicate the degree to which each of the objectives is achieved. In some cases, finding attributes may be easy, as it often is for cost objectives. For other objectives, such as geographical equity and flexibility with respect to regulatory changes, selecting an attribute may not be easy. It may be necessary to construct attributes for these cases to understand more clearly the exact meaning of the associated objectives.

After attributes are selected it is possible to assess values to combine the different attributes into a single objective function. For the evaluation of the alternative metal cask systems, we defined attributes and assessed three preliminary objective functions for individuals working on the project from Westinghouse, the Tennessee Valley Authority, and Florida Power and Light (Westinghouse, 1986). The next step should be to specify attributes and assess objective functions from individuals representing the viewpoints of other stakeholders in the problem. This information, plus the evaluation of alternatives from these perspectives, could provide a sound basis for fruitful discussion and constructive decisionmaking.

The set of objectives is potentially very valuable in communication about the project. Although members of consumer and environmental groups, regulatory agencies, and legislatures may not understand detailed implications of functional designs and technical jargon, they certainly can understand the fundamental objectives and the evaluation of alternatives in terms of these objectives. This common understanding may help provide a basis for compromise, when necessary, and consensus, if possible. It provides a foundation for the involvement of various legitimate stakeholders in the process of evaluating spent fuel management systems. Any of these stakeholders may have suggestions to improve the objectives hierarchy to make it more complete and more precise.

Note that two of the eight major fundamental objectives in the objectives hierarchy are there to interconnect this decision with other decision problems. Objectives concerning scheduling are meant to capture the implications of decisions that will have to be faced if the chosen cask system is not ready for implementation on schedule. Flexibility objectives concern the consequences of decisions that will be necessary if the technical or institutional situations that are currently appropriate for evaluating spent fuel casks change after the cask alternative is selected. These objectives are fundamental in the context of the current decision, but they are means for consequences in other related decisions.

11.3 Research on Climate Change

The possibility of global climate change is one of the major problems facing all nations on earth (see Clark, 1989). Governments, regulatory authorities, utility companies, and the public are keenly interested in this topic. There are numerous unanswered questions pertaining to possible climate change and its significance. If any major change in climate, such as a major warming, occurs, there is no question that it will have a significant impact on all societies (see Manne and Richels, 1990). There is also no scientific question that there has been an increase in carbon dioxide in the atmosphere over the last 100 years. Carbon dioxide and other greenhouse gases, such as methane, which trap heat in the earth's atmosphere, may initiate global warming and a change in climate. There are still major questions about whether global warming will occur, the degree to which it will occur if it does, the rate at which it will occur, and its implications for climate. So what should the nations of the earth do? This is definitely a monumental decision problem, one worthy of strategic thinking at all levels.

Utility companies around the world, as stakeholders in any problems concerned with climate change, are interested in making a contribution to understanding climate change and its potential impacts. As a step toward making such a contribution, the Electric Power Research Institute (EPRI) of Palo Alto, California supported the work reported in this section to address the question "What are the objectives of a comprehensive research program to address climate change issues?"

Before proceeding with any major research effort, it is useful to specify the objectives in detail. The specification of objectives indicates the reasons for the existence of a research program, promotes creative thinking to develop research tasks to achieve the objectives, and provides a basis for evaluating and monitoring the research program. Hence, it is worthwhile to develop objectives for research on climate change.

In a problem area of such breadth, it is likely that specialists in one relevant field are not aware of work in other relevant fields. Everybody concerned sees a few trees, but nobody sees the forest in which the trees stand. The work reported here is representative of an effort to see and understand the forest.

From the perspective of any stakeholder in such a problem, research objectives are means to achieve more fundamental objectives with respect to the substantive area being researched. This work therefore also outlines the utility industry's objectives with respect to climate change, and traces the links between that objectives hierarchy and the objectives hierarchy for research on climate change.

The process by which objectives were obtained in this case is relevant to many important decision situations. I held discussions to identify objectives with scientists in different fields and utility executives from different countries. The discussions included several individual interviews, some meetings with small groups, and open discussion sessions at an international workshop. Then I logically and systematically combined the information from these discussions into an objectives hierarchy for further modification and improvement.

Identifying Objectives

The objectives for research on climate change were developed as follows. First, I had detailed discussions with 13 individuals or small groups of individuals well informed about research needs concerning climate change and about the objectives of utility companies with respect to climate change. Since the intent was to develop a broad set of objectives, discussions were held with a diverse set of respondents including scientists and utility company executives. Each of the discussions yielded a list of objectives. The individual lists of objectives were then aggregated and structured to provide a basis for further discussions. Subsequently, at an international workshop, Tom Keelin and I each moderated an afternoon meeting of approximately 15 participants to articulate the objectives they considered appropriate for research on climate change. Each of these sessions also yielded a list of objectives. On the basis of the earlier discussions and the two workshop lists, I constructed two detailed objectives hierarchies. The objectives for research, structured as shown in Table 11.7, are means objectives to inform decisionmakers concerning possible climate change and to achieve the objectives of the utility industry, structured as shown in Table 11.8.

To provide an intuitive understanding of these large sets of objectives, I have broken each into five classes:

I. Understand the *science* relevant to climate change.
II. Understand the possible *impacts* of climate change.
III. Identify all the *alternatives* to address climate change issues.
IV. Facilitate the implementation of reasonable *policy*.
V. *Manage* the utility industry effectively with respect to climate change issues.

In concise terms, the respective classes are science, impacts, alternatives, policy, and management.

The objectives hierarchies were constructed as follows. Using the guidelines in Section 3.8, I identified major categories of objectives based on the interviews and discussions. The main guidelines are that no stated objectives be omitted and that the specification of objectives be consistent with the listed major objectives. There is no one "correct" set of objectives. For example, objective 2 in Table 11.8, "understand the implications of climate change," could have been broken into four separate objectives: "understand the implications of climate change to the utility industry," "understand the implications of climate change to individuals," and so on.

In interpreting the objectives, it is important to recognize that participants were asked to express their individual opinions and not necessarily those of their organizations. It is also important to recognize that the objectives suggested for a research program were not limited to ones that would be appropriate for research sponsored by individual utility companies, the utility industry, or EPRI. Participants were asked to

Table 11.7.   Objectives of research on possible climate change

I. Understand the science relevant to climate change

   1. Understand fundamental relationships between greenhouse gases and climate change

      1.1. Understand fundamental relationships in the environment (e.g., relationships among oceans, clouds, temperature, storms, rainfall, albedo, icecaps, forests, agriculture, famine)

      1.2. Understand relationships between greenhouse gases and the environment

      1.3. Understand carbon exchanges in the environment

      1.4. Explore phytosphere—how plants use water and air

      1.5. Explore photoelectric chemical processes to convert CO_2 back to methane and other organics

      1.6. Identify relationships between emissions and natural production of greenhouse gases

      1.7. Establish relationship between CO_2 emissions and CO_2 concentrations

   2. Improve predictive capability of global climate models

      2.1. Understand internal workings of global climate models

      2.2. Compare implications of global climate models

      2.3. Conduct sensitivity studies with global climate models

      2.4. Develop models to predict regional weather patterns

      2.5. Improve medium-time (6–12-month) weather forecasts

   3. Investigate what is occurring and what might occur regarding climate change

      3.1. Develop programs to examine climate over time

      3.2. Validate global climate models using information to date

      3.3. Provide information on the rate of any global climate changes

      3.4. Develop a useful set of indices to evaluate the climate

      3.5. Identify sources of major greenhouse gases and their relative importance

II. Understand the possible impacts of climate change

   4. Forecast impacts of climate change

      4.1. On utility companies (to demand, supply, operations, and finances)

      4.2. On individuals (to lifestyle and economic well-being)

      4.3. On nations (to finances, politics, economic development, business, and social)

      4.4. On society (to the environment and world order)

Table 11.7. (continued)

5. Understand differences in different countries about perceptions and priorities regarding climate change
   5.1. Investigate economic realities pertaining to global climate change
   5.2. Investigate political realities pertaining to global climate change
   5.3. Understand positions of the various stakeholders
   5.4. Investigate natural alliances of stakeholders regarding climate change

III. Identify all the alternatives to address climate change issues

6. Create alternatives that reduce greenhouse gas emissions
   6.1. Improve possibilities for efficient energy use (e.g., heating houses)
   6.2. Develop better technological alternatives (renewables, solar, gasification, hydrogen, biomass, smaller cogeneration, energy storage, etc.)
   6.3. Reduce or eliminate forest destruction
   6.4. Conduct an independent assessment of world gas reserves
   6.5. Investigate all conservation options
   6.6. Revitalize the nuclear option
   6.7. Identify integrated energy systems (i.e., production and consumption)
   6.8. Develop improved coal technologies (e.g., revolutionary—doubling of efficiency)

7. Develop plans to assist the developing world to meet its energy needs
   7.1. Promote development of infrastructure to address climate change issues
   7.2. Create financial structures to promote environmentally conscious decisionmaking in utilities of developing nations
   7.3. Understand how to transfer technological improvements to developing nations
   7.4. Predict how climate change will affect developing nations
   7.5. Incorporate viewpoints of developing nations in setting the climate change research agenda
   7.6. Evaluate alternatives for developing countries for reducing CO_2 emissions from power generation

8. Develop plans to adapt to global warming
   8.1. Develop plans for utility companies to adapt (including operating criteria)

Table 11.7. (continued)

    8.2. Develop plans for individuals to adapt
    8.3. Identify and develop carbon storage possibilities
    8.4. Investigate carbon cycle opportunities for mitigation (e.g., halophytes, accelerate growing cycle for biomass)
    8.5. Develop technology to chemically separate, collect, solidify, and use carbon dioxide

IV. Facilitate the implementation of reasonable policy

  9. Create policy options
    9.1. Address greenhouse gas emissions (supply-side options, demand-side options)
    9.2. Mitigate effects of climate change (utility contingency planning, societal contingency planning)
    9.3. Identify utility position to possibly influence UNEP agenda
    9.4. Coordinate development of energy and electricity options to address both economic and environmental impacts
    9.5. Identify mechanisms for trading CO_2 emission rights

  10. Analyze policy options
    10.1. Develop frameworks to evaluate policy options and research priorities
    10.2. Develop sound methodologies to focus on key value judgments (which can be different in different countries)
    10.3. Evaluate cost-effectiveness of national and international policy options
    10.4. Analyze national and international energy strategies (e.g., role of electricity)
    10.5. Identify benefits of reducing greenhouse gases

  11. Promote responsible and effective policy decisionmaking
    11.1. Understand the knowledge required for responsible decisionmaking
    11.2. Understand how to influence the policy debate
    11.3. Evaluate possibilities for reducing greenhouse gases in different economic sectors
    11.4. Understand social psychology of energy conservation
    11.5. Develop criteria for reasonable transfer of technologies
    11.6. Improve regulatory frameworks to address climate change issues

Table 11.7.   (continued)

---

12. Promote education about climate change issues
    12.1. Help policymakers, legislators, regulators, and the public understand risk
    12.2. Provide guiding suggestions for the processes of any proposed international negotiations regarding climate change
    12.3. Study institutional dynamics and driving forces with the goal of influencing policy
    12.4. Identify mechanisms to improve negotiations and communication on global warming

V. Manage the utility industry effectively with respect to climate change issues

13. Understand how to position the utility industry as part of the solution to possible climate change
    13.1. Investigate business opportunities of the utility industry to address climate change issues
    13.2. Investigate fair share contributions of different stakeholders (e.g., coal industry, oil industry, transportation) to address climate change issues
    13.3. Identify and appraise "high ground" that can be obtained (in generating and using electricity, in reducing emissions from other energy use)

14. Understand public opinion about the utility industry
    14.1. Develop effective techniques for communicating risk information to the public
    14.2. Understand factors that effect public opinion about utility companies
    14.3. Understand the relationships between utility company actions and the perception that they are part of the solution
    14.4. Identify political problems affecting greenhouse gas alternatives
    14.5. Understand basis of public's concerns about greenhouse gases (e.g., desire for energy conservation)
    14.6. Identify best ways of collaborating with environmentalists on greenhouse gas issues
    14.7. Identify best ways of collaborating with politicians on greenhouse gas issues (e.g., help them meet their commitments)

Table 11.7. (continued)

---

15. Coordinate utility industry contributions that address climate change issues
    15.1. Develop a research agenda for utility companies concerned with climate change issues
    15.2. Develop a research agenda for cooperative research by utility companies
    15.3. Effectively exchange information about climate change
    15.4. Understand how to shape issues of the greenhouse gas "debate"
    15.5. Investigate value of binational or multinational research centers concerning global warming

---

Table 11.8. Objectives of the utility industry pertaining to possible climate change

---

I. Understand the science relevant to climate change

  1. Understand the degree to which climate change is occurring
    1.1. Understand the science of what is occurring
    1.2. Understand why it is occurring

II. Understand the possible impacts of climate change
  2. Understand the implications of climate change
    2.1. To the utility industry
    2.2. To individuals
    2.3. To nations
    2.4. To society

  3. Understand economic and political realities around the world pertaining to possible climate change and to addressing climate change
    3.1. Coordinate climate change research efforts
    3.2. Communicate and exchange information effectively

III. Identify all the alternatives to address climate change issues

  4. Promote efficient use of energy
    4.1. Create better technological alternatives
    4.2. Develop technology to reduce emissions of carbon and other pollutants
    4.3. Revitalize the nuclear option

Table 11.8. (continued)

---

    5. Assist developing countries in addressing their future energy needs

    6. Be prepared for potential climate change
        6.1. Investigate adaptive options
        6.2. Develop contingency plans for possible climate change

IV. Facilitate the implementation of reasonable policy

    7. Understand the full range of policy options to address climate change
        7.1. Emissions policies
        7.2. Mitigation policies
        7.3. Political policies

    8. Understand the relative desirability of proposed policies

    9. Insure public policy decisions are based on sound reasoning
        9.1. Converge on critical science before international agreements are solidified
        9.2. Develop logical mechanisms to incorporate environmental realities into decisionmaking
        9.3. Develop frameworks to help decisionmaking regarding climate change

    10. Educate about what is known regarding climate change

V. Manage the utility industry effectively with respect to climate change issues

    11. Meet customer needs
    12. Position the utility industry as part of the solution to any climate change
        12.1. Have other parties (e.g., coal industry) acknowledged as key stakeholders
        12.2. Have all stakeholders doing their share to address climate change issues

    13. Enhance public image of utility industry as proactive and responsible
        13.1. Demonstrate knowledge of utility industry regarding climate change issues
        13.2. Be willing contributors to plans to level CO_2 emissions

    14. Conduct research in a cost-effective manner

---

broaden the focus for two reasons. First, more inclusive lists of objectives made it less likely that objectives appropriate for the utility industry or EPRI would be omitted. Second, the broader scope made it possible to see how any particular utility industry or EPRI research on climate change would fit into the overall research program being conducted around the world. Once a comprehensive list of objectives was explicitly provided, it would not be difficult to narrow this list to pertain to the utility industry.

The way items are listed in the tables does not indicate the relative importance of the objectives. In fact, a subobjective under one major objective may be more important than another major objective.

In the interviews and discussions, some of the objectives stated were clearly means to other objectives. In contructing the objectives hierarchies in Tables 11.7 and 11.8, I tried to eliminate those means objectives whenever possible. However, there are natural synergies in the tables. For instance, promoting responsible and effective policy decisionmaking (objective 11 in Table 11.7) would probably lead to fewer forecast impacts of climate change (objective 4) and more alternatives and plans created to address climate change (objectives 6, 7, and 8). Similarly, promoting the efficient use of energy (objective 4 in Table 11.8) would be likely to enhance the public image of the utility industry (objective 13).

Insights for Decision Opportunities, Alternatives, and Process

A very important use of the research objectives hierarchy is as a basis for communication. Anyone interested in climate change issues can peruse the objectives hierarchy for omissions. If any omissions are found, the objectives hierarchy should be modified accordingly. Also, the objectives hierarchy can be used to identify disagreements about prospective tasks and to ascertain whether those disagreements are about the expected contributions of the tasks or the relative importance of those contributions.

The research objectives in Table 11.7 can be prioritized for any individual utility company, any consortium of utility companies, or EPRI. There are two ways to determine these priorities. One is to set priorities directly for the research objectives as discussed in Chapter 5. The other is first to prioritize the objectives of the utility industry, then to determine the contribution of different levels of achievement of research objectives to the achievement of the utility industry objectives, and finally, as discussed in Chapter 4, to derive the priorities for the research objectives. Comparing the calculated priorities with those directly assessed is likely to indicate discrepancies. Understanding the basis for these discrepancies should lead to more informed priorities to better define a research program on climate change.

The list of research objectives and their priorities can be used to facilitate the creation of research tasks. Specifically, one can ask for each objective and subobjective what tasks might best achieve that objective. One can also vary the scope of the tasks by changing the costs, time, and other resources allocated. The greatest effort should be focused on the high-priority objectives.

Once attributes have been defined for the objectives these can be used as a basis for describing proposed tasks. The description of each proposed research task will indicate the degree to which the different objectives might be achieved if that task were performed. This information can then be combined with the priorities and information about the relative importance of the different possible levels of achievement to provide an overall evaluation of the research tasks.

11.4 Air Pollution in Los Angeles

High mountains surround the Los Angeles Basin on the north and east. Consequently, air pollution collects in the Basin and pollution levels often exceed national air quality standards for several pollutants. Almost everyone in the Los Angeles Basin contributes to the problem, is concerned about the problem, and must be a part of any "solution" to the problem. Responsive and responsible action needs to be taken. But what?

The Electric Power Research Institute sponsored a project to develop a methodology for involving stakeholders in decisions that affect them. As part of this project, Detlof von Winterfeldt and I elicited objectives and preliminary value tradeoffs for several stakeholders concerned about Los Angeles's air pollution. The objectives were intended to provide a common understanding of the breadth of the air pollution problem, and the value tradeoffs were intended to provide an understanding of the range of possible disagreements.

Aspects of this case are summarized here for three reasons. First, the individuals involved in expressing objectives and value tradeoffs were affiliated with a broad spectrum of stakeholders. Second, the breadth of objectives is indicative of problems that have direct effects on the public. Third, this is one of the first attempts to identify the range of agreement and disagreement among stakeholders by quantifying their interests and perceptions using value tradeoffs.

Identifying Objectives

To identify a useful set of objectives, we chose a broad set of stakeholders whose viewpoints should be included. Then we contacted individuals affiliated with each of those stakeholders and asked if we could discuss their perceptions of the Los Angeles Basin air pollution problem. Participants were affiliated with the following organizations:

American Lung Association
Automobile Club of Southern California
California Air Resources Board
California Council for Environmental and Economic Balance
Los Angeles Area Chamber of Commerce
Los Angeles City Department of Water and Power
Sierra Club
South Coast Air Quality Management District
Southern California Association of Governments
Southern California Edison
Unocal Corporation.

There are many other stakeholders in this problem, but this set covers a wide range of perspectives.

Between one and three people affiliated with each stakeholder participated in the discussions of objectives. We stressed that we were asking for personal rather than organizational perspectives to avoid the need for organizational approval and agreement on objectives. After each discussion, the objectives of that individual or individuals were structured and sent to them for consideration and revision. Subsequently, the combined objectives hierarchy in Table 11.9 was structured and also sent to the participants for comments. In the table, objectives are numbered consecutively and are listed in shortened form. For example, subobjective 4 is "minimize health implications due to air pollution causing impairment of lung function in children."

The objectives hierarchy clearly indicates that the air pollution situation is not just a physical health problem, as the Clean Air Act essentially defines it to be. In essence, the Clean Air Act says that ambient air quality should be such that the health of the groups most sensitive to air pollution is protected. The objectives hierarchy makes it clear that there are health and safety concerns, quality-of-life concerns, and economic and equity concerns.

The health and safety concerns are represented by the first two major objectives in Table 11.9. Objective 1 concerns physical health and safety impacts of air pollution and also of air pollution control strategies or requirements or technologies. Mental and emotional health are included under the psychological impacts objective 17. The concerns include any effects of air pollution on the psychological states and mental abilities of humans.

The next four major objectives address the effects of air pollution on the quality of life in the Los Angeles Basin. Objective 18 concerns degradation of visibility due to air pollution in different regions of the Basin. Objective 22 concerns the direct consequences of air pollution that lower the quality of life of individuals and families. Environmental impacts, represented by objective 34, include impacts of air pollution on flora and fauna as well as any contribution to global warming. The social impacts of objective 39 concern impacts of air pollution and air pollution control strategies on the societal structure.

The economic and equity objectives are detailed by the last three major objectives in Table 11.9. Economic costs, objective 44, include the dollar costs to individuals, business and industry, and government due to air pollution or to pollution control. Socioeconomic impacts, objective 57, concern changes in the economic system that affect individuals, businesses, and industry. These changes include lost jobs or job opportunities, lower productivity, fewer new businesses, and closing of old businesses. Objective 66, equity, concerns several different concepts about how the costs and benefits of air pollution control should be fairly distributed across many groups in society.

Assessing Value Tradeoffs

Once the stakeholders had agreed that all of their fundamental objectives were included in the combined objectives hierarchy, von Winterfeldt and I developed attributes for each of the objectives. Our intent was to quantify representative values from the individuals affiliated with the stakeholder groups in order to understand the range of differences and similarities of viewpoints. For this purpose, we chose to assess value tradeoffs among nine attributes corresponding to one key objective in

Table 11.9. Combined objectives hierarchy concerning air pollution in
the Los Angeles Basin

1. Public health and safety
    2. Due to air pollution
        3. Impairment of lung function (e.g. chronic breathing difficulty)
            4. Children
            5. Elderly
            6. Other (e.g. asthmatics)
        7. Heart attacks
        8. Cancers
            9. Lung
            10. Skin
        11. Acute health effects (e.g. difficulty in breathing, coughing,
        eye irritation, headaches, nausea)
        12. Reproductive effects
    13. Due to air pollution control
        14. Fatalities (e.g. due to vehicle accidents, less income, side effect of medication, transmission of disease, workers' accidents)
        15. Illness
        16. Injuries

17. Psychological impacts (e.g. fear, depression, embarrassment concerning surroundings, stress, reduced mental acuity and concentration)

18. Visibility
    19. In Western L.A. Basin
    20. In Eastern L.A. Basin
    21. In mountains east of L.A. Basin

22. Lifestyle impacts
    23. Enjoyment of the environment (e.g. affected by visibility, smell, deterioration of materials and products, environmental degradation, limited physical activity)
    24. Less convenience
        25. Restrictions on produce use
        26. Restrictions on vehicle use
        27. Restrictions on physical activity
        28. Restrictions on home use
            29. Limitations on where to live
            30. Forced work at home
    31. Degraded personal relationships
        32. Within families
        33. With others

Table 11.9. (continued)

34. Environmental impacts
    35. Local
        36. Tree loss in forests
        37. Degradation of private gardens, plants, and fruit trees
    38. Global (e.g. minimize L.A. contribution to Earth's warming)

39. Social impacts
    40. Restricted upward mobility
    41. Social stability and crime
    42. Conserve older neighborhoods
    43. Degradation of ethnic neighborhoods

44. Economic costs
    45. Due to pollution
        46. To individuals
            47. Low-income
            48. Other
        49. To business and industry
        50. To local government (e.g. due to federal sanctions, duplicity)
    51. Due to pollution controls
        52. To individuals
            53. Low-income
            54. Other
        55. To business and industry
        56. To local government

57. Socioeconomic impacts
    58. To individuals
        59. Lost jobs
        60. Fewer new jobs
    61. To business and industry
        62. Less productivity
        63. Fewer new businesses
        64. Closing of businesses

65. Equity
    66. With respect to economic costs (e.g. who pays: rich vs. poor, in L.A. Basin vs. out, big vs. little polluters, stockholders vs. rate payers, balanced over time)
    67. with respect to benefits and negative impacts excluding costs (e.g. balance impacts over the entire L.A. Basin region)

each of the nine major objective categories. The attributes selected, with their ranges and a unit of measurement, are presented in Table 11.10. When the unit is not the same as that of the associated attribute, the two are related by a simple calculation.

Some general assumptions used in the process are worth mentioning. There are 12 million people in the Los Angeles Basin. Of these, 4 million hold jobs. We assumed there are 3 million families. The 8 million drivers make approximately 40 million vehicle trips per day. These numbers are useful for interpreting the ranges and units of consequences in Table 11.10. For example, reduction of one percent in vehicle trips means 400,000 fewer vehicle trips daily.

We assessed value tradeoffs for individuals affiliated with nine of the eleven stakeholder groups. The assessments had three stages. First, each individual ranked the ranges of the attributes. We told participants to assume that all consequences were at the bad levels in Table 11.10 and asked which they would prefer to move to the good level. The chosen attribute corresponded to the highest-ranked objective. The respondent was then asked which would be next most important to move from bad to good. The response indicated the second-ranked objective, and so on.

The next line of questions asked how much additional annual cost would be acceptable to change the level of each attribute from bad to good level. For example, one response was that it would be worth up to $100 million to eliminate the 1,000 cases of impaired lung function. The third line of questions concerned how much it would be worth per unit of each attribute. For example, what would be the maximum acceptable cost to eliminate one adult case of 20 percent impairment of lung function for one year. The response should be $100,000 to be consistent with the $100 million to eliminate 1,000 cases. With the units and ranges, we had two ways to think about the same issue and a method to identify and reconcile inconsistencies.

Table 11.11 illustrates the reconciled unit value tradeoffs for four of the respondents. It shows reasonable consistency across individuals for some attributes and large differences for others. The attribute with the greatest agreement about the value tradeoffs was health effects, which is allegedly the reason why many people are concerned about air pollution. Most of the other attributes had differences in the neighborhood of one to two orders of magnitude. Psychological impacts had a very large range of three orders of magnitude. Individual 1 considered psychological effects essentially a consequence of the other fundamental attributes that mattered, so that to rate psychological impacts very high

Table 11.10.   Attributes for the assessment of value tradeoffs among objectives concerning Los Angeles air pollution

Attribute	Good	Bad	Unit
	Levels		
Public health and safety: Annual number of otherwise healthy adults diagnosed as having a 20% impairment in lung function	0	1,000	1 adult
Psychological impacts: Average annual number of days L.A. Basin residents say they suffer from psychological effects of air pollution	0	100	1 person-day
Visibility: Average daily miles of maximum visibility in the eastern L.A. Basin	50	10	1 mile
Lifestyle impacts: Annual percentage of "desired vehicle trips" that are banned	0	20	1 trip
Environmental impacts: Annual number of households with noticeable degradation of private gardens, plants, or fruit trees	0	1 million	1 household
Social impacts: Number of L.A. Basin residents without "upwardly mobile" job opportunities owing to pollution or pollution control	0	400,000	1 person
Socioeconomic impacts: Annual number of jobs lost	0	100,000	1 job
Costs: Total annual cost	0	$7.2 billion	$1 billion
Equity: Equity with respect to distribution of cost. Constructed scale: worst corresponds to low-income families ($10K) paying same (e.g. $1,200) as high-income families ($50K); best corresponds to proportional payments, e.g. low-income families paying $400, high-income families $2,000	proportional	equal	equal to proportional per household

Table 11.11. Assessed unit value tradeoffs for Los Angeles air pollution

Attributes	Unit value tradeoffs in dollars			
	Individual 1	Individual 2	Individual 3	Individual 4
Health and safety	$ 100,000	$ 125,000	$ 20,000	$ 50,000
Psychological	0.001	1.00	1.00	1.00
Visibility	5,000,000	25,000,000	1,000,000	1,000,000
Lifestyle	0.10	2.50	1.25	0.08
Environment	5	1,000	25	10
Social	125	10,000	3,000	100
Socioeconomic	100	40,000	1,000	1,000
Costs	1,000,000	1,000,000	1,000,000	1,000,000
Equity	16	300	1,200	300

would be double-counting. Individuals 2, 3, and 4 felt that psychological well-being was related to but distinct from the other attributes. Regarding the cost value tradeoffs they were identical by definition, since $1 million is equivalent to $1 million.

Insights for Decision Opportunities, Alternatives, and Process

The work described above was begun in 1988 and completed in early 1989. In early 1989, a "political solution" to the Los Angeles air pollution problem was announced. Its annual cost was estimated at approximately $9 billion, or $3,000 annually per family of four. The alternatives considered focused on air pollutant concentrations rather than on the consequences that matter to people as indicated in Table 11.9. The comments below are thoughts on how the problem might have been better handled.

Since air pollution is a concern to almost everyone, this problem context is an ideal one in which to get people involved. It would be reasonable to involve almost any group that wanted to participate in identifying objectives. The final list of objectives would probably be only slightly more extensive than that in Table 11.9, but the process itself would make a major contribution. The process would also cost pennies relative to the $9 billion price tag of the chosen program.

One potential decision opportunity would be to educate school-children about air pollution and its effects while involving them in structuring objectives. Teaching material could be developed that would elicit objectives from the children, tell them what they themselves might do to reduce pollution, and educate them about ways to avoid health effects of pollution. Objectives might be aggregated on a school level. This might be followed by an "air quality convention" with elected representatives of each school. This entire exercise would cost a little money, but relative to $9 billion it should be very cost-effective.

Our study suggests a large amount of useful data that should be collected. Basically, it would be useful to know the relationships between air pollution levels and the achievement of all of the objectives in Table 11.9. It would also be useful to know what consequences in terms of those objectives would be caused by actions to control air pollution.

The framework outlined could focus discussion on the pros and cons of various strategies for controlling air pollution. It could provide a basis for identifying potential conflicts by assessing value tradeoffs. However, it would be desirable to go a step further than we did in the assessments. We did not have the opportunity to bring the individual participants together to examine why their value assessments differed. In some cases, a major part of the difference may have been due to different understandings of the seriousness of what was being measured. For instance, some participants may not have understood the implications of a 20 percent impairment of lung function: would such an impairment limit the sufferer to sedentary activities, or would it simply require some moderation?

A final decision opportunity would be to develop a means-ends objectives network for all the fundamental objectives in Table 11.9. This would suggest numerous activities that would potentially be worthwhile either for reducing air pollution or for reducing the undesirable consequences of air pollution.

11.5 Design of Integrated Circuit Testers

Over the last decade, the integrated circuit industry has gone through a cycle of birth, explosive growth, and now severe competition. Few industries have evolved so quickly on the one hand and have found such severe competition on the other. As a result, the risks associated with customer and market misassessment are very significant in this industry.

In early 1984, Gary Lilien and I were approached by the Capricorn Corporation, (not its real name), a well-known Silicon Valley firm with an established reputation for producing high-quality manufacturing, test, and control equipment. The firm had made a technical break-through that it felt would give it a significant cost advantage in manufac-turing test equipment for very large-scale integrated circuits (VLSIC). Capricorn wanted to know how prospective customers would evaluate a Capricorn entry in this highly competitive market and how its product should be designed.

The analysis described here, adapted from Keeney and Lilien (1987), was part of a larger study to identify likely customers for the product, the future needs of such customers, the product's likely com-petitors for each customer, and the decision process within firms for purchasing such test equipment. This study illustrates the many inter-connections between the evaluation of alternatives using quantified val-ues and value-focused thinking using those same values.[1]

Identifying Objectives and Attributes

Several meetings with technical and marketing staff of Capricorn and a review of the technical literature yielded numerous objectives for evalu-ating VLSIC testers. By analyzing means-ends relationships we identi-fied 17 fundamental objectives from the original list of 57 objectives, many of which had subobjectives (see Healy, 1982). These fundamental objectives, listed in Table 11.12, fell into four categories: technical, eco-nomic, software, and vendor support. Attributes chosen for these objec-tives were either natural, such as picoseconds for timing accuracy, or constructed, such as the yes/no attribute for the availability of data analy-sis software.

Because the uses of the tester vary by the types of VSLIC devices tested by the customer, the range of desirable levels for attributes also varies by customer. For example, a customer may indicate that the "min-imum acceptable level" for pin capacity is 64 while the "maximum desir-able level" given current plans is 256. Then the pin capacity dimension for this customer would be evaluated only between 64 and 256.

---

1. This section contains some quantitative material; readers who are not mathemati-cally inclined may wish to skip ahead to Section 11.6.

The technical and economic objectives in Table 11.12 are easy to understand. A key software objective is whether a universal translator exists, measured by a yes/no scale. A universal translator takes VLSIC testing software developed for another manufacturer's tester and translates it for use on Capricorn's tester. Other software objectives include several forms of networking capabilities and software development time.

Vendor support objectives include service, performance, and applications support. Vendor service is measured by the time necessary to get the equipment running after it has gone down. Vendor performance is measured by the time until vendor personnel arrive at the customer's facility after such assistance has been requested. Vendor capability to assist in applications is measured by the simple yes/no attribute.

An Objective Function for Mr. Smith of Acorn Industries

Acorn Industries (not its real name) is one of the most important potential customers for Capricorn, as it is one of the five U.S. industry leaders in the manufacturing of VLSICs. After careful preliminary evaluation of the tester acquisition process, we interviewed Michael Smith, the manager of test engineering, to determine his value function. Mr. Smith was identified as "most influential" in the buying process for test equipment not only by his colleagues at Acorn but also by numerous individuals outside the firm. He seemed to serve as a key referent for many firms in the region. In addition, he maintained a detailed matrix of test equipment and evaluation of that equipment along some 25 to 30 dimensions of his own. Thus, Acorn Industries in general and Mr. Smith in particular met the "lead user" criterion discussed by von Hippel (1986).

Before beginning to assess an objective function, we asked Mr. Smith to specify a minimum acceptable level and a maximum desirable level for each attribute. His responses, which determined the range over which attributes could vary, are displayed in Table 11.12.

The independence assumptions necessary to use an additive measurable value function (see Dyer and Sarin, 1979), analogous to the additive utility function (5.3), were verified with Mr. Smith. Hence, the objective function chosen was

$$v(x_1, \ldots, x_{17}) = k_T v_T(x_1, \ldots, x_6) + k_E v_E(x_7, x_8, x_9) \qquad (11.1)$$
$$+ k_S v_S(x_{10}, \ldots, x_{14}) + k_V v_V(x_{15}, x_{16}, x_{17}),$$

Table 11.12. Objectives, attributes, and component values for VLSIC testers

Objective	Attribute	Attribute range		Normalized weights within objective category	Component value function
		Minimum acceptable level	Maximum desirable level		
Technical					
Pin capacity	X_1 = quantity	144	256	15	$v_1(x_1) = 1.93[1 - \exp(0.0065(144 - x_1))]$
Vector depth	X_2 = memory size (megabits)	1	4	20	$v_2(x_2) = -0.97E - 09[1 - \exp(6.92(x_2 - 1))]$
Data rate	X_3 = MHz	40	100	10	$v_3(x_3) = -0.31[1 - \exp(0.024(x_3 - 40)]$
Timing accuracy	X_4 = picoseconds	±500	±250	35	$v_4(x_4) = (500 - x_4)/250$
Pin capacitance	X_5 = picofarads	100	30	10	$v_5(x_5) = (100 - x_5)/70$
Programmable measurement units	X_6 = number	4	16	10	$v_6(x_6) = 1.31[1 - \exp(0.12(4 - x_6))]$
Economic					
Price	X_7 = total cost	\$2.5M	\$1.5M	50	$v_7(x_7) = 2.5 - x_7$
Uptime	X_8 = percentage	98	100	20	$v_8(x_8) = (x_8 - 98)/2$
Delivery time	X_9 = months	6	4	30	$v_9(x_9) = (6 - x_9)/2$

328

Software				
Software translator	X_{10} = percentage conversion	10	100	15	$v_{10}(x_{10}) = 2.77[1 - \exp(0.005(10 - x_{10}))]$
Networking: communications	X_{11} = yes/no	no	yes	20	$v_{11}(x_{11})$: $v_{11}(\text{no}) = 0.0$; $v_{11}(\text{yes}) = 1.0$
Networking: open	X_{12} = yes/no	no	yes	20	$v_{12}(x_{12})$: $v_{12}(\text{no}) = 0.0$; $v_{12}(\text{yes}) = 1.0$
Development time	X_{13} = mean time (months)	4	2	30	$v_{13}(x_{13}) = (4 - x_{13})/2$
Data analysis software	X_{14} = yes/no	no	yes	15	$v_{14}(x_{14})$: $v_{14}(\text{no}) = 0.0$; $v_{14}(\text{yes}) = 1.0$
Vendor support					
Vendor service	X_{15} = time until system works (hours)	4	1	30	$v_{15}(x_{15}) = -0.31[1 - \exp(0.48(4 - x_{15}))]$
Vendor performance	X_{16} = time until response (hours)	4	1	30	$v_{16}(x_{16}) = -0.31[1 - \exp(0.48(4 - x_{16}))]$
Customer applications	X_{17} = yes/no	no	yes	40	$v_{17}(x_{17})$: $v_{17}(\text{no}) = 0.0$; $v_{17}(\text{yes}) = 1.0$

where

$$v_T(x_1, \ldots, x_6) = \sum_{i=1}^{6} k_i v_i(x_i), \tag{11.2a}$$

$$v_E(x_7, x_8, x_9) = \sum_{i=7}^{9} k_i v_i(x_i), \tag{11.2b}$$

$$v_S(x_{10}, \ldots, x_{14}) = \sum_{i=10}^{14} k_i v_i(x_i), \tag{11.2c}$$

$$v_V(x_{15}, x_{16}, x_{17}) = \sum_{i=15}^{17} k_i v_i(x_i), \tag{11.2d}$$

where v is a measurable value function for evaluating testers described by $(x_1, \ldots, x_{17})$; T, E, S, and V stand for technical, economic, software, and vendor support objectives, respectively; v_T, v_E, v_S, and v_V are component measurable value functions for the four respective objective categories; k_T, k_E, k_S, and k_V are the scaling constants of the four objective categories given the ranges indicated by Mr. Smith and listed in Table 11.12; v_i is the component measurable value function for attribute X_i scaled from zero to one; x_i is a specific level of X_i; and k_i is the scaling constant for attribute X_i within its objective category. To use this model, we needed to assess 17 component value functions (the v_i), 17 scaling constants for the objectives (the k_i), and four scaling constants for the objective categories (k_j, $j = T, E, S, V$).

The measurable value function was assessed in the same manner as the utility functions described in Chapter 5. In particular, the scaling constants were determined using the identical questions and process that are used for utility functions.

Using the information assessed (see Keeney and Lilien, 1987), we calculated the parameters for the value function (11.1) and (11.2). The scaling constants for the objective categories were

$$k_T = 0.52, \quad k_E = 0.14, \quad k_S = 0.32, \quad k_V = 0.02. \tag{11.3}$$

These scaling constants were assessed from value tradeoffs and normalized sum to 1.0.

Within each objective category, we asked Mr. Smith to allocate 100 points to represent the relative values of moving the attributes from their minimum acceptable levels to their maximum desirable levels. For ease of implementation, we first assigned relative weights and then normalized them to sum to 100. The normalized weights are shown in Table 11.12. Collectively, these normalized weights and the scaling constants in (11.3) plus the component value functions, also listed in Table 11.12, define the complete objective function (11.1).

Insights for Decision Opportunities, Alternatives, and Process

This value model was used to determine the likely response of Acorn Industries to the OR9000, a new tester Capricorn had in prototype form. Acorn Industries was also interested in two other testers: the Sentry 50 and the J941. Table 11.13 presents a description of the three testers in terms of the 17 objectives and their evaluation using the value function (11.1).

With the scaling of the measurable value function, a tester described by the column of maximum desirable levels in Table 11.12 would score 100 and a tester described by the column of minimum acceptable levels would score 0. This same scoring convention was also used within each of the four objective categories.

Some evaluations in Table 11.13 are less than zero because they are lower than the minimum acceptable level. This occurred because the range was set for the testers to be used in research as well as production engineering, while the testers evaluated were basically production models. Thus, none of these testers is wholly acceptable to Acorn. This evaluation shows which of the three testers would be "least unacceptable" and indicates the characteristics of preferable testers.

Using base case evaluations, the Sentry 50 is slightly preferred to the OR9000 and both are much preferred to the J941. This follows from the overall evaluations of 15.4 for Sentry 50, 13.3 for OR9000, and -18.0 for J941. In terms of objective categories, the OR9000 dominates J941, that is, it is better than the J941 in the technical, economic, software, and vendor support categories. The Sentry 50 does not dominate the J941. The OR9000 is strongly preferred to the Sentry 50 in the economic, software, and vendor support categories. The Sentry 50 is strongly preferred to the OR9000 in the technical category. This preference is basically due to pin capacity and timing accuracy, the latter being the major factor.

The value model makes it possible to run several sensitivity analyses

Table 11.13.   VLSIC tester evaluations

Objective	Tester		
	OR9000	J941	Sentry 50
Technical			
Pin capacity	160	96	256
Vector depth	0.128	0.256	0.064
Data rate	50	20	50
Timing accuracy	±1000	±1000	±600
Pin capacitance	55	50	40
Programmable measurement units	8	2	4
Technical evaluation	− 54.9	− 78.2	10.4
Economic			
Price	$1.4M	$1.0M	$2.8M
Uptime	98	95	95
Delivery time	3	6	6
Economic evaluation	100	45	− 45
Software			
Software translator	90	90	90
Networking communications	yes	yes	yes
Networking: open	yes	no	no
Development time	3	4	4
Data analysis software	yes	yes	yes
Software evaluation	83.7	48.7	48.7
Vendor support			
Vendor service	2	4.75	6
Vendor performance	4	4	4
Customer applications	yes	yes	yes
Vendor support evaluation	55.0	37.2	34.3
Overall evaluation	13.3	− 18.0	15.4

that provide insight about decision opportunities and new alternatives. Let me give a few examples.

Note that the difference in evaluations for the Sentry 50 and the OR9000 is 15.4 minus 13.3 or 2.1 evaluation units. It is useful to know how much this difference is worth in cost. Since the range of price in Table 11.12 is $1 million, this cost translates into $k_E k_7$ evaluation units or $0.14 \times 50 = 7$ units. Hence, the 2.1 units are worth 2.1/7 of $1 million or $300,000, so the Sentry 50 is worth $300,000 more than the OR9000. This suggests that the price of the OR9000 would have to drop to approximately $1.1 million to be competitive with the Sentry 50.

Note from (11.3) that 52 percent of the evaluations within attribute ranges are due to technical objectives. Thus, this is likely to be a fruitful area in which to search for desirable alternatives. For instance, Capricorn may have some idea about the development cost of improving the OR9000's timing accuracy from the current ± 1000 picoseconds to the minimal acceptable level of ± 500 picoseconds. This change would increase the technical evaluation of the OR9000 by 70 so it would be 15.1, just slightly better than the Sentry. Multiplying this 70 by the 0.52 scaling constant for technical objectives would increase the OR9000 evaluation by 36.4 units to 49.7, which is much better then the Sentry. Since 7 evaluation units are worth $1 million, this technical improvement would be worth a price change of approximately $5.2 million. Since the current OR9000 is inferior to the Sentry by an equivalent of $300,000, an improved OR9000 with timing accuracy at ± 500 picoseconds could command an increase in cost of approximately $4.9 million per tester. Multiplying this amount by the number of testers Capricorn might expect to sell would provide some idea of the development costs that might be recouped by sales. Comparing this to expected development costs would suggest developmental strategies.

This same type of sensitivity analysis could be done for many possible upgrades of the OR9000. Comparing the expected income implications of possible sales to the forecast development costs of the different upgrades would make it possible to identify the upgrade alternatives that looked most promising for designing a high-quality product that would also be financially justifiable.

The objectives and attributes in Table 11.12 are useful for communication and information collection, particularly for marketing and sales personnel at Capricorn. Marketing should want to stress the features of the product that are both relatively important to potential purchasers and better than the competition. Sales personnel should do the same, but should also gather information from possible purchasers about their values for the different objectives. Different purchasers might naturally have different uses for the tester and might also have different values. Knowing the diversity of values among prospective purchasers of the OR9000 could help Capricorn identify and evaluate development strategies. Also, such information would allow Capricorn to customize the product as appropriate. For example, it would probably be easy to create a more responsive vendor support option for a purchaser who assigned more importance to this objective than the 2 percent for Acorn indicated in (11.3).

11.6 Collaborating on a Book

Professors Ward Edwards and Detlof von Winterfeldt had collaborated over a five-year period on a book about decision analysis and behavioral decision theory. In January 1985 the draft manuscript was finished and included approximately 1,500, double-spaced pages. Both authors wanted to revise the manuscript thoroughly before delivering it to the publisher, Cambridge University Press. The decision facing them was how best to make the revisions. On this they had different viewpoints.

My role in this decision was to elicit each collaborator's objectives separately and then to meet with both of them at once to discuss the results. On the basis of their objectives and perceptions, I suggested some alternatives to help them to achieve their objectives. This situation illustrates the usefulness of values for creating alternatives in group and negotiation contexts. Although the decision situation is relatively simple, it has several key elements that are relevant to more complex decisions.

Detlof's Perspective

Detlof's fundamental objectives for the book are presented in Table 11.14. Of these, he felt career advancement and communication of concepts of decision analysis to be the most significant. Career advancement included both academic advancement and increased opportunities for interesting consulting. The intended audience for the book was both users of decision analysis (that is, people involved in applications) and teachers of decision analysis. Thus, there was a means objective, not listed in Table 11.14, that the book be as useful as possible for teaching. This, of course, would contribute to both communication and career advancement. The third objective concerned the satisfaction of reaching a clear milestone in one's career. Detlof also hoped, naturally enough, that the book would contribute to his prestige and standing among his peers, and of course any financial reward from the book would be welcome. Detlof's final objective was to satisfy Ward's objectives with respect to the book. Specifically, Detlof thought it was important for Ward to

Table 11.14.   Detlof's fundamental objectives for the book

1. Advance career (academic and consulting)

2. Communicate important concepts of decision analysis (to practitioners and academics)

3. Achieve satisfaction of a career milestone

4. Increase prestige and respect from peers

5. Maximize any financial reward

6. Satisfy Ward's objectives

communicate certain "special messages" about aspects of decision analysis and behavioral decision theory and to achieve an important career highlight.

Detlof felt that the alternatives available for achieving the objectives of the book pertained to the process for revising the draft and submitting it to the publisher. Most of our discussion of alternatives concerned different possible processes. The range of alternatives went from handing the manuscript to the publisher with few changes to reviewing it thoroughly more than once and editing and cutting it substantially. Some of those alternatives concerned changing the focus of the book from a narrower to a broader perspective. Also, the editing could be done with a sentence focus, a paragraph focus, a chapter focus, a book focus, or combinations of these. Other variables were which of the two authors would do what and how much of the routine work (such as checking the bibliography) might be allocated to others. The process alternatives could also be differentiated by when the book would be ready for the publisher.

The purpose of discussing process alternatives was partly to whet the authors' appetite for characterizing the objectives for the process of finishing the book. Detlof's objectives for this process are given in Table 11.15. The first objective concerns the quality of the book, whereas the next two relate to how this quality is achieved. Objective 2 was to minimize the amount of hassle in completing the book. Hassle meant long, open-ended discussions of issues that had been discussed several times before, issues involving content and the style of presenting specific ideas. The third objective concerned the enjoyment of spending productive hours improving the book. The fourth objective concerned the time until the final manuscript was delivered to the publisher, as finishing

Table 11.15. Detlof's objectives for the process of finishing the book

1. Improve quality of the book

2. Minimize hassle

3. Spend productive and enjoyable time

4. Maximize freedom to pursue other activities

the manuscript would make time available for other activities. Note that there is a natural conflict between the objectives concerning freedom to pursue other activities and improved quality of the book. The more time one spends revising a book, the better the book is likely to be, but the less freedom one has to pursue other interests.

Ward's Perspective

Ward's fundamental objectives for the book are presented in Table 11.16. Ward referred to the first two objectives as much more significant than the others. Indeed, he stated that the key objective was the first one, since education of current and future generations would follow if the book was readable and coherent. Objective 3 was to achieve the satisfaction of reaching a clear milestone in a significant body of work. Objective 4 is clear. Objective 5 was to coherently state specific viewpoints on several contemporary topics in the literature on decisionmaking. Specific cases mentioned included viewpoints on cognitive illusions, the distinction between value and utility, and thoughts on the role of regret, the zero illusion, and so forth. The sixth objective was to have the book contribute to Detlof's career.

Table 11.16. Ward's fundamental objectives for the book

1. Provide a readable, coherent record of important thought

2. Educate current and future generations about these ideas

3. Achieve a key career milestone

4. Maximize sales

5. Coherently state viewpoints about contemporary topics (e.g., cognitive illusions, value-utility distinction)

6. Contribute to Detlof's career

Table 11.17. Ward's objectives for the process of finishing the book

1. Reduce length

2. Reduce redundancies

3. Improve writing style

4. Lower the required technical level for reading the book

5. Minimize completion time

Regarding alternatives to finish the book, Ward felt that the basic alternative that the authors should follow had been discussed and agreed upon. Specifically, they would make one careful pass through each of the chapters, and then the book would be ready. Ward felt that the ways in which the book could be improved were relatively clear (see process objectives in Table 11.17) and that these improvements definitely should be made. Thus, there were no large distinctions in alternatives from Ward's point of view, and hence no decision problem. There were, however, uncertainties about the impacts of following that basic alternative. For example, it was not clear how much time or work would be required for that pass through each chapter.

Since Ward had just one basic alternative, the range of possible impacts was rather narrow. Ward believed the book would not be ready in less than four months and was almost sure to be ready to send to the publisher within six months. On questioning, he gave the likelihood that the book would be ready within six months as 95 percent, excluding "acts of God" such as serious illness. When asked what alternatives might be taken if completing the book seemed likely to take longer than six months, Ward responded that he would be willing to make serious short-term alterations in his personal life in order to insure that the book would be ready in six months. Thus, one variable associated with the alternatives was intensity of the time spent revising the book.

Ward's objectives for the process of finishing the book were means to maximize the book's quality. Notably, one objective was to reduce the length of the text, as the current version was very long. Alternatives for doing this would involve eliminating material as well as tightening the writing style. A second objective was to reduce redundancies. The current version, having been written over a long period of time, stated some ideas in more than one chapter. Some of this repetition was appropriate, but some could usefully be eliminated. The third objective was to improve the writing style, primarily by tightening the text and eliminating wordy sentences. The fourth objective was to lower the level of technical knowledge required for reading the book. This would involve revising two or three of the most technical chapters. The final objective dealt with the time until completion. Ward explicitly stated that the work time was not relevant for evaluating any alternatives, because his basic alternative involved spending whatever time was required to achieve the other process objectives. Thus the only way to reduce completion time was to work more intensively, as to do less work was not considered an option.

Further discussion revealed that not all time spent on the book was of equal value to Ward. This time was divided into three categories: that spent on "dog work," that spent on reasonably interesting work, and that spent on very interesting work. Dog work included things such as insuring consistency of style in figures and tables, checking references, and obtaining permissions for quotations. Somewhat interesting work involved, for instance, having discussions with Detlof about cuts and about content. The most interesting work involved reviewing Detlof's changes and learning from this written interaction.

Comments on the Value Elicitations

Detlof and Ward had very different views of the alternatives available to complete the book. Detlof thought there were many variables that could be altered to define different alternatives. These concerned the level at which editing would take place, who would do what editing, the timing of the work on the book, and whether zero, one, or more than one passes through the book would be made. Ward felt that the only basic alternative was one complete pass through the book, and that the level of editing and the timing would be dictated by what was required to do the job. The question of who would do what work was not particularly at issue, since both Detlof and Ward assumed that they would both spend the same amount of time on finishing their book.

The two authors had very similar value structures for the book itself. In Table 11.14 and Table 11.16, Objectives 1 through 4 are basically the same. Objectives 5 and 6 are different, but objective 6 is symmetrical since each individual's concern is to achieve the other's objectives. It was interesting that part of Detlof's objective for satisfying

Ward's objectives was to get across the special messages Ward felt were important. These special messages were explicitly stated in Ward's objective 5. Ward's objectives for Detlof were more to further his career, a concern that was explicitly stated by Detlof's objective 1. It is not a surprise that Ward and Detlof agreed on the objectives of the book, since one would expect such fundamental issues to be clarified at the beginning of an effort to write a book, let alone through the five years of writing.

There were differences between their objectives with respect to the process of completing the book. Detlof's objectives dealt more with the direct impacts of the process itself, whereas Ward's objectives dealt with the impacts of the process on the book. Some of Detlof's objectives could be considered means to Ward's objectives. Detlof and Ward were both concerned with the quality of the book. Detlof expressed this concern partly by the work put into improving the book. Ward clearly stated his definition of quality by his first four objectives for the process.

Ward did not feel that there were significant value tradeoffs to make, since he focused on the one basic alternative that he felt was required. When asked about tradeoffs between reducing the number of pages in the book and increasing the number of months to completion, Ward responded that these value tradeoffs were not particularly meaningful for him within the ranges of consideration (four to six months for completion). Detlof provided rather elaborate value tradeoffs over his objectives for the process of finishing the book.

One value tradeoff was made by both authors. It concerned the relative importance of doing the most interesting, enjoyable work and doing the least interesting, hassle or dog work. Detlof stated that he would need three hours of enjoyable, productive work to compensate him for one hour of hassle work. Ward stated that he would be willing to do four hours of dog work in order to have one very interesting hour of productive, enlightening work. If we assume that both authors get the same enjoyment from productive work, it follows that the drudgery of hassle work for Detlof is twelve times as significant as the drudgery of dog work for Ward. However, in interpreting this, we must understand that those value tradeoffs apply to a specific point in time and to the specific task of finishing the book.

The authors differed in their estimates of how long it would take to finish the book. They agreed that it could not be finished in less than four months, but Ward thought the range of time would be up to six months, whereas Detlof thought it would be up to twelve months. Ward's estimate of the probability that the completion time would exceed six months was 0.05, while Detlof's was 0.75 or greater.

Insights for Decision Opportunities, Alternatives, and Process

Because of the importance of finishing the book in a timely manner, the general discussion that Detlof and Ward and I had led to their agreement that they should revise the early chapters first. This was consistent with the one-pass concept and would move them psychologically closer to finishing by providing momentum for the process.

Both authors wanted their book to be available for use in universities in the fall of 1986, so it seemed useful to ask the publisher to specify the latest time at which the manuscript could be received and yet be published in time to be available for the fall of 1986. If the publisher answered that the manuscript would have to be finished by, say, June or July 1985, this would affect the relative values of completing the book by that time or after that time.

One alternative suggested was to spend one week of joint, concentrated work on the project in February 1985, in order to identify potential bottlenecks in the process, improve momentum, and set expectations for work to be done in March and April. Clarifying expectations for March and April was important because Detlof would be out of the country for that two-month period and the two authors would be working independently.

The authors were considering adding exercises to the book. Doing so would increase its length and the time until completion but would also increase its usefulness for teaching. The latter objective, however, could be achieved with a different add-on alternative. Namely, after finishing the manuscript and sending it in for publication, the authors could write exercises and make them available separately to teachers using the text. The exercise could be added to the book in a later volume or printing if that seemed appropriate.

Although alternatives were not clearly identified in the discussion with Ward, it did appear that different alternatives with respect to editing were possible. For instance, Ward mentioned that certain chapters might be eliminated. This would save time in editing and reduce the length of the book. The tradeoff would be that certain important ideas might be lost. It seemed appropriate to make such decisions early, as other detailed revisions might be dependent upon them.

Another alternative suggested by the objectives was to reduce the time until submission by doing certain work after the book was sent to the publisher. Such work might include preparing illustrations and getting permissions for copyrighted material.

The two authors' value tradeoffs for boring and interesting work, suggested that Detlof might revise chapters to eliminate redundancies and cut unnecessary material and Ward might follow with a detailed editing. If this process was conducted so that discussions did not reconsider issues that had been previously considered in detail, this would save time and eliminate hassle for Detlof. Perhaps more important, each author would be doing the work he considers most interesting.

The different estimates of completion time suggested that it might be worthwhile to draw up a detailed schedule, including contingency plans that would trigger certain efforts if the revisions fell too far behind schedule. For instance, the authors might agree that if they got more than one month behind they would both drop everything and spend a solid week working on the book.

There was also an opportunity to take advantage of the difference in their estimates of how long it would take to finish the book. For instance, Ward might agree that if the six-month deadline passed he would devote the next two weeks to working solidly on the book. In exchange, Detlof might agree that if the book was completed within six months he would handle all of the work regarding permissions and references. The idea is that Detlof felt there was a 0.25 chance that he would get stuck with these details and a 0.75 chance that Ward would spend the extra two weeks. Ward, on the other hand, felt there was a 0.95 chance that Detlof would have to do the dog work of permissions and references and only a 0.05 chance that he himself would have to do the additional two weeks of work.

So what happened? The manuscript was sent to the publisher in just under six months. It is *Decision Analysis and Behavioral Research* by Detlof von Winterfeldt and Ward Edwards (New York: Cambridge University Press, 1986). For readers, it was well worth the six-year wait.

CHAPTER 12

Value-Focused Thinking at British Columbia Hydro

The British Columbia Hydro and Power Authority (B.C. Hydro) is a multibillion-dollar company that supplies electricity to over 90 percent of the people in British Columbia. It is a provincial crown corporation, which means that it is owned by the province of British Columbia and its activities are regulated by the British Columbia Utilities Commission. B.C. Hydro is chartered to generate, transmit, and distribute electricity. Most of the electricity is generated by hydroelectric plants, with some coal and some small local facilities in remote areas. B.C. Hydro also manages a system of interconnected transmission lines to distribute electricity throughout British Columbia and to connect to the U.S. electricity grid in the Pacific Northwest.

B.C. Hydro will naturally face many strategic decisions in the next decade. These decisions pertain to issues such as resource additions to generate electricity, the construction of transmission lines, international power agreements, arrangements with independent power producers, employee-employer relations and policies, environmental impacts, communication with the public and interest groups, and policies for addressing actual and/or perceived public risks (for example, electromagnetic fields, global warming). B.C. Hydro wants to base such decisions on good information and sound logic and make them in a coordinated manner that can be justified and openly communicated.

Many individuals have key decisionmaking roles at B.C. Hydro. Decisions about dams and dam safety are made in one department, decisions about high-voltage transmission lines in a second department, decisions about electricity prices in the province in a third department, and decisions about electricity sales to the United States in a fourth department. To facilitate the coordination of such decisions, Larry Bell, the chairman and CEO of B.C. Hydro, established an Office of Strategic Planning and appointed Ken Peterson as director. In simple but profound terms, Ken's assignment was to make B.C. Hydro the best-planned and the best-planning utility company in North America. To help him fulfill this responsibility, Ken created a Planning Committee composed of the heads of departments with major decisionmaking roles at B.C. Hydro.

It was clear to Ken that all the company's decisions should, in some sense, aim to achieve the same long-range objectives, what I call the strategic objectives. B.C. Hydro has a published mission statement and broad goals, but these are very general as is usually the case. Ken realized that they were too general to provide guidance for coordinating decisions, although they would be useful to help articulate strategic objectives.

In early 1989, Ken invited Tim McDaniels, a resource economist and risk analyst, and me to present a one-day seminar at B.C. Hydro to discuss the role of analysis in facilitating and coordinating decisions. Subsequently, I worked with Ken and Tim and other members of the Planning Committee to identify, structure, and quantify B.C. Hydro's strategic objectives.

Under ideal circumstances, all key individuals in the organization would be involved in the identification and structuring of B.C. Hydro's strategic objectives. In-depth discussions and several iterations would yield agreement on the stated list of objectives. Value judgments of various groups at B.C. Hydro would be elicited and incorporated in the process. Once the objective function was quantified, it would be thoroughly reviewed and revised as appropriate to build a consensus. Then the strategic objectives and the objective function would be communicated to interested parties outside the company. Such stakeholders would include B.C. Hydro customers, environmental groups, consumer groups, governmental organizations, and the public.

Ideals are of course easy to discuss but much harder to achieve in practice. However, work that makes progress toward such an ideal can itself make significant contributions. The work described in this chapter is an important first step.

12.1 Identification and Structuring of the Strategic Objectives

The first step in identifying and structuring objectives is to list objectives of selected individuals for the organization. For this purpose, we met separately with three people to obtain their preliminary viewpoints about B.C. Hydro objectives for the next decade. They were Victor de Buen (Senior Systems Studies Engineer), Zak El-Ramly (Manager, Policy Development), and Ken Peterson.

The general procedure to obtain information about objectives is an open discussion, as indicated in Chapter 3. When meeting with each of the three respondents, I indicated that the purpose was to have a broad discussion of all objectives that may be important to B.C. Hydro. There was no attempt to structure the discussion any further, as this might have limited its scope.

We used two devices to insure that respondents would think of objectives not only in the context of business as usual but also for situations that might not be so usual. One was to inquire about particularly undesirable alternatives and then ask why they were so undesirable or what could have gone wrong to make them undesirable. The other was to ask about particularly undesirable consequences, such as the convening of a governmental inquiry to investigate B.C. Hydro, and then pursue grounds that could have led to such a situation. Both of these devices helped identify objectives that might have been omitted if we had focused only on business as usual.

To illustrate the type of discussion that occurs in identifying objectives, I will summarize a small portion of the meeting with Ken Peterson. Early in the discussion about economics, an obvious area of concern to B.C. Hydro, Ken stated that one objective was to have efficient and fair pricing. I immediately asked, "What does efficient mean?" He responded that the pricing should reflect the social cost of resources. Then I asked, "What does social cost mean?" He said that it was a measure of the usefulness of the resources for other purposes and that it included opportunity cost. To get a better feeling for efficiency, I asked, "How might you measure efficient pricing?" Ken's response was in terms of cost per kilowatt-hour.

Next I asked the meaning of fair pricing. Ken responded that this pertained to cost sharing among customers based on value added to society by those customers. He mentioned that this concern was of relevance to the regulators.

I backed up a step and asked why pricing, be it efficient or fair, was important. Part of the response was that it led to defensible and credible resource allocation. Naturally, I asked why that was important. It was important to several stakeholders, including regulators, government agencies such as the agricultural ministry, and customers. But it was also important because pricing is the means that provides the fundamental good (electricity) for end uses. Also, efficient and fair pricing leads customers to make decisions about energy in a socially responsible manner. That is to say, it leads them to select an appropriate amount of conservation.

Pricing policy is also important because it contributes to providing cash to the provincial government. I asked, "Why is this important?" Ken's response was that it would, among other things, lead to a good relationship between the company and the government and that it would also contribute to lowering public debt.

In discussions like this one, a wide range of objectives are generated and clarified. The logic followed in the discussion should be clear from the types of questions asked. The responses indicate means-ends relationships among the objectives and specify details of the objectives. The process aims to get deeper than "motherhood and apple pie" objectives, which everyone can agree to but which serve no strategic purpose. There are still, however, various ways to interpret any of the stated objectives. In the process of structuring these objectives, identifying attributes to indicate the degree to which they are achieved, and quantifying values for them, this ambiguity is substantially reduced.

The Initial Strategic Objectives Hierarchy and Objectives Network

Two main products resulted from each of the discussions with Victor, Zak, and Ken. One product was the strategic objectives hierarchy. The other was an objectives network that related the strategic objectives to all other objectives identified in our discussions. The objectives network also indicated how the achievement of certain objectives influenced the achievement of other objectives.

Table 12.1 presents Ken's preliminary strategic objectives hierarchy for B.C. Hydro, and Figure 12.1 presents his preliminary objectives network. In the objectives network, the strategic objectives hierarchy is presented using abbreviated terms in the column in the middle of the figure. The interrelationships between corresponding objectives are also

Table 12.1.   Ken Peterson's preliminary strategic objectives hierarchy

Maximize contribution to quality of life in British Columbia

1. Maximize contribution to economic development
   1.1. Minimize cost of electricity
   1.2. Maximize quality of product (i.e., reliability)
   1.3. Maximize funds transferred to government

2. Act consistently with the public's environmental values

3. Minimize detrimental health and safety impacts
   3.1. To the public
   3.2. To employees

4. Treat customers equitably
   4.1. Equitable pricing to different customers
   4.2. Equitable compensation (in kind or money) for concentrated local impact (e.g., environmental)

5. Be recognized as a service-oriented company (i.e., corporate image)

6. Learn
   6.1. Understand and monitor public attitudes
   6.2. Understand perceived risks and how to address them
   6.3. Understand risk communication and how to provide quality risk information
   6.4. Understand and monitor public values

illustrated in the figure. An arrow from one objective to another indicates that achieving the former has an influence on achieving the latter. The strategic objectives networks of Victor and Zak are included in Figures 12.2 and 12.3.

The overall objective for all three respondents was "maximize the contribution to quality of life in British Columbia." Although there were some differences in detail, each had major objectives pertaining to economic concerns, environmental concerns, and health and safety. Also, each included objectives addressing the quality of service and equitable treatment of customers. However, pursuing these concepts in detail might show them to be exactly the same or might indicate differences.

One apparent difference concerning the environmental objectives illustrates the subtle but potentially important distinctions that can be identified by an in-depth discussion of objectives. Both Victor and Zak had a strategic objective to "minimize environmental impact." Ken's strategic environmental objective was to "act consistently with the public's environmental values." The latter accounted both for possible environmental impacts and for the relative values attached to those impacts by the public.

Each respondent had one strategic objective that was distinctive from the others. Victor's was to "be the best employer." This objective

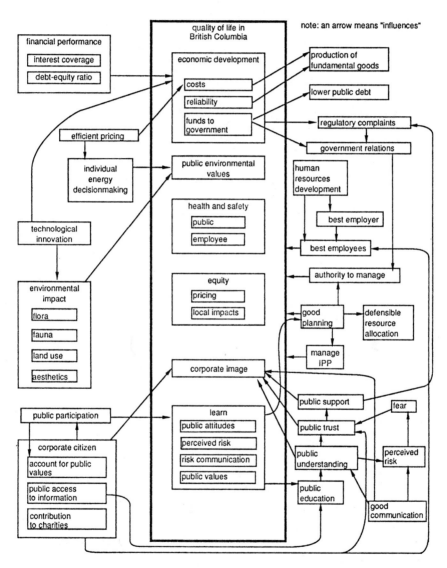

Figure 12.1. Preliminary objectives network (Ken Peterson)

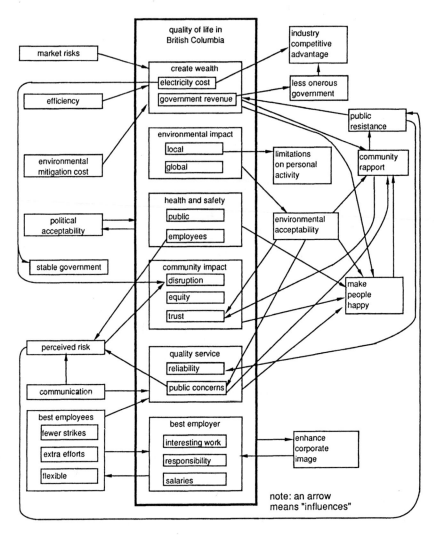

Figure 12.2. Preliminary objectives network (Victor de Buen)

was important to both Zak and Ken, but for them it was a means to more fundamental objectives. Zak had a strategic objective to "provide the basis for sound proactive decisionmaking." This was specified into the following subobjectives: understand provincial governmental objectives, provide substantial analysis for key decisions, and integrate and coordinate Hydro decisions and activities. Clearly the other respondents were not against this objective, but the issue is whether it is a strategic objective or a means for achieving the strategic objectives. To some degree, it can be both, and timing is part of the issue. For instance, if in one time period Hydro is developing the information and expertise to provide the basis for sound proactive decisionmaking, it is a strategic objective at that time. Once this basis is established, it is a means objective for achieving the other strategic objectives through sound decisionmaking.

A strategic objective stated by Ken was to "learn." This was specified to mean the following: understand and monitor public attitudes, understand perceived risks and how to address them, understand risk com-

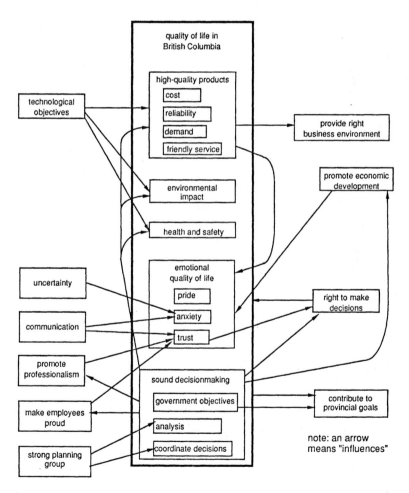

Figure 12.3. Preliminary objectives network (Zak El-Ramly)

munication and how to provide good information about risks, and understand and monitor public values. Again, neither of the other respondents was opposed to the objective of learning. The issue is simply whether it is strategic or not. And again, the issue is partially one of timing. Learning can be fundamental in one time period and a means objective at a later time.

12.2 First Revision of the Strategic Objectives and the Preliminary Attributes

After the initial discussions, I developed the material in Section 12.1 for Victor, Zak, and Ken. A few weeks later, Tim and I again met with Ken to make appropriate revisions to the preliminary strategic objectives and to specify preliminary attributes for the objectives. Ken's revised strategic objectives hierarchy together with preliminary attributes are presented in Table 12.2. The revised objectives network is not illustrated as our focus will be on the strategic objectives. We will compare Table 12.2 to Table 12.1 to see the modifications and the thought process leading to them.

There were two changes under economic development. The reliability component was pulled out of this category and a separate strategic objective concerning quality of service specified as in Victor's original objectives hierarchy. A more subtle change occurred when we focused on an attribute for the original objective "minimize cost of electricity." The objective was changed to "minimize cost of electricity use." The former might have been measured by the cost of producing electricity, whereas the latter included the costs of delivering electricity to custom-

Table 12.2.   First revision of Ken Peterson's strategic objectives hierarchy with preliminary attributes

Maximize contribution to quality of life in British Columbia

1. Maximize contribution to economic development
    1.1. Minimize cost of electricity use (average monthly bill of a residential customer)
    1.2. Maximize funds transferred to government (annual dividend payable)

Table 12.2. (continued)

2. Act consistently with the public's environmental values
   2.1. About local environmental impacts
      2.1.1. To flora (acres of forest lost)
      2.1.2. To fauna (reduction of annual Fraser River salmon run)
      2.1.3. To wildlife ecosystems (constructed scale)
      2.1.4. To land use (constructed scale)
      2.1.5. To aesthetics (constructed scale)
   2.2. About global impacts (CO_2 emissions per kilowatt generated relative to North American utility average)

3. Minimize detrimental health and safety impacts
   3.1. To the public
      3.1.1. Mortality (public person-years of life lost)
      3.1.2. Morbidity (public person-years of disability equal in severity to that causing employee lost work time)
   3.2. To employees
      3.2.1. Mortality (employee person-years of life lost)
      3.2.2. Morbidity (employee person-years of work time lost)

4. Promote equitable business arrangements
   4.1. Equitable pricing to different customers (constructed scale)
   4.2. Equitable compensation for concentrated local impacts (number of individuals felt to be inequitably treated)

5. Maximize quality of service
   5.1. Minimize outages
      5.1.1. To small customers (expected number of outages to a small customer annually)
      5.1.2. To large customers (expected number of outages to a large customer annually)
   5.2. Minimize duration of outages
      5.2.1. To small customers (average hours of outages per outage to small customers)
      5.2.2. To large customers (average hours of outages per outage to large customers)
   5.3. Improve routine service
      5.3.1. For requests for new service (elapsed time until new service is installed)
      5.3.2. For telephone inquiries (time until human answers the telephone)

6. Be recognized as public-service oriented (constructed scale)

ers. Important B.C. Hydro efforts to improve the efficiency of their transmission system would get credit with the new attribute, but not with the old one.

The environmental objective was specified to indicate that it included both local and global environmental impacts. The global environmental impacts of most concern were the possibility of the earth's warming and acid rain, and specifically the contribution of B.C. Hydro to these. Two means objectives that contribute to these environmental impacts are waste creation and waste emissions, including water and air pollution.

The health and safety objective was also elaborated to explicitly include both mortality and morbidity to both the public and employees. The usefulness of this specification became clear as we attempted to define an attribute for the original objective "minimize detrimental health and safety impacts to employees." The issue was how to combine possible fatalities, for instance from electrocution, with serious injuries from construction accidents.

The wording of the equity objective changed slightly but not substantially. The new quality of service objective specified the implications of outages to both small and large customers and of routine service requests such as new service and inquiries.

Ken decided that to be recognized as a public-service-oriented company might enhance the company's image, but that these were not identical and the former was the strategic objective. It was also noted that this objective is not identical with *being* a public-service-oriented company. Considering this, Ken concluded that B.C. Hydro was a public-service-oriented company and the objective was to be recognized as such.

The objective of learning in Table 12.1 was reclassified as a means objective contributing to all the strategic objectives. Indeed, this learning is one of the means to improve planning skills that deal with the use of what is learned. And improved planning skills are a means to better planning, and thus to better impacts in terms of the strategic objectives. Improvement in planning skills has three major components. One of these concerns doing insightful analysis, another concerns communicating about planning, and the third concerns utilizing what is learned about public values and provincial values. The communication component refers to two-way communication: communication from the public about its attitudes and values and communication to the public about options, technical information, and the basis for decisions.

12.3 Current Version of the Strategic Objectives and Attributes

The changes to the strategic objectives were documented and given to Ken for review. Then Ken, Tim, and I met again to finalize the set of strategic objectives and attributes and to quantify Ken's values. Before the meeting, Tim and I had done a little background work to help identify potentially better attributes for some of the strategic objectives. After our discussion with Ken, we felt that we now understood his values reasonably well, certainly well enough to make productive suggestions. This meeting again led to a few alterations to the strategic objectives, as can be seen in Table 12.3. One change was the addition of a third economic objective to minimize the economic implications of resource losses. This was identified as a separate objective when we were thinking about appropriate attributes for environmental objectives. The loss of environmental resources such as forests or fisheries seemed to include economic implications. These were meant to be captured by the new objective. The environmental and social impacts of resource losses remained accounted for within the listed environmental objectives.

A second change in the strategic objectives hierarchy concerned the environmental land use objective. This objective included agricultural, residential, and recreational uses of land. The implications of the first two of these are essentially economic and the implication of the third is only partially economic. The economic aspects were handled by the new economic objective. The revised environmental objective concerned environmental impacts that limit opportunities for recreation.

The third change was to reorganize the quality of service objectives. This basically changed the focus from the properties of outages, namely number and duration, to the impacts of those outages on small and large customers. The former was engineering-oriented and the latter people-oriented.

Attributes to Measure the Strategic Objectives

The overall strategic objective is to maximize the contribution to quality of life in British Columbia. This is broken down into six major objectives, most of which have several subobjectives. For each of the lowest-level objectives, it is useful to specify an attribute to measure the degree

Table 12.3.   Current version of Ken Peterson's strategic objectives
hierarchy with attributes

Maximize contribution to quality of life in British Columbia

1. Maximize contribution to economic development
    1.1. Minimize cost of electricity use (mills per kilowatt-hour in 1989 dollars)
    1.2. Maximize funds transferred to government (annualized dividend payable)
    1.3. Minimize economic implications of resource losses (cost of resource losses in 1989 dollars)

2. Act consistently with the public's environmental values
    2.1. About local environmental impacts
        2.1.1. To flora (hectares of mature forest lost)
        2.1.2. To fauna (hectares of wildlife habitat lost of Spatzizi Plateau quality)
        2.1.3. To wildlife ecosystems (hectares of wilderness lost of the Stikine Valley quality)
        2.1.4. To limit recreational use (hectares of high-quality recreational land lost)
        2.1.5. To aesthetics (annual person-years viewing high voltage transmission lines in scenic terrain)
    2.2. About global impacts (average megawatts of electricity generated using fossil fuels)

3. Minimize detrimental health and safety impacts
    3.1. To the public
        3.1.1. Mortality (public person-years of life lost)
        3.1.2. Morbidity (public person-years of disability equal in severity to that causing employee lost work time)
    3.2. To employees
        3.2.1. Mortality (employee person-years of life lost)
        3.2.2. Morbidity (employee person-years of work time lost)

4. Promote equitable business arrangements
    4.1. Equitable pricing to different customers (constructed scale)
    4.2. Equitable compensation for concentrated local impacts (number of individuals that feel they are inequitably treated)

5. Maximize quality of service
    5.1. To small customers
        5.1.1. Minimize outages (expected number of annual outages to a small customer annually)

Table 12.3.   (continued)

5.1.2. Minimize duration of outages (average hours of outage per outage to small customers)

5.2. To large customers

5.2.1. Minimize outages (expected number of annual outages to a large customer annually)

5.2.2. Minimize duration of outages (average hours of outages per outage to large customers)

5.3. Improve new service (elapsed time until new service is installed)

5.4. Improve response to telephone inquiries (time until a human answers the telephone)

6. Be recognized as public-service oriented (constructed scale)

to which the objective is achieved. That attribute explains precisely what the objective is meant to address.

Some of the attributes have already been discussed. I will briefly elaborate on aspects of the others, referring to them by the numerical designations in Table 12.3. For example, objective 1.1 is "minimize cost of electricity use," and attribute 1.1 is "mills per kilowatt-hour in 1989 Canadian dollars."

The cost of electricity is measured by the levelized cost of electricity from new sources as it enters the local grid network. Thus, attribute 1.1 addresses possible transmission losses of electricity because they affect the levelized cost of electricity. The annualized dividend paid to the provincial government of course increases costs of electricity, when all other things are held equal. Thus, objective 1.2 conflicts with objective 1.1, as is always the case when there are multiple objectives. If there is no conflict, by definition there is only a single objective.

The details of the attributes for objective 2 concerning the public's environmental values would be generated from values assessed from the public. The attributes indicated in the table concern components of environmental values and are intended to give the range over which public value might be assessed. This range is also sufficient for prioritizing the major six objectives.

For each of the objectives 2.1.1–2.1.5, there is a need to translate various environmental impacts into measurable attributes. For example, for attribute 2.1.1, various impacts to flora need to be translated into equivalent amounts of hectares of mature forest lost. Also, this attribute requires an understanding of precisely what a mature forest is. For our purposes, we assume it is densely wooded, but not of virgin timber. Similarly, impacts on fauna need to be translated into equivalent amounts of wildlife habitat lost of the quality indicated. This naturally requires environmental value judgments.

It is also necessary to convert hectares lost of one ecosystem into an equivalent loss from a second ecosystem using environmental value judgments. For example, if the relative value of one ecosystem is five times that of another, then one hectare lost of the former ecosystem is equivalent to five hectares lost of the latter. This kind of calculation makes it possible to evaluate wildlife ecosystems lost in terms of hectare-equivalents of any type of ecosystem specified.

For attribute 2.1.4, high-quality recreational land is defined to be of the quality offered by a provincial park. As above, the relative values of different types of recreational land need to be assessed to determine hectare-equivalents.

For attribute 2.1.5, we calculate as one person-day the viewing of a high voltage transmission line either from one's home or from a highway. As with other attributes, it is necessary to calculate the relative value of different aesthetic impacts. Examples of aesthetic disruption might be elimination of a free-flowing river or impairment of a natural view by man-made structures.

The possible warming of the earth and acid rain are the major concerns under global impacts. We could possibly measure these by the carbon dioxide or sulfur dioxide emitted annually, but it would be very difficult to make reasonable value tradeoffs without a better knowledge of the implications of each amount of pollution. Hence the choice of the proxy attribute of average megawatts of electricity generated using fossil fuel.

For health and safety impacts, the attributes for mortality and morbidity are the same for the public and employees. The mortality attributes give the death of a younger person greater weight than the death of an older person, since the younger person loses more expected lifetime. Morbidity can result from either injuries due to accidents or illnesses induced by emissions from power plants, for example. Specifying the level of severity as that causing employees to lose work time means that only significant morbidity is counted. It seems likely that less severe cases of morbidity would be correlated with more severe cases. Hence, in any evaluation of alternatives, it might be appropriate in sensitivity analysis to place a greater weight on the attribute measuring serious morbidity to account for correlated cases of lesser morbidity as well.

With attribute 4.1, concerning equitable pricing to different customers, three types of customers of concern are residential, commercial, and industrial. The input to the constructed scale for equity would use the price of electricity to each group relative to the cost of service delivered to that group. The most equitable situation is when all three types of customers have exactly the same ratio. The constructed scale is to measure the sum of the differences between the ratios of each group and the average of those ratios. Thus, if r_i, $i = 1, 2, 3$ is the price-to-cost ratio for the three types of customers, and if $\bar{r}$ is the average of r_1, r_2, and r_3, then the measure of equity is $\Sigma_i |r_i - \bar{r}|$.

Regarding objective 4.2, equitable compensation for concentrated local impacts, the attribute concerns only the number of people who feel they are inequitably treated by B.C. Hydro (for example, when their land is purchased against their will for a dam). The other side of the coin, that they are "too generously" treated, is dealt with indirectly by the implications on economic costs of the offers made to such individuals. These offers may pertain to direct financial compensation or to compensation in kind.

Under objective 5, quality of service, small customers are residences and small commercial users. Large customers are the others. The attributes for outages should be clear by definition. For new service, the elapsed time is the time from when the new service is requested until it is installed and operating, which can be measured in work days. The atribute for response to telephone inquiries is the time that elapses before a person—not a recording—answers the phone.

The attribute for being recognized as public service oriented is constructed. This scale has five levels of impact. An individual may perceive B.C. Hydro as very public service oriented (level 4), or as moderately (level 3), somewhat (level 2), minimally (level 1), or not at all (level 0) public service oriented. The extremes of this scale would mean that everyone considered B.C. Hydro very public service oriented or that everyone considered it not at all public service oriented.

12.4 The Quantitative Value Assessment

At this stage, Ken, Tim, and I all felt that Table 12.3 represented a good initial set of strategic objectives for B.C. Hydro. It would be useful to conduct this in-depth qualitative identification of objectives with additional members of management and then aggregate the lists. It would also be useful to quantify the values that Ken felt were appropriate for the company. The latter exercise would, of course, represent only one individual's view of B.C. Hydro. But it would demonstrate the process for others and indicate the types of insights that might be gained from the effort expended. Thus, we had a meeting to quantify values.[1]

Since the objectives and attributes were already defined, the first part of our meeting was to specify a range for each of the attributes over which the utility function should be assessed. As discussed in Section 5.4, these ranges are essential for prioritizing objectives in a meaningful way. The attributes and their ranges are presented in Table 12.4.

Table 12.4.   Attributes and ranges for Ken Peterson's value assessment

Attribute	Worst level	Best level
1.1. Levelized cost of energy from new sources at grid (1989 mills/kwh)	55	35
1.2. Annualized dividend payable (1989 dollars in millions)	0	$200
1.3. Economic cost of resource losses (1989 dollars in millions)	$20	0
2.1.1. Flora (hectares of mature forest lost)	10,000	0
2.1.2. Fauna (hectares of wildlife habitat lost— Spatzizi Plateau quality)	10,000	0
2.1.3. Wilderness ecosystem (hectares of wilderness lost—Stikine Valley quality)	10,000	0

1. This section and the following one are more quantitative than the rest of this chapter. Readers not interested in the quantitative material may wish to skip these sections and only glance at Table 12.5 before proceeding to Section 12.6.

Table 12.4.   (continued)

2.1.4.	Recreation (hectares of recreational land lost—provincial park quality)	10,000	0
2.1.5.	Aesthetic (annual person-years viewing high voltage transmission line in scenic terrain)	500,000	0
2.2.	Global environmental impact (megawatts generated using fossil fuels)	1,000	0
3.1.1.	Public mortality (annual person-years of life lost)	100	0
3.1.2.	Public morbidity (annual person-years of "severe" disability)	1,000	0
3.2.1.	Worker mortality (annual person-years of life lost)	100	0
3.2.2.	Worker morbidity (annual person-years of lost work time)	1,000	0
4.1.	Equitable pricing (constructed scale, see Section 12.3)	0.5	0
4.2.	Equitable compensation (annual average number of individuals who feel they are inequitably treated)	500	0
5.1.1.	Small customer outages (annual number/customer)	2	0
5.1.2.	Small customer outage duration (hours/outage)	24	0
5.2.1.	Large customer outages (annual number/customer)	2	0
5.2.2.	Large customer outage duration (hours/outage)	24	0
5.3.	New service (installation time in work days)	20	1
5.4.	Inquiries (time until personal response in minutes)	1	0
6.	Recognition for public service orientation (constructed scale, see Section 12.3)	0	4

The Strategic Utility Function

The strategic utility function has 22 attributes, as indicated in Table 12.4. Hence, it is not simple to write in one equation. Yet it is of a rather simple form. The main reason is that when fundamental objectives, the strategic objectives in this case, are quantified by a value assessment, the form of the utility function should usually be additive or one of the other simple forms in Chapter 5. It is when values are quantified over means objectives that the form becomes unwieldy. After summarizing the utility function, I will discuss some of the assumptions that were verified to determine it.

The overall utility function has six major components concerning, respectively, economics (1), environment (2), health and safety (3), equity (4), service (5), and public-service orientation (6). The utility function u is additive, so

$$u(u_1, \ldots, u_6) = k_1 u_1 + k_2 u_2 + \cdots + k_6 u_6, \tag{12.1}$$

where u and the u_i, $i = 1, \ldots, 6$ are scaled from 0 to 1 over the ranges in Table 12.4 and k_i, $i = 1, \ldots, 6$ are weights on the major components.

The economic utility function u_1 is given by

$$1 + ku_1(x_{1.1}, x_{1.2}, x_{1.3}) = [1 + kk_{1.1}u_{1.1}(x_{1.1})][1 + kk_{1.2}u_{1.2}(x_{1.2})]$$
$$\times [1 + kk_{1.3}u_{1.3}(x_{1.3})] \tag{12.2}$$

where all u's are scaled 0 to 1 over the ranges in Table 12.4 and the k's are relative weights corresponding to these ranges. The economic utility function is not additive as the three economic components are to some extent substitutes for each other. This represents an overall risk averseness, although not too strong, to avoid having low achievement on all three economic attributes simultaneously. This occurrence, whether due to "bad luck" or not, would give the appearance that the economic impacts were not being carefully managed. Preferential independence does hold between pairs of the three economic attributes, and each is utility independent of the others. Hence, the multiplicative utility function (6.6) of Result 3 in Chapter 5 holds.

The environmental utility function u_2 is additive between local and global impacts and additive within local impacts. The utility function can be written

$$u_2(x_{2.1}, x_{2.2}) = k_{2.1}u_{2.1}(x_{2.1}) + k_{2.2}u_{2.2}(x_{2.2}), \tag{12.3}$$

where

$$u_{2.1}(x_{2.1.1}, x_{2.1.2}, x_{2.1.3}, x_{2.1.4}, x_{2.1.5}) = k_{2.1.1}u_{2.1.1}(x_{2.1.1})$$
$$+ \ldots + k_{2.1.5}u_{2.1.5}(x_{2.1.5}) \quad (12.4)$$

and all the u's are scaled from 0 to 1 over the ranges in Table 12.4 and the k's are relative weights corresponding to these ranges.

The health and safety utility function u_3 is

$$u_3(x_{3.1.1}, x_{3.1.2}, x_{3.2.1}, x_{3.2.2}) = k_{3.1}u_{3.1}(x_{3.1.1}, x_{3.1.2})$$
$$+ k_{3.2}u_{3.2}(x_{3.2.1}, x_{3.2.2}), \quad (12.5)$$

where

$$u_{3.1}(x_{3.1.1}, x_{3.1.2}) = k_{3.1.1}u_{3.1.1}(x_{3.1.1}) + k_{3.1.2}u_{3.1.2}(x_{3.1.2}) \quad (12.6)$$

and

$$u_{3.2}(x_{3.2.1}, x_{3.2.2}) = k_{3.2.1}u_{3.2.1}(x_{3.2.1}) + k_{3.2.2}u_{3.2.2}(x_{3.2.2}) \quad (12.7)$$

and all the u's are scaled 0 to 1 over the ranges in Table 12.4 and the k's are relative weights corresponding to these ranges.

The equity utility function u_4 is

$$u_4(x_{4.1}, x_{4.2}) = k_{4.1}u_{4.1}(x_{4.1}) + k_{4.2}u_{4.2}(x_{4.2}), \quad (12.8)$$

where the u's are scaled from 0 to 1 over the ranges in Table 12.4 and the k's are relative weights corresponding to these ranges.

The quality of service utility function u_5 is

$$u_5(x_{5.1}, x_{5.2}, x_{5.3}, x_{5.4}) = k_{5.1}u_{5.1}(x_{5.1.1}, x_{5.1.2})$$
$$+ k_{5.2}u_{5.2}(x_{5.2.1}, x_{5.2.2})$$
$$+ k_{5.3}u_{5.3}(x_{5.3}) + k_{5.4}u_{5.4}(x_{5.4}), \quad (12.9)$$

where

$$u_{5.1}(x_{5.1.1}, x_{5.1.2}) = u_{5.1.1}(x_{5.1.1}) + u_{5.1.2}(x_{5.1.2})$$
$$- u_{5.1.1}(x_{5.1.1})u_{5.1.2}(x_{5.1.2}) \quad (12.10)$$

and

$$u_{5.2}(x_{5.2.1}, x_{5.2.2}) = u_{5.2.1}(x_{5.2.1}) + u_{5.2.2}(x_{5.2.2})$$

$$- u_{5.2.1}(x_{5.2.1})u_{5.2.2}(x_{5.2.2}) \qquad (12.11)$$

and all the u's are scaled from 0 to 1 over the ranges in Table 12.4 and the k's are relative weights corresponding to these ranges.

In this value assessment, it is assumed that there are 1.2 million small customers and 20,000 large customers. The utility functions for possible outages are not additive. The dependency concerns the issues of quality of impact and quantity of impact discussed in Section 6.1. In this case the quantity is measured by the number of outages and the quality is measured by their duration. If either is very low, then we need not be very concerned about the other. Quality and quantity are utility independent of each other, so the Result 4 of Chapter 5 holds.

Five discrete levels of the utility function u_6 for public-service recognition were assessed. These are

$$u_6(4) = 1, \qquad u_6(3) = 0.65, \qquad u_6(2) = 0.4,$$

$$u_6(1) = 0.15, \qquad u_6(0) = 0, \qquad (12.12)$$

where the levels are as defined in Section 12.3.

Assessed Value Tradeoffs and Risk Attitudes

To quantify value tradeoffs, we need to determine pairs of consequences that differ in two attributes and that are indifferent to each other. A relatively easy value tradeoff to make concerns two economic attributes. Using procedures discussed in Section 5.4, we found that Ken was indifferent between consequences ($x_{1.1} = 48$, $x_{1.3} = 20$) and ($x_{1.1} = 55$, $x_{1.3} = 0$). This meant that it was just worth a change in levelized cost from 48 to 55 mills per kilowatt-hour to obtain a drop in resource cost from $20 million to $0. These resource costs were direct costs due to loss of productive forests or fisheries. In making value tradeoffs, we explicitly assumed that total economic repercussions, including indirect costs, would be five times the direct costs. Hence, a $100 million cost to the provincial economy would be about as bad for quality of life in British Columbia as an increase of electricity costs from 48 to 55 mills for a year.

Impacts on wildlife ecosystems turned out to be the most heavily weighted environmental attribute given the ranges. An assessed value tradeoff was ($x_{1.3}$ = 0, $x_{2.1.3}$ = 10,000) is indifferent to ($x_{1.3}$ = 20, $x_{2.1.3}$ = 2,000) meaning that eliminating a $20 million direct resource loss would be indifferent to reducing the loss of high-quality wilderness from 10,000 to 2,000 hectares. (As a technical note, because the economic utility function is not additive, the exact value tradeoff depends on where the other two economic attributes are fixed. For this value tradeoff, they were set at $x_{1.1}$ = 40 and $x_{1.2}$ = 100.)

Regarding risk attitudes, most of the component utility functions were linear, as should be expected for most fundamental objectives. Let me mention two that were not. Concerning the annual government dividend, a payment of $50 million was felt to be indifferent to a half chance of paying either $200 million or $0. To pay nothing might be misinterpreted as denoting an emergency. This is a risk-averse attitude, as shown in Figure 12.4a.

With respect to the duration of power outages to large customers, a duration of 8 hours was indifferent to equal chances of 0 or 24 hours. Here the feeling was that part of the damage occurs rather quickly as shifts of workers may need to be sent home and as some equipment cannot immediately start up again after a shutdown. This risk-prone attitude is illustrated in Figure 12.4b.

The Scaling Constants

The most interesting results of the value assessment are probably the scaling constants. Regarding the six major objectives, the value tradeoffs were used to calculate the scaling constants in the overall utility function (12.1). The implications were as follows:

k_1 = 0.395 (economics),

k_2 = 0.250 (environment),

k_3 = 0.089 (health and safety),

k_4 = 0.012 (equity),

k_5 = 0.250 (service quality),

k_6 = 0.004 (public-service recognition),   (12.13)

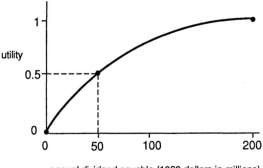

a. a risk-averse utility function for government dividend

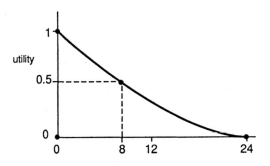

b. a risk-prone utility function for duration of outages to large customers

Figure 12.4. Two utility functions for components of B.C. Hydro's strategic objectives

where these scaling constants must be interpreted using the ranges in Table 12.4. The scaling constants indicate the relative importance of moving all the corresponding attributes from their worst levels to their best levels in Table 12.4.

By multiplying the constants k_1 through k_6 by the scaling constants for the component utility functions (12.2) through (12.12), we priori-tized the strategic objectives, taking into account the ranges for the achievement of those objectives listed in Table 12.4. The resulting prior-ities, both weights and ranks, are shown in Table 12.5. Because the component utility function for economics was not additive, normalized scaling constants were used in the calculations.

Some important insights from the quantitative value assessment are based on the scaling constants of the component utility functions. Hence, I will state those. For the economic utility function, the scaling constants $k_{1.1}$, $k_{1.2}$, $k_{1.3}$, and k in (12.2) were 0.84, 0.18, 0.30, and -0.76 respectively. Thus, the normalized scaling constants for the three attributes were 0.64 for levelized cost, 0.14 for government dividend, and 0.22 for resource costs.

The scaling constant for local environmental impacts was 0.93 in

Table 12.5.   Calculated priorities of the strategic objectives

Objective	Weight	Rank
1.1. Levelized cost	0.253	1
1.2. Annual government dividend	0.053	6
1.3. Resource cost	0.088	5
2.1.1. Flora	0.023	11
2.1.2. Fauna	0.046	7
2.1.3. Wilderness	0.093	4
2.1.4. Recreation	0.046	7
2.1.5. Aesthetic	0.023	11
2.2. Global impact	0.019	13
3.1. Public health and safety	0.045	9
3.2. Employee health and safety	0.045	9
4.1. Equitable compensation	0.008	15
4.2. Equitable pricing	0.004	17
5.1. Small customer service	0.111	3
5.2. Large customer service	0.125	2
5.3. New customer service	0.010	14
5.4. Inquiry response	0.005	16
6. Public-service recognition	0.004	17

(12.3), leaving 0.07 as the scaling constant for global environmental impacts. This is mainly due to the respective ranges of those impacts.

Public health and safety and employee health and safety were evaluated exactly the same. In both cases, the scaling constant on mortality was 0.83 and that on morbidity was 0.17.

For quality of service (12.9), the scaling constant for small customers was 0.44, for large customers 0.50, for new customer connections 0.04, and for inquiries 0.02. The almost equal constants for small and large customers were due to different factors: a single outage to a large customer is naturally much more significant than that same outage to a small customer, but an outage is likely to affect more small customers.

12.5 Insights from the Value Assessment

Value assessments provide insights about which strategic objectives are important and why. From (12.13), it is clear that the major strategic objectives that matter concern economics, the environment, health and safety, and service quality. The combined weight on equity and public-service recognition, given their ranges, is less than 2 percent. Parts of two of the four important objectives are also relatively insignificant. Global environmental impact accounts for only 7 percent of the environmental impact and is less important than any of the five separate local environmental impact categories. Within service quality, the impacts of outages account for 94 percent of the concern, with the impacts on new service and inquiries together accounting for the other 6 percent.

Collectively, 95 percent of the relevant achievement of objectives has to do with the twelve objectives addressing economic impacts, local environmental impacts, health and safety, and outages. The other six objectives, those ranked number 13 and below in Table 12.5, contribute only 5 percent.

Relative Values of Possible Impacts

Given the utility function (12.1), we can calculate for any specified impact on one attribute an equivalently valued impact on another attribute. In practice, a useful way to examine value tradeoffs is in terms of economic impacts. In this regard, however, all dollars are not equal. For example, Ken's value assessment indicated that not paying a dividend to the government (attribute 1.2) of $200 million was equally as bad as

Table 12.6.   Calculated economic value tradeoffs

Consequences	In terms of direct resource cost
Environmental values	
Each hectare of wilderness lost	$2,500
Each hectare of fauna habitat lost	1,250
Each hectare of recreation lost	1,250
Each hectare of flora lost	625
Each person-year of aesthetic degradation	13
Quality of service values	
20,000 large customers with 2 outages per year of 2 hours duration	5,000,000
1 large customer outage of 2 hours	125
1 large customer outage of 24 hours	842
1.2 million small customers with 2 outages per year of 2 hours duration	2,500,000
1 small customer outage of 2 hours	1
1 small customer outage of 24 hours	13
Decreasing new service installation time from 20 days to 1 day for 25,000 new customers	2,700,000
Reducing the telephone inquiry time from 1 minute to 0 minutes for one year	1,250,000
Health and safety values	
Public statistical fatality	3,000,000
An employee statistical fatality	3,000,000
1 year of public statistical morbidity	60,000
1 year of employee statistical morbidity	60,000
Economic values	
$10 million resource loss	10,000,000[a]
1 mill/kwh increase[b]	2,860,000

a. This is the value tradeoff by definition.

b. The calculations here are for "average" values that depend on the cost of electricity before the increase.

a loss of resources directly contributing to a $12 million resource cost, which because of indirect effects, induced a $60 million loss to the provincial economy. Ken also indicated that the value tradeoffs between resources lost and the annual government dividend would most appropriately be set jointly by B.C. Hydro and the provincial government.

Table 12.6 presents the results of calculations to determine some economic value tradeoffs in terms of the direct costs of resource losses in the province. The results should be interpreted, for example, as follows. Each hectare of wilderness lost is as bad as losing $2,500 of resources and a major electrical outage to 500,000 small customers for 24 hours is as bad as a $6.5 million resource loss (that is, $13 per customer).

12.6 Decision Opportunities

The value assessment comprised several separate tasks: listing the objectives, distinguishing between means-ends objectives and strategic objectives, identifying attributes to measure strategic objectives, and assessing an overall objective function. The results of each task suggested decision opportunities that might be worthwhile to pursue. Some of these opportunities pertain to gathering information that might be useful in significant decisions, while others are significant decisions in themselves. The following examples are illustrative of decision opportunities that can be generated by value-focused thinking.

1. *Investigate implications of resource losses on economic activity.* Objective 1.3 was to minimize economic implications of resource losses, such as the loss of productive forests or fisheries. In the assessment of the utility function, it was clear that the reduction in economic activity that would occur due to resource losses was potentially significant. Preliminarily, we assumed that the loss in economic activity would be five times the economic value of the resource loss. This suggests that it would be useful to examine the relationship between resource losses and reduced economic activity, particularly because 8.8 percent of the weight in the utility function pertained to the $20 million range for economic resources lost.

2. *Calculate the equivalent value of the environmental losses at potential hydroelectric sites.* The weight on local environmental attributes was approximately 25 percent in the utility function. It might therefore be useful to do an environmental appraisal of the implications of potential

hydroelectric developments. This would involve assessing the hectares of flora, fauna, wilderness, and recreation losses as well as the person-years of aesthetic impact. Many of these assessments are included in standard environmental impact statements. In addition, the relative values for losses of different quality would need to be assessed. This information could be used to calculate the overall equivalent value due to environmental losses using the preliminary utility function (12.1).

3. *Determine public environmental values.* This decision opportunity involves assessing the public's values about possible environmental impacts and the public's value tradeoffs between economic implications and those environmental impacts. One way to obtain the public's values would be to appoint a select committee of individuals representing the public and assess their values. Another way would be to assess values from various public stakeholder groups and combine these in some fashion. The intent would be to develop a logical measure to appraise the value the public attaches to environmental losses that might result from different alternatives in various decisions.

4. *Develop a data base on public and employee fatalities.* This decision opportunity is to create a statistical data base for all fatalities related to B.C. Hydro equipment or activities. Using this as a guide for thinking, one could generate and compare alternative actions that might reduce the number of such statistical fatalities. It might also suggest particular educational programs for the public or employees that might improve safety.

5. *Develop a utility function for equitable pricing.* The components of equitable pricing are the ratios of cost of electricity to cost of service for three classes of customers: residential, commercial, and industrial. The initial attribute did not distinguish these ratios for the three classes of customers, though a subsequent discussion with Ken indicated that this distinction would be worthwhile. The intent would be to provide a basis for evaluating pricing policy and for generating alternatives that might lead to a better pricing policy.

6. *Obtain data on "inequitably treated" individuals.* This decision opportunity would gather information on the number of people who felt they had been unfairly treated by B.C. Hydro in the recent past and why they felt mistreated. Their reasons might be, for example, that B.C. Hydro had disrupted their environment, threatened their livelihood (such as by disrupting a fishery), or created a perceived risk (such as electromagnetic fields). It might be useful to assess values for the relative

seriousness of each of these circumstances. This would provide a basis for a better evaluation of individual disruption necessarily caused by B.C. Hydro.

7. *Develop a quality-of-service utility function.* Quality of service was weighted approximately 23 percent in the value assessment. This suggests that it would be worthwhile to examine the various atributes of reliability and to assess the value tradeoffs between economic costs and quality of service. Doing so would provide information that could be useful for examining many of the strategic alternatives of B.C. Hydro that are expensive but that improve service and reduce the likelihood of outages.

8. *Model response to telephone inquiries.* The value tradeoffs indicate that transferring approximately $20 million of funds to the provincial government has the same value as reducing response time per telephone inquiry from one to zero minutes. This suggests that it might easily be worth the investment required to reduce inquiry time wherever possible, as that investment might be significantly less than $20 million. The company should gather good data on inquiry time and create and examine policies to reduce it.

9. *Examine individual decisionmaking about energy.* Individuals' decisions about electricity use can have a significant impact on the overall impacts attributable to B.C. Hydro. Consequently, it might be worth investigating how B.C. Hydro could influence that decisionmaking. A major mechanism would involve alternatives that might be considered as demand-side management. Hypothetical demand-side management alternatives might be examined in terms of the complete set of B.C. Hydro attributes to suggest designs for realistic demand-side options.

10. *Conduct a preliminary investigation of strategies involving electromagnetic fields.* It would be useful to examine potential strategies for communication about possible risks and for company actions, such as purchasing homes near high-voltage transmission lines, that pertain to electromagnetic fields. The intent would be to better understand the consequences of various alternatives that might be available to B.C. Hydro in the future. This should put B.C. Hydro in a position to act responsibly as new information about electromagnetic fields is forthcoming.

11. *Negotiations to sell power.* At this stage, it might be useful to examine hypothetical future negotiations to sell power to the United States. For such negotiations, information on the overall cost of developing the power would be relevant. This would include the equivalent cost due to

environmental damage, health and safety impacts, and the impacts on equity, quality of service, and perception of acting in the public interest as well as economic costs per se. Better information about the overall cost of power would put B.C. Hydro in a stronger negotiating position.

The intent of this list is to demonstrate one simple but critical point. An unambiguous and complete statement of strategic objectives can be a guide to identifying decision opportunities that enhance both the likelihood of achieving those objectives and the degree to which the objectives are achieved. This process, part of value-focused thinking, helps to put the decisionmaker in control of the decisions being faced rather than leave that control to others and happenstance.

CHAPTER **13**

Value-Focused Thinking for My Decisions

Value-focused thinking can be very helpful for both the big and the little decisions you make in your life. The intent of this chapter is to convince you of this fact. To do this, I will explain and illustrate how I use value-focused thinking in my own life. Why focus on me, you may ask. For one thing, applying value-focused thinking to a person's life requires understanding that person's objectives. Also, as I so strongly advocate value-focused thinking, it would be inappropriate, as well as embarrassing, if I did not use it myself. Therefore, using myself as an example seems the best way to demonstrate the breadth and depth of insights offered by value-focused thinking. Some of the decisions discussed in this chapter are extremely significant, such as whether to have a child, and others are relatively frivolous, such as whether to rent or buy a car for a summer in Europe. The point is simple: value-focused thinking can help you with any decision worth thinking about.

13.1 Strategic Objectives for Life

Over the years, I have spent considerable effort thinking about and writing down my strategic objectives for my life. This effort has been worthwhile because I have repeatedly invoked these objectives in my decisionmaking. By their nature, these objectives have not changed much over time. They define both who I am, in that they have guided my past, and who I want to be, in that they indicate where I want to go.

Let me first list and discuss my strategic objectives and then place them in the larger context of a strategic objectives network. I'll then show how both sets of objectives suggest worthwhile decision opportunities for me.

Strategic Objectives Hierarchy

It is probably not surprising that my overall strategic objective is to maximize my quality of life. This same overall objective is shared by most, if not all, individuals. What differs from one individual to another is the definition of quality of life. For me, the strategic objectives listed in Table 13.1 define quality of life. There are four major objectives: to enjoy life, to be intellectually fulfilled, to enhance the lives of family and friends, and to contribute to society. The order in which they are listed implies no prioritization. However, note that the first two concern what I get out of life and the last two concern what I offer to the lives of others.

Enjoyment of life includes fun, excitement, emotion, and experience. Collectively, these objectives capture my feelings, whereas thinking is addressed by the next objective. To be intellectually fulfilled includes learning, knowing, understanding, and reasoning. There are many natural relationships among these component objectives: learning provides knowledge which leads to understanding, all of which can be used in reasoning, which is one way that I learn. Still, in addition to being a means to others, each of the four objectives is fundamental in itself.

Enhancing the lives of family and friends is very important to me, as to most other people. In my case, the lives of my wife, Janet, and our son, Gregory, are singularly special. Because Gregory did not choose to have a relationship with us, the desire to enhance his life is of a unique nature. I clearly have a responsibility to enrich his life as much as possible, and this responsibility may contribute to my desire to do so. But for

Table 13.1. My strategic objectives

Maximize my quality of life

1. Enjoy life

2. Be intellectually fulfilled

3. Enhance the lives of family and friends

4. Contribute to society

me, the desire to enhance Gregory's life is clearly fundamental, and the responsibility is a means.

Sometimes, friends or family members get rather sick of my attempting to enhance their lives when they have not requested such divine guidance. It is hard to remain silent, though, when I think I recognize great decision opportunities for people I care about. If I care about them, I probably know something about their objectives, and if I do know something about their objectives, decision opportunities sometimes just pop into my mind. I do at least try to couch suggestions of decision opportunities as "Here is something that may be worth thinking about" rather than "Here is what you should do."

As for society, I think the idea is not to offer everyone all things on silver platters, but to have all things on silver platters that people can reach by making and taking advantage of opportunities. I do not feel that society owed me a life or owes me a living, nor do I feel that it owes those to anyone. But I believe society should provide opportunities for individuals to have a good quality of life, and I would like to contribute to society to maintain and improve its opportunities.

Strategic Objectives Network

Everything I do both contributes to and detracts from the achievement of my strategic objectives. Why? Because everything comes with both advantages and disadvantages. My intent is naturally to select those things with the greatest advantages and the smallest disadvantages. My decisionmaking is guided by the pursuit of such ends.

Figure 13.1 presents my strategic objectives network, which illustrates key means objectives of the framework in which my decisions are made. Defining these means objectives should make the framework become clear. In the figure, an arrow from one objective to another indicates that better achieving the former contributes positively toward achieving the latter.

The achievement of my strategic objectives, which are listed at the right of the figure, is directly influenced by the activities and the relationships I pursue. Thus, two means objectives are to pursue worthwhile activities and to pursue worthwhile relationships. The word "worthwhile" here is essentially defined by how well the activities and relationships help me achieve my strategic objectives: the more achievement, the more worthwhile.

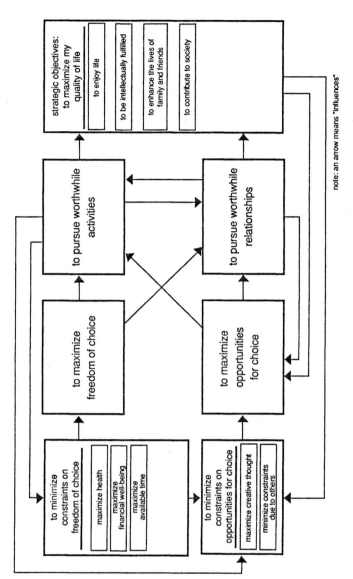

Figure 13.1 My strategic objectives network

In order to pursue anything, worthwhile or not, I must have both the opportunity and the freedom to pursue it. For instance, having the opportunity to spend a year living and working in New Zealand would not be useful if I were not free to choose this opportunity. Two further means objectives, then, are to maximize freedom of choice and to maximize opportunities for choice. The way to maximize both of these is to minimize constraints. Consequently, two additional means objectives are to minimize constraints on freedom of choice and to minimize constraints on opportunities for choice. The main constraints related to freedom of choice concern health, finances, and available time. Other constraints not listed in the figure concern political, emotional, or spiritual factors. The health constraints, which include both physical and mental health, have a natural influence on the achievement of the objective to minimize constraints on opportunities for choice. Opportunities for choice are constrained mainly by limitations on my creative thought to identify decision opportunities and by others' perceptions. For example, others may feel that I am not the right person for a particular job.

The pursuit of worthwhile activities and the pursuit of worthwhile relationships are synergistic: achievement of one enhances achievement of the other. A skiing trip may lead to a very worthwhile relationship. And good relationships can lead to new or more worthwhile activities.

Activities and relationships both affect the achievement of other means objectives. Relationships may directly lead to opportunities for choice, as when a friend says, "I have an idea about something that you may find rewarding." Activities that I pursue directly affect constraints on me. For example, activities that preserve and improve my health affect health and financial constraints. Activities that help me think about decision opportunities, such as value-focused thinking, both create opportunities and take time that otherwise could be devoted to other pursuits.

The achievement of my strategic objectives lessens any constraints on creative thought. If I am enjoying life and am intellectually fulfilled, I am likely to be more creative. If I enhance others' lives, they are likely to enhance mine. They essentially create opportunities for me as well as help me create alternatives for myself. If I contribute even a little to society, people may recognize it, and this may also create opportunities for me or stimulate my thoughts to create opportunities. As an example, if I do work of high quality, someone may offer me the opportunity to do other work that I may find interesting.

Searching for Decision Opportunities

As shown in the objectives network of Figure 13.1, one of my objectives is to minimize the constraints on creative thought. The way to do this is by thinking about decision opportunities, as discussed in Chapter 9. There are two simple notions that help in this regard. One is to understand that there are many decision opportunities always out there to be discovered, and the second is to realize that effort expended on searching for decision opportunities is likely to be rewarding. My advice, based on years of personal experience, is "Try it, you'll like it."

The list of strategic objectives and the objectives network are helpful in the search for decision opportunities. It is useful to ask yourself often whether you could do better in terms of one of your objectives or another. For example, I felt there was a distinct opportunity to communicate the ideas in this book. I thought the project would be enjoyable and intellectually fulfilling. As of the moment I'm writing this sentence, it has been. My hope is also that it will make a small contribution to others: family, friends, and readers. On the other hand, this same effort has had negative impacts by taking up time that otherwise I could have devoted to other activities or relationships.

Once I had decided to write a book on the subject matter described here, I recognized another decision opportunity pertaining to how the book would be written. It seemed as if it would be best to have some time in which to do concentrated work on it. For this purpose, I wanted to arrange a six-month sabbatical at the Harvard Business School. To do this required the support of my family, my department at the University of Southern California, and my colleagues David Bell and Howard Raiffa at Harvard. I thought about what each of them might be able to get out of my sabbatical and tried to design a winning situation for each, using ideas discussed in Section 9.6. I did get the sabbatical, and I believe that my thinking about the individual values of others involved in the decision enabled me to create a situation that contributed to their interests as well.

13.2 Guiding Involvement in Professional Activities

There are numerous professional activities in which I can participate. Such activities range from local seminars requiring roughly half a day to national scientific panels requiring ten days per year to writing a book that may require a person-year of my time. Other examples are teaching, attending conferences, doing editorial work for journals, consulting, conducting intensive courses for professionals, writing articles for journals, doing theoretical research, developing applications of theory to contemporary problems, and reading. Some of the opportunities for activities come from others, such as an invitation to be a member of a national scientific panel. Other activities grow out of my own creation of decision opportunities, such as those resulting in publications. Some activities are done alone and others are done jointly. In fact, some decision opportunities to pursue are opportunities to work with interesting people from whom I could learn and with whom I could enjoy myself.

There are many more activities than I could ever hope to participate in. Thus, by choosing some activities I de facto reject others. As a result, it is desirable to make my decisions about professional activities in a consistent manner. Clearly I do not wish to participate in an activity if doing so will prevent my participating in something better. The common framework for all my professional activities is my set of fundamental objectives for such activities. Let me briefly discuss these objectives and then indicate how I use them.

Fundamental Professional Objectives

My professional objectives are listed in Table 13.2. I use this set of objectives both to appraise any single professional activity and to appraise the collection of activities that I'm involved in.

The overall objective of my professional activity is to contribute to my quality of life as defined by my strategic objectives listed in Table 13.1. Thus, each of my professional objectives is either a part of a strategic objective or a means to one or more strategic objectives.

The first three objectives in Table 13.2 are parts of different strategic objectives. Enjoyment of professional activities is naturally part of the enjoyment of life, my first strategic objective. This enjoyment typically derives from three aspects of professional activities: who else is participating, where the activity is, and the nature of the activity. I will get more enjoyment from meeting with knowledgeable policymakers in Aspen, Colorado, to develop plans to reduce U.S. dependence on foreign oil than from working alone on a well-defined problem that nobody really cares about while sitting in hotel room 1047 in Nowheresville.

Learning from professional activities is a part of my second strategic

Table 13.2.   My fundamental professional objectives

Maximize the contribution of professional activities to my quality of life

1. Maximize enjoyment

2. Maximize learning

3. Provide service

4. Enhance professional career

5. Maximize economic gain

6. Build good professional relationships

7. Minimize the time required
   7.1. Minimize time required where I live
   7.2. Minimize time required away from home

objective concerning intellectual fulfillment. The amount of learning is also influenced by whom I'm working with and the substance of the activity. With individual consulting on a problem similar to many I have addressed before, I am basically using my existing expertise and learning only a little. On group activities addressing unique problems such as global warming, I learn a lot from the problem and from the other participants.

My third fundamental professional objective, to provide service, is a part of my strategic objective to contribute to society. This service may be for students if the activity is a course, for professionals in my field if the activity is editorial service, for clients if the activity is consulting, and for society if the work is on public issues such as selecting a site for a nuclear waste repository.

My other four professional objectives are means to the achievement of my strategic objectives. Enhancing my career is a means to future professional activities. This enhancement can come from what I learn from an activity, whom I meet during the activity, or the quality of the resulting work. Work of high quality has both direct and indirect rewards. Doing good work will create decision opportunities for me.

Objective number five concerns the financial remuneration associated with professional activity. Many activities, such as writing journal articles, giving seminars in universities, and performing editorial service bring no remuneration. Others have honoraria or consulting fees. Building good professional relationships, the sixth objective, is one means to increase both the number of professional decision opportunities in the future and the likely desirability of such opportunities.

The first six professional objectives concern the potential positive consequences of professional activities. Objective seven concerns a negative consequence, namely the amount of time an activity requires. Time I spend on one activity is time I cannot use for any other activities, whether personal or professional. I have divided this objective into time required for the activity where I live and time required away from home. All other things equal, being away from home is less desirable than being at home.

Coordinating Decisions about Professional Activity

The professional objectives in Table 13.2 are the common basis on which I evaluate professional activities. This list alone, however, does not tell me which activities I should choose to participate in. If all of my potential activities were known at the same time, I could evaluate them all and select those with the highest evaluation until my time available for professional activity was all allocated. I might pick, say, the best 16 of 45 potential activities for a given year. Collectively, these activities would form a portfolio, and I would want to ensure that the 16 did not all contribute to the same professional objectives and leave others poorly achieved. My experience in thinking about professional activities with the objectives in Table 13.2 indicates that the portfolio effects seem to take care of themselves.

My real situation has two complicating features that need to be considered. First, I do not know all possible activities at the same time. Decision opportunities occur over time, and part of my time is always committed into the future. Second, there are major uncertainties about the decision opportunities that will occur. Thus, it is important to keep some time available to participate in the very interesting activities that come up on short notice. This suggests that I need a decision rule to help me decide which activities to select and which to reject as they appear.

There are other good reasons to have a decision rule. When I look at my calendar six months to a year in the future, it appears to be wide open. Hence, if asked to participate in some activity in that period, I find it too easy to say yes. This not only commits some of my time but begins to break up the period into smaller parts. When the beginning of that period is three to six months in the future, it is already quite fragmented. The longest open period may be eight days. By the time then is now, I am overcommitted and have to turn down more interesting opportunities for both professional and personal activity.

Since I do not want to be a time-constrained person, I have established levels of the desirability of professional activities in which I agree to participate. To do this, I roughly evaluated many activities in which I have participated in terms of the objectives in Table 13.2. It was clear that some of those activities should have never been agreed to, whereas others were desirable if they didn't eliminate other useful professional activities. Still other past activities were terrific, and I should jump at the opportunity to participate in similar activities. This evaluation yielded three responses to possible professional activities: no, maybe, and yes.

These three responses are no surprise, but the way I use them is helpful to me. At any given time, there are a no-level and a yes-level. The no-level indicates the maximum overall desirability of an activity in which I will definitely not participate. It is partially defined by personal activities that I could pursue in the time that otherwise might be used for professional activities. The yes-level indicates the minimum overall desirability of an activity necessary for me to definitely participate. In between the no-level and the yes-level are activities in which I may participate. The two levels change over time. In general they fall as the time for a proposed activity approaches, as the levels are intentionally set high to avoid overcommitment. However, if some great potential projects pop up and I agree to them, the levels may rise as less time is available for other projects. This could turn a maybe into a no as the no-level rises.

To help me coordinate my professional life, I routinely think about decision opportunities for professional activities. If I am not pursuing some potentially worthwhile professional activity, I formulate a decision opportunity to figure out a way to pursue it. If some of my professional objectives are being inadequately met, I formulate a decision opportunity to decide how to rectify the situation. And sometimes when all seems well professionally, I think about decision opportunities that might make things even better. What better is there to do when I cannot fall asleep in hotel room 1047?

13.3 Decisions about Health and Safety

I make, although perhaps not explicitly, many decisions every day that affect my health and safety. You do also. Everything I do involves risks to my health or safety. Common activities such as eating, drinking, and driving present risks. Natural disasters from earthquakes to floods to hurricanes pose potential dangers. Accidents can result from human error, including my own error. The point is that almost all decisions have some health and safety implications.

There is a class of decisions that explicitly address health and safety concerns. Such decisions include, for example, whether to purchase an air bag for a car, what type of diet to follow, and what kinds of medical treatment to seek. Some activities also carry large enough risks that I consider the risks explicitly in contemplating the activity. One of many reasons that I have never smoked cigarettes is that I wish to live a long time so I may practice other "bad habits." Skydiving and serious mountain climbing are two activities with many attractions but with risks, at least to an amateur like me, serious enough to be explicitly considered.

For decisions with major implications for health and safety, I want to consider the consequences explicitly. Furthermore, I want to make those decisions consistently. This means I do not want to reduce my risk slightly through a great deal of effort and forgo simple ways to reduce it more in other contexts.

The Framework for Evaluating Health and Safety Decisions

My framework for evaluating health and safety decisions is illustrated as a part of my strategic objectives network in Figure 13.1. The activities that affect my health and safety also affect my financial well-being and time available. In other words, decisions about these activities can be evaluated in terms of the degree to which they affect the three constraints on my freedom of choice in Figure 13.1.

It is worthwhile to recognize that these three objectives are means. It was obvious to me that money and time aren't worth much if I do not use them productively. But I had to think harder about my health. Health is very important, but was it one of my strategic objectives? It occurred to me that if I had perfect health and yet did not contribute to my four strategic objectives, I would be exactly the same as a healthy tree. This clarified my thinking and I realized that health is a means to me.

So how should I think about decisions such as whether to have an expensive diagnostic test that is part of a preventive health procedure or whether to buy an air bag for my car? Basically, I wish to ask whether the time and cost are worth the health benefit. The next subsection considers the values involved in more detail.

There may be other situations in which the overall health and safety consequences are much more severe and immediate. If tomorrow I learned I had a particular form of cancer, I would want to consider my options carefully and explicitly. It would be important for me to understand how much my physical well-being might be impaired, for example by amputation, and how this would affect my freedom of choice. Available time in this context might be my time until death rather than simply time involved in a health-related activity such as a preventive procedure. In short, for decision situations of the magnitude of cancer, I would want to trace the possible implications of various alternatives through the entire objectives network in Figure 13.1 to get a better understanding of how the alternatives might influence my quality of life (see Keeney and von Winterfeldt, 1991). I am certain that carefully thinking through such difficult life-and-death decisions would provide me with insights well worth the effort.

Values for Health and Safety Decisions

One value very clear in my mind is that, for me, death from one cause is exactly as bad as death from another cause. The timing of my death and my pain and any suffering that I cause others are also important. Many people seem to act as if dying in an airplane crash is much worse than dying in a car. For me, dying in an airplane crash 15 years from now is much preferred to dying in a car crash in 14 years if both deaths are essentially instantaneous (that is, without pain or suffering). Also, for me, dying in 28 years after 5 years in a stroke-induced, relatively incapacitated state is worse than dying "healthy" in 25 years from an unexpected heart attack.

One implication of these values is that I should invest my time and funds in my safety where I can reduce the risks most effectively. Reducing my risk of dying in a car by 10 percent is worth much more than eliminating my risk of dying from eating apples treated with alar or eliminating my risk of dying in an earthquake as a resident of San Francisco. And the good news is that I usually can do much more to reduce my driving risks.

A more general implication for me is that I should avoid being overweight or in poor physical condition, which could contribute significantly to my health risks. With just a little self-control and almost no onerous effort, it is possible to eat reasonably and exercise regularly. Fortunately, both the eating and the exercising can be a part of activities and relationships with other positive consequences.

It has also been useful for me to quantify my value tradeoffs over attributes characterizing the three objectives concerning health, financial well-being, and time. Specifically, the question I addressed was how much money it would be worth to reduce my probability of dying now by one chance in a million (that is, a probability of 10^{-6}). Ron Howard of Stanford University has a computer program with actuarial statistics and a model to examine this question. The health attribute is what Ron has defined as the micromort, which is a 10^{-6} probability of dying. The financial attribute is the funds used for consumption each year. The time attribute is the time until death.

My value tradeoffs between consumption and lifetime included indifference between, for example, 30 additional years of life at a consumption level of $40,000 annually and 25 additional years at $75,000. Using Ron's model, it follows from these tradeoffs that I should be willing to pay a maximum of about $12 to reduce my immediate risk by one micromort if all other consequences are equal. His model also suggests that I should be willing to give up about 0.4 hours now to reduce my risk by a micromort. These two derived value tradeoffs can be used to calculate quickly whether some activities are worth pursuing.

As an example, my former physician suggested that I should get a colon check for cancer in conjunction with a routine physical. I naturally asked why and what were the chances I had colon cancer and what were the chances that this test would detect it. His basic answer was that I was now over 40 years old so I should have the test. This did not answer my questions; I knew my age. I wanted to know what the test might do for me and to me. Through protracted effort, and then through asking a more enlightened physician, I learned that my chances of colon cancer were about one in a million. It would probably be detected by the test if I had it. Preparing, going to and from the doctor's office, and having the test would require about four hours and cost about $100. There was no way this effort and cost were worth it to eliminate one micromort. Indeed, a separate factor was that the driving would add almost a micromort of risk. And I used the four hours to play squash, which probably contributed as much to my health and was infinitely more enjoyable than a colon check.

13.4 Professional Decisions

The previous three sections have concentrated on how I think about decision situations. The themes are always the same. One theme is to structure and understand my objectives and values first and then use these to guide my decisionmaking activities. A second theme is to search for decision opportunities and create alternatives to better achieve my objectives. And a third theme is that the objectives and values expressed provide a framework to guide consistent decisionmaking for large classes of decisions.

This and the following section provide examples of decisions in which I have used value-focused thinking. This section discusses specific professional decisions ranging from career decisions to daily interaction with colleagues. Since I always and automatically focus on values when thinking about decision situations, these examples represent only a few of the many cases that could be described. They are discussed in chronological order.

Collaborating on a Book

In the spring of 1969 I had just finished my doctoral studies in Operations Research and joined the faculty of the Department of Civil Engineering at the Massachusetts Institute of Technology (M.I.T.). My dissertation concerned the theory, assessment, and application of multi-attribute utility functions, and I had had the pleasure of having Howard Raiffa of Harvard University as my dissertation advisor. It was apparent to me that many of my personal and professional objectives would be well achieved if I could write a book on decisionmaking with multiple objectives with Howard. Regarding professional objectives, such a book would enhance my career, help build a professional relationship with Howard, and even earn a few cents. It was obvious that the collaboration would be great for me, but to become a reality it had to be desirable to Howard also.

The general situation where approval is needed from someone else to render an alternative feasible is discussed in Section 9.6. I structured what objectives Howard might have for writing such a book with me. Perhaps because of my myopia, I felt his professional objectives would be quite similar to mine listed in Table 13.2. His alternatives for achieving them were much broader than mine, though, especially at the respective stages of our careers in 1969. An additional professional objective of Howard's was to educate young people with even an inkling of promise. I was young then and he gave me the benefit of the doubt that I had an inkling of promise.

I gave considerable thought to what material we might include in a joint book on multiple-objective decisions and how we might accomplish the task together. Whenever I had the freedom to design the alternative for writing the book to be better for Howard, I did so, as it was obvious that any jointly acceptable alternative would be great for me.

In June 1969 we had a meeting and I proposed the collaboration. I acknowledged the obvious advantages to me, and talked about what advantages and disadvantages there might be for Howard. The main advantage was that a potentially significant book would be produced discussing Howard's (and my) ideas on a topic he considered important. My contribution would be to ensure that the project would definitely be completed, as I had more available time and essentially no "more important" distractions. Such a book would be a useful addition to the literature and a step toward getting the ideas of quantified values into practice for some important problems. Howard would no doubt learn some things from writing the book, and even small economic gains would be a positive consequence.

The disadvantages of such a project for Howard were clear to me. It would occupy a lot of time, and it might force him to forgo other opportunities, or he might have to renege on writing the book after we had made some progress. I could not alleviate the need for a time commitment, but I could significantly lower the negative implications of that commitment. I proposed that we should write the book on whatever time frame suited Howard, and should let the schedule evolve over time. We could have necessary meetings anywhere, anytime, and he could cancel meetings with essentially no notice if need be.

Howard agreed to write our book and I was overjoyed. The flexibility of timing turned out to be critical, as Howard was heavily involved in creating the International Institute for Applied Systems Analysis near Vienna through 1972 and served as its first director from 1972 to 1975. During that period we accumulated much more material, especially about applications of multiattribute utility, to include in the book. *Decisions with Multiple Objectives* was published in 1976. In the end, writing this book together provided a model, at least for us, of what joint authorship should be. Contributions of ideas and work time were balanced, and the product is something neither of us would have produced alone.

Teaching Responsibilities

A week after joining the M.I.T. faculty I went to have a talk with my department head, Charles Miller. This was three months before the beginning of the fall 1969 term, and many teaching responsibilities had not yet been assigned. It was generally understood that newer faculty members typically ended up teaching the courses that the more senior faculty did not want to teach. Naturally, I did not want to get stuck teaching unappealing material.

By talking with colleagues, I came to understand that one objective of the Civil Engineering Department was to become more of a systems department. They offered a few introductory courses on probability and systems analysis, but wished to offer a few more advanced courses. Many of the established faculty members had been trained in traditional civil engineering topics, such as soils and structures, and were not particularly interested in systems. I was. The opportunity was clearly there.

So I proposed to develop and teach a new graduate course titled "Analysis of Public Systems" and suggested that this teaching load would be adequate for a first semester. Professor Miller accepted my proposal and I carried out those responsibilities. By the time the last courses requiring teachers were assigned, I was in the middle of designing the new course and not available for additional fall teaching. I tried to make a bigger positive contribution to the department with the new course than I could have made as the teacher of least resort for some required course. By broadening the decision context beyond which standard course to teach, I was able to create a win-win situation for the department and me.

A Faculty Member in Europe

Since spending a summer hitchhiking through Europe, I had wanted to return to live and work in Germany for a while. While finishing my doctoral program, I became aware that Boston University offered a master's degree in business in Germany with most students being drawn from U.S. military forces stationed there. Consequently, I contacted Boston University and inquired about the possibility of being a faculty member for them in Germany. At that time, however, the program was rather new and the Business Department had many current members waiting for a chance to spend a year in Germany, the typical length of assignment.

It was apparent to me that I was in the right place but just not at the right time. Consistent with the idea in Section 9.7 of being in the right place more often, I let the Boston University faculty in charge of the program know that I would remain interested and could go for a year with little notice. As time went by I talked to them often to reaffirm my interest. By early 1972 there was no longer a backlog of faculty waiting to go to Germany, and I was offered the opportunity. I lived in Heidelberg for a year beginning in the fall of 1972 and taught in the vicinity. The year contributed tremendously to personal objectives of enjoyment and learning and led to many rewarding relationships.

Resigning from M.I.T.

In 1974 I was an associate professor in the Sloan School of Management at M.I.T. and affiliated with the Operations Research Center. Professionally, it was an exciting place to be, and I enjoyed many of my colleagues. But outside the university community I felt a lot of restrictions on the achievement of my personal objectives. Eastern Massachusetts weather is often not hospitable (I do not like high humidity and I prefer dependable weather) and Massachusetts politics are not my favorite. For me, the numerous inconveniences that occurred because of the climate and the political system were detracting too much from my enjoyment of life. I realize others find Massachusetts more congenial than I did.

This situation posed a major problem. I could stay at M.I.T. and have a great professional environment or give it up to improve personal achievement. At first, I thought of this problem within a one-year framework. The main issue was whether to resign this year or not. It always seemed better to stay. After all, I could resign next year if I felt like it.

Then I broadened the decision context to look at my entire professional career, a large part of my expected life. The one-year frame is clearly a means to this career frame. Now I considered whether I should remain at M.I.T. for my career, assuming that I would have the option, or not. It was almost transparent to me using this frame that I should leave M.I.T. Even if I stayed and had a professional career equivalent to those of the people at Harvard and M.I.T. whom I most respected, I would not be pleased with my life. In simple terms, the opportunities available to me in 1974 were much different from those available to others 20 and 30 years earlier, so my life objectives could be better pursued elsewhere.

Having made the decision that I should not stay at M.I.T. forever, I next considered when should I leave. This was now relatively easy. It would be better to leave sooner than later both for M.I.T. and for me. I felt comfortable resigning in June 1974.

Joining a Consulting Firm

After leaving M.I.T. I became a research scholar at the International Institute for Applied Systems Analysis and lived in Vienna, Austria, for two years. Then in the summer of 1976 Kesh Nair offered me a position with Woodward-Clyde Consultants in San Francisco. Woodward-Clyde was a geotechnical and environmental consulting firm with about 1,000 employees. The job was to build and head a group to apply risk analysis and decision analysis to problems concerned with issues such as earthquakes, environmental impacts, and energy supplies. This was appealing because it would be very different from my previous jobs. Hence I would have some interesting experiences and learn a lot both from coworkers in numerous disciplines and from trying to apply concepts that I had previously mainly taught in the classroom. Also, I felt the job offered an excellent opportunity to develop good professional relationships and to contribute by introducing ideas of risk and decision analysis into important fields of practice. Having graduated from U.C.L.A., I also knew that living in California fit with my personal objectives.

My major concern was that working in the "corporate world" might constrain the way I could do things, at least for eight hours a day. I felt it was important that Kesh, who would be my boss, and I agree on the firm's key objectives defining my role. Our discussion on this topic was short and effective. I said, "I assume that my overall responsibilities are to contribute professionally and financially to the firm, and that subject to that, there are essentially no other constraints on me. Is that correct?" Kesh said, "That is correct." I immediately accepted the position.

Reneging on Professional Commitments

From time to time, I find myself saddled with a commitment that I wish I didn't have. We all understand how this can happen and that it can happen even with the best of intentions and significant forethought. The world, fortunately, is dynamic. Using a simple example, let me illustrate how value-focused thinking helps me out of commitment predicaments.

In 1989, Howard Kunreuther of the University of Pennsylvania and Larry Susskind of M.I.T. asked me to be part of a two-meeting workshop on choosing sites for hazardous facilities. I was delighted and did participate in the first meeting at M.I.T. in late 1989. The second meeting was scheduled at the University of Pennsylvania on February

23, 1990. I looked forward to attending and planned to go. Other commitments intervened, however, and it became apparent in mid-February that attending the meeting would cause me a lot of difficulties.

Because I know Howard Kunreuther well, I called him and explained my predicament. I said that I would definitely attend the workshop if he felt my attendance was crucial. He politely did not laugh and say "Your attendance, crucial?" However, I also said that the time crunch for me was such that we surely should be able to create a win-win situation. Since we are friends, it was not necessary for me to come up with a concrete suggestion right then. I said that if he would let me out of my responsibility I would owe him a future favor that could be called in at his convenience. He said fine. Two months later, I spent a day with Howard in Philadelphia presenting a lecture in one of his classes and extensively commenting on material produced by the February workshop. It turned out to be win-win.

One might ask why bother with all this hassle; if you can't attend, just say so. Certainly I could have simply announced that I wasn't attending. Many reasons for doing otherwise are contained in my objectives. First, good relationships are one of my key objectives. "Tough luck" reneging does not contribute to good relationships. Enhancing the lives of friends is not accomplished by backing out of commitments to them. Finally, just dropping the commitment would have been throwing away a decision opportunity. Even if simply discarding the commitment to attend had been better for me than attending, which it was not, my task, and later our task, was to create a third alternative that would be better than these both for me and for Howard. It turned out that way.

Personal Publication Policy

One of the major objectives in my strategic objectives network in Figure 13.1 is to maximize opportunities for choice. Professional opportunities can include working on an important problem, working with interesting people, or attending conferences in fascinating places. Such opportunities sometimes appear to come out of nowhere. When others have such offers to make, I would like to be in their minds as a possible recipient. It is like being in the right place at the right time. But the right place is in their minds, so how do I get there?

I view this situation as a constant decision opportunity. From my professional objectives, it seems that one of the best things I can do to promote opportunities is to enhance my professional career and build good professional relationships. One effective way to do these things is to publish articles in respected peer-reviewed professional journals. Such articles, along with books, are the main tangible products of my work. It is through these articles that news of my interests and abilities, or lack thereof, is spread. So I have a policy that I should write articles and books. These activities not only contribute directly to all four of my strategic objectives but also create many opportunities to contribute more to these objectives.

13.5 Personal Decisions

By now you may be bored with reading about me. If this is the case, please shut the book and end your misery, because this section is in some sense more of the same. My intent, though, is still to convince you that value-focused thinking can be very helpful to you. The personal examples in this section push this point as far as I can to show you that value-focused thinking can contribute to the quality of your life. The examples are discussed in chronological order.

Dating

An important class of decisions to me when I was a teenager involved dating. My basic objective was to have dates with girls who were both interesting and fun. When I asked someone new for a date, the scenario often went like this: "Would you like to go to a movie with me on Friday?" "I can't, I already have plans." "How about Saturday?" "On Saturday, I'm going home (from college) for the day." "Are you free Sunday?" "Sunday I've got to study." You may think I should have been getting the message. I did get a message, but I did not know which message it was. Either the girl was not so subtly saying "no, never" or she was probably interesting and fun and therefore busy. I needed a diagnostic test to tell me which message she was sending.

Although my ideas about values were not as well formulated then as now, I realized that what mattered was whether she wanted to go out with me, not whether she was available next Friday. I would try to get the principle straightened out using clearly stated objectives. I'd say something like "Let's see if we have a common interest. I would like to go out with you. The question is whether you would like to go out with me. If the answer is yes, we can work out the time and place. If the answer is no, then I will stop bothering you and wasting my time." I liked this question because either response, if honest, immediately led to a better circumstance than before. And if the response was not honestly given, I was probably better off not going out with her. With a dishonest "no," I clearly wouldn't call again. With a dishonest "yes," I would call and call, which would both tax her imagination to come up with creative excuses for turning me down and irritate her a little. As I am a fan of poetic justice, I like this very simple example of clarifying stakeholder values for group decisions, as discussed in Section 8.3.

Meeting Janet

Many of the best things of life seem to occur from being in the right place at the right time. As Section 9.7 discusses, you can increase the frequency with which these "best things" occur by being in better "right places" and being there more often.

During my two years living in Austria, I learned to ski. I enjoyed the sport, and I liked many of the people who went skiing; at a minimum we had one thing in common. So a natural way for me to meet people was skiing.

In March 1977 I had a business meeting in Houston on a Monday and had to travel from my home in San Francisco. A weekend of time is a resource that can be used, and naturally will be used. I checked the airfares and found that a stop in Aspen to ski on the way to Houston would essentially be free. I spent the weekend there and had two great days of skiing. And I met Janet, who is now my wife.

The point of this simple story is not that with value-focused thinking you will meet someone you will eventually marry and without it you will not. All people who are married met their spouse in some way. But in situations like this, value-focused thinking increases your chances; let us say it doubles your chances. Randomness or luck or whatever you wish to call it still plays a major role, but you will be lucky twice as often. Over a lifetime, that means twice as many great things in life.

Commuting from San Francisco to New York

Janet lived in New York City when we met, and as mentioned, I lived in San Francisco. It would have been easy to assume that we could not have a reasonable relationship across 3,000 miles. But our objectives were clear: we wanted to see each other. With the principle established, only the details of the logistics remained. This is the core of value-focused thinking. Understand your objectives first and then figure out how to achieve them.

After several cross-country visits, we wanted to spend a longer period of time together. We agreed that it would be nice if I could live in New York for three or four months. For this I would need the authorization of Kesh Nair, my boss at Woodward-Clyde. To go to New York, I could either ask for unpaid leave, one year after joining the firm, or try to remain on the payroll. I preferred the latter.

To create such an alternative I simply had to reconsider Kesh's objectives for my employment. Recall that these were for me to contribute professionally and financially to the firm. I proposed to go to New York and contribute more to both objectives than in San Francisco. To do this, I would work in New York and bill clients for 40 hours per week, whereas my average weekly billing was about 32 hours in San Francisco. This increase would not be too difficult because I would not be involved in time-consuming activities such as office meetings and "overhead activities" during my New York stay. Also, I told Kesh he could count on me to return to San Francisco or go anywhere else during the New York visit if an important need arose. Kesh accepted the proposal, I worked productively those four months, and Janet and I had a wonderful time.

Frequent Flyer Programs

With the advent of frequent flyer programs, air travel decisions became more complex. Each airline has a different program with different rules, although they all are organized on the same basic principles. A passenger who flies on an airline accumulates miles in a personal account. These miles are often not equal to the actual miles flown, as there are bonuses, multiples of actual miles, and minimums. An airline promoting its Los Angeles to San Francisco route may award a bonus of 1,000 miles per flight. Flying first class may award double the actual miles flown. A minimum of 750 miles may be awarded for any flight.

Once miles are accumulated in your account, you can use them for free travel. For example, for 30,000 miles you may choose a free round-trip coach ticket for anywhere in the United States that the airline flies, whereas 150,000 miles may provide two first-class tickets to Asia and back.

The existence of such programs poses many potential problems.

What airline should I fly from San Francisco to Boston? If I want mileage on Trans World Airlines, is it worth waiting two additional hours in an airport or should I go earlier on a United Airlines flight? What is the value of paying an additional fee to fly first-class if double miles are then awarded?

Dealing with such issues every time I plan a trip would be inconvenient, irritating, and a waste of time. But the rewards of the frequent flyer programs are such that it is worth it to me to do some thinking about them. What I want is a simple and consistent way to include frequent flyer considerations in my decisions about flying. To do this, I use value tradeoffs to connect all flight decisions as discussed in Section 10.3.

The cost of flights and convenience are the major components that matter to me. I am accustomed to making such value tradeoffs. Hence, I have developed a simple scheme to convert frequent flyer mileage into dollars. For each airline, I pick an award that is representative of those that I may use. For TWA, my representative award is a round-trip ticket in the United States for 20,000 miles. As I would expect to use such an award for transcontinental travel, this is currently worth about $600 to me. Hence, TWA miles are currently worth three cents each. As airfares change over time, this value clearly changes. On Delta, my representative award is two round-trip coach tickets from the United States to Europe for 110,000 miles. This has a current value of about $1,800 to me or 1.6 cents each mile. Thus, if I am comparing TWA and Delta flights of 2,000 miles, the frequent flyer value on TWA is $60, whereas on Delta it is $32. I simply subtract those "savings" from airfares when I make decisions about flights. Using these value tradeoffs, I can logically address the frequent flyer aspects of flight decisions with just a few seconds of thought.

Overseas Automobile Purchase

In the summer of 1983, my friend and colleague Detlof von Winterfeldt and I had plans to be in Europe for five weeks. The first week was scheduled at a conference at Les Arcs in the French Alps and the other four weeks we would be working together on a project with the Nuclear Research Center near Aachen, Germany. We would need a car for those five weeks. The two readily apparent alternatives were to rent one and to borrow a car from Detlof's parents, who lived in southern Germany. Neither of these appealed to us so we thought a little harder. Another alternative was to buy a car, but that would be expensive and then we would have to get rid of it somehow. Then we thought about buying a used car, which might be somewhat less expensive. If we had ever considered a constraint on cost, even at a high level such as $1,500 for the five weeks, alternatives of purchasing a car would have been out of the question.

Fortunately, the U.S. dollar was relatively high versus the German mark at this time. This would not lower by much the new car prices in the U.S., but it would significantly lower the effective cost (measured in dollars) of used cars in Germany, which naturally followed the mark price. With Detlof's knowledge of the used car market in Germany, we decided to try to buy a low-mileage Mercedes or Porsche for use in Europe. Then, by coordinating alternatives as discussed in Section 7.7, we would ship it to the United States, convert to U.S. standards, and sell it. By using available resources, namely family and friends in Germany, to help find potential cars for purchase, Detlof arranged to buy a 1980 Mercedes 380 S.L. coupe for about $20,000 shortly after we arrived in Germany.

Our first stop was Les Arcs, which was a picturesque four-hour drive south of Geneva. It was fun with the top down. At the conference, other friends complained about their 12-hour trip from Geneva by bus, train, and funicular up the mountain. They asked us, "How did you get up here?" We smugly said, "Bought a Mercedes and drove up." Half the people thought we were crazy and the other half thought we were the only attendees with any sense.

That car served us very well in Europe and also on a few occasions after it returned to California. We sold it in late 1984 for a price that covered all of our expenses for purchase, shipping, and conversion to U.S. standards, as well as all of our uses. It was the proverbial free lunch in the form of a free car.

Renting an Apartment in Passau

From October through December 1985, I had the privilege of being a Visiting Professor at the University of Passau in Germany. My wife and I hoped to live in the historical center of this medieval small city. We found a pleasant small furnished apartment, but the landlord would not rent it for just three months. As there were very few furnished apartments in Passau, we were willing to pay 50 percent more than the requested rent to have the apartment. We offered to pay a higher rent, not mentioning how much, but the landlord still said no. I pursued his reasoning and found out that his concern was that he might not be able to rent the apartment in January and he did not want a nonproductive resource. One of his objectives was to have the apartment rented. I proposed to rent the apartment for four months, October through January, and the landlord accepted this at the standard rent. We had our apartment and the landlord was also pleased.

It is useful to note that the landlord could have received more total rent for a three-month rental period. For whatever reasons, this did not satisfy his objectives. I believe that he had constraints in his mind about the range of feasible alternatives for renting his apartment. My task was to understand his objectives, whether I thought they were reasonable or not, and create an alternative acceptable to him and to us.

Having a Child

A rather different type of decision from traveling the autobahns of Germany or renting an apartment is whether or not to have a child. Anyone who can read this sentence knows that the decision to have a child is an extremely important one. The consequences are monumental to the parents and to the child.

One cannot get a lot of practice making decisions about whether or not to have a first child. There was clearly no way that Janet and I could get good at making this decision by accumulating experience. For me, it was almost imperative to complement my intuitive thinking and feelings on the subject with thought facilitated by my strategic objectives network in Figure 13.1. It was obvious to me that this could not and should not provide the answer about whether we should have a child. However, if the process lent any insight or made me feel more comfortable with the resulting decision, it would well be worth it.

What I did was compare, qualitatively, life with and without a child by considering each of the sets of objectives in Figure 13.1. Since we had no children at the time of the comparison, we knew the qualitative implications of that state of affairs. I examined having a child in terms of changes from this status quo.

A child would affect many of the constraints in the first two boxes of Figure 13.1. There would clearly be much greater constraints on time and somewhat greater constraints on financial resources. On the other hand, just keeping up with a child would probably positively contribute to both our physical and mental health. It would also naturally enhance creative thought. A child would not place constraints on opportunities. Indeed, it would likely increase them. The main constraint would be due to the time available to pursue them.

Because of time spent with the child, certain activities and relationships would naturally be allocated less time. But the time with the child would also be spent pursuing worthwhile activities. With a child, we thought, on average we would be pursuing activities and relationships more and sleeping and sitting around less in the next 20 years. Parenthetically, and jumping ahead, the comment about less sleep seems to be one of the few universal truths.

It seemed clear that a child would, on average, positively influence the achievement of each of my four strategic objectives. Having a child would be an experience with a lot of joy, excitement, and emotion. I would certainly learn a great deal; I would have to. At a minimum, with a child, I would have one more family member whose life to enhance. But enhancing my child's life would bring me unparalleled rewards. Regarding contribution to society, there would be a possibility that the child would make a crucial contribution. Also, a child would perhaps make me more attuned to life for future generations and, therefore, more creative and eager to make contributions myself.

This review of my objectives did help my thinking, and it helped my feelings. It also helped Janet and me in our discussions about a child. We decided to have a baby, and our son was born in June 1987.

Naming Our Child

In the early spring of 1987, Janet was becoming a bit concerned that I had not yet seriously concentrated on possible names for our child. We knew it was to be a boy, so I felt we had at least eliminated about 50 percent of all potential names. Janet saw it as a decision opportunity to get me to think hard about a name. She said, "Why don't we each write down the objectives of his name?" If you have read even a small part of this book, you know that I could not say no to that proposition. The foundation of value-focused thinking is the idea that objectives should be considered prior to alternatives on important decisions. And, especially from our child's point of view, the choice of what name he would bear was surely an important decision.

Janet and I had agreed that our son's middle and last names would be Lee and Keeney, which are respectively her and my "maiden" names. So what we needed to choose was his first name. We each listed our

Table 13.3.   Objectives for our son's name

1. Single spelling

2. Not a unisex name

3. Reasonable initials

4. Understandable pronunciation
   4.1. With last name
   4.2. With middle and last name

5. No obvious "unwanted" nickname

6. Not unique

7. Not extremely common

8. Not religious

9. Not named after anyone

10. Has a nice rhythm
    10.1. With last name
    10.2. With middle and last names

11. Nice-sounding in foreign languages

12. Appealing (i.e., you feel predisposed to talk to or meet the person)

13. No "ee" sounds

---

objectives and then combined the list to produce that in Table 13.3. These are our own objectives for our child's name and of course have no implications for what other parents should name their children. The order of the list in Table 13.3 does not imply prioritization.

Whether a name meets some of the objectives, such as having a single spelling, is immediately clear. Whether a name has a nice rhythm is essentially our subjective judgment. Let me clarify some of the objectives.

A unisex name is one appropriate for both boys and girls, like Chris or Robin. With initials, there may be undesirable three-letter combinations. With L and K as the second and third initials, only ELK and ILK may be a problem. A name we both like is Eric or Erik. However, besides having more than one spelling, this name is hard to pronounce with Keeney. The last syllable of Eric runs into the first of Keeney and sounds like Airy Keeney or the British Harry Keeney.

As for unwanted nicknames, there is no way to eliminate random nicknames. Whether you name your son Jonathan or Godfrey probably does not greatly influence the chance that his nickname will be Bullfrog. But it may influence whether his nickname will be God, which is also an unwanted nickname from our perspective. On the other hand, with objective 12, "appealing" implies that you would readily answer the phone if so-and-so, whom you didn't know, called. If someone said, "It's for you, God calling," you would probably answer.

A unique name is Dwiezel. Common names and religious names are obvious. We didn't want to name our son after anyone (for example Ralph, Jr.), which is the point of objective 9. As for rhythm, we preferred a first name of three syllables to one syllable, which we preferred to two. Nice-sounding in foreign languages meant that the name with American pronunciation would sound pleasant to non-Americans. For example, one of the names that we liked was Scott. We asked Germans, Russians, and French people about names, and all said Scott did not appeal to them. Since Lee Keeney has three "ee" sounds, we thought it would be nice to avoid another "ee" in the first name, which is the intent of objective 13.

After listing our objectives, we looked through books of names. We first wrote down any possible contender, and this provided about 30. Using the objectives, we cut the list to seven realistic possibilities. We lived with these for a while and zeroed in on three finalists: Jeffrey, Scott, and Gregory. None were perfect in terms of our objectives. Jeffrey can alternately be spelled Geoffrey, is two syllables, and has an "ee" sound. Scott didn't sound good to non-Americans, has one syllable, and rendered the full name a little difficult to understand. Gregory is a somewhat religious name and also has an "ee" sound. Our son's name is Gregory.

13.6 Value-Focused Thinking and You

The fundamental point of this chapter: value-focused thinking can help you! You need to do some work to get this help, but I believe that you will find that the benefits are definitely worth it.

Clarifying and explicitly stating your strategic objectives should have a high benefit-to-effort ratio for you. Indeed, even if your objectives are fairly clear but not explicitly written down, writing them down should lead to further clarification. These strategic objectives not only will help you make wiser decisions but, more important, should help you recognize and create new decision opportunities.

For specific decisions, clearly articulated fundamental objectives should help you to better understand the decisions you face and to create fruitful alternatives. Articulating your objectives should put you in a better position to explain yourself to others as well as to yourself.

Although value-focused thinking is much broader than alternative-focused thinking, they are not competitive approaches. At some stage in the deliberation about any decision situation, alternatives must be compared. At this stage, value-focused thinking and alternative-focused thinking are quite similar, as discussed in Section 2.6. It is before this stage in a decision, and indeed in whether the particular decision is ever addressed, that value-focused thinking and alternative-focused thinking are completely different.

It may initially be difficult for you to articulate, review, and revise your objectives. You may get the feeling that you are not "solving" your decision problems when you are just thinking about your objectives. You may feel it is merely a hypothetical philosophical exercise to articulate your values, whereas the decision problems facing you are real. But whether or not you label thinking about your values as hypothetical, the results of that thinking can help with any of the real decisions that you make. One good decision opportunity can repay you for a lot of "hypothetical" thinking.

As you gain experience, thinking about your objectives should get easier and easier and the results should get better and better. There are three reasons for this. First, as with all endeavors, practice makes perfect, or at least, practice makes better. It is useful to practice by articulating your values for easier decision situations if you plan to use value-focused thinking for difficult decisions. Second, as you structure your values, you will necessarily tackle some complex and involved value issues. As you sort these out, you will learn more about yourself. A better self-understanding makes it easier to clarify difficult value issues. Third, as you continue to structure and understand your values, they will begin to form a coherent pattern. Numerous frames of reference based on previously articulated values facilitate thinking about your values in a new decision context.

To recapitulate, value-focused thinking will help you in three major ways: to recognize and identify decision opportunities for yourself, to create better alternatives for your decision problems, and to develop an enduring set of guiding principles for your life.

References

Ackoff, R. L. 1978. *The Art of Problem Solving*. New York: Wiley.

———— 1981. "The Art and Science of Mess Management." *Interfaces, 11*, no. 1, 20–26.

Ackoff, R. L., and E. Vergara. 1981. "Creativity in Problem Solving and Planning: A Review." *European Journal of Operational Research, 7*, 1–13.

Adams, J. L. 1979. *Conceptual Blockbusting: A Guide to Better Ideas*. 2d ed. New York: Norton.

Alpert, M., and H. Raiffa. 1981. "A Progress Report on the Training of Probability Assessors." In D. Kahneman, P. Slovic, and A. Tversky, eds., *Judgment under Uncertainty: Heuristics and Biases*. New York: Cambridge University Press.

Bell, D. E. 1977a. "A Decision Analysis of Objectives for a Forest Pest Problem." in D. E. Bell, R. L. Keeney, and H. Raiffa, eds., *Conflicting Objectives in Decisions*. New York: Wiley Interscience.

———— 1977b. "A Utility Function for Time Streams Having Interperiod Dependencies." *Operations Research, 25*, 448–458.

———— 1982. "Regret in Decision Making under Uncertainty." *Operations Research, 30*, 961–981.

———— 1984. "Bidding for the S.S. *Kuniang*." *Interfaces, 14*, no. 2, 17–23.

———— 1985. "Disappointment in Decision Making under Uncertainty." *Operations Research, 33*, 1–27.

Broome, J. 1982. "Equity in Risk Bearing." *Operations Research, 30*, 412–414.

Brownlow, S. A., and S. R. Watson. 1987. "Structuring Multi-attribute Value Hierarchies." *Journal of the Operational Research Society, 38*, 309–317.

Buede, D. M. 1986. "Structuring Value Attributes." *Interfaces, 16*, no. 2, 52–62.

Clark, W. C. 1989. "Managing Planet Earth." *Scientific American, 261*, 18–26.

Coombs, C. H. and G. S. Avrunin, 1977. "Single-Peaked Functions and the Theory of Preference." *Psychological Review, 84*, 216–230.

Dawes, R. M. 1988. *Rational Choice in an Uncertain World.* San Diego: Harcourt Brace Jovanovich.

Debreu, G. 1960. "Topological Methods in Cardinal Utility Theory." In K. J. Arrow, S. Karlin, and P. Suppes, eds., *Mathematical Methods in the Social Sciences, 1959.* Stanford: Stanford University Press.

de Neufville, R., and R. L. Keeney. 1972. "Use of Decision Analysis in Airport Development for Mexico City." in A. W. Drake, R. L. Keeney, and P. M. Morse, eds., *Analysis of Public Systems.* Cambridge, Mass.: M.I.T. Press.

Diamond, P. A. 1967. "Cardinal Welfare, Individualistic Ethics and Interpersonal Comparison of Utility: Comment." *Journal of Political Economy, 75,* 765–766.

Dole, S. H., H. G. Campbell, D. Dreyfuss, W. D. Gosch, E. D. Harris, D. E. Lewis, T. M. Parker, J. W. Ranftl, and J. String, Jr. 1968. "Methodologies for Analyzing the Comparative Effectiveness and Costs of Alternate Space Plans." RM-5656-NASA, vols. 1 and 2. Santa Monica: Rand Corporation.

Dyer, J. S., and R. K. Sarin. 1979. "Measurable Multiattribute Value Functions." *Operations Research, 27,* 810–822.

Edwards, W. 1968. "Conservatism in Human Information Processing." In B. Kleinmuntz, ed., *Formal Representation of Human Judgement.* New York: Wiley.

Edwards, W., and D. von Winterfeldt. 1987. "Public Values in Risk Debates." *Risk Analysis, 7,* 141–158.

Einhorn, H. J., and R. M. Hogarth. 1981. "Behavioral Decision Theory: Processes of Judgment and Choice." *Annual Review of Psychology, 32,* 53–88.

Evans, J. S. 1991. "Strategic Flexibility for High Technology Manoeuvres: A Conceptual Framework." *Journal of Management Studies, 28,* 69–89.

Fischer, G. W., N. Damodaran, K. B. Laskey, and D. Lincoln. 1987. "Preferences for Proxy Attributes." *Management Science, 33,* 198–214.

Fishburn, P. C. 1965. "Independence in Utility Theory with Whole Product Sets." *Operations Research, 13,* 28–43.

———— 1970. *Utility Theory for Decision Making.* New York: Wiley.

———— 1984. "Equity Axioms for Public Risk." *Operations Research, 30,* 901–908.

Fishburn, P. C., and R. K. Sarin. 1991. "Dispersive Equity and Social Risk." *Management Science, 37,* 751–769.

Fisher, R., and W. Ury. 1981. *Getting to Yes: Negotiating Agreement Without Giving In.* Boston: Houghton Mifflin.

Ford, A. 1979. "Breaking the Stalemate: An Analysis of Boom Town Mitigation Policies." *Journal of Interdisciplinary Modeling and Simulation, 2,* 25–39.

Ford, A., and P. C. Gardiner. 1979. "A New Measure of Sensitivity for Social System Simulation Models." *IEEE Transactions on Systems, Man, and Cybernetics, SMC-9,* 105–114.

Gardiner, P. C., and W. Edwards. 1975. "Public Values, Multi-Attribute Utility Measurement for Social Decision Making." In M. F. Kaplan and S. Schwartz, eds., *Human Judgment and Decision Processes.* New York: Academic Press.

Gorman, W. M. 1968a. "The Structure of Utility Functions." *Review of Economic Studies, 35*, 367–390.

———— 1968b. "Conditions of Additive Separability." *Econometrica, 36*, 605–609.

Graham, J. D., and J. W. Vaupel. 1981. "Value of a Life: What Difference Does It Make?" *Risk Analysis, 1*, 89–95.

Grayson, C. J. 1960. *Decisions under Uncertainty: Drilling Decisions by Oil and Gas Operators.* Boston: Division of Research, Harvard Business School.

Gustafson, D. H., and D. C. Holloway. 1975. "A Decision Theory Approach to Measuring Severity in Illness." *Health Services Research*, Spring, 97–106.

Hammond, J. S., III. 1967. "Better Decisions with Preference Theory." *Harvard Business Review, 45*, 123–141.

Healy, J. 1982. "A VLSI-ATE Selection Matrix." *Solid State Technology*, November, 81–88.

Hilborn, R., and C. J. Walters. 1977. "Differing Goals of Salmon Management on the Skeena River." *Journal of the Fisheries Research Board of Canada, 34*, 64–72.

Hogarth, R. 1987. *Judgment and Choice.* 2d ed. New York: Wiley.

Howard, R. A., and J. E. Matheson. 1984. "Influence Diagrams." In R. A. Howard and J. E. Matheson, eds., *The Principles and Applications of Decision Analysis.* Menlo Park, Calif.: Strategic Decisions Group.

Huber, G. P., V. Sahney, and D. Ford. 1969. "A Study of Subjective Evaluation Models." *Behavioral Science, 14*, 483–489.

Jungermann, H., I. von Ulardt, and L. Hausmann. 1983. "The Role of the Goal for Generating Actions." In P. Humphreys, O. Svenson, and A. Vari, eds., *Analyzing and Aiding Decision Processes.* Amsterdam; North-Holland.

Kahneman, D., P. Slovic, and A. Tversky, eds. 1982. *Judgment under Uncertainty: Heuristics and Biases.* Cambridge, England: Cambridge University Press.

Kaufman, G. M. 1963. *Statistical Decision and Related Techniques in Oil and Gas Exploration.* Englewood Cliffs, N.J.: Prentice-Hall.

Keefer, D. L., and C. W. Kirkwood. 1978. "A Multiobjective Decision Analysis: Budget Planning for Product Engineering." *Journal of the Operational Research Society, 29*, 435–442.

Keeney, R. L. 1968. "Quasi-Separable Utility Functions." *Naval Research Logistics Quarterly, 15*, 551–565.

———— 1972. "Utility Functions for Multiattributed Consequences." *Management Science, 18*, 276–287.

———— 1974. "Multiplicative Utility Functions." *Operations Research, 22*, 22–34.

———— 1977a. "A Utility Function for Examining Policy Affecting Salmon on the Skeena River." *Journal of the Fisheries Research Board of Canada, 34*, 49–63.

———— 1977b. "A Preliminary Model of Adversary Preferences." In *Proceedings of the Lawrence Symposium on Systems and Decision Sciences.* North Hollywood, Calif.: Western Periodicals.

———— 1979. "Evaluation of Proposed Pumped Storage Sites." *Operations Research, 27*, 48–64.

———— 1980. *Siting Energy Facilities.* New York: Academic Press.

———— 1981. "Analysis of Preference Dependencies among Objectives." *Operations Research, 29,* 1105–1120.

———— 1982. "Evaluating Mortality Risks from an Organizational Perspective." in M. W. Jones-Lee, ed., *The Value of Life and Safety.* Amsterdam: North-Holland.

———— 1984. "Ethics, Decision Analysis, and Public Risks." *Risk Analysis, 4,* 117–129.

———— 1988. "Structuring Objectives for Problems of Public Interest." *Operations Research, 36,* 396–405.

Keeney, R. L., R. Kulkarni, and K. Nair. 1979. "A Risk Analysis of an LNG Terminal." *Omega, 7,* 191–201.

Keeney, R. L., J. F. Lathrop, and A. Sicherman. 1986. "An Analysis of Baltimore Gas and Electric Company's Technology Choice." *Operations Research, 34,* 18–39.

Keeney, R. L., and G. L. Lilien. 1987. "New Industrial Product Design and Evaluation Using Multiattribute Value Analysis." *Journal of Product Innovation Management, 4,* 185–198.

Keeney, R. L., and V. Ozernoy. 1982. "An Illustrative Analysis of Ambient Carbon Monoxide Standards." *Journal of the Operational Research Society, 33,* 365–375.

Keeney, R. L., and H. Raiffa. 1976. *Decisions with Multiple Objectives.* New York: Wiley.

———— 1991. "Structuring and Analyzing Values for Multiple-Issue Negotiations." In H. P. Young, ed., *Negotiation Analysis.* Ann Arbor: University of Michigan Press.

Keeney, R. L., O. Renn, and D. von Winterfeldt. 1987. "Structuring Germany's Energy Objectives." *Energy Policy, 15,* 352–362.

Keeney, R. L., and G. A. Robilliard. 1977. "Assessing and Evaluating Environmental Impacts at Proposed Nuclear Power Plant Sites." *Journal of Environmental Economics and Management, 4,* 153–166.

Keeney, R. L., R. K. Sarin, and R. L. Winkler. 1984. "Analysis of Alternative National Ambient Carbon Monoxide Standards." *Management Science, 30,* 518–528.

Keeney, R. L., and A. Sicherman. 1983. "Illustrative Comparison of One Utility's Coal and Nuclear Choices." *Operations Research, 31,* 50–83.

Keeney, R. L., and D. von Winterfeldt. 1986. "Improving Risk Communication." *Risk Analysis, 6,* 417–424.

———— 1991. "A Prescriptive Risk Framework for Individual Health and Safety Decisions." *Risk Analysis, 11,* 523–533.

Keeney, R. L., and R. L. Winkler. 1985. "Evaluating Decision Strategies for Equity of Public Risks." *Operations Research, 33,* 955–970.

Keeney, R. L., and E. F. Wood. 1977. "An Illustrative Example of the Use of Multiattribute Utility Theory for Water Resource Planning." *Water Resources Research, 13,* 705–716.

Keller, L. R. 1985. "An Empirical Investigation of Relative Risk Aversion." *IEEE Transactions on Systems, Man, and Cybernetics, SMC-15,* 475–482.

Keller, L. R., and J. L. Ho. 1988. "Decision Problem Structuring: Generating Options." *IEEE Transactions on Systems, Man, and Cybernetics, 18,* 715–728.

Kleindorfer, P. R., H. C. Kunreuther, and P. J. H. Schoemaker. 1992. *Decision Sciences: An Integrative Perspective.* Cambridge, England: Cambridge University Press.

Koopmans, T. C. 1960. "Stationary Ordinal Utility and Impatience." *Econometrica, 28,* 287–309.

———— 1972. "Representation of Preference Orderings Over Time." In C. B. McGuire and R. Radner, eds., *Decision and Organization.* Amsterdam: North-Holland.

Krantz, D. H. 1964. "Conjoint Measurement: The Luce-Tukey Axiomatization and Some Extensions." *Journal of Mathematical Psychology, 1,* 248–277.

Krantz, D. H., R. D. Luce, P. Suppes, and A. Tversky. 1971. *Foundations of Measurement,* vol. 1. New York: Academic Press.

Krischer, J. P. 1976. "Utility Structure of a Medical Decision-Making Problem." *Operations Research, 24,* 951–972.

LaValle, I. H. 1968. "On Cash Equivalents and Information Evaluation in Decisions under Uncertainty." *Journal of the American Statistical Association, 63,* 252–290.

Lave, L. B. 1983. "Testimony at a NHTSA Statutory Hearing Regarding Initial Determination of Defect." National Highway Transportation Safety Administration Hearing, May 4.

Luce, R. D., and J. W. Tukey. 1964. "Simultaneous Conjoint Measurement: A New Type of Fundamental Measurement." *Journal of Mathematical Psychology, 1,* 1–27.

MacCrimmon, K. R., and D. A. Wehrung. 1986. *Taking Risks.* New York: Free Press.

Manheim, M. L., and F. Hall. 1967. "Abstract Representation of Goals: A Method for Making Decisions in Complex Problems." In *Transportation: A Service,* Proceedings of the Sesquicentennial Forum. New York: New York Academy of Sciences–American Academy of Mechanical Engineers.

Manne, A. S., and R. G. Richels. 1990. "CO2 Emission Limits: An Economic Analysis for the USA." *Energy Journal, 11,* no. 2, 51–85.

Maslow, A. H. 1968. *Toward a Psychology of Being.* 2d ed. Princeton, N.J.: Van Nostrand.

McClelland, G. H., and J. Rohrbaugh. 1978. "Who Accepts the Pareto Axiom? The Role of Utility and Equity in Arbitration and Decisions." *Behavioral Science, 23,* 446–456.

McGarvey, R. 1989. "Getting Your Goals." *USAir Magazine,* July, 26–30.

McNeil, B. J., S. G. Pauker, and A. Tversky. 1988. "On the Framing of Medical Decisions." In D. Bell, H. Raiffa, and A. Tversky, eds., *Decision Making: Descriptive, Normative, and Prescriptive Interactions.* Cambridge, England: Cambridge University Press.

Merkhofer, M. W. 1977. "The Value of Information Given Decision Flexibility." *Management Science, 23,* 716–727.

Meyer, R. F. 1970. "On the Relationship among the Utility of Assets, the Utility of Consumption, and Investment Strategy in an Uncertain, but Time Invariant World." In J. Lawrence, ed., *OR 69: Proceedings of the Fifth International Conference on Operational Research.* London: Tavistock.

————— 1976. "Preferences over Time." In R. L. Keeney and H. Raiffa, *Decisions with Multiple Objectives.* New York: Wiley.

Miller, J. R., III. 1970. *Professional Decision Making.* New York: Praeger.

Miser, H. J., and E. S. Quade, eds. 1985. *Handbook of Systems Analysis: Overview of Uses, Procedures, Applications, and Practice.* New York: North-Holland.

Patton, F. H. 1986. *Forces of Persuasion.* Englewood Cliffs, N.J.: Prentice-Hall.

Pitz, G. F., N. T. Sachs, and T. Heerboth. 1980. "Procedures for Eliciting Choices in the Analysis of Individual Decisions." *Organizational Behavior and Human Performance, 26,* 396–408.

Pollak, R. A. 1967. "Additive von Neumann-Morgenstern Utility Functions." *Econometrica, 32,* 122–136.

Pratt, J. W. 1964. "Risk Aversion in the Small and in the Large." *Econometrica, 32,* 122–136.

Pratt, J. W., H. Raiffa, and R. O. Schlaifer. 1964. "The Foundations of Decision under Uncertainty: An Elementary Exposition." *Journal of the American Statistical Association, 59,* 353–375.

Raiffa, H. 1968. *Decision Analysis.* Reading, Mass.: Addison-Wesley.

————— 1969. "Preferences for Multi-Attributed Alternatives." RM-5868-DOT/RC. Santa Monica: Rand Corporation.

————— 1982. *The Art and Science of Negotiation.* Cambridge, Mass.: Harvard University Press.

————— 1985. "Post-Settlements." *Negotiation Journal, 2,* no. 1, 9–12.

Raiffa, H., W. Schwartz, and M. Weinstein. 1978. "Evaluating Health Effects of Social Decisions and Programs." In *EPA Decision Making.* Washington, D.C.: National Academy of Sciences.

Raisbeck, G. 1979. "How the Choice of Measures of Effectiveness Constrains Operational Analysis." *Interfaces, 9,* no. 4, 85–93.

Richard, S. F. 1975. "Multivariate Risk Aversion, Utility Independence, and Separable Utility Functions." *Management Science, 22,* 12–21.

Ride, S. 1987. *Leadership and America's Future in Space.* Washington, D.C.: National Aeronautics and Space Administration.

Russo, J. E., and P. J. H. Schoemaker. 1989. *Decision Traps.* New York: Doubleday.

Saaty, T. L. 1980. *The Analytical Hierarchy Process.* New York: McGraw-Hill.

Sarin, R. K. 1985. "Measuring Equity in Public Risk." *Operations Research, 33,* 210–217.

Savage, L. J. 1954. *The Foundations of Statistics.* New York: Wiley.

Shachter, R. D. 1986. "Evaluating Influence Diagrams." *Operations Research, 34,* 871–882.

Sicherman, A. 1982. "Decision Analysis Computer Program." In *Decision Framework for Technology Choice, vol. 2: Decision Analysis User's Manual.* EPRI Report EA-2153. Palo Alto, Calif.: Electric Power Research Institute.

Simon, H. A. 1969. *Science of the Artificial.* Cambridge, Mass.: M.I.T. Press.

——— 1982. *Models of Bounded Rationality.* Cambridge, Mass.: M.I.T. Press.

Slovic, P., B. Fischhoff, and S. Lichtenstein. 1977. "Behavioral Decision Theory." *Annual Review of Psychology, 28,* 1–39.

——— 1979. "Rating the Risks." *Environment, 21,* 14–20, 36–39.

Smith, G. R. 1989. Logical Decision: Multi-Measure Decision Analysis Software. Golden, Colo.: Logical Decisions, Inc.

Southern California Edison. 1983. "SCE Corporate Goals." Los Angeles: Southern California Edison Company.

Swalm, R. O. 1966. "Utility Theory—Insights into Risk Taking." *Harvard Business Review, 44,* 123–136.

Tversky, A., and D. Kahneman. 1974. "Judgment under Uncertainty: Heuristics and Biases." *Science, 185,* 1124–1131.

——— 1981. "The Framing of Decisions and the Psychology of Choice." *Science, 211,* 453–458.

U.S. Environmental Protection Agency. 1980. "Carbon Monoxide: Proposed Revision to the National Ambient Air Quality Standards." 40 CFR Part 50. *Federal Register, 45,* 161.

von Hippel, E. 1986. "Lead Users: A Source of Novel Product Concepts." *Management Science, 32,* 791–805.

von Neumann, J., and O. Morgenstern. 1947. *Theory of Games and Economic Behavior.* 2d ed. Princeton, N.J.: Princeton University Press.

von Winterfeldt, D. 1980. "Structuring Decision Problems for Decision Analysis." *Acta Psychologica, 45,* 71–93.

——— 1987. "Value Tree Analysis: An Introduction and an Application to Offshore Oil Drilling." In P. R. Kleindorfer and H. C. Kunreuther, eds., *Insuring and Managing Hazardous Risks: From Sevesco to Bhopal and Beyond.* New York: Springer.

von Winterfeldt, D., and W. Edwards. 1986. *Decision Analysis and Behavioral Research.* Cambridge, England: Cambridge University Press.

Walker, W. E. 1988. "The Generation and Screening of Alternatives in Policy Analysis." In H. J. Miser and E. S. Quade, eds., *Handbook of Systems Analysis: Craft Issues and Procedural Choices.* New York: North-Holland.

Westinghouse Electric Corporation. 1986. *Phase 1 Study of Metallic Cask Systems for Spent Fuel Management from Reactor to Repository.* Report WTSD-TME-085. Madison, Pa.: Westinghouse Waste Technology Services Division.

White House. 1988. *Fact Sheet on National Space Policy.* Washington, D.C.: Office of the White House Press Secretary, January 25.

Zeleny, M. 1982. *Multiple Criteria Decision Making.* New York: McGraw-Hill.

Index of Applications and Examples

General Index

Harvard University Press is a member of Green Press Initiative (greenpressinitiative.org), a nonprofit organization working to help publishers and printers increase their use of recycled paper and decrease their use of fiber derived from endangered forests. This book was printed on 100% recycled paper containing 50% post-consumer waste and processed chlorine free.